Fostering Organizational Culture for Provider Well-Being:

The 5S's Well-Being Framework

Minhaj Qidwai
https://orcid.org/0009-0003-0770-481X

American Institute of Healthcare Quality, USA & Unet Consultants, Pakistan

Arfa Masihuddin
https://orcid.org/0009-0006-4697-6318

Rufayda, Karachi, Pakistan

IGI Global
Scientific Publishing
Publishing Tomorrow's Research Today

Vice President of Editorial Melissa Wagner
Director of Acquisitions Mikaela Felty
Director of Book Development Jocelynn Hessler
Production Manager Mike Brehm
Cover Design Jose Rosado

Published in the United States of America by
IGI Global Scientific Publishing
701 East Chocolate Avenue
Hershey, PA, 17033, USA
Tel: 717-533-8845 | Fax: 717-533-7115
Website: https://www.igi-global.com E-mail: cust@igi-global.com

Library of Congress Cataloging-in-Publication Data

No LCCN (CIP Data Pending)
ISBN13: 9798260005828
Isbn13Softcover: 9798260005835
EISBN13: 9798260005842

British Cataloguing in Publication Data
A Cataloguing in Publication record for this book is available from the British Library.

Table of Contents

Detailed Table of Contents

Healthcare providers face increasing burnout, job dissatisfaction, and workforce shortages, necessitating a holistic approach to well-being. The 5Ss' Approach—comprising Self, Society, State, Systems, and Spirituality—offers a comprehensive framework integrating individual resilience, social support, governmental policies, institutional structures, and existential well-being. Drawing on Schein's organizational culture model and the JD-R framework, this approach highlights the interplay of personal agency, teamwork, regulatory mechanisms, leadership, and spiritual grounding. Case studies from Magnet hospitals and state-led initiatives validate its effectiveness. To safeguard the workforce, healthcare institutions must prioritize transformational leadership, digital innovation, and policy reforms. The 5Ss' model demands systemic implementation to enhance provider resilience and sustain high-quality patient care.

Healthcare providers are at the risk of mental health challenges due to long working hours, workloads, insufficient social support, lack of autonomy (Piras et al., 2020; Yalim et al., 2024); rigid policies, toxic work culture, and lack of reinforcement (Tawfik et al., 2019).Implementing wellness initiatives should be adaptable and responsive to feedback from healthcare providers (Wilkie et al., 2021). This chapter aims to propose effective and evidence-based programs to ensure the mental wellbeing of healthcare providers and increases the credibility of the organization itself. Developing wellness programs, such as managing stress and burnout, dealing

This chapter examines the perception of quality of work life (QWL) among healthcare providers in private-sector tertiary care hospitals in Karachi, Pakistan. The research involved 42 healthcare providers from three hospitals, using in-depth interviews. The findings revealed that QWL is a combination of a well-paying job, a good work-life balance, a comfortable working environment, supportive leadership, and family support. Organizational factors affecting QWL include fair monetary compensation, increased workload, lack of infrastructure, decision-making autonomy, and feedback from leadership. Emotional and practical support from colleagues significantly influences QWL by mitigating workplace stress. Family expectations were recognized as a factor influencing QWL, as healthcare providers frequently encounter challenges in fulfilling unrealistic demands. Initiatives to improve QWL include introducing confidential mental health services, support facilities, and personal development skills. The results are shown using the 5Ss framework: Self, Society, State, Systems, and Spirituality. Key themes include workload and burnout, leadership behavior, infrastructure gaps, peer and familial support, and a lack of recognition. The chapter proposes human-centered and policy-driven interventions to improve QWL in resource-constrained healthcare settings. Healthcare organizations should establish wellness committees to promote a positive work culture and improve QWL.

Effective policies for healthcare providers health are mandatory for maintaining perfect workflow and their safety in workplace. Policies bring about workload management, supportive environment, fair reward system and a healthy culture of organisation. Governance brings about structure, transparency and accountability from workers and fosters collaboration among stakeholders. Thus, policies shape the environment of an organisation and governance runs the organisation flawlessly. This chapter will explore the critical role of policy in shaping organisational culture, beginning with theoretical underpinnings of culture and governance. It will examine how policies serve as ethical and legal anchors in clinical practice and explore their role in promoting accountability and safety. Finally, it will examine regulatory frameworks that reinforce patient safety and support continuous improvement.

Preface

INTRODUCTION

Healthcare systems around the world are experiencing unprecedented transformation and pressure. Rapid technological advances, increasing patient expectations, complex regulatory requirements, and persistent resource constraints have reshaped the work environment of healthcare providers. While these changes have improved many aspects of healthcare delivery, they have also intensified the demands placed upon those who serve on the frontlines of care. Physicians, nurses, allied health professionals, and administrators often work long hours under conditions that challenge their physical, emotional, and mental well-being.

In recent years, the global healthcare community has become increasingly aware of the profound consequences of provider burnout. Exhaustion, moral distress, and disengagement not only affect the lives of healthcare providers but also have direct implications for patient safety, service quality, and the sustainability of healthcare organisations. Despite the recognition of this growing crisis, efforts to address provider well-being have frequently been fragmented—focusing on isolated interventions rather than addressing the broader organisational culture in which healthcare professionals operate.

This book emerges from the recognition that meaningful and sustainable change requires a holistic and integrated approach. *Fostering Organizational Culture for Provider Well-Being: The 5S's Framework Approach* introduces and explores the *5Ss model—Self, Society, State, Systems, and Spirituality*, conceptualised by *Dr. Minhaj Qidwai*. The framework offers a comprehensive lens through which healthcare organisations can examine the complex factors shaping provider well-being and organisational culture.

The 5Ss model recognises that healthcare providers do not function in isolation. Their professional lives are influenced by multiple interacting dimensions. The *Self* represents the personal resilience, emotional intelligence, and professional growth that empower individuals to navigate the challenges of healthcare practice. *Society* reflects the broader cultural and social dynamics that shape expectations, relationships, and organisational behavior. *State* encompasses governance, leadership, policy frameworks, and institutional responsibility in creating environments that protect and support providers. *Systems* focus on the structures, processes, and operational mechanisms that determine efficiency, safety, and workflow within healthcare organisations. Finally, *Spirituality* highlights the often overlooked dimension of meaning, compassion, ethical clarity, and inner purpose that sustains healthcare professionals in their vocation of healing.

The chapters in this edited volume bring together contributions from scholars, practitioners, and healthcare leaders who share a commitment to transforming healthcare workplaces. Through theoretical insights, empirical research, practical strategies, and real-world case studies, the contributors explore how each of the 5Ss can be applied in diverse healthcare contexts. Together, these chapters demonstrate how a culture that prioritises provider well-being ultimately leads to improved patient outcomes, stronger professional relationships, and more resilient healthcare systems.

An important and distinctive feature of this framework is the inclusion of *spirituality* as a core pillar. Healthcare is not merely a technical profession; it is fundamentally a human and moral endeavor. By acknowledging the spiritual dimension of care—understood broadly as the search for meaning, purpose, compassion, and ethical responsibility—healthcare organisations can foster deeper connections between providers and those they serve. This dimension encourages reflection, empathy, and a sense of vocation that strengthens both professional satisfaction and patient trust.

This book is intended for a diverse audience including healthcare leaders and managers, healthcare providers, human resource professionals, organisational development specialists, and academicians. Our hope is that the ideas presented in this volume will stimulate dialogue, inspire innovation, and support the development of healthier and more compassionate healthcare organisations.

As editors, we are deeply grateful to the contributors who have generously shared their knowledge, research, and experiences. Their collective insights enrich this volume and reflect a shared vision of healthcare systems that value not only efficiency and outcomes but also the well-being of the people who make care possible.

We also acknowledge the dedication of healthcare providers across the world who continue to serve patients and communities with resilience and compassion despite immense challenges. It is our sincere hope that the 5Ss framework presented in this book will contribute to shaping organisational cultures that support, empower, and sustain them.

Ultimately, fostering a positive organisational culture is not simply an administrative goal—it is a moral and professional imperative. By investing in the well-being of healthcare providers, we strengthen the very foundation of healthcare delivery and move closer to a future where both caregivers and patients can thrive.

In this volume, each chapter contributes to the evolving understanding of how organisational culture influences the well-being of healthcare providers and how the 5Ss framework—Self, Society, State, Systems, and Spirituality—can guide transformative change in healthcare institutions. As editors, we have structured this book so that readers move progressively from conceptual foundations to practical strategies and applied insights drawn from diverse healthcare settings.

CHAPTER OVERVIEWS

Chapter 1, authored by Deepa Mukherjee, introduces the foundational concepts of the 5Ss framework and situates them within established organisational and behavioural theories. Drawing on Schein's model of organisational culture and the Job Demands–Resources (JD-R) framework, the chapter illustrates how personal resilience, supportive teamwork, regulatory policies, leadership structures, and spiritual grounding collectively shape provider well-being. Through examples such as Magnet hospitals and state-supported initiatives, the chapter demonstrates how the integration of these dimensions can mitigate burnout and strengthen healthcare organisations. As the opening chapter of the book, it provides readers with a comprehensive overview of the 5Ss model and establishes the conceptual basis for the discussions that follow.

Chapter 2, written by Aqsa Yaqoob, Amena Ali, and Minhaj Qidwai, expands the framework by focusing on the implementation of organisational wellness management programs designed to support healthcare providers. The authors highlight the increasing psychological burden faced by healthcare professionals due to demanding workloads, insufficient autonomy, and toxic workplace cultures. The chapter proposes evidence-based wellness interventions, including stress management, mindfulness and meditation, counselling services, cognitive behavioral therapy, and peer-support mechanisms. By presenting adaptable wellness initiatives that respond to provider feedback, the chapter demonstrates how healthcare organisations can strengthen both workforce resilience and institutional credibility through the practical application of the 5Ss framework.

Chapter 3, by Zoella Ali, examines the "Self" dimension of the 5S model within one of the most demanding healthcare environments—the emergency room. Drawing on research conducted among emergency healthcare providers in Pakistan, the chapter explores how emotional awareness, psychological resilience, and supportive leadership influence individual well-being. The findings reveal notable differences between public and private sector institutions in terms of available psychological support structures. The study further highlights the importance of empathetic leadership and peer support networks in reducing burnout and improving workplace satisfaction. Through these insights, the chapter underscores the critical role of organisational commitment to mental health support in strengthening the resilience of frontline healthcare professionals.

Chapter 4, authored by Sobia Ali, Sofia Ali, and Aabdar Hidayat, continues the exploration of the "Self" dimension by examining the concept of self-empowerment among healthcare providers. Challenging the rigid stereotypes that often depict providers either as emotionally detached or unrealistically flawless professionals, the authors present a human-centered narrative of physician well-being. Through qualitative insights and direct reflections from healthcare providers, the chapter explores why burnout affects some individuals more than others and how personal awareness, emotional intelligence, and reflective practice can strengthen resilience. By encouraging providers to recognise their own vulnerabilities and strengths, the chapter highlights the importance of nurturing inner capacity to sustain compassionate care.

Chapter 5, written by Rohit Kumar and Shameen Arif, shifts the focus to the "Systems" dimension by examining organisational efficiency within healthcare settings. The authors explore how resource allocation, infrastructure, and workplace culture influence the well-being of healthcare workers. The chapter emphasises the role of data-driven decision making, including the use of well-being surveys to inform organisational reforms and equitable resource distribution. It also highlights the potential of digital technologies and artificial intelligence to automate administrative tasks and streamline workflows. By integrating systems thinking with compassionate leadership, the chapter presents strategies for building healthcare organisations that are both operationally efficient and supportive of provider well-being.

Chapter 6, contributed by Muhammad Ijaz, further develops the systems perspective by presenting a systems-based approach to healthcare management. In the face of growing technological advancements, regulatory complexity, and increasing patient demands, healthcare leaders must adopt integrated approaches to organisational design. This chapter illustrates how systems thinking can help leaders diagnose inefficiencies, align processes, and coordinate human and technological resources more effectively. Through this lens, the chapter demonstrates how adaptive and high-functioning healthcare organisations can be created to improve both patient care and workforce satisfaction.

Chapter 7, authored by Arfa Masihuddin and colleagues, offers an empirical exploration of healthcare providers' quality of work life within tertiary care hospitals in Karachi, Pakistan. Based on qualitative interviews with physicians, surgeons, and nurses across multiple clinical departments, the chapter identifies key organisational and systemic factors influencing professional well-being. Themes such as workload pressures, leadership behavior, infrastructure limitations, peer support, and recognition emerge as critical determinants of job satisfaction. Interpreting these findings through the lens of the 5Ss framework, the authors propose human-centered and policy-oriented strategies aimed at improving the quality of work life in resource-constrained healthcare environments.

Chapter 8, written by Tahirah Atif, addresses the "State" dimension of the framework by examining the role of policy and governance in shaping organisational culture within healthcare institutions. The chapter highlights how well-designed policies serve as ethical and legal anchors for clinical practice while promoting transparency, accountability, and collaboration among stakeholders. Through theoretical discussion and real-world examples, the author demonstrates how regulatory frameworks and governance structures contribute to safe work environments, balanced workloads, and patient safety. This chapter reinforces the critical role of policy leadership in fostering a culture that supports both providers and patients.

Chapter 9, by Minhaj Qidwai and Tehrim Toqir, introduces the G.R.A.S.P. model—Governance, Resource Allocation, Accountability, Sustainability, and Profitability—as a complementary framework for evaluating organisational impact. The chapter emphasises that meaningful organisational outcomes require careful alignment between inputs, processes, outputs, and long-term impact. By examining the key variables that shape the organisational ecosystem, the authors demonstrate how strategic management decisions can influence workplace culture and ultimately improve the well-being of healthcare providers. The G.R.A.S.P. model thus provides healthcare leaders with a practical tool for assessing and strengthening organisational performance within the broader context of the 5Ss philosophy.

Chapter 10, authored by Sadaf Naveed and Memona Guldost Khan, explores the often overlooked dimension of spirituality in healthcare organisations. The chapter argues that spiritual awareness can play a vital role in helping healthcare providers manage emotional stress, moral distress, and burnout. Through examples of leadership practices, institutional rituals, and chaplaincy programs from international healthcare settings, the authors illustrate how spirituality can be integrated into organisational culture in an inclusive manner. The chapter also addresses challenges such as cultural diversity and secular resistance, while proposing strategies for developing supportive policies and evaluation tools that measure the impact of spiritual care on both provider well-being and patient outcomes.

Chapter 11, written by Hira Aziz, concludes the volume by reflecting on the deeper meaning of spirituality in the medical profession. The chapter presents a thoughtful narrative on how healthcare providers are often trained to prioritize patient care while neglecting their own well-being. By emphasizing spirituality as a source of purpose and resilience, the author highlights its role in restoring balance within the demanding world of healthcare practice. The chapter argues that when providers reconnect with the deeper meaning of their work, they are better equipped to sustain compassion, maintain resilience, and continue serving humanity with dedication.

Collectively, these chapters demonstrate the breadth and depth of the *5Ss framework* as a holistic approach to transforming organisational culture in healthcare. Through theoretical insights, empirical research, and practical applications, the contributors offer valuable guidance for leaders, practitioners, and scholars seeking to build healthcare environments that support both provider well-being and high-quality patient care.

CONCLUSION

As editors, we believe that the well-being of healthcare providers is not merely an individual concern but a fundamental determinant of organisational culture, patient safety, and the sustainability of healthcare systems. The chapters in this volume collectively demonstrate that improving provider well-being requires a multidimensional perspective—one that moves beyond isolated interventions and instead addresses the broader ecosystem in which healthcare professionals live and work.

The 5Ss framework—Self, Society, State, Systems, and Spirituality—offers such a holistic lens. By recognising the interconnected roles of personal resilience, supportive social environments, enabling policies, efficient organisational systems, and meaningful spiritual engagement, the framework provides a comprehensive pathway for transforming healthcare organisations into spaces where providers can thrive. When these dimensions are aligned, healthcare institutions can cultivate cultures of compassion, accountability, collaboration, and continuous improvement.

We hope that the insights presented in this book will inspire healthcare leaders, policymakers, educators, and practitioners to reflect critically on their own organisational environments and to adopt innovative strategies that prioritise the well-being of those who deliver care. Ultimately, strengthening the culture of healthcare organisations is not only an investment in providers but also in the communities and patients they serve.

It is our sincere hope that this book will contribute to ongoing dialogue, research, and action aimed at building healthcare systems that are resilient, humane, and sustainable—systems in which healthcare providers are empowered to deliver compassionate care while maintaining their own sense of purpose, balance, and well-being.

Minhaj Qidwai
American Institute of Healthcare Quality, USA & Unet Consultants, Pakistan

Arfa Masihuddin
Rufayda, Karachi, Pakistan

Acknowledgements

The book, "Fostering Organizational Culture for Provider Wellbeing", came from the collection of chapters for our first book, "Impact of Organizational Culture and the Well-Being of Healthcare Providers". After a successful call for chapters for the former, it was decided that given the number of rich submissions that we had received, it would improve the thematic focus of the topic to publish the submissions as two separate books. For this, we are truly grateful to the IGI Publishing team.

We sincerely thank the chapter contributors for placing their trust in this project and sharing their valuable research and insights. We also deeply appreciate the members of the Editorial Advisory Board and the peer reviewers, whose thoughtful and rigorous evaluations enhanced the quality of every chapter. Together, their contributions demonstrate a unified dedication to advancing the well-being of healthcare providers across the globe.

Above all, I would like to extend my deepest appreciation to my co-editor, Dr. Arfa Masihuddin, for taking the lead in compiling the book very diligently. A special mention for our project managers, Dr. Tehrim Toqir and Dr. Emmama Sattar for their unwavering support across every phase of the project.

With regards,

Prof Dr. Minhaj A Qidwai, *Editor*

Dean Faculty of Allied Health and Medical Sciences

Faculty Member American Institute for Healthcare Quality

The prevalence of burnout in the healthcare workforce has become a public health emergency, and one that needs to be addressed on an urgently. It directly co-relates to provider wellbeing, which, in turn, is proportional to compassionate patient care and better clinical outcomes. Hence, the publication of this book serves to fulfill a greater purpose, and I am deeply grateful to the IGI Publishing team for facilitating the publication of "Fostering Organizational Culture for Provider Wellbeing."

I would also like to thank our valuable contributors for sharing their research and insights, and for believing in the greater purpose of this book.

Another special thank you to my co-editor, Dr. Minhaj Qidwai, who trusted me with the execution and compiling of this publication.

To our project managers, Drs Emmama Sattar and Tehrim Toqir – you two have been incredible, sturdy team members.

I would also like to thank my family and my husband -your patience, support, and encouragement has ensured the completion of this book. To my son-you're so little, and, yet, so patient as you shared your mother with her academic projects. I hope that if you ever decide to walk the path of healthcare, you will find the organizational cultures across the globe to be more compassionate and empowering.

Regards,

Dr. Arfa Masihuddin, *Editor*

Founder, Rufayda – Care for Healthcare

Chapter 1

Impact of Organizational Culture and Well-Being of Healthcare Providers:

The 5S Approach - An Overview of Self, Society, State, Systems, Spirituality

Deepa Mukherjee
http://orcid.org/0000-0003-3007-2040
SGT University, India

ABSTRACT

Healthcare providers face increasing burnout, job dissatisfaction, and workforce shortages, necessitating a holistic approach to well-being. The 5Ss' Approach—comprising Self, Society, State, Systems, and Spirituality—offers a comprehensive framework integrating individual resilience, social support, governmental policies, institutional structures, and existential well-being. Drawing on Schein's organizational culture model and the JD-R framework, this approach highlights the interplay of personal agency, teamwork, regulatory mechanisms, leadership, and spiritual grounding. Case studies from Magnet hospitals and state-led initiatives validate its effectiveness. To safeguard the workforce, healthcare institutions must prioritize transformational leadership, digital innovation, and policy reforms. The 5Ss' model demands systemic implementation to enhance provider resilience and sustain high-quality patient care.

DOI: 10.4018/979-8-2600-0582-8.ch001

1. INTRODUCTION

Organizational culture is a key factor that affects how people work together, their job satisfaction, their level of engagement, and their overall health. We cannot overstate the significance of a supportive and adaptive organizational culture in the healthcare sector, where professionals operate in high-stress environments (Schein, 2010). Healthcare providers frequently encounter challenges such as long working hours, emotional exhaustion, and administrative burdens, which, if left unaddressed, can lead to burnout, reduced productivity, and compromised patient care (Dyrbye et al., 2017; Shanafelt et al., 2015). Given these challenges, fostering a culture that promotes resilience, collaboration, and holistic well-being is essential for sustaining high-quality healthcare delivery.

The importance of organizational culture in healthcare has been widely recognized in management and healthcare research. Schein's (2010) model of organizational culture provides a foundational perspective, emphasizing that culture consists of deeply ingrained values, shared beliefs, and behavioral norms that shape interactions within an institution. Similarly, Mannion and Davies (2018) highlight that healthcare culture influences everything from decision-making and teamwork to ethical practice and patient safety. Organizations that cultivate a positive work culture—characterized by effective leadership, transparent communication, and emotional support—tend to exhibit higher staff retention, reduced stress levels, and improved patient outcomes (Scott et al., 2003; Wong & Cummings, 2007). Conversely, a toxic work culture, marked by hierarchical rigidity, lack of autonomy, and poor work-life balance, has been associated with increased staff turnover and suboptimal healthcare service delivery (West et al., 2016).

The intersection of organizational culture and healthcare provider well-being is especially pertinent in the context of increasing workload pressures, workforce shortages, and the growing complexity of patient needs (Laschinger et al., 2014; Aiken et al., 2012). Burnout among healthcare professionals has reached alarming levels worldwide, with studies indicating that over 50% of physicians and nurses report symptoms of emotional exhaustion, depersonalization, and reduced personal accomplishment (Maslach & Leiter, 2016; Reith, 2018). Addressing these concerns requires a multidimensional approach that considers workplace factors and recognizes the broader social, policy, and personal determinants of well-being (Bakker & Demerouti, 2007; Gonzalez et al., 2021).

In response to these challenges, the *5Ss' Approach* has emerged as a comprehensive framework for understanding and enhancing healthcare provider well-being. This approach encompasses five interconnected dimensions: (Qidwai, 2024)

1. *Self*—Individual resilience, self-care practices, and personal development.

2. *Society*—Social support, team cohesion, and interpersonal relationships.
3. *State*—Government policies, healthcare regulations, and workforce development.
4. *Systems*—organizational structures, leadership styles, and technological integration.
5. *Spirituality*—existential well-being, meaning in work, and holistic self-fulfillment.

The *5Ss framework builds on existing models of organizational culture by combining personal, institutional, and systemic points of view. This gives a complete picture of how to improve the well-being of healthcare providers* (Harris & Larson, 2021). Unlike conventional approaches that focus solely on stress management or policy reforms, this model underscores the interplay between individual self-care, supportive workplace relationships, regulatory environments, and the intrinsic motivation derived from professional and spiritual fulfillment (Krasner et al., 2009; Epstein & Krasner, 2013).

By exploring each of these dimensions in depth, this chapter aims to provide a nuanced understanding of how healthcare organizations can cultivate a culture that supports provider well-being and enhances patient care. In doing so, it offers evidence-based recommendations for fostering resilience, optimizing institutional policies, and promoting a sustainable healthcare workforce (Thornicroft et al., 2020; Patel et al., 2018). Through a combination of theoretical insights and practical applications, the *5Ss' Approach* presents a pathway toward a healthier, more engaged, and more effective healthcare workforce.

2. THEORETICAL UNDERPINNINGS AND CONCEPTUAL FRAMEWORK

A robust understanding of organizational culture within healthcare necessitates the integration of multiple theoretical perspectives. Schein's (2010) model, which distinguishes between artifacts, espoused values, and underlying assumptions, provides a foundational lens for examining how culture is both manifested and sustained in organizations. Complementing this perspective, the Job Demands-Resources (JD-R) model (Bakker & Demerouti, 2007; Bakker et al., 2014) highlights how work demands and available resources interact to influence burnout and engagement among healthcare providers.

The 5Ss' approach extends these models by incorporating broader contextual and existential factors. It posits that provider well-being is not solely determined by immediate workplace conditions but is also influenced by individual self-care practices, social relationships, governmental policies, organizational systems, and spiritual beliefs. This integrated framework encourages a holistic analysis, prompting healthcare leaders to address multiple layers of influence—from personal resilience to state-level regulatory support—to promote a healthier workforce (Harris & Larson, 2021; Gonzalez et al., 2021).

3. SELF: INDIVIDUAL FACTORS IMPACTING HEALTHCARE PROVIDER WELL-BEING

3.1 Personal Resilience and Self-Care

At the heart of the 5Ss' approach is the concept of self, which focuses on the individual attributes, attitudes, and behaviors of healthcare providers. Personal resilience, self-awareness, and effective stress management are critical components that enable providers to cope with the rigors of their profession (Shanafelt et al., 2015). Numerous studies have demonstrated that interventions aimed at enhancing self-care—such as mindfulness training, stress reduction techniques, and cognitive behavioral strategies—can significantly reduce burnout and improve job satisfaction (Krasner et al., 2009; West et al., 2016).

3.2 Professional Development and Empowerment

In addition to self-care practices, continuous professional development and empowerment are key to bolstering individual well-being. Empowered providers who engage in lifelong learning and skill development tend to exhibit higher levels of confidence and job satisfaction (Laschinger & Leiter, 2006; Spence Laschinger et al., 2015). Leadership training, mentorship programs, and reflective practice initiatives are essential strategies that help individuals build the resilience necessary to thrive in complex healthcare environments (Epstein & Krasner, 2013).

4. SOCIETY: SOCIAL DYNAMICS AND INTERPERSONAL RELATIONSHIPS

4.1 The Role of Social Support and Teamwork

Society, as conceptualized in the 5Ss' Approach, refers to the social and interpersonal dynamics that exist within and beyond the healthcare organization. A positive organizational culture is characterized by robust social support networks and effective teamwork, which are critical for mitigating stress and enhancing overall well-being (Manojlovich, 2005; Salas et al., 2008). Collaborative practices, such as interdisciplinary team meetings and peer support groups, foster a sense of community and shared purpose among healthcare providers (Dyrbye et al., 2017).

4.2 Organizational Justice and Social Capital

Research in organizational behavior underscores the importance of fairness and social capital in promoting employee satisfaction (Colquitt et al., 2013; Tyler & Blader, 2003). When healthcare providers perceive that they are treated equitably and that their contributions are valued, they are more likely to exhibit higher levels of engagement and commitment. Social capital, built through trust and mutual respect among colleagues, further reinforces a supportive work environment that can buffer the adverse effects of high job demands (Putnam, 2000; Adler & Kwon, 2002).

5. STATE: THE ROLE OF GOVERNMENT POLICIES AND REGULATIONS

5.1 Policy Frameworks and Healthcare Funding

The dimension of state encompasses the governmental policies, regulations, and funding mechanisms that shape the healthcare landscape. State-level interventions, such as workforce development initiatives, labor regulations, and public health policies, play a crucial role in determining the resources available to healthcare providers (World Health Organization [WHO], 2013; Patel et al., 2018). Adequate funding and supportive regulatory frameworks are essential for ensuring that healthcare organizations can implement programs aimed at reducing burnout and improving provider well-being (Aiken et al., 2012).

5.2 Regulatory Oversight and Professional Standards

In addition to funding, regulatory oversight and the establishment of professional standards are critical for maintaining high-quality care. Policies that promote safe staffing levels, continuous professional development, and ethical practice contribute to a healthier work environment and better patient outcomes (Vahey et al., 2004; McHugh et al., 2011). Moreover, state-sponsored initiatives such as the Mental Health Action Plan and national accreditation programs serve to standardize best practices and create accountability within healthcare institutions (Saxena et al., 2007).

6. SYSTEMS: INSTITUTIONAL STRUCTURES AND ORGANIZATIONAL INFRASTRUCTURE

6.1 Organizational Structure and Leadership

Systems refer to the internal organizational structures, management practices, and technological infrastructures that underpin healthcare delivery. Effective leadership is a cornerstone of positive organizational culture, with transformational leadership styles shown to significantly reduce burnout and enhance job satisfaction (Bass & Riggio, 2006; Cummings et al., 2010). Clear communication, participative decision-making, and robust feedback mechanisms are essential elements that contribute to a cohesive and supportive work environment (Laschinger et al., 2014).

6.2 Digital Health and Communication Systems

Advances in digital health technologies have revolutionized the way healthcare organizations function. Telemedicine, electronic health records (EHRs), and integrated communication platforms not only streamline workflows but also facilitate real-time collaboration among providers (Firth et al., 2019; Fortney et al., 2015). These innovations contribute to improved care coordination and reduce the administrative burdens that often contribute to provider stress (Becker et al., 2018). Furthermore, digital training and e-learning platforms support continuous professional development, thereby strengthening the overall capacity of the healthcare workforce (Lora et al., 2020).

7. SPIRITUALITY: THE ROLE OF SPIRITUAL AND EXISTENTIAL WELL-BEING

7.1 Spirituality as a Source of Resilience

The final dimension, spirituality, highlights the importance of spiritual well-being as a source of personal resilience and meaning. For many healthcare providers, spiritual beliefs and practices offer a framework for coping with the challenges and emotional demands of their work (Koenig, 2012). Spirituality—whether expressed through formal religious practices, meditation, or personal reflection—can foster a sense of purpose and inner strength, which in turn contributes to improved mental health and overall well-being (Pargament, 1997; Cotton et al., 2006).

7.2 Integration of Spirituality into Organizational Culture

Incorporating spirituality into the organizational culture means recognizing and meeting the different spiritual needs of healthcare workers. This may include the provision of quiet spaces for reflection, the incorporation of mindfulness and meditation programs, and the encouragement of work-life balance practices that honor personal values (Howden, 2004; Benefiel, 2003). Research suggests that organizations that embrace spiritual dimensions tend to report higher levels of employee satisfaction and reduced incidences of burnout (Nelson, 2010).

8. INTEGRATION OF THE 5SS: A SYNERGISTIC MODEL

The true strength of the 5Ss' approach lies in its integrative capacity—each dimension interacts with and reinforces the others to create a comprehensive support system for healthcare providers. For example, personal self-care practices are more effective when supported by strong social networks (Society) and facilitated by clear policies and adequate resources (State). Similarly, robust institutional systems (Systems) can enhance the delivery of spiritual and emotional support (Spirituality), leading to a more resilient and engaged workforce (Thornicroft et al., 2020).

This holistic model underscores the necessity of multifaceted interventions that address both individual and collective needs. Healthcare organizations must adopt strategies that not only focus on immediate workplace improvements but also consider broader systemic and existential factors. The integrated 5Ss' model provides a roadmap for developing comprehensive interventions that promote well-being at all levels—from the individual to the organizational and societal.

9. CASE STUDIES AND PRACTICAL APPLICATIONS

9.1 Case Study: A Magnet Hospital Initiative

One illustrative example comes from Magnet-designated hospitals, which have long emphasized the importance of supportive organizational cultures. These institutions have implemented programs that integrate self-care workshops, interdisciplinary team meetings, and digital communication tools to enhance provider well-being (Kutney-Lee et al., 2009; McHugh et al., 2011). In these settings, providers report lower levels of burnout, higher job satisfaction, and improved patient care outcomes, demonstrating the efficacy of a holistic approach that aligns closely with the 5Ss' framework.

9.2 Community Health Centers and Digital Innovations

Community health centers, another example, have utilized telehealth and digital training platforms to assist non-specialist health workers. By incorporating e-learning modules and real-time communication systems, these centers have effectively reduced the isolation often experienced by providers in remote areas (Fortney et al., 2017; Lora et al., 2020). Moreover, initiatives that include peer support groups and mindfulness training sessions have further strengthened the social and spiritual dimensions of care, contributing to a more resilient workforce.

9.3 Government-Led Initiatives

State-level initiatives, such as the WHO's Mental Health Gap Action Programme (mhGAP), highlight the importance of comprehensive policies in bridging the treatment gap in mental health care. These programs, which integrate training for non-specialist providers with robust regulatory frameworks, demonstrate how governmental support (state) can significantly enhance the effectiveness of community-based care models (WHO, 2013; Patel et al., 2011).

10. IMPLICATIONS FOR PRACTICE AND POLICY

The integrated 5Ss' approach has significant implications for both practice and policy. For healthcare organizations, adopting this model means prioritizing interventions that address individual self-care, foster supportive social environments, ensure robust state and regulatory support, optimize organizational systems, and nurture the spiritual well-being of staff. Practical steps may include:

- **Developing Comprehensive Training Programs:** Incorporate modules on self-care, teamwork, digital literacy, and spiritual well-being into professional development curricula (Kazdin, 2017; Epstein & Krasner, 2013).
- **Enhancing Leadership Practices:** Promote transformational leadership that supports open communication, participative decision-making, and continuous feedback (Bass & Riggio, 2006; Cummings et al., 2010).
- **Investing in Digital Infrastructure:** Expand telehealth services, electronic health records, and e-learning platforms to streamline operations and facilitate continuous professional growth (Firth et al., 2019; Becker et al., 2018).
- **Strengthening Regulatory Support:** Advocate for state policies that ensure adequate staffing levels, equitable resource distribution, and ongoing workforce development (Aiken et al., 2012; Saxena et al., 2007).

- **Integrating Spiritual Care:** Establish programs and spaces that support spiritual practices, including mindfulness sessions, meditation breaks, and reflective practices (Koenig, 2012; Pargament, 1997).

For policymakers, the 5Ss' framework points out that there must be a multi-pronged approach that combines funding, regulation, and innovative program design. State and federal agencies must work together to make rules that support the overall development of the workforce and make sure that healthcare providers have the tools they need to give high-quality, patient-centered care (Patel et al., 2018; WHO, 2013).

11. FUTURE DIRECTIONS AND RESEARCH GAPS

While the 5Ss' Approach offers a robust framework for understanding the multifaceted influences on healthcare provider well-being, further research is necessary to refine and validate its components. Longitudinal studies examining the interplay between individual self-care practices and broader organizational and state-level interventions would provide valuable insights. Moreover, research exploring the efficacy of digital and spiritual interventions in diverse healthcare settings is needed to identify best practices and scalable models (Thornicroft et al., 2020; Kazdin & Rabbitt, 2013).

Addressing gaps will require interdisciplinary collaboration among researchers, healthcare practitioners, and policymakers, with a focus on developing integrated, evidence-based interventions that align with the holistic principles of the 5Ss' Approach.

12. CONCLUSION

The well-being of healthcare providers is a critical determinant of the quality of patient care, and it is profoundly influenced by organizational culture. The 5Ss' Approach—encompassing Self, Society, State, Systems, and Spirituality—offers a comprehensive framework for understanding and enhancing provider well-being. By addressing individual needs, fostering supportive social environments, ensuring robust policy and regulatory support, optimizing organizational systems, and integrating spiritual dimensions, healthcare organizations can build a resilient workforce capable of meeting the complex demands of modern healthcare.

This holistic approach not only improves job satisfaction and reduces burnout but also translates into better patient outcomes, stronger interprofessional collaboration, and more efficient healthcare delivery. As the healthcare landscape continues to evolve, the integrated 5Ss model provides a roadmap for sustainable workforce development and a call to action for continuous research and policy innovation.

REFERENCES

Adler, P. S., & Kwon, S. (2002). Social capital: Prospects for a new concept. *Academy of Management Review*, *27*(1), 17–40. DOI: 10.2307/4134367

Aiken, L. H.. (2012). Nurse staffing and patient outcomes: Cross-national findings. *Journal of Advanced Nursing*, *69*(11), 2425–2434. DOI: 10.1111/j.1365-2648.2011.05722.x

Aiken, L. H., Sloane, D. M., Bruyneel, L., Van den Heede, K., Griffiths, P., Busse, R., Diomidous, M., Kinnunen, J., Kózka, M., Lesaffre, E., McHugh, M. D., Moreno-Casbas, M. T., Rafferty, A. M., Schwendimann, R., Scott, P. A., Tishelman, C., van Achterberg, T., & Sermeus, W. (2012). Nurse staffing and education and hospital mortality in nine European countries: A retrospective observational study. *Lancet*, *383*(9931), 1824–1830. DOI: 10.1016/S0140-6736(13)62631-8 PMID: 24581683

Bakker, A. B., & Demerouti, E. (2007). The Job Demands-Resources model: State of the art. *Journal of Managerial Psychology*, *22*(3), 309–328. DOI: 10.1108/02683940710733115

Bakker, A. B., Demerouti, E., & Sanz-Vergel, A. I. (2014). Burnout and work engagement: The JD–R approach. *Annual Review of Organizational Psychology and Organizational Behavior*, *1*(1), 389–411. DOI: 10.1146/annurev-orgpsych-031413-091235

Bass, B. M., & Riggio, R. E. (2006). *Transformational leadership* (2nd ed.). Lawrence Erlbaum Associates. DOI: 10.4324/9781410617095

Becker, A. E.. (2018). Community-based mental health services in developing countries: New models and innovations. *World Psychiatry; Official Journal of the World Psychiatric Association (WPA)*, *17*(2), 168–174. DOI: 10.1002/wps.20599 PMID: 29856555

Benefiel, M. (2003). Mapping the terrain of spirituality in organizations research. *Journal of Organizational Change Management*, *16*(4), 367–377. DOI: 10.1108/09534810310484136

Cotton, S.. (2006). Spirituality in the workplace: Perspectives on theory, research, and practice. *Journal of Management, Spirituality & Religion*, *3*(2), 189–203. DOI: 10.1300/J085v03n02_12

Cummings, G. G., MacGregor, T., Davey, M., Lee, H., Wong, C. A., Lo, E., Muise, M., & Stafford, E. (2010). Leadership styles and outcome patterns for the nursing workforce and work environment: A systematic review. *International Journal of Nursing Studies*, *47*(3), 363–385. DOI: 10.1016/j.ijnurstu.2009.08.006 PMID: 19781702

Dyrbye, L. N., Shanafelt, T. D., Sinsky, C. A., Cipriano, P. F., Bhatt, J., Ommaya, A., West, C. P., & Meyers, D. (2017). Burnout among healthcare professionals: A call to explore and address this underrecognized threat to safe, high-quality care. *NAM Perspectives*, *7*(7), 1–10. DOI: 10.31478/201707b

Epstein, R. M., & Krasner, M. S. (2013). Physician resilience: What it means, why it matters, and how to promote it. *Academic Medicine*, *88*(3), 301–303. DOI: 10.1097/ACM.0b013e318280cff0 PMID: 23442430

Firth, J.. (2019). Digital interventions for improving mental health and well-being: A systematic review. *The Lancet. Psychiatry*, *6*(6), 500–510. DOI: 10.1016/S2215-0366(19)30027-4

Fortney, J. C.. (2015). Telepsychiatry and integrated care in mental health workforce development. *Psychiatric Services (Washington, D.C.)*, *66*(9), 972–979. DOI: 10.1176/appi.ps.201400372

Fortney, J. C.. (2017). Practice transformation in primary care: Bridging the gap between mental health and primary care. *Psychiatric Services (Washington, D.C.)*, *68*(2), 101–108. DOI: 10.1176/appi.ps.201600166 PMID: 27582237

Gonzalez, P.. (2021). Organizational justice and mental health: Impact on workforce well-being. *Journal of Health Organization and Management*, *35*(3), 227–243. DOI: 10.1108/JHOM-05-2020-0170

Harris, J., & Larson, P. (2021). The role of organizational justice in the workplace: Implications for employee well-being in healthcare. *Journal of Health Organization and Management*, *35*(3), 227–243. DOI: 10.1108/JHOM-05-2020-0170

Howden, S. (2004). Workplace spirituality and organizational performance. *Journal of Management, Spirituality & Religion*, *1*(2), 119–138. DOI: 10.1300/J161v01n02_08

Kazdin, A. E. (2017). Innovations in mental health workforce development: Advancing evidence-based practices. *The American Psychologist*, *72*(6), 483–495. DOI: 10.1037/amp0000235

Kazdin, A. E., & Rabbitt, S. M. (2013). Novel models for delivering mental health services and reducing the burdens of mental illness. *Clinical Psychological Science*, *1*(2), 170–191. DOI: 10.1177/2167702612463566

Koenig, H. G. (2012). Religion, spirituality, and health: The research and clinical implications. *ISRN Psychiatry, 2012*, 1–33. DOI: 10.5402/2012/278730 PMID: 23762764

Krasner, M. S.. (2009). Association of an educational program in mindful communication with burnout, empathy, and attitudes among primary care physicians. *Journal of the American Medical Association, 302*(12), 1284–1293. DOI: 10.1001/jama.2009.1384 PMID: 19773563

Kutney-Lee, A.. (2009). Magnet hospital staff nurses report lower burnout and higher job satisfaction. *Health Affairs, 28*(5), 144–153. DOI: 10.1377/hlthaff.28.5.144

Laschinger, H. K. S.. (2014). Workplace empowerment, incivility, and burnout: Impact on staff nurse recruitment and retention outcomes. *Journal of Nursing Management, 22*(8), 1027–1038. DOI: 10.1111/jonm.12103 PMID: 23758834

Laschinger, H. K. S., & Leiter, M. P. (2006). The impact of nursing work environments on patient safety outcomes: The mediating role of burnout engagement. *The Journal of Nursing Administration, 36*(12), 659–667. DOI: 10.1097/00005110-200605000-00019 PMID: 16705307

Lora, A.. (2020). Workforce training for integrated mental health care: A systematic review of programs and outcomes. *Journal of Mental Health (Abingdon, England), 29*(1), 12–20. DOI: 10.1080/09638237.2019.1670160 PMID: 28644705

Mannion, R., & Davies, H. T. O. (2018). Understanding organizational culture for healthcare quality improvement. *BMJ (Clinical Research Ed.), 363*, k4907. DOI: 10.1136/bmj.k4907 PMID: 30487286

McHugh, M. D.. (2011). Nurse engagement in hospital quality improvement: A multi-level analysis. *Health Services Research, 46*(3), 903–920. DOI: 10.1111/j.1475-6773.2010.01220.x

Nelson, B. (2010). Spirituality, leadership, and organizational culture: The development of spiritual intelligence. *Journal of Management Development, 29*(3), 218–230. DOI: 10.1108/02621711011025355

Pargament, K. I. (1997). *The psychology of religion and coping: Theory, research, practice*. Guilford Press.

Patel, V.. (2011). The mental health treatment gap in low- and middle-income countries: A systematic review. *Bulletin of the World Health Organization, 89*(9), 658–666. DOI: 10.2471/BLT.07.045479

Patel, V.. (2018). Integrating mental health into primary care: A global perspective. *Lancet, 392*(10161), 1553–1567. DOI: 10.1016/S0140-6736(18)31612-X PMID: 30314863

Putnam, R. D. (2000). *Bowling alone: The collapse and revival of American community*. Simon & Schuster.

Qidwai, M. A. (2024). The 5Ss' Approach for Managing Health of Client, Family, and Community. *National Journal of Health Sciences*, *9*(4), 231–234. DOI: 10.21089/njhs.94.0231

Saxena, S., Thornicroft, G., Knapp, M., & Whiteford, H. (2007). Resources for mental health: Scarcity, inequity, and inefficiency. *Lancet, 370*(9590), 878–889. DOI: 10.1016/S0140-6736(07)61239-2 PMID: 17804062

Schein, E. H. (2010). *Organizational culture and leadership* (4th ed.). Jossey-Bass.

Shanafelt, T. D., Hasan, O., Dyrbye, L. N., Sinsky, C., Satele, D., Sloan, J., & West, C. P. (2015). Changes in burnout and satisfaction with work-life balance in physicians and the general US working population between 2011 and 2014. *Mayo Clinic Proceedings, 90*(12), 1600–1613. DOI: 10.1016/j.mayocp.2015.08.023 PMID: 26653297

Spence Laschinger, H. K.. (2015). Impact of workplace empowerment on new graduate nurses' workplace incivility and burnout. *Nursing Outlook*, *63*(2), 186–194. DOI: 10.1016/j.outlook.2014.09.008 PMID: 26833252

Thornicroft, G.. (2020). Innovations in mental health workforce development: Challenges and future directions. *World Psychiatry; Official Journal of the World Psychiatric Association (WPA)*, *19*(3), 380–382. DOI: 10.1002/wps.20773

Tyler, T. R., & Blader, S. L. (2003). The group engagement model: Procedural justice, social identity, and cooperative behavior. *Personality and Social Psychology Review*, *7*(4), 349–361. DOI: 10.1207/S15327957PSPR0704_07 PMID: 14633471

West, C. P., Dyrbye, L. N., Erwin, P. J., & Shanafelt, T. D. (2016). Interventions to prevent and reduce physician burnout: A systematic review and meta-analysis. *Lancet, 388*(10057), 2272–2281. DOI: 10.1016/S0140-6736(16)31279-X PMID: 27692469

WHO. (2013). *Mental Health Action Plan 2013-2020*. World Health Organization.

Yammarino, F. J.. (2005). Transformational leadership and team performance: Integrating team process and contextual moderation perspectives. *The Leadership Quarterly*, *16*(4), 475–493. DOI: 10.1016/j.leaqua.2005.05.008

Chapter 2
5S Approach for Efficacy of Organizational Wellness Management on the Well-Being of Healthcare Providers:
5S – Self, Society, State, Systems, and Spirituality

Aqsa Yaqoob
http://orcid.org/0009-0000-1742-9346
University of Karachi, Pakistan

Amena Zehra Ali
http://orcid.org/0000-0002-0032-3163
University of Karachi, Pakistan

Minhaj A. Qidwai
http://orcid.org/0009-0003-0770-481X
Al-Kawthar University, Pakistan

ABSTRACT

Healthcare providers are at the risk of mental health challenges due to long working hours, workloads, insufficient social support, lack of autonomy (Piras et al., 2020; Yalim et al., 2024); rigid policies, toxic work culture, and lack of reinforcement (Tawfik et al., 2019).Implementing wellness initiatives should be adaptable and responsive to feedback from healthcare providers (Wilkie et al., 2021). This chapter

DOI: 10.4018/979-8-2600-0582-8.ch002

aims to propose effective and evidence-based programs to ensure the mental wellbeing of healthcare providers and increases the credibility of the organization itself. Developing wellness programs, such as managing stress and burnout, dealing with difficult people, anger management, navigating social interaction, mindfulness and meditation programs, counselling and peer support, cognitive behavior therapy. Crisis management etc. these programs are effective in improving practice efficiency and help balance job demands and reduce work-life conflict.

INTRODUCTION

As humans we all require proper care and attention for our health needs, failing which can result in short-term or long-term negative health consequences. We can end up getting sick or being vulnerable to some deadly illnesses. Sometimes the issues are much beyond simple caring and so we end up needing the help of a trained professional, a health care professional, to provide us with the necessary guidelines on how to resolve our situations.

A health care provider can range from primary care physicians to specialists. With the advancements of research and technology, the horizon of health care has broadened, including experts of complex and advanced health care issues. The lists include, but are not limited to, doctors, nurses, paramedics, counselors, therapists, diagnosticians, lab technicians, etc. The service they provide also ranges from simple advice about drinking water to giving radiotherapy or conducting MRI scans. They guide the patients regarding how to make healthy decisions for themselves (Smith, 2025) and to follow through with the compliance on medical advice.

Working in various health care facilities and hospitals, these professionals, while caring for us, go through their own silent crises as well. This is because health care or medical practice is by itself a very demanding profession. Along with the usual health-related issues that they experience (being humans). Working hours, organizational policies, work pressures, stress, and other work-related factors affect their well-being. Then there is work-family balance, as they all have to meet the family needs. (Masood et al., 2022). The irony in this situation is that while the purpose of health care is to promote well-being and reduce illnesses, the ones providing this care often end up suffering themselves. This does not just directly affect the individual involved, but it indirectly affects the quality of care they provide, resulting in poor patient outcomes.

Health care providers are the basic backbone of health care systems, their role being very crucial (Smith, 2025). Through these agents, the required health care reaches people in need. While reaching others, they themselves are working under immense stress from high patient influx, difficult and complicated cases, and interpersonal pressures and conflicts. There are different emotional responses of seeing patients' sufferings and deaths (McNeely, 2005). To add to the stress, there are night shifts and lengthy day shifts too. Despite having the correct medical knowledge, the risk of medical error is there, which can be dangerous for the lives of the patient and; sometimes these errors cannot be undone (Chou, et al., 2014). They usually result in occupational stress (Masood, et al., 2014), poor wellbeing, psychological distress, and burnout (McNeely, 2005; Colling & Murray, 1996; Maslach & Schaufeli, 1993). These are the negative psychological outcomes that lead to or exacerbate the medical conditions commonly known as psychosomatic illness (Zhang, 2011).

5SS (SELF, SOCIETY, STATE, SYSTEMS AND SPIRITUALITY) AND HUMAN WELLNESS MANAGEMENT

The World Health Organization (WHO) defines health as "a dynamic state of complete physical, mental, and social well-being and not merely the absence of disease or infirmity." WHO has lately debated on adding the fourth dimension of Health-Spirituality (Dhar et al., 2011; World Health Organization, 1985). A holistic approach is necessary to ensure human wellness and its management, taking into account these four dimensions of human health.

The 5Ss' (Self, Society, State, Systems, and Spirituality) approach of Dr. Minhaj Qidwai is a Human Wellness Management integrated approach, derived from the three fundamental aspects of human existence: the body, soul, and spirit; and their eight dimensions. The *body* is the physical and material part of a human being. *Soul* is the realm of decision-making, containing the mind, will, emotions, and personality. While Spirit is considered the innermost part of a person, the connection to the divine or a higher power. Considering the three aspects of body, soul, and spirit, human wellness can be considered as encompassing eight mutually interdependent dimensions: physical, intellectual, emotional, social, spiritual, occupational, financial, and environmental (Ardell, 1999; World Health Organization, 2010). In order to ensure human wellness management within organizations, the concept of wellness needs to be considered.

Figure 1.

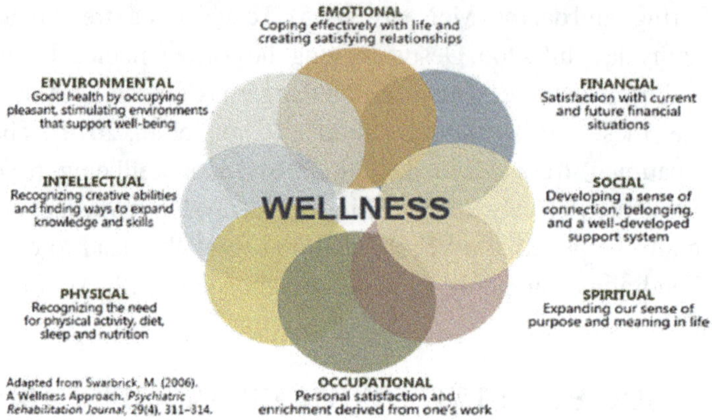

Management of self is the key in bringing any change, either locally or globally. However, understanding of a healthcare worker is essential to intervene and manage health. The healthcare professional is equipped with the required knowledge, and the curriculum is geared towards the curative, symptomatic, and preventive management. However, wellness management requires the smooth functioning of health systems. The World Health Organization (2010) proposes a health system revolving around six building blocks contributing to the strengthening of health systems. The cross-cutting components, such as leadership/governance and health information systems, provide the basis for the overall policy and regulation of all the other health system blocks. Key input components to the health system include specifically financing and the health workforce. A third group, namely medical products and technology and service delivery, reflects the immediate output of the health system, i.e., the availability and distribution of care. Subsequently, health and wellness management care is beyond that of current teachings in a healthcare institution and needs an integrated approach with interventions from all the 5Ss (Self, Society, State, Systems, and Spirituality). Let us consider the 5Ss on an individual basis:

1. Self

Healthcare providers can help individuals understand their physical, emotional, and mental health needs through education and self-assessment tools. Promoting healthy behaviors such as regular exercise, balanced nutrition, stress management techniques, and adequate sleep can empower individuals to take control of their health. Providing resources for personal development, goal setting, and skill-building can help people find meaning and fulfillment. Understanding and managing personal well-being is crucial, as is helping others within the organization.

Stress rate among healthcare providers (HCPs) is high, which often results in poor mental and physical health (Cakirpaloglu et al., 2024; Hofmann, 2018); compromised patient care quality (Burton et al., 2017; Hofmann, 2018); result in frequent job shifts, absenteeism, and financial costs for healthcare institutions (Hofmann, 2018). The self-perception of a stressful person is that they are unlovable, a failure, and worthless. As a result, he constantly strives for the best because he places high demands on himself. For instance, I am expected to be flawless, to work beyond regular hours, and so forth. Consequently, he experiences feelings of stress, overwhelm, and pressure. As a result, he indulges in overworking behaviors and perfectionistic tendencies.

It is crucial for healthcare setups to initiate wellness programs. Stress management plays an important role in improving quality of life, efficiency, concentration, and job performance of a person (Cakirpaloglu et al., 2024; Odigie, 2016; Shapiro et al., 2005). Below are the several steps to follow for the management of stress (Riggenbach, 2013, p. 45).

Stress Management

Step 1: To identify the triggers of stress. It is necessary because once they identify them, they will better be able to search for solutions. e.g. What makes you feel stressed? What do I think in that situation? How do I feel? The last time I felt stressful was...

Step 2: The second step is to identify coping strategies. Because coping makes the outcome either positive or negative. e.g., What do I do when I feel stressed? Are these coping mechanisms healthy or not? Do these coping mechanisms give rise to my unhealthy behavior?

Step 3: Modifying the unhealthy coping is a necessary step. As a result, you will learn healthy coping to deal with it, and it will also help you in the future.

- Replace negative coping strategies with positive ones.
- Find out the ways to solve the problem without getting too stressed.
- Ask the trustworthy person about the different solutions.
- Do a cost-benefit analysis of the decision.

Step 4: Replacing negative thoughts is the key to overcoming stress.

- Check the theme of negative thoughts in stressful situations.
- Replace them with less negative thoughts and practice it.

- Replace less negative ones with positive ones.

Step 5: Make a list of self-care strategies that can replace unhealthy coping and practice them daily. For example, go for a walk, eat healthy, sleep well, do exercise, watch television, play your favorite sport, read a book, and talk to an old friend.

Setting Goals

Setting goals to manage stress is the turning point of wellness management. One of the most popular and often applied frameworks for goal setting is the SMART model. It was initially presented in an essay in the Management Review in 1981 (Doran, 1981) and showed a positive result when used for both individuals.

Goal: *Improve time management by making a to-do list of daily tasks.*

Specific: Every goal ought to be as precise and well-defined as feasible. Although you might have more than one aim, each one needs to be distinct. *Make a to-do list of tasks for a day.*

Measurable: Every objective needs to have precise measurements that allow it to be assessed, either for progress or the final objective. *Complete 70% of the task by following the list.*

Achievable: Although it's simple to overdo it when creating objectives, aiming for something that is ultimately unachievable can sap your motivation. Set modest, attainable goals. You may always expand and add to them. *Allocate a time of day to note progress.*

Relevant: This is the point at which setting aside time to organize your objectives might be beneficial. Pursuing a goal that doesn't align with your basic beliefs or life goals is pointless. Verify that each objective pertains to you. *Work productively by managing time; this will decrease stress and increase performance.*

Time-Bound: To stay motivated and engaged, make sure you give yourself reasonable due dates for each objective and the necessary actions. *Start and follow the routine for 4 weeks.*

Emotional Regulation

Emotional regulation is a critical skill for healthcare providers, directly impacting their well-being, job performance, patient safety, and the quality of care delivered. Effective emotional regulation helps providers manage stress, prevent burnout, and maintain high standards of patient care, even in emotionally charged or high-pressure environments. HCPs with strong emotional regulation skills experience less workplace stress and are less likely to suffer from burnout or compassion fatigue, supporting both short- and long-term well-being and resilience (Weilenmann et al., 2018; Kharatzadeh et al., 2020; Kadović et al., 2022; Buruck et al., 2016; Santo et al., 2024). Emotional regulation training leads to improvements in psychological well-being, reduces depression, anxiety, and stress, and increases job satisfaction among nurses and other healthcare workers (Kharatzadeh et al., 2020; Buruck et al., 2016).

a. Validation

Accept the fact that you are feeling some emotions, which may be either positive or negative. Most people get irritated because they do not accept their emotions. When they accept and validate their emotions, they will come to a better position to regulate them.

b. Understanding Emotions

Understanding emotions is a key to emotional regulation. Question yourself, why am I feeling this way? What do my emotions do for me? Understand the fact that if you change the way you feel about something, you will change the whole system.

- Observe your emotions.
- Explain it.
- Give a name to it.

c. Changing Emotions

In difficult situations, it's crucial to consider the bigger picture and adjust your response accordingly. If your emotions are appropriate, respond assertively. If not, modify them. For instance, if you're angry in a conflict, consider the thought behind the emotion. If you're feeling motivated and happy, change the thought that brought the emotion. This will help you focus on improving your treatment and patient care, ultimately leading to a more productive day.

d. Problem Solving

A. The first step in problem solving is to think about the problem.
B. Write down the possible and realistic solutions of the problem.
C. Collecting the information about the problem.
D. What are the costs and benefits of the solution?
E. What is the appropriate solution of the problem?
F. Visualizing the outcome.

e. Build Mastery and Healthy Coping

People can work on their shortcomings in order to make themself emotionally balanced. Maladaptive copings should be replaced with more positive ones. Here is a list of some copings on which people can work to make themself happy. For example, making goals, traveling, engaging in outdoor activities, exercise, meditating, doing yoga, or Zumba, running, jogging, walking, doing groceries, take sun baths, etc.

f. Building Self-confidence

Low self-esteem can be a significant issue, often triggered by negative thoughts and unhealthy coping mechanisms. To address this, it is essential to identify triggers, such as feeling low or anxious, and identify common feelings. It is also crucial to identify distorted thoughts and unhealthy coping strategies that can lead to negative consequences. To replace negative coping with healthy ones, it is essential to challenge negative thoughts and replace them with rational ones. This can be achieved by using the downward arrow technique to identify core beliefs and rating their strengths. For example, if you believe that failing a project will result in failure, staying in the same position, or not providing a good life for your family, you can modify the negative core belief to "can succeed." Collecting evidence for negative and healthy beliefs is another step in the process. It is essential to identify your values as a person and write down the values that are most important to you. By taking these steps, you can work towards improving your self-esteem and overcoming the negative thoughts that contribute to low self-esteem.

2. Society

Encouraging participation in community activities, support groups, and peer networks can enhance social connections and provide emotional support. Recognizing the impact of factors such as income, education, employment, and access to healthcare on overall wellness, and advocating for policies to address health disparities. Collaborating with community organizations and stakeholders to create initiatives that promote health education, prevention, and access to healthcare services. Individuals knowledgeable with the 5Ss concept will consider the well-being of society and thus be able to contribute to community wellness.

Building Social Skills

Building social skills is a building block of promoting wellness on societal levels. Social psychologists have created various methods for assisting people in acquiring social skills, which they can learn. Cognitive therapy is essential in changing the way the people view other people. It helps them form more reasonable expectations for social interactions. For example, they discover that most individuals are extremely sensitive to criticism. It is essential to establish and maintain social connections with other people. So that we may feel connected to our friendships, intimate partners, family, and neighbors. Commitment comes in a way to build social relations. It is a deep desire to uphold a relationship that adds to the longevity of professional partnerships. Additionally, certain personality traits are linked to having a successful professional relationship. Some people seem to be better at keeping up professional relationships than others. There is compatibility, shared personality traits, and commitment that make a relationship better (Baron et al., 2011).

Managing Anger

Anger is defined as "a feeling of displeasure and annoyance in response to perceived provocation" (APA). Anger is an emotional response, while aggression is a behavior that grows from the need to control. Aggression is defined as "a person's forceful action, whether it is physical or psychological, with the intention of making harm to another person" (APA). Both anger and aggression are different from each other and are positively correlated. People can feel anger without being aggressive and they can be aggressive without feeling anger. For example, patients feel angry because of the illness without acting aggressive. Similarly, an employee aggressively competes with another employee for a promotion without feeling angry. Aggression has always been considered an unacceptable response. However, there are two types of aggressive behavior: socially appropriate conduct and socially inappropriate conduct.

For example, HCPs compete with each other in order to take positions and opportunities, a boxer fights with a competitor to win the challenge, and employees work hard to win the promotion. These are the examples of socially appropriate conduct. A student teases another student and calls for a fight, a passenger on a flight takes another passenger's window seat and does not want to give it back, and a driver honks at other cars and verbally abuses others. These are the types of socially inappropriate conduct. There are many ways through which a person can prevent aggressive behavior.

- Looking into the bigger picture of a situation.

Sometimes a situation gets worse when people focus on one aspect of the problem. By looking into the bigger picture and more aspects of the problem, HCPs can manage to handle it in more different ways that could be healthy.

- Distract yourself from the situation.

Sometimes it does not help when people try to deal with the problem immediately. Distracting yourself from the situation for some seconds makes a change in your emotional state.

- Ask yourself, what made you feel angry?

This is very important because people need to understand that the situation itself is not negative, but the meaning they attach to it makes it negative. Check what meaning you have attached to the situation and what triggered you?

- Initiate self-talk to reduce anger.

Talking to yourself positively helps to distract from the active situation. You can use some phrases for yourself to calm you down.

- Assertively communicate with others.

Talking with others in an assertive manner leads to reducing aggression. By communicating what you feel, you let others understand your side of the story and similarly, you also get to know their side too.

3. State

Supporting policies that promote wellness, such as healthcare reform, mental health parity laws, and initiatives to address public health issues like substance abuse and obesity. Ensuring healthcare systems adhere to standards of quality, safety, and accessibility through regulatory oversight and accreditation processes. Investing in healthcare infrastructure, workforce development, and prevention programs to improve population health outcomes. Becoming a good and law-abiding citizen. He will ensure ethical practices within the organization.

Healthcare providers face crises due to several reasons, including poor organizational management, pandemics, lack of resources, system failures, etc. The outcome of these crises impacts the mental and physical well-being of an HCP. COVID-19 has become the major source of intense workload, redeployment of staff, and increased risk of getting infected. HCPs are at more risk of depression, anxiety, burnout, PTSD, and insomnia during crisis (Abbas, 2021; Hertelendy et al., 2020; Xu et al., 2021). Mental health crisis also leads to an emergency situation and shed the light on crisis management among HCPs (DeLeo et al., 2022).

Crisis management focuses on building resilience (Emami et al., 2024) and decentralizing key functions (e.g., prioritization, financing, service delivery) to regional or local authorities, ensuring rapid and context-specific responses (Shchyrina et al., 2022). Leadership skills, strategic thinking, emotional intelligence, and collaboration are the key competencies for health care leaders to make rational and difficult decisions and keep the team in loop (Sacopulos & Greeter, 2023; Sahu et al., 2024). Effective crisis management focuses on the two-way clear and timely communication with the higher authorities to resolve the crisis (Paul, 2024; Tomić et al., 2024).

Identify Crisis: When There is an Acute Risk of Harm to Self and Others

- Self-harm, suicide attempts, suicidal talks
- Expressing suicidal/homicidal/violent intent
- Displaying aggressive/agitated behavior
- Evidence of being in a state of displaying extremely disruptive behavior, or being unresponsive

Providing Support

- HCP in crisis has been identified
- Calls for an emergency (made for crisis management)
- Do not let the HCP alone after identification of crisis
- Please ensure that crisis management is provided to the HCP.
- Keep the follow-up.

4. System

Implementing integrated healthcare delivery models that coordinate services across various settings (e.g., primary care, mental health, social services) will provide comprehensive and coordinated care. Leveraging health information technology to improve communication, care coordination, and patient engagement, such as electronic health records, telemedicine, and mobile health apps. Adopting quality improvement methodologies to identify areas for improvement, optimize processes, and enhance patient outcomes within the healthcare system. Understanding the WHO Health systems, planning will be easy to integrate wellness into organizational structures.

Effective Communication

Effective communication in healthcare providers is essential because it is essential in providing quality care, resulting in a reduction in errors, improvement in patient outcome, and increased team collaboration. Understanding the cultural sensitivity is important in dealing with people with diverse backgrounds to address the barriers, communicate clearly, and take beneficial actions (Ratna, 2019). It also helps in reducing conflicts, enhance team collaboration, and create positive work environment (Dartiguelongue & Cafiero, 2021; Vrućan, 2022). Before learning how to communicate effectively, it is essential to understand the communication styles people have. There are four communication styles, which have been metaphorically related to animals to remember and understand them in the easiest way.

a. Passive Turtle

Passive turtle types of people prefer to remain quiet rather than to speak. If they speak, they have a soft tone with poor eye contact to the extent that others do not listen to them and devalue their opinion, reinforcing them to remain quiet in future situations. Because of their passive nature, they do not express their needs, desires, and wants and prioritize others' needs over theirs. Even if they express their needs, they constantly apologize for self-expression because they perceive themselves as not important. This allows others to take advantage of them, and they do not complain about it. They do not freely express their thoughts because of their sensitivity to criticism. They also are afraid of rejection and disapproval; that is why they find it difficult to confront and often end up pleasing.

b. Aggressive Tiger

Aggressive tiger types of people speak loudly with intense eye contact (eyes opened widely, eyebrows pulled down, upper lids pulled up), without considering others' opinions or even listening to them. They are unwilling to compromise and use verbal or physical force to keep their word. Their boundaries are rigid, which leads to maximum distance in their relationships. They grow easily frustrated and become rude and controlling. And to be in control, they constantly criticize and humiliate others, pointing out their weaknesses. These behaviors violate the rights of others because they do not think others' needs are as important as theirs.

c. Passive-aggressive Cat

Passive-aggression people share mixed features of passive and aggressive communication. They consider it difficult to confront others while being angry and hostile at the same time. They give importance to their needs but are unable to express them and often end up being frustrated and aggressive. Their characteristics are similar to as aggressive but like passive, they cannot communicate or express it.

d. Assertive Owl

Assertive owls have a confident tone and body language, appropriate eye contact, and a relaxed facial expression. They clearly express their needs and wants, stand up for the right of self and respect the rights of others; listen to others without interrupting; and are willing to compromise if there is a need. They are wise, calm, and observant and think before speaking. They use "I statements": "I understand what you are saying but I have to disagree." Assertiveness is a style of communication in which a person feels confident enough to speak up for himself in a firm and respectful manner without feeling guilty.

Assertive Communication Techniques (Smith, 2011).

I- Broken Record

It is a power struggle technique of avoiding conflict without being passive or aggressive. You just need to say your opinion or point again and again and stick to your point without being anxious or nervous, so this exercise helps you to deal with others who get illogical or manipulative. Initially you will feel uncomfortable raising up to your point and sticking to it.

Examples:

Patient: I got a checkup from you last week and I am not getting well because you did not give me adequate medicines.
Doctor: I apologize that the medicine I prescribed you did not work on you. Did you take the medicine timely?
Patient: Umm, I took the medicine twice and I do not feel any better, so I did not continue it as you said to take it for three days.
Doctor: I see; the reason it did not work out is you did not comply with the treatment. I suggest you take medicine for three days; sometimes medicines take time to show improvements.
Patient: No, I took it twice and I do not want to take it again; just change my medicine.

Doctor: I insist you take this medicine for three days; thereafter, we will see if this does not work out, and I will change it.

II- Fogging

In this skill, you learn to listen to others' opinions, criticism, and truth of other persons without getting uncomfortable but maintaining your separate opinion. This exercise helps you to engage in active listening but at the same time helps you to go on to your point.

For example, if your colleague calls you "lazy and useless," you could fog with "Nobody is perfect; you are entitled to your opinion, but I think of myself differently than your opinion."

III- Free Information

It is the skill that shows the acknowledgment of basic prompts given by a partner in casual discussion to show what is important to that individual. It allows you to feel less shy going into discussion while simultaneously making it easy for partners to talk about themselves easily.

IV- Negative Assertion

This skill teaches us to accept our weaknesses and faults without being apologetic and defensive and verbally accept them without being ashamed or embarrassed. At the same time, using constructive criticism will help you feel accepted.

V- Workable compromise

It is always a helpful skill in assertive communication, in which you figure out the best and most appropriate solution to the conflict while maintaining the respect of yourself and the other person.

Conflict Resolution

Conflict is a mental struggle resulting from incompatible or opposing needs, drives, wishes, external or internal demands, sharp disagreement or opposition of interests, or ideas (Merriam-Webster, n.d.). Conflict is a multidimensional phenomenon, including the outcome of both constructive and destructive nature.

Constructive when	Destructive when
Builds a strong relationship with improved communication	dispute hurts a relationship
Develops common goals and reaches to the resolution	there is no agreement reached
Emotions and thoughts are share with respect	there are uncontrolled emotions, anger, and raised
Leads to win-win outcome	the conflict prevents from reaching goals

There is a need to resolution when conflict is destructive because it increases the stress, absenteeism, and mental health problems (Kelly & Al-Rawi, 2020; Kim et al., 2017; Koibichuk et al., 2021; McKibben, 2017); effects teamwork, communication, and collaboration (Kelly & Al-Rawi, 2020; Kim et al., 2017; McKibben, 2017); lead to staff turnover or decreased productivity (Kim et al., 2017; Almost et al., 2016; Koibichuk et al., 2021).

Conflict in healthcare settings strongly affects the well-being of healthcare professionals and organizational performance and results from toxic or high-stress environments, unclear rules and boundaries, or complex organizational structures. Common forms include task conflict (differences in opinions), process conflict (disagreements over logistics), and relationship conflict (interpersonal incompatibility). Relationship conflict is often the most destructive and prevalent, leading to negative outcomes such as decreased job satisfaction and increased errors (Kelly & Al-Rawi, 2020; Piryani & Piryani, 2019).

Conflicts stem from individual traits (e.g., self-focus, low emotional intelligence), interpersonal issues (e.g., poor communication, bullying), and organizational factors (e.g., unclear roles, ambiguous workflows) (Kim et al., 2017; Almost et al., 2016; Koibichuk et al., 2021; Piryani & Piryani, 2019). Cultural differences and differing values also contribute, especially in diverse teams and patient populations (Sinskey et al., 2019; Piryani & Piryani, 2019). There are several conflict management styles people use to resolve conflict.

Conflict management style	Description	Application in healthcare settings
Avoiding	Withdraw from conflict	Use when issue is minor
Accommodating	Yielding others' needs	Useful For maintaining harmony
Compromising	Finding a middle ground	Common in time-pressured situations
Competing	Asserting one's viewpoints	Appropriate in emergencies
Collaborating	Working together for a win-win solution	Ideal for complex ongoing issues

Steps to Resolve Conflict (Lambert & Myers, 1999)

Think about some current conflict, preferably in the workplace.

- Who was involved?
- What were the reasons behind the conflict?
- What methods were used to resolve it?
- Were these methods different than the earlier methods? If so, how?

Identify the source of conflict.

- List all the possible external factors you can think of that can cause conflict.

Lack of available personnel, poorly functioning equipment, inefficient performance, time constraints, contradictory goals, hostile work environments, inadequate scheduling, over-limiting work rules, poorly crafted institutional policies, unclear lines of authority, declines in business, lack of capital for investment, and costs out of control.

- List all the possible external factors you can think of that can cause conflict

Incorrect assumptions, different values, poor work habits, biases, prejudices against the unfamiliar, ingrained and early personal experiences, unrealistic expectations and perceptions, personal uncertainties, inflexibility, and failure to assume responsibilities.

- List the behaviors of others that you find annoying enough to bring about conflict.

Miscommunication, constant interruption, cursing, shouting, clash of styles, inattentiveness, impolite behavior, over-emotionalism, disrespect, judgmental comments, constant bragging, and repeated excuses.

Dealing With "Triggers"

- Neutralize the situation by detachment.
- Mentally detach yourself.
- Step back from the situation and take a few deep breaths.
- Give yourself and the other person some space.

- Recognize others' feelings. When you realize that a hot button has been pushed, give careful thought to your next move in order to avoid pushing more or adding to the hurt.
- Allow things to cool down. Collect more data. Ask questions that will help you get a deeper understanding of the situation.
- Look for commonalities and use positive language. Focus on the goals you both have in common. Use "we" language, as in "We both would like to…"

Emotional Intelligence

Organizations can cultivate EI among healthcare professionals through workshops focused on self-awareness, communication, and empathy-building. They can encourage emotionally intelligent leadership that fosters trust and motivation among teams. Promoting psychological safety and emotional support in healthcare settings. Encouraging practices that help healthcare workers recognize and regulate their emotions.

Emotional intelligence (EI) is characterized by *"a person's potential to perceive, use, understand, and manage emotions in an effective and healthy manner."* To enhance cognitive processes and decision-making, use emotions to promote creativity, problem-solving, and thinking. Recognize the significance of emotions, their causes, and their evolution to control them effectively in order to accomplish wellbeing (Mayer & Salovey, 1993; Mayer et al., 2008; Salovey & Grewal, 2005).

Emotional intelligence in HCPs can be developed through training. Previous literature suggested that nurses who have gone through the EI training reported low level of stress and aggression, high level of resilience and effective coping, result in improved patient care (Castillo et al., 2013; Mao et al., 2021; Saikia et al., 2023; West et al., 2020); improve the skill to identify and manage emotion (Kotsou et al., 2018; Nélis et al., 2009). EI training increases effective communication skills, teamwork, and leadership skills among HCPs (Grant, 2007; Hen & Sharabi-Nov, 2014; Shrivastava et al., 2022) and emotion-guided decision-making tasks (Alkozei et al., 2019). EI is associated with better conflict resolution skills among healthcare professionals. Higher EI helps staff manage emotionally charged situations, leading to improved teamwork and reduced workplace conflict (Carminati, 2021; Theodoratou & Papadopoulos, 2024).

How to Develop Emotional Intelligence?

- Recognize the emotions of self and others.
- Analyze: What makes us feel this way?
- Ask yourself, what needs are unmet?

- Share your opinion in an empathetic way and listen to them.
- Communicate effectively with clear words, active listening, and summarizing their opinion so that misunderstanding will not take place.

Recognizing Emotions

This is the most crucial of the three emotional intelligence foundations. Answer the unique questions listed below in order to understand your feelings.

- Where did they come from first?
- What thoughts are going through your head just before the emotion arises?
- What kind of thought causes this emotion? When you are about to experience an emotion, think about what led to its development.
- What belief or idea briefly echoed in your mind before they manifested? Asking
- "Why do I feel this way?" will help you if you can't recall any previous thoughts.

Finding the cause will provide HCPs with crucial understanding about the types of thinking that cause these emotional states to arise within their body.

Where did They Begin, and When?

Every feeling has a home in your body. It's interesting to note that various people express the same feelings differently. When an emotion arises, close your eyes and determine exactly where in your body it is, as well as where the emotion originates.

- Find out how the feeling manifests itself. Is it a leisurely birth or an explosive explosion?

How did These Emotions Develop and How Strong Were They?

Noticing the effect of emotions on your body. From where it is coming and going. What makes it happen? To make things simpler, attempt to visualize its exact form, shape, color, size, temperature, etc. As a result, you will gain insight about your Consider how emotions function in your body. Additionally, consider how strong or weak the emotion is.

How and Where are They Decreasing?
How Much Time do They Last?

Consider a situation when the expressed feeling vanishes. It begins to evaporate for what reason? Has sufficient time passed, or was it the product of some particular thought? How does the emotion end—does it revert to its original state or perhaps just suddenly vanish? How long did this feeling last—maybe a few minutes or hours?

Manage Your Emotions

Once you have all the answers to the aforementioned questions, you will have amassed a priceless body of knowledge regarding the particular emotion you are experiencing. You've probably never known this much about one particular emotion before, but it will inspire you to move forward. Knowing where it originates, how it develops, and when it takes over gives you the power to control it. Regarding any feelings you may be experiencing, ask yourself these questions. After some time, it becomes unnecessary to actively consider it and intentionally figure it out. You will feel everything in your body naturally and instantly know all about it.

The third goal is to raise the level of control to a more complex one. Effective mind control is the key to managing your emotions. Prior to anything else, you must realize that your mind always provides the meaning to the world around you (Goleman, 2020).

Perspective Taking

It sometimes takes moving from one position to another to understand someone else's point of view. Making assumptions is something most of us do from time to time. Although it's possible that our assumptions are correct, quite often they are flawed. Carried to an extreme, unverified assumptions can escalate and put the entire resolution process on a slippery slope. Remember, the other person may also be making assumptions about you, and these may be just as invalid as your assumptions about him or her. Collecting the data, checking out the assumptions, and reevaluating first impressions are important steps in any conflict situation.

Boundary Setting

Respect yourself. Your needs, wants, and rights are as important as anyone else's. It's fine to express what you want so long as you are respectful toward the rights of others. Express your thoughts and feelings calmly. Take responsibility for your emotions. Express them in a calm and factual manner. Try starting sentences with "I feel…." Plan what you're going to say. Know your wants and needs. Consider how you can articulate your needs and wants before engaging in a conversation. Come up with specific sentences and words you can use. Say "no" when you need to. You can't make everyone happy all the time. When you need to say "no," do so clearly, without lying about the reasons. Offer to help find another solution.

5. Spirituality

Emotional exhaustion, stress, and ethical dilemmas resulting in compassion, fatigue, and burnout compromise the well-being of healthcare providers and often end up in compromised patient care. According to the World Health Organization (2019), "burnout is a state of physical, mental, and emotional exhaustion caused by chronic stress that results in reduced professional efficacy, feelings of negativity or cynicism, or a sense of detachment related to one's job, patients, and colleagues." Burnout is common in HCPs and is caused by the constant exposure to stressful situations (Athimni et al., 2023; Halouani et al., 2023). Considering the factor of spirituality at the workplace gives meaning to professional life and it has been found to be effective in reducing mental health challenges. Spirituality is defined as the *"quality of being concerned with the human spirit or soul as opposed to material or physical things"* (Brown, 1993).

A person's interactions with themselves, their community, and their surroundings are the indicators of their spiritual health. Spirituality is an innate ability that develops when a person is born and evolves in accordance with spiritual needs. Religion and spirituality are not the same, because religion usually consists of a structured set of beliefs, rituals, and practices, whereas spirituality may be attained without religion or religious rites. Spirituality is exhibited by people via their relationship with God, but it may also be displayed by those who don't believe in supernatural forces. It is crucial to acknowledge the significance of spirituality in overall well-being (Moreira-Almeida et al., 2016).

One aspect of wellness management, which encompasses both wellness management and psycho-spiritual integration, is spirituality. It acknowledges that humans look for meaning and purpose in life, which includes growing a profound appreciation for the breadth and depth of life and the forces of nature in the cosmos. Adding the concept of spirituality in healthcare organizations enhances the outcome. Leaders' adoption of workplace spirituality has a big impact on workers' empathy and ethical conduct. Empathy is a crucial mechanism for the positive effects of a workplace that values spirituality, which tends to encourage moral conduct and emotional bonds among employees. A cycle of good conduct and spiritual development is reinforced when leaders who exhibit humility and empathy set an example for their subordinates. This improves the spiritual environment of the workplace and inspires them to act with more empathy and ethical awareness (Lalani, 2020; Reisinger, 2024).

Meditation plays an important role in reducing stress, but it is important to practice it daily because of its effectiveness. Meditation has both physical and psychological benefits. It helps in maintaining peace of mind. As a result, a person who practices meditation becomes mentally relaxed, resulting in satisfaction. Furthermore, it reduces physical illnesses and balances the hormones, resulting in better sleep, a favorable appetite, and proper bowel movement. A person who practices meditation does not get easily irritated or lack concentration. Core mindfulness is the higher level to basic meditation; as a result, people become more aware, quiet, focused, and clear; they become less stressed and more self-accepted, develop positive energy, and become joyful, optimistic, energized, and loving (Álvarez-Pérez et al., 2022).

The FICA Spiritual Assessment Tool, developed by Dr. Christina Puchalski and her colleagues at the George Washington Institute for Spirituality and Health, is an evidence-based tool designed to assess patients' spiritual needs in healthcare settings. It helps healthcare professionals understand how their values, beliefs, and faith impact their choices and lives. The tool includes questions and actions that help staff explore their sources of strength, community support, spiritual practices, and the impact of belief systems on their approach to care.

The HOPE Spiritual Assessment is another tool that represents sources of hope, organized religion, individual spirituality and practices, and influences on end-of-life decisions and medical treatment. It offers a thorough review of patients' spiritual practices and beliefs and how they affect healthcare decisions. The SPIRIT tool stands for Spiritual Belief System, Individual Spirituality, Spiritual Community Integration, Ritualized Practices and Restrictions, Medical Care Implications, and Planning Terminal Events.

The Spiritual History Tool (SPIRIT) stands for Spiritual Belief System, Individual Spirituality, Spiritual Community Integration, Ritualized Practices and Restrictions, Medical Care Implications, and Planning Terminal Events. It includes questions and actions that help healthcare providers recognize their deeper purpose behind their work, personal spirituality and practices, integration with the community, and rituals/practices & restrictions.

Tazkia e Nafs emphasizes the importance of developing spiritual awareness from a religious perspective. Life can throw challenges, but how we respond shows how much we trust that God is always there for us. Leaning on our faith in God is the best way to heal our hearts, as demonstrated by the Prophet Ayyub during his tough times. This journey brings in more love for God, making our heart feel lighter and stronger. Spiritual awareness is crucial in dealing with emotional distress, such as feeling upset, let down by loved ones, or feeling useless or anxious. We experience these feelings when our connection with Allah SWT weakens, leading us to overlook the blessings in life. By understanding the first four verses of Surah Ar-Rahman, we can better combat negative emotions such as feeling stressed, upset, or anxious.

SUMMARY

In the healthcare sector, healthcare professionals play a crucial role in addressing various situations and promoting well-being. Their work involves various emotional responses, such as stress, work-family balance, and the need for medical knowledge. These responses can lead to occupational stress, poor wellbeing, psychological distress, and burnout, which can exacerbate medical conditions. A holistic approach, derived from Dr. Minhaj Qidwai's 5Ss approach, is needed to ensure human wellness and its management. Healthcare providers can help individuals understand their physical, emotional, and mental health needs through education and self-assessment tools. Promoting healthy behaviors, such as regular exercise, balanced nutrition, stress management techniques, and adequate sleep, can empower individuals to take control of their health.

Stress management plays an important role in improving quality of life, efficiency, concentration, and job performance. To improve emotional regulation, healthcare providers should validate their emotions, understand them, and adjust their response accordingly. In difficult situations, it's vital to see the bigger picture and address multiple aspects of the problem. Supporting policies that promote wellness, such as healthcare reform, mental health parity laws, and initiatives to address public health issues, and investing in healthcare infrastructure, workforce development, and prevention programs can improve population health outcomes.

Crisis management focuses on building resilience, decentralizing key functions, and ensuring rapid and context-specific responses. Leadership skills, strategic thinking, emotional intelligence, and collaboration are key competencies for health care leaders to make rational and difficult decisions and keep the team in the loop. In healthcare, understanding and managing emotions is crucial for providing effective patient care and fostering trust. Effective communication is essential for providing quality care, reducing errors, and improving patient outcomes. Cultural sensitivity is essential in dealing with diverse backgrounds and addressing barriers. The role of the system in healthcare is essential for ensuring a positive work environment.

Conflict in healthcare settings can lead to stress, absenteeism, and mental health problems. Conflict management styles include avoiding, accommodating, compromising, competing, and collaborating. Emotional intelligence (EI) is crucial for healthcare professionals to manage emotions effectively and create a healthy work environment. EI training can improve communication skills, teamwork, and leadership skills, leading to better conflict resolution skills and reduced workplace conflict. Recognizing emotions, analyzing their causes, and taking responsibility for feelings are essential steps in conflict resolution. Spirituality is an important part of helping healthcare workers deal with mental health problems. Burnout, a state of physical, mental, and emotional exhaustion caused by chronic stress, can lead to reduced professional efficacy, negative feelings, and detachment from patients and colleagues. By understanding and managing emotions, healthcare providers can better support their patients and maintain a positive work environment.

REFERENCES

Abbas, J. (2021). Crisis management, transnational healthcare challenges and opportunities: The intersection of COVID-19 pandemic and global mental health. *Research in Globalization, 3*, 100037–100037. DOI: 10.1016/j.resglo.2021.100037

Alkozei, A., Smith, R., Demers, L., Weber, M., Berryhill, S., & Killgore, W. (2019). Increases in Emotional Intelligence After an Online Training Program Are Associated with Better Decision-Making on the Iowa Gambling Task. *Psychological Reports, 122*(3), 853–879. DOI: 10.1177/0033294118771705 PMID: 29699472

Almost, J., Wolff, A., Stewart-Pyne, A., McCormick, L., Strachan, D., & D'Souza, C. (2016). Managing and mitigating conflict in healthcare teams: An integrative review. *Journal of Advanced Nursing, 72*(7), 1490–1505. DOI: 10.1111/jan.12903 PMID: 26822008

Álvarez-Pérez, Y., Rivero-Santana, A., Perestelo-Pérez, L., Duarte-Díaz, A., Ramos-García, V., Toledo-Chávarri, A., Torres-Castaño, A., León-Salas, B., Infante-Ventura, D., González-Hernández, N., Rodríguez-Rodríguez, L., & Serrano-Aguilar, P. (2022). Effectiveness of Mantra-Based Meditation on Mental Health: A Systematic Review and Meta-Analysis. *International Journal of Environmental Research and Public Health, 19*(6), 3380. Advance online publication. DOI: 10.3390/ijerph19063380 PMID: 35329068

Ardell, D. B. (1999). Definition of wellness. *Ardell Wellness Report, 18*(1), 1–5.

Athimni, Z., Chouchen, A., Kalboussi, H., Nsiri, L., Ferhi, F., Aloui, A., Gaddour, A., Bouhoula, M., Maoua, M., Brahem, A., Maalel, O., Chatti, S., Kacem, I., & Mrizak, N. (2023). Burnout Syndrome and its associated factors among anesthesia technicians in a Teaching Hospital in the central region of Tunisia. *European Psychiatry : the Journal of the Association of European Psychiatrists, 66*(S1), S462–S463. DOI: 10.1192/j.eurpsy.2023.992

Baron, R. A., Byrne, D., & Branscombe, N. R. (2011). *Social psychology* (13th ed.). Pearson Education.

Brown, L. (1993). *Oxford English Dictionary*. Clarendon Press.

Burton, A., Burgess, C., Dean, S., Koutsopoulou, G., & Hugh-Jones, S. (2017). How Effective are Mindfulness-Based Interventions for Reducing Stress Among Healthcare Professionals? A Systematic Review and Meta-Analysis. *Stress and Health, 33*(1), 3–13. DOI: 10.1002/smi.2673 PMID: 26916333

Buruck, G., Dörfel, D., Kugler, J., & Brom, S. (2016). Enhancing well-being at work: The role of emotion regulation skills as personal resources. *Journal of Occupational Health Psychology, 21*(4), 480–493. DOI: 10.1037/ocp0000023 PMID: 26974495

Cakirpaloglu, S., Cakirpaloglu, P., Skopal, O., Kvapilová, B., Schovánková, T., Vévodová, Š., Greaves, J., & Steven, A. (2024). Strain and serenity: Exploring the interplay of stress, burnout, and well-being among healthcare professionals. *Frontiers in Psychology, 15*, 1415996. Advance online publication. DOI: 10.3389/fpsyg.2024.1415996 PMID: 38984287

Carminati, L. (2021). Emotions, Emotion Management and Emotional Intelligence in the Workplace: Healthcare Professionals' Experience in Emotionally Charged Situations. *Frontiers in Sociology, 6*, 640384. Advance online publication. DOI: 10.3389/fsoc.2021.640384 PMID: 33889607

Castillo, R., Salguero, J., Fernández-Berrocal, P., & Balluerka, N. (2013). Effects of an emotional intelligence intervention on aggression and empathy among adolescents. *Journal of Adolescence, 36*(5), 883–892. DOI: 10.1016/j.adolescence.2013.07.001 PMID: 24011104

Chou, L. P., Li, C. Y., & Hu, S. C. (2014). Job stress and burnout in hospital employees: Comparisons of different medical professions in a regional hospital in Taiwan. *BMJ Open, 4*(2), e004185. DOI: 10.1136/bmjopen-2013-004185 PMID: 24568961

DeLeo, K., Maconick, L., McCabe, R., Broeckelmann, E., Rains, S., Rowe, S., & Johnson, S. (2022). Experiences of crisis care among service users with complex emotional needs or a diagnosis of 'personality disorder', and other stakeholders: Systematic review and meta-synthesis of the qualitative literature. *BJPsych Open, 8*(2), e53. Advance online publication. DOI: 10.1192/bjo.2022.1 PMID: 35197131

Dhar N, Chaturvedi S, Nandan D. (2011). Spiritual health scale 2011: Defining and measuring 4th dimension of health. Indian Journal of Community Medicine 36:275 82.

Dimensions of Wellness. University of Maryland. Your Guide to Living Well. [Last accessed June 27, 2017]. https://umwellness.wordpress.com/8-dimensions-of-wellness/

Emami, S., Lorenzoni, V., & Turchetti, G. (2024). Towards Resilient Healthcare Systems: A

Goleman, D (2020). *Emotional Intelligence: Improve your Social Skills and Emotional Agility for a better life, success at work, and happier relationships.*

Grant, A. (2007). Enhancing coaching skills and emotional intelligence through training. *Industrial and Commercial Training*, *39*(5), 257–266. DOI: 10.1108/00197850710761945

Halouani, N., Koukane, M., Elleuch, O., Turki, M., Samet, A., Jemil, F., Ellouze, S., & Aloulou, J. (2023). Burnout and its associated factors in healthcare workers during the COVID-19 pandemic. *European Psychiatry : the Journal of the Association of European Psychiatrists*, *66*(S1), S804–S804. DOI: 10.1192/j.eurpsy.2023.1702

Hen, M., & Sharabi-Nov, A. (2014). Teaching the teachers: Emotional intelligence training for teachers. *Teaching Education*, *25*(4), 375–390. DOI: 10.1080/10476210.2014.908838

Hertelendy, A., Ciottone, G., Mitchell, C., Gutberg, J., & Burkle, F. (2020). Crisis Standards of Care in a Pandemic: Navigating the Ethical, Clinical, Psychological, and Policy-making Maelstrom. *International Journal for Quality in Health Care : Journal of the International Society for Quality in Health Care*. Advance online publication. DOI: 10.1093/intqhc/mzaa094 PMID: 33128564

Hofmann, P. (2018). Stress Among Healthcare Professionals Calls Out for Attention. Journal of Kadović, M., Mikšić, Š., & Lovrić, R. (2022). Ability of Emotional Regulation and Control as a Stress Predictor in Healthcare Professionals. *International Journal of Environmental Research and Public Health*, *20*(1), 541. Advance online publication. DOI: 10.3390/ijerph20010541

Kelly, J., & Al-Rawi, Y. (2020). Recognising, understanding and managing high conflict behaviours in healthcare. *Postgraduate Medical Journal*, *97*(1144), 123–124. DOI: 10.1136/postgradmedj-2020-139173 PMID: 33184149

Kharatzadeh, H., Alavi, M., Mohammadi, A., Visentin, D., & Cleary, M. (2020). Emotional regulation training for intensive and critical care nurses. *Nursing & Health Sciences*, *22*(2), 445–453. Advance online publication. DOI: 10.1111/nhs.12679 PMID: 31975520

Kim, S., Bochatay, N., Relyea-Chew, A., Buttrick, E., Amdahl, C., Kim, L., Frans, E., Mossanen, M., Khandekar, A., Fehr, R., & Lee, Y. (2017). Individual, interpersonal, and organisational factors of healthcare conflict: A scoping review. *Journal of Interprofessional Care*, *31*(3), 282–290. DOI: 10.1080/13561820.2016.1272558 PMID: 28276847

Koibichuk, V., Dźwigoł, H., & Stenko, S. (2021). *Conflict Management in Health Care Institutions*. Health Economics and Management Review., DOI: 10.21272/hem.2021.4-07

Kotsou, I., Mikolajczak, M., Heeren, A., Grégoire, J., & Leys, C. (2018). Improving Emotional Intelligence: A Systematic Review of Existing Work and Future Challenges. *Emotion Review*, *11*(2), 151–165. DOI: 10.1177/1754073917735902

Lalani, N. (2020). Meanings and Interpretations of Spirituality in Nursing and Health. *Religions*, *11*(9), 428. Advance online publication. DOI: 10.3390/rel11090428

Lambert, J., & Myers, S. (1999). *50 Activities for Conflict Resolution Group Learning and Self Development Exercises*. HRD Press.

Mao, L., Huang, L., & Chen, Q. (2021). Promoting resilience and lower stress in nurses and improving inpatient experience through emotional intelligence training in China: A randomized controlled trial. *Nurse Education Today*, *107*, 105–130. DOI: 10.1016/j.nedt.2021.105130 PMID: 34543939

Maslach, C. & Schaufeli, WB. (1993). Historical and conceptual development of burnout. Prof Burnout .1–16.

Masood, A., Salik, S., & Masroor, U. (2022). Relationship of Occupational Stress with Psychosomatic Symptoms and Mental Wellbeing in Medical Professionals: An Exploratory Study. [JDUHS]. *Journal of the Dow University of Health Sciences*, *17*(1), 36–42. DOI: 10.36570/jduhs.2023.1.1655

Mayer, J., Roberts, R., & Barsade, S. (2008). Human abilities: Emotional intelligence. *Annual Review of Psychology*, *59*(1), 507–536. DOI: 10.1146/annurev.psych.59.103006.093646 PMID: 17937602

Mayer, J., & Salovey, P. (1993). The intelligence of emotional intelligence. *Intelligence*, *17*(4), 433–442. DOI: 10.1016/0160-2896(93)90010-3

McKibben, L. (2017). Conflict management: Importance and implications. *British Journal of Nursing (Mark Allen Publishing)*, *26*(2), 100–103. DOI: 10.12968/bjon.2017.26.2.100 PMID: 28132555

McNeely, E. (2005). The consequences of job stress for nurses' health: Time for a check-up. *Nursing Outlook*, *53*(6), 291–299. DOI: 10.1016/j.outlook.2005.10.001 PMID: 16360700

Merriam-Webster. (n.d.). Conflict. In Merriam-Webster.com dictionary. Retrieved June 2, 2025. https://www.merriam-webster.com/dictionary/conflict

Merriam-Webster. (n.d.). Confidence. In Merriam-Webster.com dictionary. Retrieved June 2, 2025, from https://www.merriam-webster.com/dictionary/confidence

Moreira-Almeida, A., Sharma, A., Van Rensburg, B., Verhagen, P., & Cook, C. (2016). WPA Position Statement on Spirituality and Religion in Psychiatry. *World Psychiatry; Official Journal of the World Psychiatric Association (WPA), 15*(1), 87–88. Advance online publication. DOI: 10.1002/wps.20304 PMID: 26833620

Nélis, D., Quoidbach, J., Mikolajczak, M., & Hansenne, M. (2009). Increasing emotional intelligence: (How) is it possible? *Personality and Individual Differences, 47*(1), 36–41. DOI: 10.1016/j.paid.2009.01.046

Odigie, A. (2016). STRESS MANAGEMENT FOR HEALTHCARE PROFESSIONALS.

Paul, J. (2024). Strategies for Effective Crisis Management in Healthcare Systems: Patient Safety and Lessons Learned. *Medical Research Archives, 12*(7). Advance online publication. DOI: 10.18103/mra.v12i7.5424

Piryani, R., & Piryani, S. (2019). Conflict Management in Healthcare. *Journal of Nepal Health Research Council, 16*(41), 481–482. DOI: 10.33314/jnhrc.v16i41.1703 PMID: 30739920

Ratna, H. (2019). *The Importance of Effective Communication in Healthcare Practice*. HPHR Journal., DOI: 10.54111/0001/W4

Riggenbach, J. (2013). *The CBT Toolbox: A Workbook for Clients and Clinicians. Premier Publishing and Media.* CMI Education Institute, Inc.

Sacopulos, M., & Greeter, A. (2023). Effective Crisis Leadership in Healthcare. *Physician Leadership Journal, 10*(5), 60–62. Advance online publication. DOI: 10.55834/plj.7146928492

Sahu, N., Sriram, S., Samrat, B., Jayakumar, S., Choudhary, A., Garg, A., & Naregal, P. (2024). *Assessing Healthcare Leadership Competencies in Crisis Management.* Health Leadership and Quality of Life., DOI: 10.56294/hl2024.371

Saikia, M., George, L., Unnikrishnan, B., Nayak, B., & Ravishankar, N. (2023). Thirty years of emotional intelligence: A scoping review of emotional intelligence training programme among nurses. *International Journal of Mental Health Nursing*. Advance online publication. DOI: 10.1111/inm.13235 PMID: 37772479

Salovey, P., & Grewal, D. (2005). The Science of Emotional Intelligence. *Current Directions in Psychological Science, 14*(6), 281–285. DOI: 10.1111/j.0963-7214.2005.00381.x

Santo, L., Michaux, R., & Pohl, S. (2024). The Effect of Emotional Coworker Support on Work Engagement Among Pediatric Health Care Providers: The Mediator Role of Emotional Regulation. *Western Journal of Nursing Research, 1939459241296965*(12), 963–969. Advance online publication. DOI: 10.1177/01939459241296965

Shapiro, S., Astin, J., Bishop, S., & Cordova, M. (2005). Mindfulness-Based Stress Reduction \ for Health Care Professionals: Results From a Randomized Trial. *International Journal of Stress Management, 12*(2), 164–176. DOI: 10.1037/1072-5245.12.2.164

Shchyrina, K., Koshova, S., & Parkhomenko-Kutsevil, O. (2022). Foreign experience of anti-crisis management of medical institutions. ScienceRise. *Medical Science*, (2(47)), 49–54. Advance online publication. DOI: 10.15587/2519-4798.2022.256383

Shrivastava, S., Martinez, J., Coletti, D., & Fornari, A. (2022). Interprofessional Leadership Development: Role of Emotional Intelligence and Communication Skills Training. *MedEdPORTAL: the Journal of Teaching and Learning Resources, 18*, 11247. Advance online publication. DOI: 10.15766/mep_2374-8265.11247 PMID: 35634034

Sinskey, J., Chang, J., Shibata, G., Infosino, A., & Rouine-Rapp, K. (2019). Applying Conflict Management Strategies to the Pediatric Operating Room. *Anesthesia and Analgesia, 129*(4), 1109–1117. Advance online publication. DOI: 10.1213/ANE.0000000000003991 PMID: 30633050

Smith, M. (2011). *When I Say No, I Feel Guilty: How to Cope, Using the Skills of Systematic Assertive Therapy*. Bantam.

Smith, Y. (2025). Primary Healthcare Providers. *News Medical Life Sciences*. https://www.news-medical.net/health/Primary-Healthcare-Providers.aspx

Theodoratou, M., & Papadopoulos, A. (2024). Emotional Intelligence, Psychological Distress, and Conflict Resolution Among Healthcare Professionals. *European Psychiatry : the Journal of the Association of European Psychiatrists, 67*(S1), S832–S833. Advance online publication. DOI: 10.1192/j.eurpsy.2024.1737

Tomić, Z., Vegar, V., & Radalj, M. (2024). CRISIS COMMUNICATION IN HEALTHCARE. Medicina Academica Integrativa. https://doi.org/DOI: 10.47960/3029-3316.2024.1.1.11

Vrućan, V. (2022). Management, Communication in the Health Institution. Quality of Life (Banja Luka) -. *Apeiron (Clayton, Vic.), 22*(1). Advance online publication. DOI: 10.7251/QOL2201058V

Weilenmann, S., Schnyder, U., Parkinson, B., Corda, C., Von Känel, R., & Pfaltz, M. (2018). Emotion Transfer, Emotion Regulation, and Empathy-Related Processes in Physician-Patient Interactions and Their Association With Physician Well-Being: A Theoretical Model. *Frontiers in Psychiatry*, *9*, 389. Advance online publication. DOI: 10.3389/fpsyt.2018.00389 PMID: 30210371

West, E., Singer-Chang, G., Ryznar, R., Ross, D., Czekajlo, M., Hoang, T., Alson, R., Berbel, G., Moloff, A., Safaoui, M., Nevins, N., & Laporta, A. (2020). The Effect of Hyper-Realistic Trauma Training on Emotional Intelligence in Second Year Military Medical Students. *Journal of Surgical Education*, *77*(6), 1422–1428. Advance online publication. DOI: 10.1016/j.jsurg.2020.04.020 PMID: 32624450

World Health Organization. (1985). Handbook of Resolutions and Decisions, (2) 5-6. http://www.who.int/ hia/evidence/doh/en

World Health Organization. (2010). Monitoring the building Blocks of health systems: A handbook of indicators and their measurement strategies https://iris.who.int/bitstream/handle/10665/258734/9789241564052-eng.pdf

Xu, N., Lv, A., Li, T., Li, X., Huang, M., & Su, Y. (2021). Experiences of healthcare providers during the coronavirus pandemic and its impact on them: Protocol for a mixed-methods systematic review. *BMJ Open*, *11*(2), e043686. Advance online publication. DOI: 10.1136/bmjopen-2020-043686 PMID: 33637546

Zhang, X., Smith, D. R., Zheng, Y., & Wang, R. S. (2011). Occupational stress and psychosomatic complaints among health professionals in Beijing, China. *Work (Reading, Mass.)*, *40*(2), 239–245. DOI: 10.3233/WOR-2011-1224 PMID: 21876278

Chapter 3
Empowering Emergency Room Healthcare Providers:
A Study on the "Self" Dimension of Well-Being Within the 5S Model Framework

Zoella Ali
http://orcid.org/0009-0004-2362-0517
Ziauddin University, Pakistan

ABSTRACT

Emergency Rooms have been one of the most emotionally and physically demanding workplaces in healthcare. This chapter will focus on the emotional and psychological wellness of ER health care providers with various roles, experiences, and institutions in Pakistan and how it impacts the "Self" dimension. Research revealed insights related to emotional awareness, mental and physical resilience. Private institutions received better ratings in terms of psychological support structures compared to the public sector. Moreover, with the support of leadership and supervisors displaying higher self-awareness and empathy, their employees reported better job satisfaction, stronger team dynamics, and a reduction in workplace burnout. Thematic analysis of coping strategies and reflections on emotionally triggering incidents signified the role of peer support networks. This research offered recommendations highlighting the critical need for systematic level interventions. These findings aim to support health care institutions in integrating mental health support strategies for clinical settings.

DOI: 10.4018/979-8-2600-0582-8.ch003

INTRODUCTION

Emergency rooms are dynamic, high-stakes environments that require quick decision-making and emotional resilience to distinguish between life and death. They are often referred to as the "frontline" of healthcare institutions, serving as the first point of care for patients in critical emergency situations, including traumatic injuries, acute infections, or psychiatric emergencies. The role of healthcare service providers is critical in such unpredictable and fast-paced settings, as they ensure the clinical stability of patients while managing administrative chaos and provide calm and impactful responses under high-pressure environments. As gatekeepers of providing life-saving interventions, communicating with distressed families, and navigating operations with limited resources, uncertainty, and overutilized facilities, accompanied by emotionally charged situations, are a few dynamics that are the realities of healthcare providers.

The actions of healthcare providers directly impact patient health and survival, as well as short-term and long-term outcomes. Healthcare providers play a pivotal role in developing trust in healthcare systems, enabling communities to access the necessary care. Healthcare institutions operate in high-pressure environments where errors can have life-threatening consequences. Thus, such environments are assessed based on their ability to perform consistently, backed by their medical expertise, as well as on their psychological wellness, emotional regulation, and resilience. Due to a lack of adequate support mechanisms and effective coping strategies, healthcare workers are susceptible to burnout, psychological distress, emotional exhaustion, and compassion fatigue.

On a global scale, burnout is rising at an alarming rate among ER professionals. According to a 2019 study by the World Health Organization (WHO), burnout is now considered a professional phenomenon triggered by the mismanagement of chronic workplace stress (WHO, 2019). Burnout in emergency healthcare workers is linked to higher medical errors (Tawfik et al., 2018), reduction in patient satisfaction (Panagioti et al., 2018), and mental health triggers such as anxiety, depression, and suicidal deliberations (Moss et al., 2016).

Within ER, the external environment is highly uncertain and cannot be significantly influenced; therefore, empowering individuals to be resilient is paramount in ensuring sustainable performance and psychological well-being. In clinical practices, the role of the "Self" encompasses internal mechanisms for emotional regulation, reflection on decisions, trauma processing, and maintaining a sense of purpose, which in turn supports clinical performance. Traditional medicine typically focuses on clinical expertise and technical knowledge while maintaining a negligible focus on reflective practices and stress management. This results in the deterioration of services provided by healthcare workers, as they induct younger professionals who are not well-prepared to manage the psychological demands of a high-stress and uncertain environment.

THEORETICAL BACKGROUND

This chapter will center around the 5S framework by Dr. Minhaj Qidwai (2024), which incorporates five key pillars of health, including "Self," "Society," "State," "Systems," and "Spirituality." This chapter will focus on the "Self" dimension of the 5S framework in the context of emotional resilience (ER) by highlighting the experiences of healthcare professionals, such as house officers and residents, and exploring the emotional strain they face, the coping mechanisms they employ, their effectiveness, and the role of institutional support systems. Moreover, this chapter establishes that empowering the "Self" has a positive impact on the systematic improvements while also reinforcing individual resilience. This feature allows healthcare workers to engage their patients empathetically, be effective in team collaboration, and support compassionate and ethical care. More importantly, the dimension The concept of "Self" will connect individual empowerment to the broader framework of the 5S model by recognizing that personal well-being is influenced by social norms, organizational and institutional systems and policies, as well as spiritual alignment.

LITERATURE REVIEW

Globally, healthcare systems are facing a rise in workplace stress, emotional fatigue, and a lack of engagement in professional environments, all of which are broadly classified as "burnout." The World Health Organization (WHO) has categorized burnout as a phenomenon common in occupational ecosystems that emerges from chronic workplace stress (WHO, 2019). Emergency services in the medical profession pose a high risk of burnout, which not only impacts job satisfaction but also has an adverse effect on patient well-being and safety, clinical service outcomes, and overall organizational performance (Panagioti et al., 2018). Various research publications, such as those by Moss et al. (2016) and Tawfik et al. (2018), have highlighted a clear link between workplace stress and burnout, characterized by an increase in medical errors, reported patient dissatisfaction, and self-destructive thoughts. Moreover, systematic disregard for the emotional labor prevalent in healthcare contributes to increased psychological distress and adversely impacts the retention of healthcare professionals (West et al., 2018). Following the COVID-19 era, this issue has intensified, highlighting the increasingly prevalent gaps in the provision of psychological safety for frontline healthcare workers (Restauri & Sheridan, 2020).

Emergency care settings are disproportionately exposed to the performance burden due to the urgent and fast-paced demands being routed towards healthcare providers. ER professionals deal with patients' traumatic injuries, death, and uncertainties, resulting in cumulative psychological distress, which is commonly known as "Second Victim Syndrome" (Sexton et al., 2000). Compared to their counterparts in other clinical disciplines, emergency room physicians and nurses are more vulnerable to emotional fatigue and a loss of empathic engagement referred to as "depersonalization" (Dyrbye et al., 2017).

Swancott et al., in a 2024 scoping review, highlighted that ER professionals face significant strain due to systematic issues, including long working hours, limited to no institutional support, irregular scheduling, and a high influx of patients, in addition to routine clinical demands. These realities create an environment that encourages emotional collapse, rendering healthcare providers vulnerable as their coping mechanisms are not institutionalized (Poncet et al., 2007).

Traditionally, historical reforms have concentrated on altering shift patterns, managing workloads, and enhancing patient management systems. However, these approaches have largely overlooked the physiological dimensions necessary for sustaining resilience and empathy in clinical settings, which are highly demanding (Shanafelt & Noseworthy, 2017).

Interventions such as "Mindfulness-Based Stress Reduction" (MBSR) can provide immediate relief if integrated with a broader organizational framework. However, their adoption and applications are inconsistent and are not systematically incorporated into the core framework of medical education (Krasner et al., 2009). Moreover, most current interventions are reactive in nature and initiated after the onset of burnout, instead of functioning as preventive measures in clinical environments (Reith, 2018). Perceptions of inequality in workload management can increase the risk of burnout and reduce self-efficacy. Reliance on digital systems creates additional stress from the constant need for data entry and alert management.

Organizational culture is a critical factor in providing support or hindering the development of an air of emotional regulation and resilience among healthcare professionals. Psychological safety has been recognized as a foundational element in ensuring effective teamwork within high-pressure work environments such as emergency departments (Edmondson, 1999). A workplace that is devoid of a supportive work culture, even with the most effective individual-focused interventions, loses efficacy. The literature suggests that organizational culture is critical in encouraging learning from mistakes, open communication, and allowing room for vulnerability (Keller et al., 2019).

Research also suggests that healthcare professionals with high emotional intelligence have lower burnout levels and improve patient interaction (Weng et al., 2011). Resilience is defined as the ability to adapt to and recover from adverse situations while sustaining psychological wellness, which is a fundamental trait for clinicians who operate in high-stress environments. According to Cooper et al. (2020), individuals displaying a higher level of emotional resilience are better equipped to preserve mental health, reduce workforce attrition, and maintain effective performance in a high-stress environment. Despite these efforts, resilience remains insufficiently integrated into training programs for emergency departments in a systematic or strategic way (Stacey et al., 2019).

Self-efficacy, or the belief in one's ability to handle difficult clinical situations, has a direct impact on how healthcare professionals handle high-acuity patient care situations. Cao et al. (2023) found that ER nurses with higher self-efficacy displayed more effective coping mechanisms and were less prone to emotional exhaustion and depersonalization. Although these constructions are backed by research, these principles are still treated as secondary within the medical instruction and institutional policy making (Versel et al., 2023). Backed by robust empirical evidence supporting the importance of psychological competencies in clinical effectiveness, they remain largely overlooked within both the medical education and the structural design of healthcare systems. Marshall et al. (2021) have argued that the failure of organizations in promoting these competencies has led to increased burnout, especially in ER settings.

The lack of alignment between theoretical frameworks and their implications in the real world is especially evident in the way healthcare institutions address the well-being of their staff. Most of the systems opt for a "system-first" or a "policy-driven" methodology, which leads to marginalization of personal empowerment, emotional regulations, and the role of self-awareness in sustaining a culture suitable for resilient teams (West et al., 2016). Although systematic interventions can lead to short-term respite from stress, they lack application and sustainability in promoting long-term resilience unless internal competencies are built up, such as emotional intelligence, stress management, and the ability to make sense (Montgomery, 2014).

Within the 5S model of Qidwai (2024), Society, State, and Systems receive frequent and ongoing institutional attention through various protocols, infrastructure, and laws; however, the "Self" dimension is critically underrepresented despite it being a key pillar. The 5S model is unique in its ability to offer a vigorous alternative for a comprehensive framework of health by integrating Self, Society, State, Systems, and Spirituality. According to Qidwai, the dimension of "Self" encompasses personal competencies, including mindfulness, personal development, work-life balance, and resilience—factors that are critical for healthcare professionals while operating in high-stress emergency departments. West et al. (2014) assessed a comprehensive set of wellness programs for physicians aimed at enhancing mindfulness and self-awareness and reported a significant decline in depersonalization and emotional exhaustion because of these interventions. Moreover, Travis et al. (2016) stated that resilience-focused training is effective in reducing stress and improving overall life satisfaction among healthcare professionals. Nonetheless, insufficient institutional and academic focus on the issue leads to a disjointed approach to well-being. In essence, structural reforms can address the surface-level issues, but empowering the "Self" is crucial to addressing the deeper roots of professional concerns.

Despite the conceptual strength of the 5S model, especially its "Self" component, it remains largely unexplored in medicinal literature. Limited research is available that shows the impact of interventions targeted at "Self" on clinical outcomes, emotional regulation, or burnout resilience among ER professionals, depicting a significant gap in the existing literature. There is a significant theoretical alignment between the foundational models in psychology and organizational behavior, as well as Qidwai's 5S model. Goleman's EI model, WHO's multidimensional definition of health (1948), and Bandura's theory of self-efficacy are a few examples of the theories that propose that individual well-being is a prerequisite for patient and society care.

Additionally, burnout has received significant research attention, but there is a scarcity of studies that highlight the interventions showing the impact of individual development under "Self" in the emergency care setting. For early-career clinicians, the gap is particularly large, as house officers and residents transitioning into professional practice are more prone to psychological vulnerabilities (Thomas et al., 2018). In low-middle-income countries such as Pakistan, healthcare professionals face distinct structural challenges such as a lack of resources and necessary staff, political instability, and a lack of psychological support, placing additional strain on their emotional resilience. Ahmad et al. (2022) highlighted that the lack of culturally suited wellness programs in healthcare institutions in Pakistan has contributed to intensifying burnout and emotional disengagement in emergency support staff.

To conclude, psychological competencies such as self-efficacy, resilience, and emotional intelligence are key to the effective manifestation of "Self" and are critical for emergency care providers facing continuous stress. Despite the theoretical recognition of the importance of the "Self" dimension of the 5S framework, it remains underutilized in its applications in ER settings.

METHODOLOGY

This research will deploy a mixed-methods approach as its research design, incorporating both quantitative and qualitative approaches to explore the psychological resilience, self-awareness, and emotional wellness of healthcare providers working in ER settings. This design will enable a comprehensive understanding of the measurable as well as qualitative and lived experiences and subjective insights of ER professionals.

Participants for the research were probed through a structured sampling from a variety of healthcare backgrounds, including public and private healthcare facilities in urban areas of Pakistan. We specifically targeted the survey at ER healthcare professionals, such as house officers, residents, nurses, and other emergency care staff. Sampling was done through non-probability purposive sampling to ensure the participation of respondents who had direct experience in emergency health care services. This survey included 56 respondents, representing a diverse range of genders, roles, and years of experience.

Data collection was done through a structured survey questionnaire that included both open-ended qualitative questions and closed-ended questions, such as on a Likert scale. The questionnaire assessed the demographics of respondents, their emotional resilience, self-awareness, and regulation; work-life balance; support from supervisors and organizations; exposure to training and workshops focused on mental health and emotional intelligence; and personal strategies adopted to cope with workplace stress. The Likert scale questions used a 5-point format ranging from "Strongly Disagree" to "Strongly Agree," while the qualitative section allowed participants to elaborate on aspects that impact their emotional state, their understanding of well-being, and potential institutional improvements. Cultural adaptation was done to enhance clarity and fitness in the context, and the content was reviewed and validated by expert reviews.

Data collection through a survey was done digitally, employing Google Forms to ensure ease of accessibility and maintain the anonymity of participants. The survey complied with ethical norms and principles of research, such as a consent statement at the beginning, and clarified the voluntary nature of involvement, along with the confidentiality of responses. Data collection was done over an 8-week period. The size of the sample was established by response accessibility during the course of study.

For data analysis, descriptive and inferential statistics methods were deployed to explore the relationship between emotional resilience, institutional support, and various indicators of burnout. Analysis was done through the Python programming language available through Google Colab, which offered a flexible, accessible, and interactive environment to perform statistical analysis and visualize the data. Moreover, thematic analysis was done to extract themes from qualitative data.

FINDINGS AND ANALYSIS

The data collected through the survey from Emergency Room (ER) professionals within various public and private healthcare settings in Pakistan offers new perspectives on the emotional landscape and the psychological resilience, reinforcing the frontline services. Responses of 56 healthcare professionals were analyzed, working across a diverse range of roles, experience levels, and institutions. Several patterns emerged while evaluating the dimension of "Self" within the 5S framework, focusing on emotional resilience, self-efficacy, and overall wellness through the lived experiences of individuals involved in emergency care services. Figure 1 provides a snapshot of the Likert scale responses, showing a healthy variation and diversity in responses.

Figure 1. A snapshot of Likert scale responses

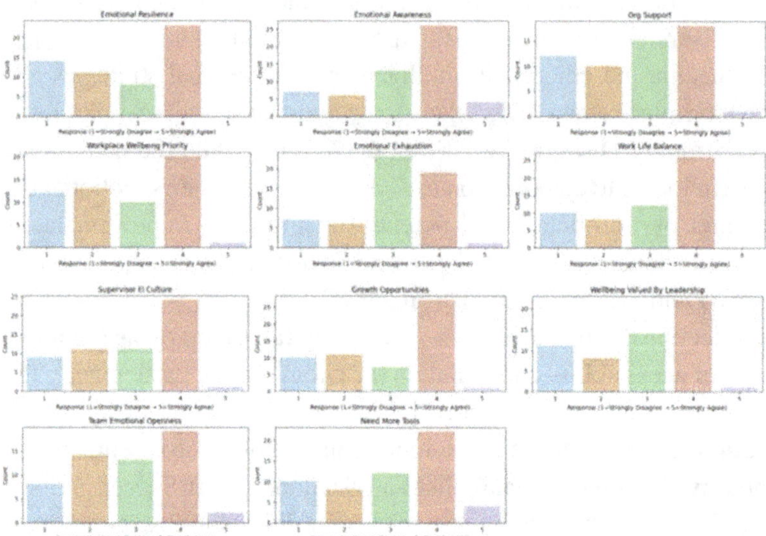

Figure 2 shows the distribution of emotional exhaustion with varying levels of meaningfulness associated with work. It is usually expected that a healthy perception of meaningfulness in work serves as a buffer against burnout and emotional exhaustion. However, the data shows that even among the professionals who find their work "always" meaningful, a significant level of exhaustion is prevalent.

Figure 2. Distribution of Emotional Exhaustion across Levels of Perceived Work Meaningfulness

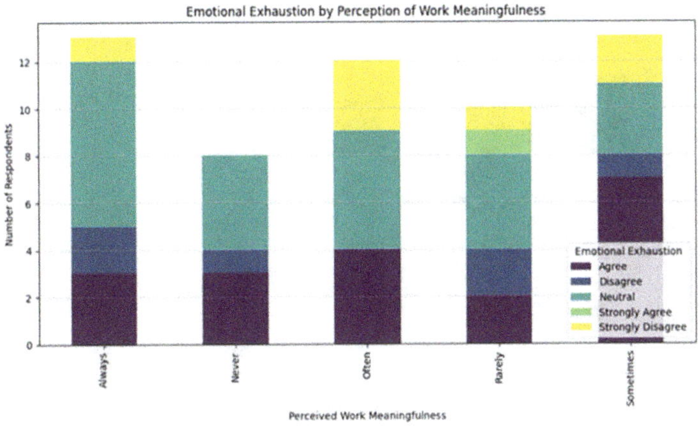

Moreover, a significant number of respondents, especially those in senior roles, rated their exhaustion levels as "high" after their ER shifts [Figure 3].

Figure 3. Boxplot comparing emotional exhaustion levels by professional role.

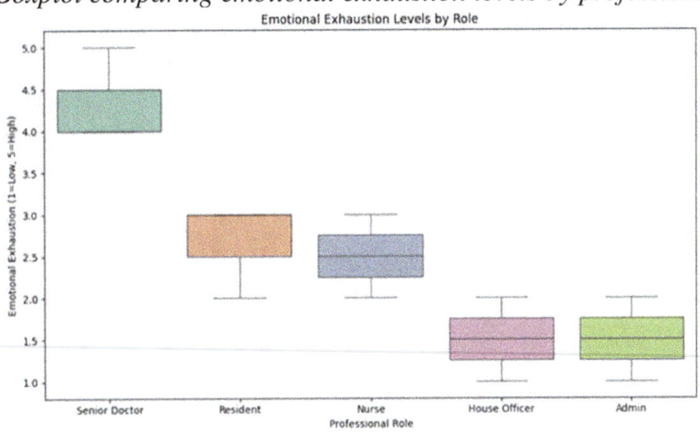

This aligns with the widely reviewed and published literature suggesting that senior medical officers often bear the weight of critical decision making and face emotional fatigue without the lack of proportional institutional support (Shanafelt et al, 2015).

On the other hand, the same group of professionals claimed a high level of meaningfulness associated with their work, which suggests that purposefulness at work is not the key to coping with chronic stress [Figure 4].

Figure 4. Emotional Exhaustion by Work Meaningfulness

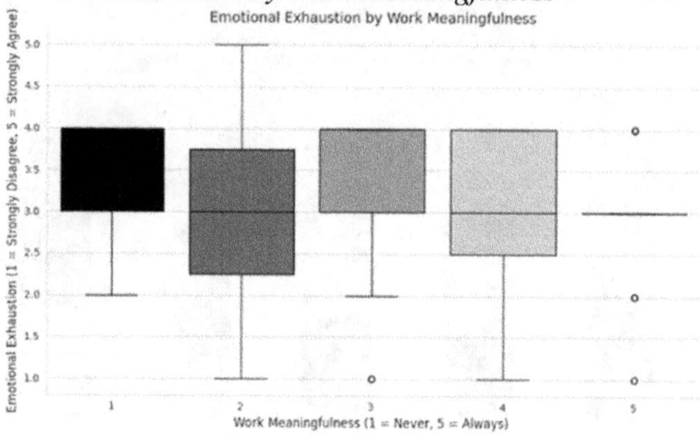

This illustrates the necessity to create systematic buffers that offer psychological support within the ER landscape. This duality is reflective of Goleman's (1995) claim that emotional intelligence without a structure reinforcing it can lead to burnout instead of creating resilience.

Analysis also highlighted the variation in different roles or professionals at different stages of their careers processing emotional challenges differently. Professionals in the early part of their careers, such as postgraduate trainees and nurses, reported frequent emotional exhaustion and lack of structured support from their supervisors or institutions, while the consultants and administrative staff reported slightly better coping ability, although the feeling of being underrepresented remained prevalent [Figure 5].

Figure 5. Boxplot on Right: Boxplot showing Emotional Exhaustion levels by role (1 = Low, 5 = High). Residents and nurses exhibit higher median exhaustion scores.

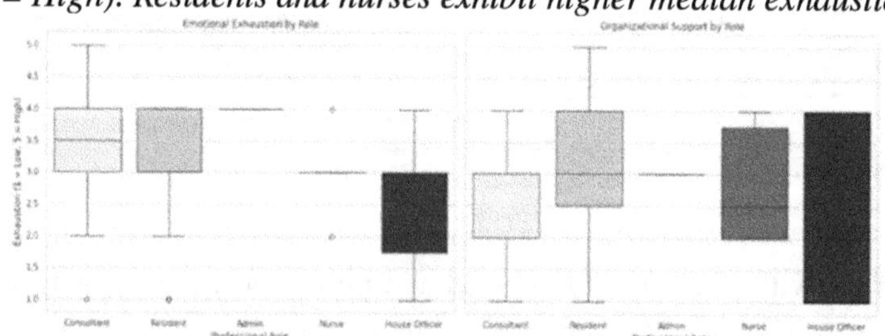

Boxplot on Left: Boxplot of Perceived Organizational Support by role (1 = Strongly Disagree, 5 = Strongly Agree). Lower support perception among house officers and residents is evident.

Figure 5 illustrates that the interquartile range for residents and nurses accumulates at the high end of the scale, indicating ongoing psychological strain. Likewise, examining perceived organizational support among job roles akin to groups, such as residents and house officers, reveals low median ratings of support from their respective institutions. The institutional hierarchy and experience level can significantly influence stress management and the accessibility of support structures. These findings reinforce the need for systematic support to ensure targeted emotional resilience for staff in their early careers.

Professionals who have more experience in the ER showed greater emotional awareness and were resilient; this can be due to their adaptive learning over the course of their careers [Figure 6].

Figure 6. Average emotional resilience and emotional awareness scores varied across ER experience groups. Respondents with over 10 years of experience reported the highest levels of emotional awareness and consistently stable resilience, suggesting that long-term exposure contributes to adaptive emotional regulation.

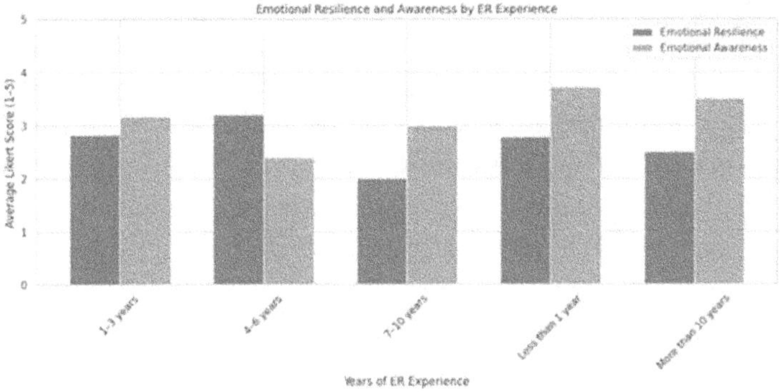

This resilience is self-taught, having been gained through the process of trial and error rather than institutional support, which supports the argument that it should be actively inculcated and not left to random chance or an individual's experience. While accessing organizational support for ER staff's psychological wellness, responses showed a variation with facility types. ER personnel working in public/government hospitals rated organizational support on a higher range than their counterparts in military or teaching hospital institutions [Figure 7].

Figure 7. Average Perception of Organizational Concern for Mental Well-being by Facility Type.

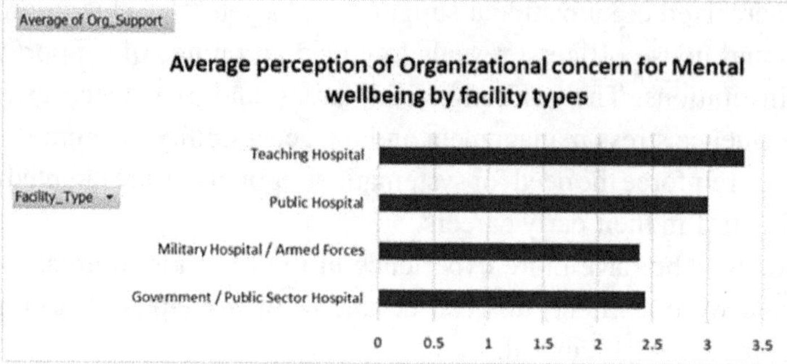

This suggests a variation in institutional policies instead of sectoral differences. Organizational culture, and especially leadership's role in the well-being of ER staff, define the psychological safety network in the ER. Figure 8 illustrates a heatmap with the correlation between supervisors' support for promoting emotional intelligence in work culture and other associated factors of well-being. A high positive correlation is observed between EI-supportive culture and the value of leadership to create wellness, with r=0.25, openness in the team showed an r=0.23, and the organization's prioritizing wellness of ER staff r=0.14. On the other hand, EI culture showed a negative correlation with emotional exhaustion, with r=-0.23, reflecting a positive influence of EI in reducing emotional fatigue.

Figure 8. Heatmap displaying the correlation between supervisor-promoted emotional intelligence (EI) culture and various workplace wellness factors.

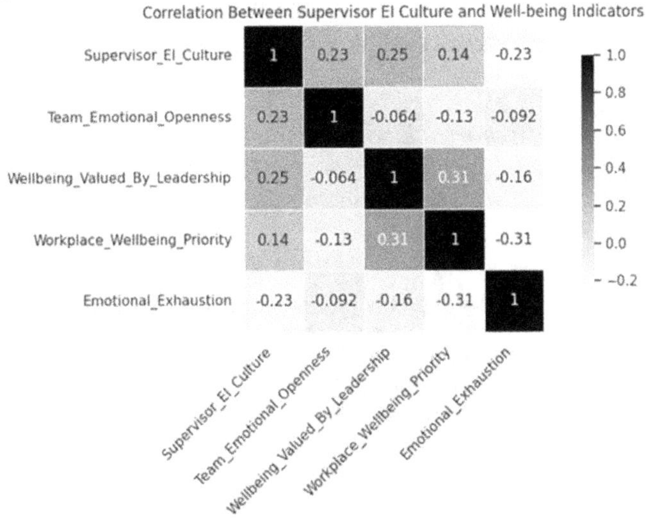

Supervisors displaying self-awareness and psychological insight testified to a higher level of satisfaction, stronger communication within the team, and reduced occurrences of burnout. These findings support the work done by Laschinger et al. (2014), which shows that the leadership team can serve as buffers in reducing the stress faced by frontline staff.

To assess the nature of EI and mental health-related training and existing institutional focus, respondents were presented with open-ended survey questions to assess whether they have received any such training and how the overall experience has been. The responses were unstructured and text-based, so qualitative categorization was created to systematically structure them. After rectifying the typographical errors, to ensure clarity without losing the respondents' original intent, a thematic coding process was done. Responses were analyzed to shortlist key descriptives, and frequently occurring patterns and categories were established. Three broad categories were created based on the responses. *Structured training* represents any formal workshops, seminars, and institutional programs hosted by the respective organizations or healthcare institutions. *Self-initiated* includes any personal efforts that support learning on the subject, such as podcasts, online courses, or self-reflection journals, etc., not supported by institutions. *No training* responses indicate a lack of experience, whether self-initiated or through institutionally mandated initiatives, and this category includes responses that were vague or did not directly answer the question, making it difficult to confidently classify them into other categories.

After manually reading the responses and assigning them to one of the four categories using keywords and the context, categorization was completed by tallying the responses in each category. Counts of each category and its sub-items were then converted to proportions and plotted as a pie chart, shown in Figure 9.

Figure 9. Distribution of Reported Emotional Intelligence or Mental Health Training.

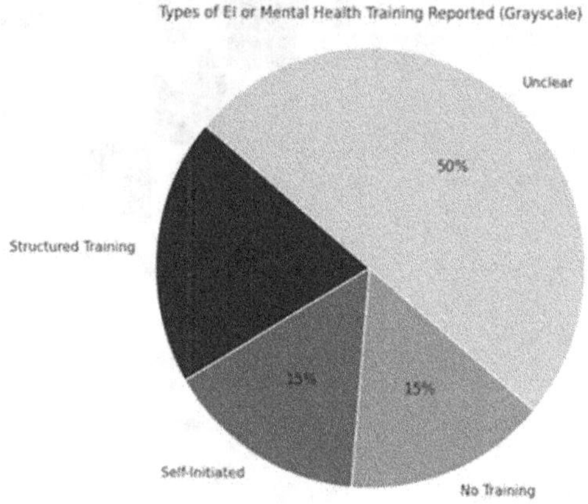

The chart shows how ER professionals in the sample described their exposure to EI or mental health training. 20% of the respondents showed that they received some form of structured institutional training, 15% focused on getting some form of training by taking initiatives themselves, while another 15% indicated a lack of any training. The result suggests that among the respondents who received the training, the impact of this training was positive but was infrequent and not incorporated into the everyday work life or culture of the organization, and the efforts couldn't be sustained. This finding is indicative of the need to shift from unstructured and ad hoc training and interventions to structured and inclusive institutional programming, a key call to action in this chapter.

Figure 10 shows levels of emotional exhaustion varying within different roles and organizational support.

Figure 10. Average Emotional Exhaustion by Role Across Perceived Organizational Support Levels

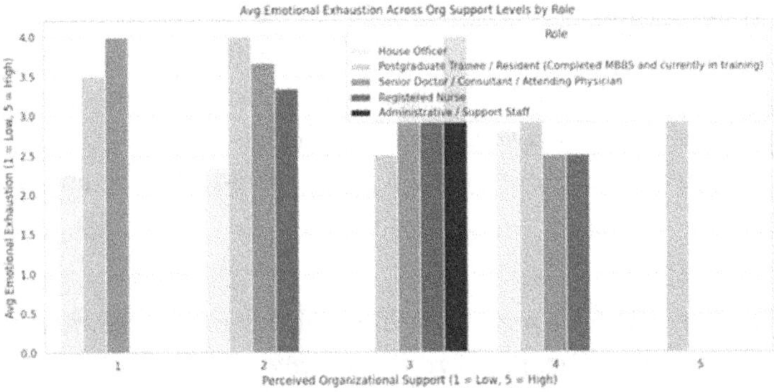

Residents and professionals in early careers reported high levels of emotional fatigue with low support from their institutions. With improvements in organizational support, exhaustion levels decline significantly in various roles. Thus, emotional exhaustion is inversely linked to organizational support, especially among staff working on the frontlines in the ER. The finding supports the proposition that systematic structures and backings are critical in mitigating burnout in ER staff, particularly prevalent in frontline and early mid-career professionals. Interestingly, healthcare professionals working 41-50 hour shifts reported high levels of work-life balance, with an average of ~3.4, while those working fewer hours reported low levels of satisfaction (while sample sizes are kept at n>5 for each category) [Figure 11].

Figure 11. Average self-reported work-life balance scores across weekly ER shift categories.

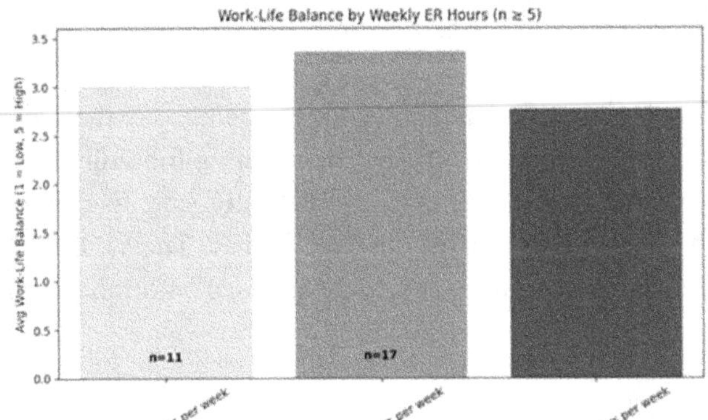

This suggests that work-life balance might not be directly linked to the number of hours and might be influenced by other factors such as autonomy of decision-making, seniority of role, and coping mechanisms. Given the low number of respondents in the 51+ work hours section, it is crucial to carefully review this trend.

To show the relationship between emotional awareness and emotional resilience, a regression line is plotted between the two variables. Figure 12 shows a positive trend suggesting that high self-awareness is associated with the ability to address emotions better.

Figure 12. Scatter plot with regression line illustrating the relationship between emotional awareness and emotional resilience among ER professionals.

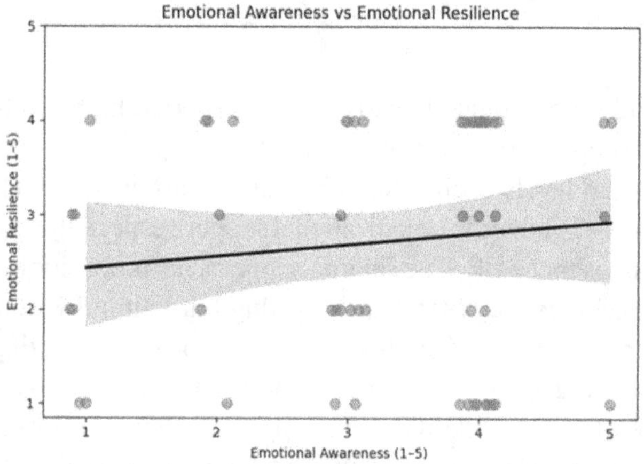

A scatterplot shows that individuals with high emotional awareness reported stronger emotional resilience. Although the trend is not statistically strong, it strengthens the perspective that self-awareness will serve as the foundation for emotional regulation.

Professionals who identified greater levels of openness in their teams rated lower emotional exhaustion. This is reflective of the existing literature that suggests team dynamics can create a buffer and offer emotionally safe spaces to rely on while working in high-stress environments such as the ER. The violin plot in Figure 13 represents emotional exhaustion with varying levels of emotional openness in teams.

Figure 13. Emotional Exhaustion Across Levels of Team Emotional Openness.

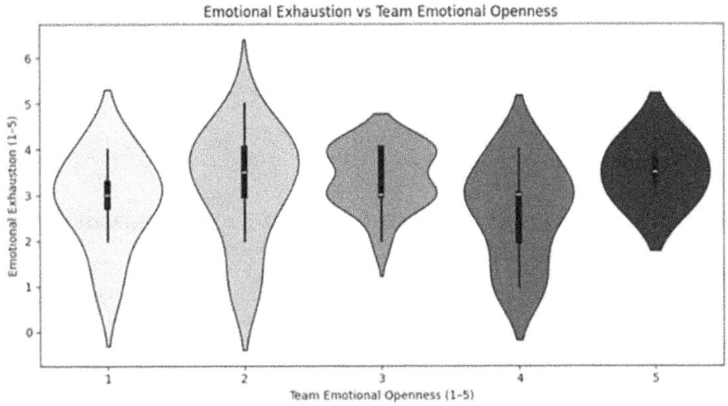

The interquartile range is reflected in the central box of the violin, while the width of the violin signifies the distribution density. Although the plot shows variation, it shows a noticeable trend indicating that higher emotional honesty and open discussion in teams are linked to lower levels of emotional exhaustion.

When examining the demand for training and tools linked to emotional support, residents showed high self-reported needs along with consultants [Figure 14].

Figure 14. Average Perceived Need for Emotional Support Tools by Role (n ≥ 5)

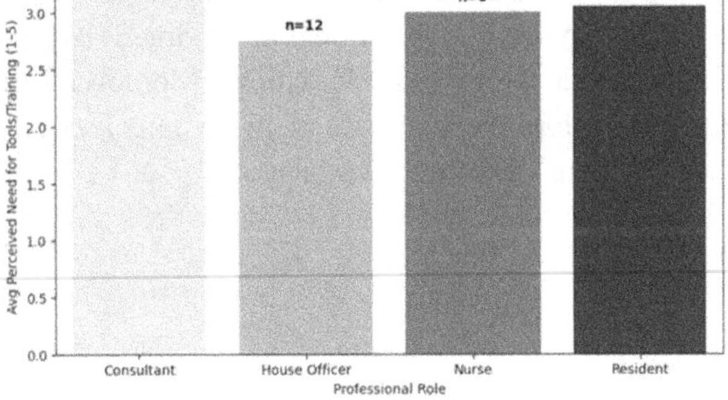

The bar chart shows Likert scale scores for the respondents, which measure the need for additional emotional support tools and training. The sample included 5 or more responses per role, where a high average demand was reported by Residents n=19 (in their early careers), along with consultants n=18 and house officers n=12. This trend reflects the high expectations and demanding working environment that these groups encounter in the ER setting. A high overall demand across different roles shows that there is a systematic lack of effective psychological support and resources.

The data collected for research is pivotal in understanding the role of leadership in regulating burnout in the ER setting. Figure 15 shows average emotional exhaustion linked with varying levels of leadership support.

Figure 15. Impact of Perceived Leadership Support on Emotional Exhaustion

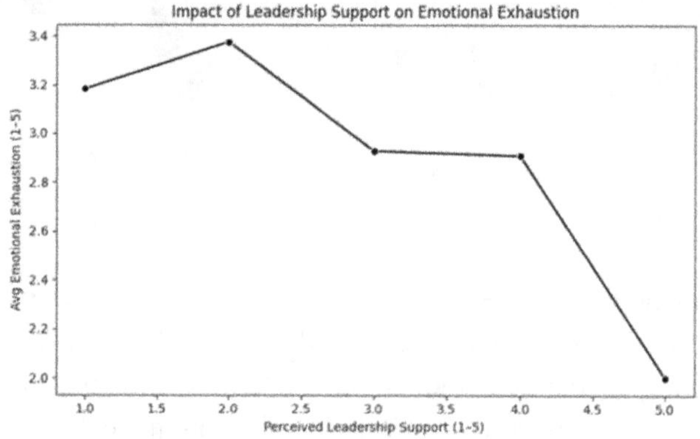

The data shows an inverse relationship between emotional exhaustion and the increase in support from leadership. When leadership support was rated at the highest level of 5, the reported levels of emotional exhaustion were at their lowest. This trend is in sync with the existing literature that suggests that emotional intelligence and leadership support are critical in serving as buffers against stress and emotional fatigue while working in ER settings. Moreover, Figure 15b shows a bivariate analysis to explore the influence of EI on perceived culture supported by supervisors and the team's emotional openness.

Figure 16. Relationship between perceived Supervisor Emotional Intelligence (EI) Culture and Team Emotional Openness.

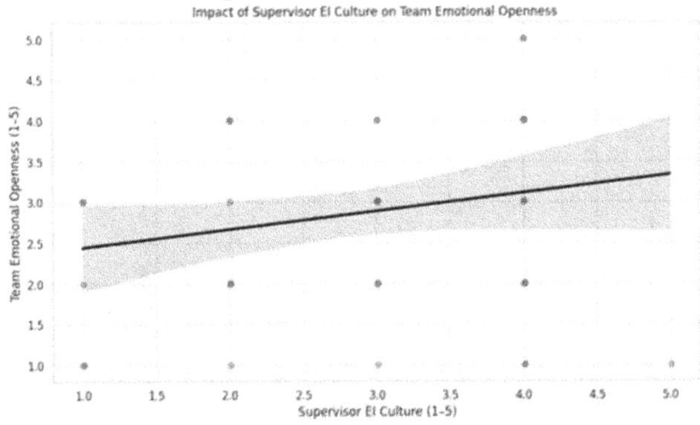

A positive linear relationship displayed reflects that teams where supervisors display emotional intelligence in their conduct, such as self-regulation, awareness, and empathy, have high levels of openness within their team. This relationship aligns with literature highlighting leadership with high EI that leads to improved trust, communication, and resilience in the team. This suggests that emotionally aware leadership can complement structural support in promoting a psychologically safer emergency room culture.

Research conducted through the survey included several open-ended reflections on top of the structured and closed-ended responses. Open-ended questions allow reflection on the coping strategies adopted by individuals and their recommendations to improve institutions regarding EI, self-efficacy, and overall mental health support in the ER settings. These qualitative responses were filtered through the frequency analysis of word clouds to disclose the key themes and dominant patterns. Figure 16 on coping strategies records a high dose of emotional regulation by individuals, support from their peers, and remaining mindful are some of the key strategies used by ER professionals. Several key words, such as "stay," "short," "shift," and "emotional," represent the high-pressure, high-stress, nuanced nature of ER environments. Key themes include emotional composure, short breaks between shifts, spiritual practices, and emotional composure. Several participants reflected on taking "quick moments" or "short breaks" to reconnect and rest during emotionally challenging shifts, as indicated by the word cloud in Figure 16.

Figure 17. Coping Strategies Word Cloud

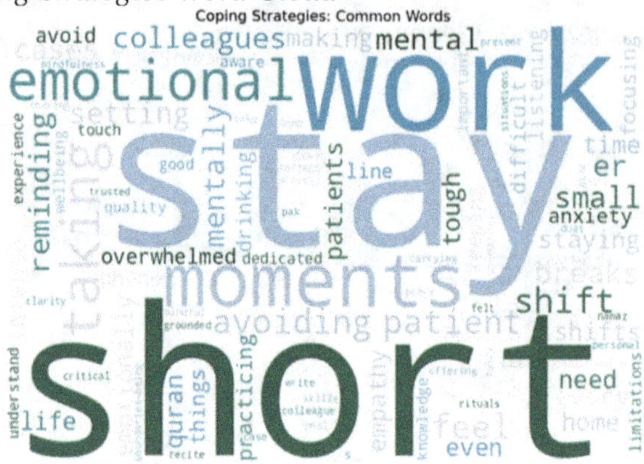

One remarkable finding of the research, as represented by the open-ended questions, is that faith-driven actions and gestures play a significant role in coping with high-stress situations. A high frequency of words representing clarity, namaz, Quran, and dua, along with words such as empathy and clarity, reflects respondents' belief in them being internal mechanisms effective in maintaining composure and clinical functioning under highly stressful situations. Figure 17 shows a word cloud in response to the open-ended question asking about institutional support for mental health support in the ER, where the responses represented key themes suggesting structural and institutional interventions.

Figure 18. Suggestions for Institutional Improvement Word Cloud

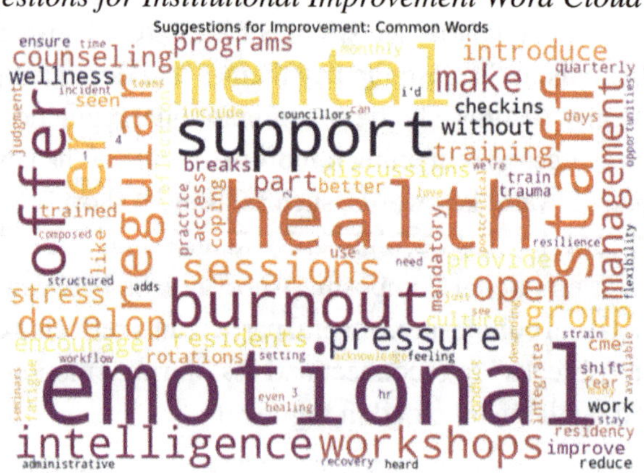

Key themes that emerged in the analysis include EI training, prevention programs aimed at reducing burnout, counselling, and leadership involvement. Strong support and a call to action are seen in the frequency of terms used, such as "support," "regular," "sessions," "emotional," and "health," reflecting a strong support base for mental health practices that are rooted in the workplaces and are sustainable in the future.

Respondents actively supported "counselling sessions," "wellness workshops," "Check-ins," and "open discussions in groups," suggesting that most of the professionals advocate proactive and institutionalized support systems instead of short-term and reactive practices. Moreover, recurrence of words such as "management," "provide," "culture," "staff," and "encouragement" underpins the role of leadership in promoting a psychologically safe work environment that supports development of emotional intelligence. There is a need to promote work cultures that acknowledge burnouts, provide mental health support, and encourage and integrate practices for emotional wellness, making psychological safety a critical aspect in this profession instead of being recognized as a luxury.

A notable influence is seen in gender-based variations where psychological responses to ER demands are represented across three variables, as shown in Figure 18, with emotional exhaustion, awareness, and work-life balance.

Figure 19. Gender Differences in Emotional Exhaustion, Emotional Awareness, and Work-Life Balance

The figure shows that male respondents recorded higher emotional exhaustion. However, the interquartile range for both genders overlaps significantly. On the other hand, female respondents reported greater emotional awareness with lower variation in scores. For work-life balance, there is a similar distribution, suggesting that institutional or role-specific dynamics have a stronger influence as compared to gender. These findings, although less significant, are reflective of the subtle differences in how emotional labor is processed. Gender division in the display of emotions can be a result of societal gender norms around self-regulation, professional expectations, and support groups. While adopting emotional training and support mechanisms, a gender-sensitive approach is critical to ensure that training and support mechanisms are beneficial in multidisciplinary teams.

DISCUSSION

The research findings indicate the dynamics of emotional wellness among healthcare professionals in emergency rooms in Pakistan, highlighting key social, psychological, and systematic factors that shape their experiences. This discussion highlights exploratory data analysis, visual patterns observed, statistical results analyzed, and the key qualitative insights to allow analysis for health policies, wellness of the workforce, and the institutional frameworks to guide effectiveness. One of the constraining findings of this research is the concurrence of emotional exhaustion with the perception of high meaningfulness associated with work. The study suggests that although purposefulness is psychologically rewarding, it does not provide immunity to healthcare professionals from workplace and especially ER-related burnout due to working in highly stressful situations in emergency wards. Boxplots and the comparison of means for different groups suggested that those professionals who rated their work highly on the meaningfulness scale still showed moderate to high exhaustion levels. This is reflective of "Compassion Fatigue," where higher emotional contribution with no supportive system leads to burnout and exhaustion regardless of the internal motivation.

This finding calls for the inclusion of systematic psychological buffers, despite the strong internal motivations of professionals. Institutional structures should incorporate routine debriefing, interventions, building emotional skill sets, and changing shift designs based on how straining the last shift has been. Without these support structures, there is a risk of motivation becoming a double-edged sword, which can drive professionals into breakdown instead of safeguarding them from it.

Role-Based Differences in Stress and Support

This research highlights variations in the way consultants, residents, and postgraduate trainees experience emotional burdens of their roles and perceive the support received from their institutions. When respondents were asked to reflect upon their past experiences or incidents that were emotionally draining for them, key emerging themes were "helped," "senior," "family," "death," and "coworker," suggesting the levels of stressful events that are dominant in emergency care services.

Figure 20. Wordcloud reflecting emotional incidents and their responses. Dominant themes from emotional reflections are highlighted.

Often, these incidents triggered emotional strain and team interactions, and support was provided. The frequently used word “helpful” suggests that healthcare professionals have to rely on support structures in the form of peer networks during the “emotionally” charged situations, such as the death and near-death experiences of patients. These words reflect the emotional impact of these events, suggesting that there may be high levels of unprocessed stress that remain neglected. Peer support and hierarchical support systems have been effective in severe cases, helping ER staff understand how these high-stress events are interpreted and experienced.

Several reflections provided references to high-impact or traumatic experiences with expressions of fatigue and emotional charge. Co-occurrence of patterns of burnout and seeking peer support suggests that although ER professionals manage to stay resilient by taking support from their peers, there is a lack of structured debriefing or availability of formal support systems after dealing with critical life-deaths and traumatic incidents. Moreover, professionals in their early careers are especially susceptible to higher levels of exhaustion and may not be aware of the options available to seek support. The presence of high stress in early careers is not solely due to a lack of experience but can also be a reflection of power dynamics, unfair workload distribution, and marginalization within the healthcare profession. On the other hand, consultants showed higher levels of self-reported emotional stability, reflective of the protective privilege that comes with seniority.

These findings are crucial for designing policies that target ER professionals. Emotional wellness and EI interventions must be directed at professionals in early to mid-careers and especially in roles where decision-making power is limited and institutional voice is low and not structured. Mentoring programs that promote empathy and share the emotional burdens of ER professionals are critical for connecting these experiential loose ends.

Supervisors' Emotional Intelligence Serving as a Cultural Lever within Teams

This research examined the correlation between the perceived emotional intelligence of supervisors and their teams' comfort with emotional openness. Although Spearman and Pearson correlation (0.24-0.23) did not provide significant results, they suggested a positive relationship between the two factors. This highlights the role of leaders in embodying EI to foster psychological openness within their teams. Emotional intelligence is crucial for cultural transformation. Supervisors play a crucial role in navigating the dynamics of their team in strongly hierarchical institutions where leadership cascades from top to bottom. Institutions must invest in leadership development and their emotional intelligence to promote emotional literacy, vulnerability, and empathy, not just for patients but also for their peers, while managing managerial productivity and efficiency.

Channeling Resilience Through Experience

Professionals who had more than 10 years of experience in the ER had significantly higher resilience and self-awareness. Violin plots and bar charts supported this notion, highlighting that experience, which is reflective of experiential and adaptive learning, safeguards them from emotional burdens. However, we should not overly rely on this finding, as it could hinder the growth and development of young professionals. Building resilience with time can have certain costs, such as long-serving ER professionals may rely on coping strategies that disengage them emotionally or focus on hiding the distress, which are not suitable as long-term survival strategies.

It is critical to build resilience and instill it early in careers instead of relying on professionals to build it as a side effect with longer service. Institutions should introduce modules that provide early- and mid-career training on mindfulness, create a peer support network, and formalize reflective practices to ensure quick adoption of effective coping strategies among early-career professionals.

Perception of Mental Health Value Depending on Organizational Type

We observed a notable difference in how private and governmental institutions perceived their professionals' concern for psychological wellness. Private institutions rated their workplaces as more supportive, while the public sector reflected neglect and skepticism. This disparity can be reflective of the differences in availability of resources, leadership styles, and responsiveness of HR. These insights demand immediate attention from policymakers. If such critical matters remain unattended, government institutions and hospitals serving a significant patient population may face severe consequences. Introducing infrastructure and support systems that support mental health, ranging from spaces to rest to availability of institutional psychologists, should be introduced as a core part of public health spending and must not be treated as a luxury or optional intervention.

Work-Life Balance and Intensity/length of Shifts

Hours spent per week in the ER are negatively associated with the work-life balance ratings. The bar plot indicated that longer shift workers reported poor work-life balance and are more prone to psychological vulnerabilities. These findings are reflective of the literature that emphasizes the impact but are more relevant in this study, considering the local context where long shifts, along with resource scarcity, are the norm. Institutions must introduce unbiased and data-driven shift scheduling to prevent the accumulation of burnout cases.

A reflection of coping strategies by professionals suggested recurring patterns and terms, such as resorting to prayers and spiritual connections to provide respite and strength during high emotional fatigue. Research has demonstrated that a relational and behavioral tendency to seek peer support and gratitude from patients can boost morale levels.

This research has reinforced the belief that emotional wellness in ER healthcare systems is not a factor of individual motivation or resilience but is a collective outcome of the way organizational culture is built up, organizational designs are reinforced, and the role of leadership in perpetuating a conducive work environment. Pakistan's institutions and especially public ones, need to integrate the emotional well-being of ER professionals into their strategic frameworks and should offer them as fundamental pillars of clinical expertise.

This research can serve as a framework to introduce reforms that are not just corrective in nature but are actionable, ranging from shifting structures to leadership development and promoting open discussions in teams while ensuring sufficient resources and a network are available for mental health and wellness. Prioritizing our ER workforce's mental health reflects our systematic integrity and operational focus.

RECOMMENDATIONS

Based on the survey insights gathered from strategic and operational aspects of ER healthcare professionals' need for psychological wellness, several interventions are recommended to support individual resilience and enhance institutional support mechanisms. One of the most consistent patterns that came out of the analysis was how supervisors and leaders and their emotional intelligence affected how teams worked together. Incorporating structured training and the implementation of EI modules, along with incentives to place more value on intelligent leadership, will help embed EI in the culture of hospitals and institutions. This guarantees that the organization's critical values align with recognition systems and performance appraisals.

Early- to mid-career postgraduate trainees have shown higher susceptibility to burnout and emotional exhaustion. These residents and professionals stepping into early careers have to navigate overwhelming clinical demand, uncertain and long work shifts, and a lack of knowledge about coping strategies. Healthcare institutions, especially ER departments, must tailor interventions specific to roles, such as increasing exposure for trainees through rotational breaks, workshops structured around resilience, and support networks led by peers within cohorts. By integrating such interventions into academics, it will lay the groundwork for a cultural shift and ensure that such support is not viewed as a one-off exception, but is embedded into the entire professional lifecycle, from induction to ongoing learning.

The number of hours spent per week in the ER has a direct correlation with diminishing work-life balance. Professionals working an average of 40+ hours have rated their wellness as significantly lower than their peers, even after adjusting for their roles and experience. Healthcare institutions must reinforce scheduling policies with protected meal and rest breaks to prevent shift workload from spilling over. Sleep deprivation and disruption in circadian rhythm contribute to fatigue and burnout, where disturbed sleep impairs cognitive functions. Inadequate sleep further impacts resilience in high-pressure environments.

This requires that sufficient human resources are available to cover up the emergencies and deal with patients when required. Additionally, implementing caps on maximum shift hours will allow better control from a systematic perspective. By providing flexible scheduling options, ER empowers residents to promote personal organization by allowing them to better manage their responsibilities and time. This will promote a reduction in burnout and improve cognitive engagement of residents to provide and sustain higher standards of patient care.

Insights from the survey indicated that respondents who experienced higher levels of stress were still able to maintain a sense of meaningfulness. This is representative of a latent strength that can be fostered further. To harness this further, institutions should integrate practices in self-reflection in routine work, such as monthly sessions on “meaningfulness in medicine” or debriefings with teams that will allow staff to rethink the impact they are creating and the value generated by them.

Disparity in mental wellness was another key finding across various types of facilities. Private hospitals placed greater value on psychological health. This could be linked to better investment and availability of resources or policies. Such gaps can be bridged by allocating donor- and NGO-backed mental health programs as a priority to government hospitals. Contextual adaptations within the public sector can explore several private sector best practices. Inter-facility benchmarking can promote healthy competition and facilitate the sharing of learnings across both streams, as several interventions can be managed by peer-led initiatives or volunteer work. These mediations can ensure that emotional well-being is not considered as a privilege reserved for one sector with sufficient resources but is available as a standard basic need across all healthcare settings.

Reflections and responses highlighted various coping mechanisms such as prayer, peer support, mindfulness, and physical exercise. Although many professionals expressed a concern for the unavailability of formal guidance channels, they also expressed emotional strain in handling such situations. To give professionals more power, it is important to start campaigns that promote healthy ways to deal with stress, like storytelling sessions where peers can share their own successful ways of dealing with stress.

Data plays a critical role in streamlining the introduction and implementation of control channels. Instead of manual and limited assessments or check-ups, hospitals can adopt dashboards that allow the tracking of burnout with AI, creating predictions based on EI levels and the psychological scoring of teams in real time. Such analysis can be done through quarterly surveys to measure and assess various attributes that can be linked to actionable KPIs. Strategic decision-making, including resource allocation, workflow designs, and hiring practices, can benefit from the data available on such tools.

Although individual interventions drive long-term and systematic changes, they must be reinforced by central policy reforms that can integrate emotional health within the broader theme of patient safety and quality care. A prevention strategy within care providers will do This approach serves as a preventive strategy for patients. This can be done through the state-level inclusion of psychological wellness in the accreditation criteria. This can be achieved by mandating EI and psychological wellness training for new hires, and by establishing a standard operating procedure that incorporates emotional support as a fundamental component of quality care. This process will require collaboration and initiative from policymakers and regulatory authorities to implement systematic changes by institutionalizing these practices.

Professionals shared their reflections on emotionally draining experiences, their impact, and the coping mechanisms they employ. Most of the professionals shared experiences dealing with highly critical cases that leave an impact on their mental health; however, the lack of sufficient avenues for support in such circumstances is evident in all cases. The discussion calls for the implementation of formal, routine debriefs after critical incidents to allow processing in a prudent way. Within institutions and hospitals, buddy systems can be introduced as peer support, which is emphasized by professionals during times of uncertainty and after dealing with critical cases. These processes can be enhanced by leveraging data within decision-making through recruitment, job rotations, and employee retention policies, especially within ER.

An underlying issue in creating support networks is the stigma attached to psychological support seeking. By introducing awareness campaigns and leadership encouragement, we can destigmatize and provide job security by separating judgments based on support from leaders and peers. Moreover, cross-departmental experience sharing around wellness programs, implementation of flexible schedules, and mental wellness services can especially benefit government institutions by learning from the private sector.

It is critical to note that professionals in their early careers, especially those under 5 years, have shown more vulnerability to burnout and psychological fatigue. For these reasons, early career professionals can be prioritized for resilience training and prioritized accordingly.

LIMITATIONS & FUTURE RESEARCH DIRECTIONS

Research conducted for this chapter and its analysis offer valuable insights to improve existing mental health wellness approaches by accessing the psychological experiences of ER professionals. However, several limitations exist within the existing landscape, limiting the interpretation of insights and offering more opportunities to conduct further inquiry in the future and refine the research methodologies.

Although the data sample is diverse and targets various public and private hospitals, the respondents were not uniformly distributed. This can be seen with low representation from administrative staff and nurses. Additionally, a higher representation of private hospitals and institutions can add bias towards the evaluation of support mechanisms for respective institutions. Future research studies should adopt strategies that include more stratified strategies for research participants to ensure representation across the ER hierarchical system that is reflective of the actual dynamics of the ER.

This research survey is heavily dependent on self-reported data, which is associated with social desirability bias, particularly in areas such as emotional resilience, satisfaction linked to the workplace, and the ease of access and willingness to ask for psychological help. Due to prevailing professional norms around the subject of mental health, several participants might have over- or under-reported the frequency and level of emotional fatigue compared to what they have actually faced. It is recommended that future research endeavors triangulate these conclusions through careful assessments or introduce statistical methods to nullify the extreme variations and smooth out the respective factors.

This research also captured responses and reflections at a point instead of a time series. A longitudinal study would have allowed monitoring of patterns and more reflective insights to enhance the research. Emotional fatigue, resilient mindset, and developing institutional support and peer networks are not fixed in time and are constantly evolving with policy, leadership, and personnel shifts. A longitudinal study in the future can enhance the understanding of support systems, stress factors, and coping mechanisms through various stages of professionals in the ER and broader crisis management, such as during a pandemic or systematic overloads.

Moreover, the analysis relied on frequency patterns and word clouds while employing a thematic study of the open-ended questions about coping mechanisms, reflecting on emotional incidents, and using the current method of analysis. A more detailed thematic analysis of the content can be done via quantitative software and grounded theory to yield rich insights into the way language is used for communication, cultural appropriation, and moral concerns. Future studies should utilize sentiment analysis and narrative-based inquiry to uncover more nuanced experiences often overlooked by quantitative analysis.

Findings from the study pointed to differences between public and private facility types when exploring mental health. However, the study lacked the ability to create interactive models and only aggregated facility-level insights at a broader level, with limited clustering. Future studies can employ a multi-pronged approach to account for institutional dynamics such as patient inflow, resource allocation, and employee-to-patient ratios, along with leadership and organizational culture, to probe the differences between the two major institutions.

Utilization of digital tools is on the rise in this age of rapid technological advancements and accessibility. The research, however, did not account for the utilization of any digital wellness tools and technologies. Incorporation of AI-based forecasting of patient inflow, workload prediction, and an employee feedback system were not assessed. As ERs worldwide are adopting digital wellness tools, future assessments should incorporate the usage, effectiveness, and adoption of the readily available technology advancements to create mental health support systems for frontline professionals.

Lastly, the study's conclusions are driven from a specific geographical and cultural context rooted in South Asia, and such findings cannot be directly replicated in global systems such as in East Asia or the Global North, where the cultural meaning of work-life balance, emotional labor, and institutional adoption differ greatly. We recommend a comparative study approach for varied geographies to facilitate understanding of local context and develop widely adaptable frameworks.

The study is limited in empirical evidence because it could not be determined whether a link exists between medical errors, workplace stress, and burnout, as such cases cannot be easily assigned a cause-and-effect relationship under current medical administration and data-gathering policies.

CONCLUSION

This chapter has presented a layout of the psychological strain and the emotional distress experienced by healthcare professionals in Pakistan. With a detailed study employing survey data that included both closed-ended and open-ended questions and reflections, it's evident that healthcare professionals are prone to deeper vulnerabilities while trying to exhibit remarkable resilience working in Emergency Rooms (ERs). The subject's limited attention has prevented a systematic approach to addressing these vulnerabilities.

Although several respondents reported higher professional commitment and the emotional meaning of their work, they expressed feelings of frequent burnout and insufficient institutional support. Especially prevalent among early-career professionals, the systematic lack of psychological safeguards was prominent. On the other hand, seasoned professionals displayed greater coping ability due to their experiential learning, although they equally voiced concerns about a lack of organizational recognition and emotional negligence. Moreover, seasoned professionals and supervisors in leadership roles contributed to the creation of effective peer support networks; their empathy, better self-efficacy, active listening, and team cohesion significantly improved the team's morale, while the opposite effect was observed in teams where leaders failed to establish emotional connections and provide support. The results suggested a transformational role of leadership in creating emotionally resilient teams.

Moreover, qualitative insights suggested that coping methods are informal and make the processing of emotional incidents ineffective; however, peer support networks and patient gratitude were rated as respites from this emotional turmoil. These findings suggest the rehabilitation of healthcare systems and call for policymakers' attention to be proactive in inducing a culture of care. This can be manifested through briefing sessions, stronger peer support networks, and resilience training not just for ER professionals but for institutional leaders and supervisors.

This study is critical in understanding the emotional labor faced by ER professionals and the role of institutions in providing support systems. By adopting these findings and recommendations, healthcare institutions can move the narrative of patient wellness beyond mere medical care and also offer care for their service providers by focusing on psychological safety, emotional wellness, and professional sustainability that will benefit not just the ER professionals but also elevate the service level for the patients they serve.

REFERENCES

Ahmad, S., Khalid, R., & Fatima, S. (2022). Occupational stress and coping strategies in emergency room physicians in Pakistan: A mixed-methods study. *International Journal of Mental Health Systems, 16*(1), 45. DOI: 10.1186/s13033-022-00522-9 PMID: 36056370

Bandura, A. (1997). *Self-efficacy: The exercise of control.* W.H. Freeman.

Cao, J., Wang, S., & Li, J. (2023). Self-efficacy and burnout among emergency nurses: A cross-sectional study. *International Journal of Nursing Studies, 134*, 104382. DOI: 10.1016/j.ijnurstu.2022.104382

Cooper, A. L., Brown, J. A., & Rees, C. S. (2020). Resilience in emergency service workers: An integrative literature review. *International Emergency Nursing, 49*, 100814. DOI: 10.1016/j.ienj.2019.100814

Dyrbye, L. N., Shanafelt, T. D., & Sinsky, C. A.. (2017). *Burnout among health care professionals: A call to explore and address this underrecognized threat to safe, high-quality care.* National Academy of Medicine., DOI: 10.31478/201707b

Edmondson, A. (1999). Psychological safety and learning behavior in work teams. *Administrative Science Quarterly, 44*(2), 350–383. DOI: 10.2307/2666999

Goleman, D. (1995). *Emotional intelligence: Why it can matter more than IQ.* Bantam Books.

Krasner, M. S., Epstein, R. M., & Beckman, H.. (2009). Association of an educational program in mindful communication with burnout, empathy, and attitudes among primary care physicians. *Journal of the American Medical Association, 302*(12), 1284–1293. DOI: 10.1001/jama.2009.1384 PMID: 19773563

Laschinger, H. K. S., Wong, C. A., Cummings, G. G., & Grau, A. L. (2014). Resonant leadership and workplace empowerment: The value of positive organizational cultures in reducing workplace incivility. *Nursing Economics, 32*(1), 5–16. PMID: 24689153

Marshall, A. P., Austin, D. E., Chamberlain, D., & New, K. (2021). Burnout and emotional intelligence in emergency department nurses: A review. *Journal of Nursing Management, 29*(2), 241–251. DOI: 10.1111/jonm.13126

Montgomery, A. (2014). The inevitability of physician burnout: Implications for interventions. *Burnout Research, 1*(1), 50–56. DOI: 10.1016/j.burn.2014.04.002

Moss, M., Good, V. S., Gozal, D., Kleinpell, R., & Sessler, C. N. (2016). An official critical care societies collaborative statement: Burnout syndrome in critical care healthcare professionals: A call for action. *American Journal of Critical Care, 25*(4), 368–376. DOI: 10.4037/ajcc2016133 PMID: 27369038

Panagioti, M., Geraghty, K., Johnson, J., Zhou, A., Panagopoulou, E., Chew-Graham, C., & Esmail, A. (2018). Association between physician burnout and patient safety, professionalism, and patient satisfaction: A systematic review and meta-analysis. *JAMA Internal Medicine, 178*(10), 1317–1330. DOI: 10.1001/jamainternmed.2018.3713 PMID: 30193239

Poncet, M. C., Toullic, P., Papazian, L., Kentish-Barnes, N., Timsit, J.-F., Pochard, F., Chevret, S., Schlemmer, B., & Azoulay, É. (2007). Burnout syndrome in critical care nursing staff. *American Journal of Respiratory and Critical Care Medicine, 175*(7), 698–704. DOI: 10.1164/rccm.200606-806OC PMID: 17110646

Qidwai, M. A. (2024). The 5Ss' approach for managing health of client, family and community. *National Journal of Health Sciences, 9*(4), 231–234. DOI: 10.21089/njhs.94.0231

Reith, T. P. (2018). Burnout in United States healthcare professionals: A narrative review. *Cureus, 10*(12), e3681. DOI: 10.7759/cureus.3681 PMID: 30761233

Restauri, N., & Sheridan, A. D. (2020). Burnout and posttraumatic stress disorder in the COVID-19 pandemic: Intersection, impact, and interventions. *Journal of the American College of Radiology, 17*(7), 921–926. DOI: 10.1016/j.jacr.2020.05.021 PMID: 32479798

Sexton, J. B., Thomas, E. J., & Helmreich, R. L. (2000). Error, stress, and teamwork in medicine and aviation. *BMJ (Clinical Research Ed.), 320*(7237), 745–749. DOI: 10.1136/bmj.320.7237.745 PMID: 10720356

Shanafelt, T. D., Hasan, O., Dyrbye, L. N., Sinsky, C., Satele, D., Sloan, J., & West, C. P. (2015). Changes in burnout and satisfaction with work-life balance in physicians and the general US working population between 2011 and 2014. *Mayo Clinic Proceedings, 90*(12), 1600–1613. DOI: 10.1016/j.mayocp.2015.08.023 PMID: 26653297

Shanafelt, T. D., & Noseworthy, J. H. (2017). Executive leadership and physician well-being. *Mayo Clinic Proceedings, 92*(1), 129–146. DOI: 10.1016/j.mayocp.2016.10.004 PMID: 27871627

Stacey, G., Felton, A., Joy, D., & Morris, M. (2019). Embedding resilience training into nursing education: An integrative review. *Nurse Education Today, 76*, 79–87. DOI: 10.1016/j.nedt.2019.01.014

Swancott, L., Armstrong, N., Roland, D., Walters, H. L., & Kirk, K. (2024). Emergency department workforces' experiences and perceptions of well-being from an international perspective: A scoping review. *BMJ Open*, *14*(7), e087485. DOI: 10.1136/bmjopen-2024-087485 PMID: 38986554

Tawfik, D. S., Profit, J., Morgenthaler, T. I., Satele, D. V., Sinsky, C. A., Dyrbye, L. N., Tutty, M. A., West, C. P., & Shanafelt, T. D. (2018). Physician burnout, well-being, and work unit safety grades in relationship to reported medical errors. *Mayo Clinic Proceedings*, *93*(11), 1571–1580. DOI: 10.1016/j.mayocp.2018.05.014 PMID: 30001832

Thomas, L. R., Ripp, J. A., & West, C. P. (2018). Charter on Physician Well-being. *Journal of the American Medical Association*, *319*(15), 1541–1542. DOI: 10.1001/jama.2018.1331 PMID: 29596592

Travis, D. J., Lizano, E. L., & Mor Barak, M. E. (2016). 'I'm So Stressed!': A Longitudinal Model of Stress, Burnout and Engagement among Social Workers in Child Welfare Settings. *British Journal of Social Work*, *46*(4), 1076–1095. DOI: 10.1093/bjsw/bct205 PMID: 27559215

Versel, J. L., Plezia, A., Jennings, L., Sontag-Milobsky, I., Adams, W., & Shahid, R. (2023). Emotional Intelligence and Resilience "PROGRAM" Improves Well-being and Stress Management Skills in Preclinical Medical Students. *Advances in Medical Education and Practice*, *14*, 1309–1316. DOI: 10.2147/AMEP.S437053 PMID: 38028369

Weng, H. C., Chen, H. C., & Chen, H. J.. (2011). Doctors' emotional intelligence and the patient–doctor relationship. *Medical Education*, *45*(8), 835–842. DOI: 10.1111/j.1365-2923.2011.03985.x PMID: 21752080

West, C. P., Dyrbye, L. N., & Shanafelt, T. D. (2018). Physician burnout: Contributors, consequences and solutions. *Journal of Internal Medicine*, *283*(6), 516–529. DOI: 10.1111/joim.12752 PMID: 29505159

World Health Organization. (2019). *Burn-out an "occupational phenomenon": International Classification of Diseases*. Retrieved from https://www.who.int/mental_health/evidence/burn-out/en/

KEY TERMS AND DEFINITIONS

Emotional Exhaustion: A state of mental and emotional depletion due to extended exposure to high-stress environments such as the ER.

Psychological Safety: A perception among employees that they can freely and openly express themselves without fear of judgment or retaliation.

Reflective Practices: A process where healthcare providers access and reflect on their experiences, especially after emotionally intense and challenging situations, to drive insights and discuss coping methods and support professional growth.

Peer Support: Formal and informal ways that colleagues interact with each other to provide practical assistance. This includes experience sharing and offering help where needed.

Narrative Analysis: A qualitative method of research where free texts are interpreted. This paper was used to explore emotional themes, coping methods, and dynamics of psychological wellness to drive insights.

Emotional Resilience: The capacity of healthcare providers to adapt to stress and recover from emotionally draining incidents to ensure effective delivery of service without the loss of cognitive abilities.

Burnout: Emotional exhaustion when driven by work-related factors. It is accelerated by trauma exposure, longer shifts, and minimal institutional support.

Chapter 4
Self- Empowering Healthcare Providers:
Building Inner Strength for Better Care

Sobia Ali
http://orcid.org/0000-0001-7601-4634
Ayub Medical College, Abbottabad, Pakistan

Sofia Ali
http://orcid.org/0009-0001-6055-6989
Ayub Medical College, Abbottabad, Pakistan

Aabdar Hidayat
http://orcid.org/0000-0002-5415-4318
Aga Khan Univerisity, Karachi, Pakistan

ABSTRACT

The rigid stereotypes associated with healthcare providers neglect the human aspects of their personalities and often portray them to be either deficient in communication skills or as flawless professionals who can handle every situation perfectly. This chapter pans at the healthcare provider in the perspective of self and self-empowerment. The authors build a narrative for physician well-being by trying to answer why is provider well-being important? Why and how do things go wrong? Why is it that some develop the burnout syndrome while others don't? And finally how can providers help themselves? Verbatim quotes from healthcare providers interviewed for several qualitative studies are embedded within the text.

DOI: 10.4018/979-8-2600-0582-8.ch004

INTRODUCTION

"That physician will hardly be thought very careful of the health of the others who neglects his own." - Galen

The culture in popular media portrays an ideal healthcare professional either as a selfless healer who is available around the clock, always leading, unshaken by suffering, and possessing endless knowledge or, on the opposite end of the spectrum, as a greedy, arrogant, and emotionally cold person who is a poor communicator and only talks in jargon. Rigid stereotypes in medicine have led to the inconsideration of the humanistic side of healthcare professionals, leading to burnout and exhaustion.

It is estimated that globally, 39% of healthcare workers report symptoms of burnout (Nagarajan et al., 2024). Between 2011 and 2014, the prevalence of burnout increased by 9% in US healthcare workers, with no change in other professions, denoting the gravity of its situation, particularly in healthcare. This condition is associated with a concomitant rise in some serious consequences for healthcare providers, institutions, and healthcare systems (Dyrbye et al., 2017). Worker mental health has become central to ensuring quality care delivery to populations due to shifts in epidemiological disease patterns, increasing life expectancies, and a greater frequency of public health emergencies that strain already weak health systems. A mentally strained worker cannot provide quality healthcare and is more likely to make medical errors due to clouded judgment and slower reflexes. Medical errors as a result of a compromised provider's well-being can be viewed as the most important link in the chain of consequences faced by the patients and society, negatively affecting lives and damaging healthcare trust. Most of these errors are unintentional and stem more from working conditions and burnout than from incompetence or a lack of knowledge (Hall et al., 2016).

The alarming rates of rise in dissatisfaction and exhaustion in healthcare can be attributed to the fast pace of modern life, greater competition in achieving better lifestyles, and a strife for financial gains rather than connecting to a meaningful purpose in life. An added strain on mental health is the social media distraction, which portrays anything apart from aesthetically pleasing as inferior and raises expectations for the general public as well as health personnel in all aspects of life. The ease in communication comes at the price of a lesser ability to disconnect and revive mental peace (Shanafelt et al., 2003).

The current body of literature focuses on physician distress rather than wellness, and although fragmented efforts have been made to redefine and redirect healthcare provider wellness, there is little consensus on the interventions, which are self-centric and allow a provider to empower themselves rather than waiting for the system or society to address their concerns about their well-being.

SECTION IA: THE IMPORTANCE OF PROVIDER WELL-BEING

"I joined the profession thinking of herself as the young blood who could bring change and heal the suffering humanity. I continued to work for years with all enthusiasm, pouring all my attention and energies into my profession. Slowly, I felt like every day was turning into a slow blur, I could not feel happy anymore. I kept snapping at my colleagues and felt the emotional weight of every patient loss. I was lucky that my supervisor recognized I was getting burnt out. A short getaway helped me reset. I was encouraged to seek counselling. Mindfulness training and resilience coaching helped me understand I did not need to over-extend myself to practice compassion. I learnt that sometimes saying "no" is also a form of caring."

A substantial body of evidence suggests that burnout has deep and long-term effects on the physical, mental and social health of providers and several organizational and system level implications.

Personal Safety:

Healthcare providers often work in emotionally charged settings where escalation to violence is not uncommon, especially in low-resource health systems where public sector hospitals are run on public funds and provider security is not a primary priority. Workplace violence is a known predictor of burnout (Giménez Lozano et al., 2021; Lim et al., 2022). But there is limited literature available on the role of burnout and provider exhaustion as a predictor for workplace violence.

"Sometimes we will see the emergency patient; the patient has an MI, so we gave him an acute coronary syndrome treatment and I'm referring the patient and I'm telling them that we have only one ambulance and the ambulance has gone, has taken the other patient, so they start fighting with me, saying, "Why do you not have another ambulance?" (Wright, 2025) These are the kinds of situations that healthcare providers have to deal with, adding to their anxiety and eventually, inducing apathy.

A burnt-out worker is more likely to display apathy, commit medical errors, and show a reduced threshold for agitation and anger with a limited capacity to resolve conflicts, all of which may precipitate or worsen violence against workers in healthcare settings. Long work hours and sleepless shifts can also jeopardize the personal safety of healthcare professionals. A shift longer than 16 hours can lead to a greater risk for motor vehicle crashes or near-miss events.

"I've been paying for a hotel after night shifts because I know I won't be safe to drive because I have lots of colleagues who've crashed after night shifts. It's

like being under the influence of four or five pints of beer. I've fallen asleep on the M4 motorway once, coming home from a night shift." (Hodgson et al., 2024)

Emotional Exhaustion:

It is natural for physicians to feel emotionally involved with their patients. If these emotions are not managed, they can compromise patient care by causing excessive attachment or detachment, as well as impact the physician's mental health by triggering feelings of failure, guilt, or anger toward the patient, their family, and the system overall. (Meier, 2001). Vicarious trauma can also result from the cumulative effects of exposure to secondary trauma encountered daily in hospitals by witnessing the patients' suffering. Such events can alter a provider's worldview and may lead to compassion fatigue and emotional exhaustion. Emotional exhaustion is often a harbinger of impending burnout and more serious risks to the physician's well-being.

"The first day at my very first job, I went to the ward and they gave me a night shift. A very fine-looking patient suddenly collapsed, held my hand while I was checking his blood pressure, said something, and died mid-sentence. His adult son cried and screamed for an hour. Have never recovered from it."

Cognitive Dissonance:

A stressed person is more likely to make decisions that do not reflect their personal values or beliefs. Cognitive dissonance about health-promoting behaviors and attitudes is common in overworked individuals. An inability to practice what a person preaches all day can deepen a sense of helplessness and a feeling of anguish. A provider who emphasizes the importance of sleep, a healthy diet, and stress reduction after a 36-hour sleepless shift, surviving on barely scraps for food in extremely stressful circumstances, and handling life and death feels the conflict between ideals and practice and realizes the counterintuitive effects of these behaviors on their well-being.

Quality of Patient Care:

In professional settings, poor provider well-being is associated with worse patient safety and hence, lower patient satisfaction (Hall, 2016). Provider well-being significantly influences health system performance, making it a valid indicator. It indirectly reflects patient care and the quality of healthcare provided through a system. (Wallace et al., 2009).

Malpractice and Litigation:

Medical errors resulting from impaired decision-making put the patient's health in danger and warrant litigation against the provider or institution, not only incurring costs but also damaging the reputation of both. The effects of such allegations can be profound and long-term, resulting in a cycle of shame and ostracization that further precipitates burnout. Second Victim Syndrome is the term introduced for the consequences faced by providers who make a medical error. If not properly handled, the subsequent trauma can lead to Post-Traumatic Stress Disorder (PTSD) (Madan et al., 2024).

Addiction, Depression, and Suicidal Ideation:

Previous studies (Shanafelt et al., 2012) have reported extreme cases of burnout, substance abuse, depression, and suicidal ideation. Providers at the front-line specialties, who encounter emergencies, uncertain call hours, and death, are more vulnerable to the extreme consequences of burnout due to the extent of responsibility and a lack of control over the work environment. In the absence of support from the surroundings, it can cause grave outcomes for the providers.

"Dead people can't be put on trial, so the obvious solution is for me not to be alive," Dr. Michael McPhillips wrote in his suicide note in 2022 (Madan et al., 2024).

SECTION IB: THE BREAKDOWN OF PHYSICIAN WELL-BEING: PATHWAYS TO DISTRESS

The pursuit of euthymia in healthcare is harder than in other professions due to the variable and intense emotional experiences involved in patient management, leading to an emotional load as well as physical presence and strain. The term 'allostasis' was introduced by Sterling & Eyer in 1988 and refers to the maintenance of a stable state in response to external stimuli. It is different from the term 'homeostasis' as it involves adjustment in the 'baselines' in response to stressors. Allostatic load/ overload ensues from a dysregulated allostasis and is a concept somewhat more complex than 'stress' as used in literature. While some consequences of allostatic load help an individual cope with stressful situations, an overload is detrimental. Allostatic overload can result from repeated activation of allostatic systems, inability to recover from this activation after a stressful stimulus is removed, or inadequate activation of allostatic systems resulting in activation of counter-regulatory systems (McEwen, 1998).

Based on the concept of allostatic load, the continuous loop of dysregulation resulting from the build-up of smaller stressors and leading to a breakdown can be compared to an "allostatic avalanche." The varying combination of work demands, life demands, and personal health concerns is a precursor and determines the extent of physical and emotional labor a worker has to handle. The balance can be greatly affected by the presence of uncertainty in the work environment, acting as a mediator and potentiating the effects of job and work demands. Specialties with uncertain work schedules, call timings, or the presence of an unpredictable superior at the workplace can add to the physical and mental load carried by the profession. According to the effort-recovery model (Meijman & Mulder, 1998), the physical and mental load can produce effects on the body at the physiological level, which can lead to pathological changes if sustained for a long time. These effects are called load reactions.

While the focus on life-changing events as major contributors to stress is well discussed in literature (De Hert, 2020; Edú-Valsania et al., 2022; Fava et al., 2023; Gauche et al., 2017), the greatest contribution to stress may be from a combination of smaller stressors formed by an inattention to detail in daily life activities ranging from workplace to home. These factors combine to create distractions for workers, which can significantly impact their mental and physical health. These distractors are majorly determined by the socioeconomic status of the worker as well as the workplace design and setup, and handling them can not only improve the well-being of healthcare workers but also improve the socioeconomic disparities seen within the healthcare workers that result in attrition and the urban-rural divide in low-resource settings. While they might be categorized as job or life demands by some, it is suggested that they be placed in a separate category, as these can be avoided and are not necessarily to be tackled by the healthcare worker. These are present in the background and enhance the effect of other stressors.

As an example, a healthcare worker who lives in a dingy building that needs frequent repairs, has to commute daily to work, and has no help with house chores will face a greater mental load when at the workplace. Similarly, a provider who has to tackle frequent power outages and has no access to basic amenities or equipment at the workplace will be more likely to proceed to the burnout spiral than someone who only has to focus on patient dealing in a comfortable environment.

The complicated interplay between sympathetic and parasympathetic nervous systems, mediated by hormones like cortisol and catecholamines, results in behavioral and physiological responses that lead to a pressured lifestyle. Activities that release endorphins and serotonin are important for recovery from the effects of allostatic overload. (McEwen, 2008).

Several theories have been put forward to explain the origins of stress-related physical and psychological diseases. One of the most popular models to describe the origin of work stress is Karasek's JDC Model. The model is based on job demand-control and places jobs into one of the four quadrants: high strain, active, passive, and low strain, according to the job decision latitude and presence of work stressors. The model was validated with data from several countries. A certain level of discretion in fulfilling the job responsibilities by empowering the workers can change the position of a job on this grid. While work stressors are mostly embedded in the job design, job decision latitude acts as a modulator for stress release. If poor job decision latitude places enough strain on the employee to neglect his needs, the stress can manifest as "mental strain" (Karasek, 1979).

The individual response to stress and the development of disease is highly variable in practice (Zakreski & Pruessner, 2020). Allostatic load has been operationalized for quantitative analysis in terms of load reactions such as the presence of primary chemical messengers like cortisol, DHEA sulfate, epinephrine, and norepinephrine, and secondary markers that reflect the cumulative effect on specific organs in response to the primary mediators, like blood pressure, waist-hip ratio, cholesterol levels, and glycated hemoglobin. (Rodriquez et al., 2019).

Chronic stress developing as a result of recurrent or excessive workload leads to an alteration of the allostatic mechanisms of the body, leading to overload of these systems after a certain threshold. Under ideal circumstances, a person will essentially be protected by this overload in case of a work-life imbalance, or if ample opportunity for recovery from stress is available. Without these protective systems, physical and psychosocial effects will begin to manifest. Allostatic load and overload progress over several stages before it reaches a point where it triggers or worsens physical or psychological problems, as depicted in Figure 1. Biomarkers for allostatic load gradually increase over each stage from barely noticeable to showing marked derangement when the effects become visible as disease. Subtle signs and symptoms can be noticed in stage 1, like sleep disturbances, demoralization, or irritability, which may be brushed off until stage 2, when significant social impairment is observed. In this phase, there is a noticeable dysfunction of environmental mastery, resulting in feeling overwhelmed by even minor inconveniences. It is often at stage 3 when the effects eventually warrant medical attention by the individual, though it is in the initial stages that the load reactions are reversible (Fava et al., 2023).

Figure 1. The progression of allostasis and allostatic overload over stages.

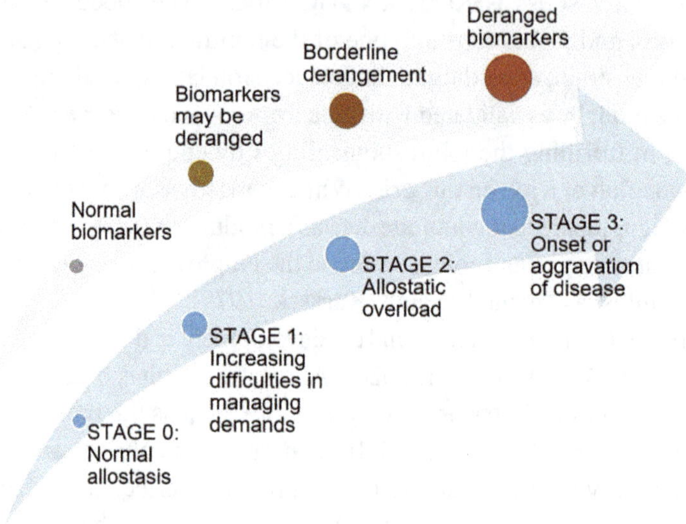

It leads to a gradual worsening of health concerns, and consequently, the physical and mental load associated with work enters a continuous vicious cycle, leading to collapse and burnout in the long run. Figure 2 summarizes these mechanisms.

Figure 2. Mechanism of developing allostatic avalanche and its effects. Inhibiting the buffering effect of work-life balance increases the likelihood of allostatic overload leading to adverse outcomes and a vicious cycle.

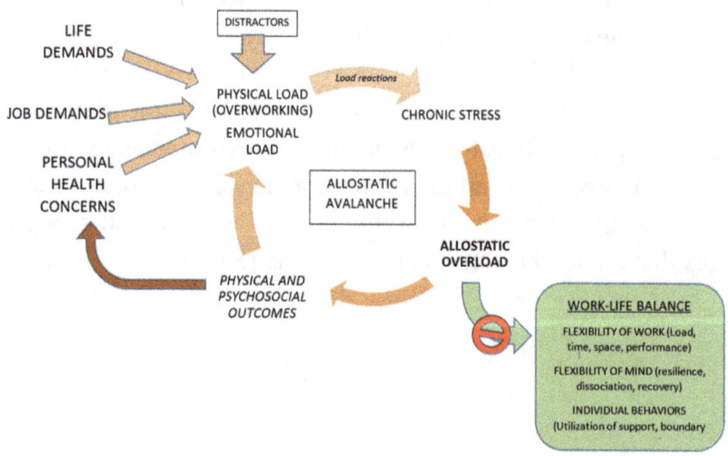

BACKGROUND

Section IIA: Motivation and Burnout

Motivation is defined by Ryan & Deci (2020) as "energy, direction, persistence, and equifinality—all aspects of activation and intention." Motivation drives change, productivity, and behaviors. It can be external when influenced by environmental factors and internal when influenced by intrinsic needs or wishes. Motivation is a complex phenomenon that has been a topic of interest in a wide range of behavioral and social sciences to influence human behavior.

Motivational drivers of Empowerment

In healthcare, motivation is a key concept in psychology and neuroscience as well as educational instruction in the biopsychosocial perspective. The classical theories of motivation initially explored the concept in the 20th century, viewing motivation as a rigid attribute. These theories are based on human psychology. Later on, several contemporary theories built upon the concept, adding an element of flexibility, variability, and practicality in the labor markets. These theories form the basis of all interventions designed for worker well-being implemented in the present day. This section explores them in depth with an emphasis on Maslow's hierarchy as the foundational framework applied to a healthcare worker's needs.

Classical Theories:

Maslow's Hierarchy:

Perhaps the most widely cited work regarding motivation and human needs is the hierarchy of needs described by Abraham Maslow. According to the theory, human needs can be described as a series of 'prepotent' needs according to their urgency and priority. Interestingly, Maslow did not originally propose the visualization of this hierarchy as a pyramid, which is widely depicted throughout literature. This illustration has inaccurately led to the conceptualization of human needs as a rigid sequence where progression to the next level is considered possible only after the fulfillment of the previous levels. (Maslow, 1954)

Maslow's theory was not based on empirical data and only focused on challenging the orthodox Darwinistic notion, "survival of the fittest." It has since received critique for not considering the sociocultural variation in collectivistic and individualistic societies and labels the hierarchy as 'ethnocentric.' The absence of family values or collective goods in the hierarchy makes it inapplicable in different societies, where collective harmony may be considered the peak human experience, in contrast to self-actualization (Hofstede, 1984). The order of these needs may be more flexible at the individual level; however, in the context of healthcare workers, Maslow's hierarchy can be applied as a simplification of their needs to guide policies and interventions aimed at their empowerment. With the advent of modern lifestyles, the hierarchy can now be revised to include modern-day needs as applied to healthcare providers.

Physiological Needs. These needs are universal for a species or a group and are also called survival needs. These are the same for healthcare providers as in other occupations, like food, water, and space. A comfortable working space with adequate resting space and ample time available for breaks are the basic necessities for retaining a worker.

Safety Needs. At present, the safety needs of a person are very different from those proposed by Maslow decades ago. An upsurge in conflicts, disasters, and environmental threats has expanded the role of this level. Financial security, as well as digital safety, can also be considered part of a person's modern safety needs. Personal safety is an intrinsic requirement for rational thinking and so a healthy relationship with the patient. When a healthcare provider's safety needs aren't satisfied, the workforce is on the verge of leaving. Financial incentives alone, often, cannot compensate for the deficiency of physical safety, so retention of staff in high-conflict zones is a challenge despite the higher compensation packages offered.

Interpersonal Needs. This level represents the need to develop meaningful relationships and a sense of belonging. A healthcare provider is surrounded by several connections in personal life and the workplace, maintaining both of which requires a delicate balance and time allocation for either. A disruption in any string of these connections due to a lack of time or overburdening can be considered a threat to the work-life balance. Similarly, if the healthcare worker's attention shifts more towards one aspect, they risk losing the balance. We can metaphorically compare this attention to a rolling ball that maintains a complex balance of human connections, as illustrated in Figure 3.

Figure 3. Visualization of work-life balance as a function of worker attention as conceptualized by the authors

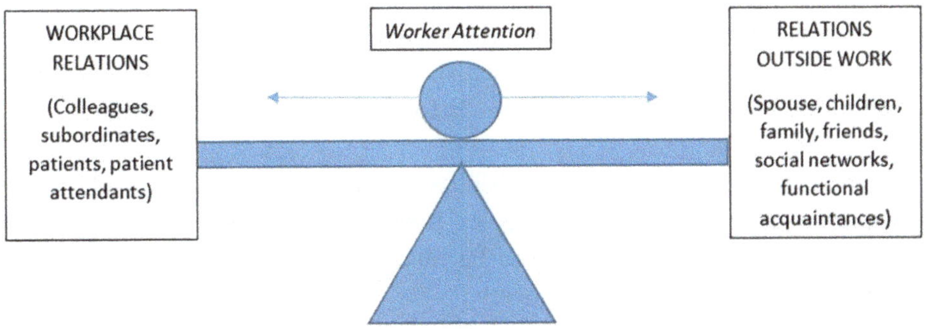

The presence of individuals who require extra attention in their personal lives, like a sick child or an elderly parent, can contribute as distractions that need to be accommodated in the workplace schedules and policies. While human resource managers may view such providers as undesirable candidates during recruitment, the adjustment of such variables leads to a boost in the motivation and hence greater productivity on the part of the worker.

Esteem Needs. This level encompasses the intrinsic human desire to feel satisfied about oneself and to feel worthy and adequate. After joining the medical profession by being chosen from among such a large number of applicants, the perceived social value and education and training involved enable improving the quality of life, hence relating the profession to privilege and enhanced self-esteem by virtue of social comparison. Self-worth, a concept based on a more stable intrinsic belief about oneself rather than achievement, is highly relevant. These terms are not distinguished in Maslow's writings but are important to be differentiated in the context of modern psychology.

Anyone can be self-confident about their worth, but not everyone can be a high achiever, leading to lower self-esteem. Ignoring esteem needs or seeking external validation may generate a sense of inferiority complex that can hamper the progress to actualize self or distort reality, where it seems possible for only a few people to fulfill their esteem needs. While these needs are fulfilled intrinsically, the direction often needs to be refined with the help of Cognitive Behavioral Therapy (CBT) to direct self-talk in a positive direction.

Deficit motivates the first four levels of Maslow's hierarchy. Incentives and rewards are based on fear of losing these needs and hence are common to all to reach a stable state where they can focus on themselves. The next two levels may not be experienced by all and are termed "B-motivation" or the "motivation of being" by Maslow in his later publications.

Self-actualization. This level represents the epitome of human experience in Maslow's earlier writings but is later superseded by the aspects of spirituality. It is not a state but rather a transient experience of perceiving reality and acquiring an awareness of wholeness as a human. The term does not mean that all other needs in all situations are fulfilled for a self-actualized person, but rather means that self-actualization helps reflect on these needs from a clearer perspective and makes better choices in life.

In the backdrop of healthcare provision, self-actualization allows a professional to become the best version of themselves. Recognition of one's creative potential and pursuing professional excellence becomes possible through self-reflection, lifelong learning, and finding purpose.

Self-transcendence. The ultimate human experience is defined in Maslow's words as, "The very highest and most inclusive or holistic levels of human consciousness, behaving and relating, as ends rather than means, to oneself, to significant others, to human beings in general, to other species, to nature, and to the cosmos."

This pertains to finding a deeper purpose in life and engaging in activities that are beyond self-interest, taking into consideration one's legacy and impact on the world. It necessitates transforming one's positive and negative life experiences into strengths and opportunities for personal growth.

ERG Theory:

This theory depicts human needs as a combination of three components: existence, relatedness, and growth. The order of these needs is not emphasized, and multiple pursuits can be followed simultaneously (Alderfer, 1969).1

Herzberg's Two Factor Theory:

Herzberg theorizes that human motivation is achieved through motivation and hygiene factors. Motivational factors increase workplace satisfaction by appealing to intrinsic requirements like recognition and achievement, while hygiene factors prevent dissatisfaction by covering extrinsic needs like remuneration (Herzberg, 1966).

McClelland's Theory:

This theory focuses on acquired needs of humans rather than innate needs. It postulates that humans are motivated by a combination of the need for achievement (Nach), affiliation (Naff), or power (Npow) (McClelland, 1961).

McGregor's X and Y Theories:

These two theories are based on negative and positive assumptions about typical workers. Theory X views workers as operating for self-interest, so a soft or a harsh approach may be used to achieve work output. Theory Y assumes that workers are internally motivated and feel more responsible for their work. It creates a healthier and more flexible environment for the employees (McGregor, 1960).

Contemporary Theories:

The contemporary theories view motivation as a more complex and dynamic idea and are grounded in real-world observations. A more modern approach to motivation recognizes the variability in motivation for different individuals across different settings.

Self-determination Theory:

This theory views motivation as a spectrum ranging from amotivation, extrinsic motivation, and intrinsic motivation, with different regulatory styles and processes governing each phase. It places intrinsic motivation at the highest level and relates it to ownership, interest, enjoyment, and inherent satisfaction, and contrasts it to an extrinsic locus of causality, which is regulated by external pressures. There is an emphasis on the social contexts of human activity and integration, like autonomy, competence, and relatedness. According to SDT, these psychological requirements of humans appeal to the personal development of any human existing in a social setup and so can lead to a seamless adaptation to instruction and regulation (Ryan & Deci, 2020).

Vroom's Expectancy Theory:

Victor Vroom's expectancy theory is concerned with the cognitive antecedents of motivation. It states that effort, performance, and the resulting outcomes are mutually connected. As per the theory, greater motivation results from the notion that greater effort yields a better performance and eventually rewards that are preferable for an employee. Vroom postulates that motivation is a product of expectancy, instrumentality, and valence: expectancy refers to the estimate of the probability that an effort will lead to a specific level of performance, instrumentality indicates the likelihood that a particular performance will result in a certain outcome or reward, and valence represents the estimated preference of an employee for that reward (Simone, 2015; Vroom, 1964).[1]

Social Cognitive Theory:

This theory posits that a person can exert self-motivation and self-control. It discusses the elements of intentionality of human agency, whether it is direct personal agency or proxy agency to allow others to act on one's behalf, or collective agency in groups. It recognizes the concept of General Self-Efficacy (GSE) and emphasizes the role of forethought, self-reflection, environmental influences, and outcome expectancies as sources for motivation (Bandura, 2001; Gerçek & Özveren, 2025).

Table 1 summarizes these theories and links them to some practical interventions.

Table 1.Theories of motivation translated into practical interventions

Classical Theories			
Theory	**Drivers**	**Application in healthcare**	**Practical interventions**
Maslow's hierarchy	Unmet needs	Adequate rest, mental safety & sense of purpose	Protected breaks, safe staffing ratios, wellness programs for staff
Herzberg's two-factor theory	Motivators: Recognition, Achievement Hygiene: Pay, workload, work conditions	Recognition programs alongside workload management to improve morale	Rewards for clinical excellence, mentorship, fair schedules, clear career progression
ERG Theory (Alderfer)	Existence, Relatedness, Growth	Providing growth opportunities even if basic needs are met	Continuing Professional Development (CPD), Cross-training, Supportive team culture, stable compensation, safety
McClelland's Theory	Achievement, Affiliation, Power	Assign roles aligned with personal drivers	Leadership development tracks, team-building for affiliation seekers, advanced skills training for achievers
McGregor's X and Y theory	Theory X: Low motivation Theory Y: Self-driven motivation	Empowerment under Theory Y leadership improves initiative & retention	Shared governance, participatory decision-making, coaching leadership styles
Contemporary Theories			
Theory	**Drivers**	**Application in healthcare**	**Practical interventions**
Self-determination theory	Autonomy, Competence, Relatedness	Autonomy in clinical decisions	HCP-led initiatives, continuing education, collaborations, peer-support groups
Vroom's Expectancy theory	Expectancy, Instrumentality, Valence	Linking extra effort to meaningful outcomes	Transparent promotion criteria, performance-based incentives, skill-based pay
Social Cognitive Theory (Bandura)	Self-efficacy, Observational learning, Reinforcement	Modeling best practices & building confidence in new competencies	Simulation training, Role modeling, mentorship, positive feedback loops

Burnout: Dimensions and Measurement

The term "burnout" was popularized after the extensive and detailed work by Freudenberger and then later by Christina Maslach in the 1970s. Freudenberger originally describes it as

"A state of fatigue or frustration brought about by devotion to a cause, way of life, or relationship that failed to produce the expected reward and that ultimately leads to a reduction in commitment and effectiveness at work." (Freudenberger, 1974)

The definition has evolved over the years and there have been multiple scholarly perspectives that have attempted to deconstruct the idea. Maslach defines the concept from a three-dimensional perspective: emotional exhaustion, depersonalization, and diminished self-value, and emphasizes more the social and situational factors rather than the permanent traits of people (Maslach et al., 1997).

International Classification of Diseases (ICD-11):

The International Classification of Diseases and Related Health Problems, eleventh revision (ICD-11), recognizes burnout as a factor that influences health status or contact with health services. It maintains the Maslach definition of burnout as a trifecta of symptoms induced by work-related stress. However, this definition has been criticized for a lack of clear distinction from depressive symptoms and a lack of clear clinical underpinning (Bianchi & Schonfeld, 2023).

Burnout is essentially considered a multi-domain phenomenon. For practical purposes, several inventories have been developed to quantify burnout and identify thresholds when an intervention must be administered. The most commonly used psychometric tool for quantification of burnout is the Maslach Burnout Inventory (MBI) (Maslach & Jackson, 1981). It was originally developed for personnel in clinical care, but later versions cover a wider range of occupations. Several questionnaires have been successfully developed and validated for the measurement of burnout and its dimensions. Some of these popular instruments include the Oldenberg Burnout Inventory (Demerouti et al., 2003), Copenhagen Burnout Inventory (CBI) (Kristensen et al., 2005), Shirom-Melamed Burnout Questionnaire (SMBQ) (Shirom & Melamed, 2006), Questionnaire for Evaluation of Burnout Syndrome (CESQT), also known as the Spanish Burnout Inventory (SBI) (Gil-Monte, 2009), Burnout Clinical Subtypes Questionnaire (BCSQ-12) (Montero-Marín et al., 2011), and Burnout Assessment Tool (BAT) (Schaufeli et al., 2020).

The Burnt-Out Subtypes:

Burnout can be viewed as a spectrum, and the progression holds significance when applying interventions. Three subtypes of burnout have been described according to the levels of professional dedication and changes in personality over time. (Edú-Valsania et al., 2022; Montero-Marín, 2016)

Frenetic Subtype:

Workers show high dedication and involvement in work in this subtype. This relates to an active coping style with excessive indulgence in work, with extensive hours spent on the same job or taking up multiple jobs at the same time.

Under-challenged Subtype:

This type is seen in fields that are considered monotonous and repetitive in nature. The workers often utilize avoidance and escapism as a coping mechanism for the lack of challenge in their jobs.

Worn-out Subtype:

This type is associated with jobs where the effort-reward balance is perceived to be inefficient and is coped with by distance and detachment from the job. If an opportunity arises, the worker prefers to change jobs in search of better reciprocity for effort.

Gauche et al. used a qualitative approach to explore the job and personal demands of employees at risk of burnout. The study highlights several important aspects of burnout which may not be covered by the quantitative approach, attempting to bridge the compartmentalization in occupational and non-occupational aspects of burnout and summarizes three main themes derived from their work, viz., job demands, life demands, and health concerns (Gauche et al., 2017). *Table 2* shows that burnout progresses through a series of various phases before converting into a syndrome. A variation in the description of these phases exists in literature but the themes are essentially similar. An earlier diagnosis warrants a swifter recovery and better career prospects.

Table 2. The 12 stages of burnout (Frudenberger, 1982) vs the 5 stages of burnout (De Hert, 2020).

Stage 1	Enthusiasm	"It is easy; I will prove them wrong."	Honeymoon (*Enthusiasm*)
Stage 2	Hard work	"One more extra shift won't hurt."	
Stage 3	Neglecting needs	"I don't have time for this."	
Stage 4	Displacing of conflicts	"I feel this way because the staff is lazy."	Onset of stress (*Stagnation*)
Stage 5	Value revision	"Birthdays aren't important anyways."	

continued on following page

Table 2. Continued

Stage 6	Denial	"This isn't stress, just the weather."	Chronic stress *(Frustration)*
Stage 7	Withdrawal	"I don't want to meet anyone; I'm not going to the dinner."	
Stage 8	Behavioral changes	"I lashed out at the children because they were loud."	
Stage 9	Depersonalization	"I have not been feeling like myself lately."	Burnout *(Apathy)*
Stage 10	Numbness	"I need to feel alive again."	
Stage 11	Depression	"I am lost and completely exhausted."	
Stage 12	Burnout	"I cannot function normally; my life is falling apart."	Chronic Burnout *(Intervention)*

"I joined the specialty of my choice three years back. I got the specialty that I love, the specialty in which I could see myself evolving and spending the rest of my life in. It was 'love at first sight.' I was a motivated person, with the belief that I could face all the troubles of residency with firmness and dedication to my goal. I was soon to be proven wrong. Three years in, I have suffered through two nights where I was about to harm myself, had multiple episodes of panic attacks, had several crying sessions in the hospital parking lot, and lost my dream team, with which I initially thought to keep forever in touch and work to advance our specialty. I was not this person before my residency.
Residency is challenging. I was well aware of the challenges that I might face during my residency, but I had not appropriately judged the value of practicing wellness while I was daily exposed to various types of physical, mental, emotional, and social challenges. During residency training, we spend most of our time in the hospital, struggle to get decent sleep of six hours and try to juggle time for our family and friends. It is easy to forget oneself in all this." (Khalil et al., 2023)

ANALYSIS

Section IIB: Individual characteristics effecting burnout

Apart from the broader factors that influence burnout, several personal and system-level characteristics are central to the risk of its manifestation. These characteristics vary significantly between countries and are influenced by the training received prior to entering the workforce.

Family Structure:

Family structure is the most important predictor of work-family conflict in family-oriented societies. Marital status, cohabitation, number, and age of children constitute the family structure. While this social construct is not always under control, it has profound effects on personal decisions and the requirement for social support.

Career Stage:

Healthcare providers in residency or in early careers are more prone to the effects of burnout due to their position at the foundational levels of the professional hierarchy, giving them limited control over workplace decisions (Geurts et al., 1999; Thomas, 2004). However, the 'light at the end of the tunnel,' that is, the prospects of a more independent and fulfilling career ahead, can act as a cushion against negative experiences encountered during a grueling residency.

Personality Traits:

Freudenberger (1974) recognized the role of personality traits and mindsets in the development of burnout and put the healthcare worker, who is in his words "dedicated and committed," or a worker "who has a need to give," at the greatest risk of burnout. Decades later, when the terminology has become more complex and specific, this still holds true.

Four out of the five attributes included in the Five Factor Model (openness to experience, conscientiousness, extraversion, and agreeableness) are associated with lesser burnout, while neuroticism, alexithymia, and a type A personality pattern with a competitive nature are shown to enhance the effects of burnout (Edú-Valsania et al., 2022).

Gender Dimension:

"It's hard to be the golden boy when you're neither a boy nor golden." (Elliott et al., 2010)

Female healthcare providers in all fields are often seen with higher levels of emotional exhaustion, less self-compassion, and reported professional fulfillment and hence burnout (Qamar et al., 2024; Rotenstein et al., 2021). It is reported that globally, women show a 30% to 60% higher odds of burnout as compared to their male counterparts (Dyrbye et al., 2017). Women often feel overwhelmed by the extra work, lower pay, and less time for activities that focus on themselves after work. A crucial aspect is the social responses to female gender, which can range from gender bias and microaggressions to harassment at work. Professional isolation and work devaluation in certain sub-specialties, which are deemed male-dominated, are also typically common in societies with misogynistic attitudes and gender inequality (Lyubarova et al., 2023). Role incredulity is another common gender bias in medical fields when women are regarded as less appropriate for leadership and command roles, and their expertise is regarded as less valuable than their male counterparts by colleagues as well as patients. The narrow window of acceptable behavior in the middle of assertiveness and femininity keeps women in medicine limited and leaves them reflecting on their demeanor more often than their male colleagues, who can be more expressive (Temkin et al., 2024). While the female workforce constitutes 70% of the total healthcare workers, a disparity is also seen in the proportion of women in leadership positions. Senior managers, who have not personally experienced female issues, make the decisions that affect these workers (Betron et al., 2019).

Biases, discrimination, and gendered expectations for female physicians to provide longer and more thorough communication to the patient and families lead to a disproportionate rate of burnout among women physicians compared to men (Linzer & Harwood, 2018). Women often experience a lack of personal achievement, which contributes more to burnout risk than depersonalization and emotional exhaustion. Personal identity, roles and norms, interpersonal relationships, and power dynamics predispose women to several disadvantages throughout their careers, and they have to pursue a significantly different pathway as compared to their male counterparts, as described in *Figure 4*. Females are usually given lesser authority in discriminatory settings, which is to be carried over a steeper and more uneven slope throughout their careers with an eventual "Glass Ceiling Effect" at the highest managerial positions, where invisible barriers like unacknowledged discrimination impede the advancement of women or minorities to the top of the hierarchy despite the qualifications and skills needed for it. The inherent misogynist views and the so-called "male privilege" in strongly patriarchal societies give a head start to the male counterparts with better educational opportunities even at the foundational level.

Figure 4. Comparison of career trajectories for male and female healthcare workers.

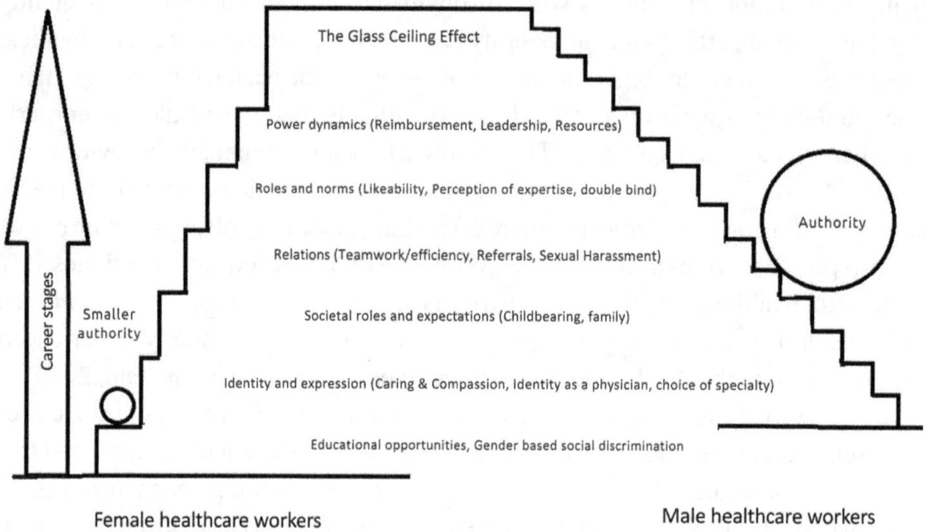

(Elements from "Women's work": Gender and the physician workforce, by Temkin et al, 2024, Social science and medicine, 351(1), 116556 (https://doi.org/10.1016/j.socscimed.2023.116556)

Disparities regarding social institutions and gender roles play a major part in women's lives in most settings, particularly in patriarchal societies where the unequal distribution of domestic chores and childcare tasks puts an unequal burden on the female gender.

> *"Women must work at least 120% more than men just to stay even. Women must realize that they are not going to have a 50/50 split at home. This may happen in the future, but it is not the case currently. (Guptill et al., 2018)*

Factors like overtime, extra shifts, or overburdening due to understaffing can worsen the situation more for women with familial commitments. A female resident, speaking to one of the authors, reflects on the trivialization of women's efforts.

> *"I feel like Atlas sometimes; I keep carrying the crushing mom guilt on my shoulders daily to keep saving sick people, but in return what am I getting? Ungrateful people treating me like I somehow owe it to them."*

Perhaps stemming from the fact that healthcare provision was historically associated with the male gender are the modern job designs, which do not take into consideration that the female reproductive years are the same as those years when a male is working to establish his career without any childbearing responsibilities. The conformity with a tacit standard of a resident who works like there is no life outside work was incorporated into the medical curriculum in the pre-World War

II era when doctors and nurses were the only healthcare providers, skill acquisition was the main focus for the diagnosis of a limited number of diseases and a patient could be easily followed throughout the natural history of a disease (Cassell, 1999; Robinson & Gottlieb, 1999). Over the past decades, the scope of medicine has dramatically changed with task sharing and shifts to a diverse category of medical and paramedical sciences. The burden of disease has shifted from acute conditions to chronic ones, which are now more frequent, necessitating a change in the paradigm of medical care towards preventive medicine that is time-consuming and not immediately rewarding. The residency training, however, has undergone little innovation, especially in LMICs, where the evidence-policy gap is huge.

Another downside of the lack of flexibility and innovation in residency programs is that residency is often perceived as a constant struggle. When the health workforce is considered as only a group and not a collection of individuals, those who require extra support or mentorship may fall behind and consider abandoning the profession altogether, while those with a potential for creativity may feel marginalized or undervalued and so consider different setups or systems. This attrition is particularly seen in commercialized health systems where profits are prioritized over the well-being of healthcare workers, and demoralization due to social, political, and administrative pressures is rampant. If, due to any cause, a provider survives the grind and enters the same system, they become the "dinosaur physician," as Mendelsohn (2022) puts it, who was trained in the dark ages of residency, where the mainstay of training was a lack of trainee well-being and extensive working hours. It leads to a perpetual cycle of creating a similar environment for the incoming trainees they are responsible for, in the name of better training, and to bring them to a standard they were compared to, without regard for the inevitable changes in lifestyles that occur over time.

Yarnell et al. (2019), in a very interesting study, show that the differences in self-compassion do not vary by biological or perceived gender but by feminine or masculine gender roles. When adjusting for these roles, no difference in self-compassion was observed. The study found that socialization as a masculine gender role had the greatest impact and significantly predicted differences in self-compassion. The 'entitlement' associated with masculinity or the 'nurturing and selfless' attitudes associated with femininity were considered the background for such differences.

The initiative to break this repetitive cycle may take a long time, and failing to take it will worsen marginalization for women in general. A gender-transformative health workforce can be developed only with gender-transformative policies and partnerships employing social behavioral change strategies to overcome gender biases in education, recruitment, and service provision of the workforce.

SECTION IIC: INDIVIDUAL STRATEGIES FOR PHYSICIAN WELL-BEING

When a professional enters the medical field, their thinking is molded to rationality, mostly working towards an objective diagnosis and cure. Medicine is a field dealing with a person as a whole, but the division of specialties, subspecialties, and superspecialties has created a strong demarcation among the domains of expertise and fragmented patient care. To use a holistic approach, one cannot deny the importance of integrating the subjective elements of human health to form a complete picture of health and disease. The creation of collaborative multidisciplinary teams to manage patients is also crucial for this approach to be effective, which warrants the provider to not only act individually but also respect the team dynamics. As the scope of dimensions that providers must consider in their workplace continues to expand, they must adapt to meet these needs, even when the surrounding factors lack support.

Over time, researchers have observed successful patterns in their respective fields and attempted to decipher the formula for well-being and fulfillment. While there is no panacea, there are a few traits, which can be intrinsic or acquired as a provider navigates their surroundings, that ensure a healthcare provider remains an asset to the system and the society rather than a passive participant. However, it is never an individual who can tackle everything; it is a combination of several factors coming together, as highlighted by the previous section.

Self-care and Self-discipline:

Healthcare providers are more likely to neglect their health and well-being and forgo medical care and sick leaves (presenteeism). Female gender, young age, working in suburban areas, and chronic illness are factors associated with a tendency to self-neglect (Cohidon et al., 2022). This is based on several notions about the medical profession, where a doctor's health is perceived as an indicator of their competence.

Self-care is the cornerstone of physical and mental well-being, as it places the responsibility of well-being in one's own hands instead of placing it on external factors, which are often not in everyone's control. It largely ameliorates mechanization or the feeling of leading a robotic life and facilitates recovery from allostatic overload by reversing the load effects. Self-care, however, needs to be regular and disciplined for achieving optimum well-being.

Self-care not only includes healthy habits like sufficient quality sleep, physical activity, and relaxation exercises but also encompasses activities that promote psychological detachment from work during off-job hours. Psychological detachment protects the worker by disengaging the nervous system from work-related stressors.

Women and people with children find it easier to detach from work, as they have greater participation in household activities (Sonnentag & Kruel, 2006). Detachment may also be achieved by pursuing any skill-based hobby that enhances a sense of control and mastery or engaging in socialization or voluntary work. Sports, video or computer games (Reinecke, 2009), and vacations with little to no interference by work-related issues (Sinsky et al., 2024) have also been shown to enhance recovery from stress and reduce burnout.

Self-awareness:

Self-awareness is the capacity to consider one's feelings, emotions, and behaviors in a situation and realize how they impact oneself, those surrounding them, and their environment. Except for a few, most settings do not incorporate self-awareness education in clinical teaching. Integrating self-awareness into practice entails the acceptance of one's limitations, setting clear Establishing clear boundaries and maintaining clarity are essential to avoid maladaptive perfectionism and obsession (Sabo & Vachon, 2011).

At the personal level, other than boundary management, mindfulness meditation and reflective writing are evidenced as effective methods to enhance self-awareness (Ouliaris, 2019). Implementation of these practices at the group level can be most effective to ensure better compliance and to allow for group analysis in case of reflective writing, but personal journaling can be beneficial for venting and processing emotions for healthcare personnel.

Self-compassion and Mindfulness:

Compassion is deeply rooted in the idea that human experiences are imperfect and that a negative experience must be acknowledged to connect to a person undergoing it to identify avenues for help, whether it is someone else or one's own self. Neff (2023) describes self-compassion as a combination of overlapping but conceptually distinct elements, viz., presence for oneself in the time of adversity, human connection, and a balanced awareness of discomfort or present-moment experience termed mindfulness. Self-compassion is seen as distinct from self-esteem, which involves standing out in a crowd or seeking social approval to feel more valued and may be linked to some degree of narcissism. In contrast, self-compassion involves recognizing the flow of experiences without making comparisons, making it a more suitable coping strategy for stress than prioritizing the development of self-esteem.

In healthcare, where compassion fatigue is common for both patients and providers, self-compassion involves recognizing the allostatic load experienced in workplace settings and practicing mindfulness regarding personal stress, attachment, attention, and emotions (Conversano et al., 2020). The importance of Mindfulness-Based Stress Reduction (MBSR) Interventions is well-recognized. These include interventions like OASIS & BREATHE stress management programs, educational modules, acupuncture, meditation, choir singing, yoga, massage, self-care or gratitude coaching, and moral distress or compassion fatigue management workshops. Teaching providers wellness techniques, relaxation techniques, positive psychological approaches, focus group discussions, and CBT have also shown significant improvements in different dimensions of burnout (Cohen et al., 2023). In some regions, the incorporation of these interventions into HR policies is far from a reality as institutions downplay the importance of workforce well-being. Therefore, we need to implement these interventions either individually or in groups. Healthcare professionals' hectic schedules and denial of stress impede the adoption of such interventions, despite their perceived benefits (Valley & Stallones, 2018).

> *"Illness doesn't belong to us. It belongs to them, the patients. Doctors need to be taught to be ill. We need permission to be ill and to acknowledge that we are not superhuman." (Mckevitt & Morgan, 1997)*

Healthcare workers are often portrayed as selfless messiahs and considered self-indulgent if they put their well-being as a priority. This stereotype has led healthcare workers to internalize a sacrificial mindset and has created expectations of constant availability from patients. When healthcare workers attempt to negotiate their interests or remuneration, they often face a negative portrayal in the media. The stigma related to seeking help can be worsened if the upward mobility in career or leadership positions is reserved for providers who portray themselves as stronger by not seeking help even when required; this entails discrimination against providers who recognize the threshold where help must be sought and have better awareness of their well-being needs.

General Self-efficacy:

General self-efficacy represents the perceived competence of a person. It is the ability to view setbacks as temporary and adapt effectively to challenging circumstances. The idea is based on Bandura's SCT theory and recognizes the roles of previous or vicarious experiences in motivation. However, it is distinct from resilience, as it covers not only adverse but all kinds of tasks or challenges and comes into play before or during an event. Persons with a greater GSE are shown to have greater well-being and resilience to adversity (Gerçek & Özveren, 2025).

Future Work Self:

The Career Construction Theory visualizes career ambition as an interaction between an individual and a society and compares it to a life story as opposed to a linear process where fixed options in an area are available. Career adaptability, based on the four dimensions of concern, control, curiosity, and confidence, guides the pursuit of how a professional views the future in their career pathway (Savickas, 2019). Zhang et al. (2022) define the future working self as a personal vision that drives ambition. Planning for the future, taking ownership, and exploring available choices to shape them according to different scenarios can allow a person to actively adapt to uncertainties faced in their professional journey.

The essence of career adaptability is the recognition of stagnation and the willingness to start anew when necessary. Both future work self and career adaptability can constructively contribute to psychological well-being by motivating professionals to engage in proactive career behavior and enhancing job satisfaction when their hopes and aspirations are met. (Strauss et al., 2012) Opportunities that align with the personal vision and goals of a healthcare provider can impart them a sense of accomplishment, leading to greater job satisfaction and personal motivation.

Emotional Intelligence:

Emotional intelligence (EI) is the capacity to manage one's emotional states, comprehend the influence of emotions on impulses and relationships, and apply this comprehension to prevent or resolve conflicts, thereby enhancing interactions with others (Dâmbean & Gabor, 2021; Salovey & Mayer, 1990). In healthcare, EI also involves a constructive processing of emotions that arise during patient care, particularly in seriously ill patients or those requiring long-term care. It is easier to tackle these emotions by acknowledging them and identifying the possible sources of unprocessed emotions that may affect the patient-provider relationship. Stepping back from the situation, gaining perspective, and identifying behaviors originating from these emotions can help identify possible solutions to improve both patient outcomes and provider mental health (Meier, 2001).

EI is essential to develop empathy, cooperation, effective conflict management, retaining individuality in teams and maintaining a positive individual identity. Individual performance and team dynamics can benefit from EI, making it an asset for the human resource management systems. (Ugoani, 2021) While different conceptual models define EI either as an ability or a trait, it is known that it is not a static attribute and can be improved by training for better performance (Gilar-Corbi et al., 2019). EI is operationalized as the Emotional Quotient (EQ), which can be measured as a scale for practical application and is closely related to Adversity

Quotient (AQ), which is an operational measure of mental resilience in the wake of difficulty and untoward circumstances (Chadha, 2021).

The incorporation of EQ and AQ measures in entry and licensing examinations for HCPs can be a useful strategy to help choose more effective leaders in healthcare, but harnessing this potential is a paradox. It can create a more resilient workforce with better patient outcomes if employed fairly, but on the other hand, it can potentially worsen the inequities and stress among healthcare providers.

Work-life Balance:

The effort-recovery model (Meijman & Mulder, 1998) describes that the recovery from allostatic overload is possible if a person can achieve a balance between work, life, and personal demands, curbing its progress to burnout syndrome. The specialties that report the lowest work-life balance report the highest levels of burnout, like general surgery, surgical subspecialties, and gynecology & obstetrics (Shanafelt et al., 2012).

A sound work-life balance requires an efficient time and attention allocation and maintaining an equilibrium between both work and personal commitments. Working more than 50 hours per week and workplace conflict are shown to be the most important factors associated with burnout (Wright, 2025). This issue closely relates to flexibility in work and mind as well as individual behaviors, as summarized in Figure 2 previously. Flexibility of work can be described in terms of various aspects like time, space, and workload.

Studies show that the odds of burnout in healthcare providers with perceived low workplace flexibility are significantly higher as compared to jobs with a flexible work environment. Familial demands, variable responsibilities of different specialties, and gender affect this relationship between burnout and workplace flexibility (Maglalang et al., 2021). Telemedicine gained popularity after the unprecedented exigencies created by the COVID-19 pandemic and contributed to making spatial flexibility in healthcare organizations largely acceptable.

While work flexibility is an organizational and policy-level construct, marital status and specialty options are personal choices that determine the requirement for flexibility. However, inability to practice control over these personal aspects of life to compensate for autonomy at work can, regardless, increase the sense of despondency, which itself contributes to burnout.

Family Work Conflict (FWC), which signifies family interference with work, and Work Family Conflict (WFC), which indicates work interference with family, are directional descriptions of how work and family may affect each other. The direction of FWC or WFC and the type of flexibility (time, place, and availability expectation) have significant effects on the overall well-being of human resources

(Allen et al., 2013). As explained in the next section, the COVID-19 pandemic changed the prevalent practices in flexibility for all workers with wider acceptability of telemedicine and patient self-care.

The extent of FWC is shown to be greater for women, particularly those who are mothers (Alotaibi & Aldossry, 2024). On one hand, flexible working arrangements can promote workforce participation by women in human-capital-intensive fields like medicine by reducing both FWC and WFC, but on the other, if inequitably offered to all employees, this can deepen normative gender roles by enhancing the expectation of women being available for the family. It also allows males in the field to use the opportunity to expand their work sphere, and hence a greater gender pay gap (Chung & Van Der Lippe, 2020). Work-life balance reduces stress, increases productivity and commitment, and improves the general Quality of Life (QoL) for healthcare providers (Mitra et al., 2024).

Job Crafting:

Job crafting is the introduction of small alterations in the tasks or social interactions to shape the organizational and social environments at the workplace. This involves minute changes in task execution, social interactions, or the cognitive perception of the job. It is driven by needs for control, positive self-image, and human connection at work and varies according to the autonomy offered by the job design, level of monitoring, and task boundaries. Job crafting can be a useful self-development tool if driven by internal motivation (Wrzesniewski et al., 2013; Wrzesniewski & Dutton, 2001).

Job crafting, however, must not be confused with sycophancy or workplace politics, where the motivation is external and the means used to achieve control and positive self-image ignore the aspect of human connection and focus on manipulation to achieve personal advantage, like promotions or lighter duties. This is seen in work environments where team members have unclear roles and receive minimal formal training in team dynamics and conflict resolution.

Resilience Training:

A policy gap is identified where incorporation of resilience training is essential for a curriculum designed to keep the requirements of an ever-evolving healthcare system in mind. The long-asked question here is, *"They are trained in medicine, but are they trained for medicine?"*

While some educational systems have integrated some means to build resilience and avoid burnout in physicians by implementing restricted working hours and making self-screening and availability of confidential mental health services mandatory, most medical education programs do not address these concerns (Parks-Savage et al., 2018). The American Medical Association (AMA) addresses burnout and resilience training at the individual level through its STEPS Forward module (Finkelstein, 2018), revolving around a change in perspective, considering the bigger picture, connecting to find meaning, and seeking support outside of work. It can be a resource for self-reflection and building resilience in healthcare providers.

Digital empowerment:

The digital revolution in recent years is rapidly changing every sector, including medicine, with more rapid-paced care, electronic record keeping, and AI-assisted decision-making tools that save time and effort but add a layer of complexity to practice for providers who might not be as digitally adept, particularly in low-resource settings or working at senior positions.

Wellness apps, which can even be linked with wearable tracking devices for physical activity and health parameters, can help provider awareness and act as a supplemental resource for individual or self-adopted practices for well-being and mindfulness. Such digital tools, when properly utilized to boost efficiency, have been shown to empower providers, boost performance, and increase the sense of achievement and control in the job. They can also enhance patient care and reduce some burden for physicians.

Another innovation, observed over the recent years, is the journaling of experiences and feelings by healthcare providers on social media platforms. If patient confidentiality is preserved, this method is not only effective but also has the added benefit of acting as an awareness tool for the general public and may also allow connectedness and empathy for the care provider by giving their voice a better reach. However, this can be a double-edged sword, as it can result in depersonalization and misinformation peddling for sensationalism. A resident expresses these concerns on a social media platform:

> *"Majority of times, we think and react to issues very far away from us in person and ideology mainly because social media dynamic drives us into thinking that if I didn't speak up, I wouldn't be a good person. Expressing and talking about these issues is not per se a bad thing, but it is seriously affecting our actions. We as a community feel more for engagement from social media, for recognition, and to be seen as someone we are not. That is a dangerous pursuit."*

The exploration of human aspects of the use of digital technologies reveals that suboptimal use of health information technologies and inefficient work processes can be associated with burnout, leading to feelings of frustration and reduced job satisfaction among up to 28% of HCPs in a study. Another aspect is workflows with interruptions and higher cognitive burden resulting in alert or tech fatigue, which necessitates that digital tools are designed to strike a balance between reducing workload and promoting critical thinking among HCPs when dealing with provided information (Wosny et al., 2023).

Previous literature suggests that users' perceived benefits and expectations of performance strongly influence their intention to adopt and use health care technology. Insufficient training, infrastructure deficiencies, and usability issues are significant barriers influencing the usage of digital health tools. Integrating specialized training into educational programs is crucial for preparing healthcare professionals to navigate the evolving digital landscape. (Alotaibi et al., 2025)

SECTION III: BRINGING IT TOGETHER: EMPOWERMENT IN THE BROADER VIEW

Cultural and system-level differences in LMICs:

Healthcare workers (HCWs) in low- and middle-income countries (LMICs) face severe burnout and mental health challenges driven by high workloads, limited resources, and structural system weaknesses, which threaten both their well-being and patient safety. Evidence shows elevated rates of stress, depression, anxiety, and moral injury among HCWs in LMICs, yet most interventions focus narrowly on individual coping strategies rather than addressing organizational, policy, and occupational health and safety (OHS) determinants (Headrick et al., 2024).

A unique aspect of practicing in LMICs is the extensive dependence of patients on quacks, the use of traditional medicine and healers and illegal practices, which worsen health problems till the patient has to enter the healthcare system with complications, leading to frustration and a greater workload for the physician. The lack of regulations, absence of a strong referral network, primary health care networks and general practice in rural and disadvantaged areas leads to this distrust in modern medicine in LMICs (Kim et al., 2020).

Burnout among healthcare workers in LMICs is deeply rooted in structural barriers that extend far beyond personal coping capacity. Chronic shortages of essential resources, ranging from staff and supplies to digital infrastructure, force clinicians to shoulder excessive workloads under constant pressure. Fragmented communication systems and inadequate managerial support often compound these constraints, limiting opportunities for professional collaboration, feedback, or shared decision-making. Workers, already stretched to their limits, bear the direct burden of inefficiency when organizational processes fail to function smoothly.

A physician's reflection illustrates how systemic dysfunction undermines both care continuity and professional fulfillment:

"Then you have also a system which is, I would call it, dysfunctional to some extent, in the sense that it, there is no coordination the coordination of care is not there in the government sector, because if the patients are seen like on a conveyor belt, you see a patient today. Tomorrow, you see another one. The other day you see. So, there's no real continuity of care." (Wright, 2025)

Such environments create moral distress, as clinicians are forced to provide care that conflicts with their professional values and cultural expectations of patient-centeredness. In many LMICs, strong relational norms such as continuity, compassion, and community connection are core to healthcare identities. Yet systemic pressures reduce interactions to rapid, transactional encounters, weakening those relational foundations and heightening emotional exhaustion (Villagran et al., 2023). Additionally, hierarchical workplace cultures commonly seen in LMIC health systems can limit psychological safety, discourage upward communication, and reduce the likelihood that workers seek help or speak out about unsafe practices. Limited recognition systems and minimal autonomy further diminish self-efficacy and sense of agency, contributing to feelings of depersonalization and disengagement (Wright, 2025).

Ultimately, burnout in LMICs is not simply the result of scarce resources; it arises from the interaction of cultural values with system-level deficiencies. Addressing it, therefore, requires culturally informed reforms that strengthen coordination of care, enhance communication, support leadership responsiveness, and honor the deep-rooted human relationships that define healthcare in these contexts.

Empowerment in the Post-COVID Era:

The COVID-19 pandemic changed the world for everyone but presented some unique challenges and lessons for healthcare systems. It highlighted vulnerabilities in healthcare systems and provider resilience. An accelerated cycle of development of burnout and other mental health issues was seen with the uncertainty, moral distress, and strain associated with working with a crisis with inadequate preparation to face it. The need for well-being programs, anonymous reporting mechanisms, and continued psychological support for healthcare workers was highlighted in all settings, especially LMICs (Dzau et al., 2020).

Importantly, resource-limited environments were not the sole source of these challenges. A study conducted on family physicians in Canada highlights the deficiency of a larger infrastructure even in developed countries with little to no preparedness for this scale of a pandemic, which burdened healthcare providers with challenges beyond their scope of practice.

"I think the other thing is that many people added their Internet or phone connection. Their cell service is just not adequate where they live. So, we are asking

them to do that, but then at the same time, they do not have the resources, or some financially do not have—like, they run out of minutes on their phone or things like that." (Anaraki et al., 2022)

The prolonged nature of the pandemic further intensified these pressures. A persistent crisis was the harbinger of several waves of worsening mental health problems. High burnout symptoms in response to the work environment during the first pandemic wave were the main predictor of both high burnout and depressive symptoms during later periods of the crisis, regardless of the intensity of frontline work or participation in psychological support (Appelbom et al., 2024). These findings demonstrate how early strain rapidly calcified into chronic distress, emphasizing the importance of proactive rather than reactive support systems.

Wider adoption of telemedicine and digital tools during this era created the wider possibility or expectation of providing care remotely and from home. While it improved the quality of patient care, enhanced workflow efficiency, and ensured better information availability, negative outcomes such as increased workload, heightened patient safety risks, outdated or missing information, and disruptions in workflow were also identified as relevant, even with modern clinical information systems (Wosny et al., 2023). Digital transformation, while expanding access, also introduced new complexities that many systems were ill-prepared to handle. Together, these experiences make it clear that while healthcare workers demonstrated extraordinary dedication, the pandemic revealed the limits of relying solely on individual resilience. Sustaining well-being in prolonged and complex crises requires strong organizational structures, coordinated system support, and policies that safeguard the workforce.

CONCLUSION

It Takes a Village: Organizational enablers of empowerment

While this chapter emphasizes the personal aspects of physician well-being, it is critical to acknowledge that individual resilience alone cannot secure wellness. Healthcare professionals navigate complex socio-ecological systems in which national health policies, institutional culture, and collaborative efforts significantly influence their psychological safety and professional efficacy. As Dzau et al. (2020) note, there is an unavoidable trickle-down effect: structural weaknesses at higher levels inevitably manifest as stress and overload for frontline clinicians.

These systematic challenges are not unique to LMICs; even well-resourced health systems struggle to sustain their workforce. A family physician interviewed in a high-income context commented:

"Well, we have got a very fragile system here. So, we do not have enough physicians to start with... very fragile and it has worsened. People, I think, have just become burned out. So, we have had a few in the last month... we have had – somebody is leaving; somebody is retiring; somebody else just retired. So, we lost three physicians in a month. So, that is a huge challenge..." (Anaraki et al., 2022)

Such experiences underscore that burnout is not only a personal experience but also a symptom of structural failure. The presence or absence of organizational and policy scaffolding directly influences healthcare providers' well-being, retention, and health-related quality of life. Headrick et al. (2024) argue that comprehensive, multi-tiered approaches that include workforce protections, supportive workplace environments, adequate staffing, and national policy engagement are essential. Their work across four LMICs demonstrates that locally adapted, evidence-based technical assistance can shift mental health initiatives from isolated programs to integrated occupational health and safety priorities, highlighting that sustainable burnout prevention in LMICs requires government commitment, financing, and system-level reform, not just individual resilience training.

Organizational enablers such as responsive leadership, opportunities for staff voice, supportive supervision, clear guidelines and protocols, adequate staffing, and effective teamwork act as critical facilitators (O'Brien et al., 2022). Aligning these elements not only protects healthcare workers but also truly empowers them. Empowerment fortifies professional autonomy, reinvigorates work, and enables clinicians to maintain ethical care standards amidst challenging situations. Building a culture of well-being requires a village: systems that care for those who care for others.

REFERENCES

Alderfer, C. P. (1969). An empirical test of a new theory of human needs. *Organizational Behavior and Human Performance*, *4*(2), 142–175. DOI: 10.1016/0030-5073(69)90004-X

Allen, T. D., Johnson, R. C., Kiburz, K. M., & Shockley, K. M. (2013). Work–family conflict and flexible work arrangements: Deconstructing flexibility. *Personnel Psychology*, *66*(2), 345–376. DOI: 10.1111/peps.12012

Alotaibi, A., & Aldossry, T. (2024). Work-life balance of working mothers in the healthcare industry in Riyadh, Saudi Arabia. *Journal of Social Service Research*, *50*(1), 14–24. DOI: 10.1080/01488376.2023.2271037

Alotaibi, N., Wilson, C. B., & Traynor, M. (2025). Enhancing digital readiness and capability in healthcare: A systematic review of interventions, barriers, and facilitators. *BMC Health Services Research*, *25*(1), 12663. Advance online publication. DOI: 10.1186/s12913-025-12663-3 PMID: 40186200

Anaraki, N. R., Mukhopadhyay, M., Karaivanov, Y., Wilson, M., & Asghari, S. (2022). Living and working in rural healthcare during the COVID-19 pandemic: A qualitative study of rural family physicians' lived experiences. *BMC Primary Care*, *23*(1), 01942. Advance online publication. DOI: 10.1186/s12875-022-01942-1 PMID: 36550406

Appelbom, S., Nordström, A., Finnes, A., Wicksell, R. K., & Bujacz, A. (2024). Healthcare worker burnout during a persistent crisis: A case–control study. *Occupational Medicine*, *74*(4), 297–303. DOI: 10.1093/occmed/kqae032 PMID: 38738440

Bandura, A. (2001). Social cognitive theory: An agentic perspective. *Annual Review of Psychology*, *52*(1), 1–26. DOI: 10.1146/annurev.psych.52.1.1 PMID: 11148297

Betron, M., Bourgeault, I., Manzoor, M., Paulino, E., Steege, R., Thompson, K., & Wuliji, T. (2019). Time for gender-transformative change in the health workforce. *Lancet*, *393*(10171), e25–e26. DOI: 10.1016/S0140-6736(19)30208-9 PMID: 30739706

Bianchi, R., & Schonfeld, I. S. (2023). Examining the evidence base for burnout. *Bulletin of the World Health Organization*, *101*(11), 743–745. DOI: 10.2471/BLT.23.289996 PMID: 37961064

Cassell, E. J. (1999). Historical perspective of medical residency training: 50 years of changes. *Journal of the American Medical Association*, *281*(13), 1231. DOI: 10.1001/jama.281.13.1231-JMS0407-6-1 PMID: 10199439

Chadha, N. (2021). Adversity quotient: Surviving rather than giving up. *Psychology (Savannah, Ga.)*, *58*(2), 5942–5947. DOI: 10.17762/pae.v58i2.3068

Chung, H., & van der Lippe, T. (2020). Flexible working, work–life balance, and gender equality: Introduction. *Social Indicators Research*, *151*(2), 365–381. DOI: 10.1007/s11205-018-2025-x PMID: 33029036

Cohen, C., Pignata, S., Bezak, E., Tie, M., & Childs, J. (2023). Workplace interventions to improve well-being and reduce burnout for nurses, physicians and allied healthcare professionals: A systematic review. *BMJ Open*, *13*(6), e071203. Advance online publication. DOI: 10.1136/bmjopen-2022-071203 PMID: 37385740

Cohidon, C., Mahler, L., Broers, B., Favrod-Coune, T., Moussa, A., & Sebo, P. (2022). Primary care physicians' personal and professional attributes associated with forgoing own care and presenteeism: A cross sectional study. *International Journal of Public Health*, *66*, 1604442. Advance online publication. DOI: 10.3389/ijph.2021.1604442 PMID: 35242001

Conversano, C., Ciacchini, R., Orrù, G., Di Giuseppe, M., Gemignani, A., & Poli, A. (2020). Mindfulness, compassion, and self-compassion among health care professionals: What's new? A systematic review. *Frontiers in Psychology*, *11*, 1683. Advance online publication. DOI: 10.3389/fpsyg.2020.01683 PMID: 32849021

Dâmbean, C. A., & Gabor, M. R. (2021). Implications of emotional intelligence in human resource management. *ECONOMICS*, *9*(2), 73–90. DOI: 10.2478/eoik-2021-0016

De Hert, S. (2020). Burnout in healthcare workers: Prevalence, impact and preventative strategies. *Local and Regional Anesthesia*, *13*, 171–183. DOI: 10.2147/LRA.S240564 PMID: 33149664

Demerouti, E., Bakker, A. B., Vardakou, I., & Kantas, A. (2003). The convergent validity of two burnout instruments: A multitrait-multimethod analysis. *European Journal of Psychological Assessment*, *19*(1), 12–23. DOI: 10.1027//1015-5759.19.1.12

Dyrbye, L. N., Shanafelt, T. D., Sinsky, C. A., Cipriano, P. F., Bhatt, J., Ommaya, A., West, C. P., & Meyers, D. (2017). Burnout among health care professionals: A call to explore and address this underrecognized threat to safe, high-quality care. *NAM Perspectives*, *7*(7). Advance online publication. DOI: 10.31478/201707b

Dzau, V. J., Kirch, D., & Nasca, T. (2020). Preventing a parallel pandemic — A national strategy to protect clinicians' well-being. *The New England Journal of Medicine*, *383*(6), 513–515. DOI: 10.1056/NEJMp2011027 PMID: 32402153

Edú-Valsania, S., Laguía, A., & Moriano, J. A. (2022). Burnout: A review of theory and measurement. *International Journal of Environmental Research and Public Health, 19*(3), 1780. DOI: 10.3390/ijerph19031780 PMID: 35162802

Elliott, B. A., Dorscher, J., Wirta, A., & Hill, D. L. (2010). Staying connected: Native American women faculty members on experiencing success. *Academic Medicine, 85*(4), 711–716. https://journals.lww.com/academicmedicine/fulltext/2010/04000/staying_connected__native_american_women_faculty.32.aspx. DOI: 10.1097/ACM.0b013e3181d28101 PMID: 20354388

Fava, G. A., Sonino, N., Lucente, M., & Guidi, J. (2023). Allostatic load in clinical practice. *Clinical Psychological Science, 11*(2), 345–356. DOI: 10.1177/21677026221121601

Finkelstein, C. (2018). *Protect against burnout and encourage self-care*. American Medical Association.

Freudenberger, H. J. (1974). Staff burn-out. *The Journal of Social Issues, 30*(1), 159–165. DOI: 10.1111/j.1540-4560.1974.tb00706.x

Gauche, C., De Beer, L. T., & Brink, L. (2017). Exploring demands from the perspective of employees identified as being at risk of burnout. *International Journal of Qualitative Studies on Health and Well-being, 12*(1), 1361783. Advance online publication. DOI: 10.1080/17482631.2017.1361783 PMID: 28784048

Gerçek, M., & Özveren, C. G. (2025). From self and career perceptions to life satisfaction: A sequential mediation approach to general self-efficacy, future work self, career anxiety, and life satisfaction in the emerging workforce. *International Journal for Educational and Vocational Guidance*. Advance online publication. DOI: 10.1007/s10775-024-09721-3

Geurts, S., Rutte, C., & Peeters, M. (1999). Antecedents and consequences of work–home interference among medical residents. *Social Science & Medicine, 48*(9), 1135–1148. DOI: 10.1016/S0277-9536(98)00425-0 PMID: 10220015

Gil-Monte, P. R. (2009). Validez factorial del «Cuestionario para la Evaluación del Síndrome de Quemarse por el Trabajo» (CESQT) en una muestra de maestros mexicanos [Factorial validity of the "Burnout Assessment Questionnaire" (CESQT) in a sample of Mexican teachers]. *Salud Mental, 31*, 205–214.

Gilar-Corbi, R., Pozo-Rico, T., Sánchez, B., & Castejón, J.-L. (2019). Can emotional intelligence be improved? A randomized experimental study of a business-oriented EI training program for senior managers. *PLoS One, 14*(10), e0224254. Advance online publication. DOI: 10.1371/journal.pone.0224254 PMID: 31644585

Giménez Lozano, J. M., Martínez Ramón, J. P., & Morales Rodríguez, F. M. (2021). Doctors and nurses: A systematic review of the risk and protective factors in workplace violence and burnout. *International Journal of Environmental Research and Public Health, 18*(6), 3280. DOI: 10.3390/ijerph18063280 PMID: 33810020

Guptill, M., Reibling, E. T., & Clem, K. (2018). Deciding to lead: A qualitative study of women leaders in emergency medicine. *International Journal of Emergency Medicine, 11*(1), 47. DOI: 10.1186/s12245-018-0206-7 PMID: 31179933

Headrick, E. G., McCarten-Gibbs, M., Coley, R., Avila, G., Mina, J., Villa, R. C., & Fernando, L. H. (2024). Care for staff: A novel technical assistance approach to promote occupational mental health among healthcare workers in lower and middle income country settings. *Workplace Health & Safety, 72*(4), 144–152. DOI: 10.1177/21650799241247154 PMID: 38629824

Herzberg, F. I. (1966). Work and the nature of man. *WORLD (Oakland, Calif.).*

Hodgson, K. L., Lamport, D. J., & Laville, A. (2024). "Are you OK doctor?" An expanded health belief model exploration of doctors' experiences and perspectives of on-shift health behaviour. *International Journal of Qualitative Studies on Health and Well-being, 19*(1), 2388795. Advance online publication. DOI: 10.1080/17482631.2024.2388795 PMID: 39104181

Hofstede, G. (1984). The cultural relativity of the quality of life concept. *Academy of Management Review, 9*(3), 389–398. DOI: 10.2307/258280

Karasek, R. A. (1979). Job demands, job decision latitude, and mental strain: Implications for job redesign. *Administrative Science Quarterly, 24*(2), 285–308. DOI: 10.2307/2392498

Khalil, M. T., Rathore, F. A., & Dy, R. (2023). Wellness in residency: Addressing the neglected need in lower middle-income countries. *Journal of Pediatric Rehabilitation Medicine, 16*(3), 457–462. DOI: 10.3233/PRM-230031 PMID: 37694319

Kristensen, T. S., Borritz, M., Villadsen, E., & Christensen, K. B. (2005). The Copenhagen Burnout Inventory: A new tool for the assessment of burnout. *Work and Stress, 19*(3), 192–207. DOI: 10.1080/02678370500297720

Lim, M. C., Jeffree, M. S., Saupin, S. S., Giloi, N., & Lukman, K. A. (2022). Workplace violence in healthcare settings: The risk factors, implications and collaborative preventive measures. *Annals of Medicine and Surgery (London), 78*, 103727. Advance online publication. DOI: 10.1016/j.amsu.2022.103727 PMID: 35734684

Linzer, M., & Harwood, E. (2018). Gendered expectations: Do they contribute to high burnout among female physicians? *Journal of General Internal Medicine, 33*(6), 963–965. DOI: 10.1007/s11606-018-4330-0 PMID: 29435727

Lyubarova, R., Salman, L., & Rittenberg, E. (2023). Gender differences in physician burnout: Driving factors and potential solutions. *The Permanente Journal, 27*(2), 130–136. DOI: 10.7812/TPP/23.023 PMID: 37303223

Madan, R., Das, N., Patley, R., Nagpal, N., Malik, Y., & Math, S. B. (2024). Consequences of medical negligence and litigations on health care providers – A narrative review. *Indian Journal of Psychiatry, 66*(4), 317–325. DOI: 10.4103/indianjpsychiatry.indianjpsychiatry_799_23 PMID: 38778854

Maglalang, D. D., Sorensen, G., Hopcia, K., Hashimoto, D. M., Katigbak, C., Pandey, S., Takeuchi, D., & Sabbath, E. L. (2021). Job and family demands and burnout among healthcare workers: The moderating role of workplace flexibility. *SSM - Population Health, 14*, 100802. Advance online publication. DOI: 10.1016/j.ssmph.2021.100802 PMID: 33997249

Maslach, C., & Jackson, S. E. (1981). The measurement of experienced burnout. *Journal of Organizational Behavior, 2*(2), 99–113. DOI: 10.1002/job.4030020205

Maslach, C., Jackson, S. E., & Leiter, M. P. (1997). Maslach Burnout Inventory. In Zalaquett, C. P., & Wood, R. J. (Eds.), *Evaluating stress: A book of resources* (3rd ed., pp. 191–218). Scarecrow Press.

Maslow, A. (1954). *Motivation and personality*. Harper & Row.

McClelland, D. C. (1961). *The achieving society*. Van Nostrand. DOI: 10.1037/14359-000

McEwen, B. S. (1998). Stress, adaptation, and disease: Allostasis and allostatic load. *Annals of the New York Academy of Sciences, 840*(1), 33–44. DOI: 10.1111/j.1749-6632.1998.tb09546.x PMID: 9629234

McEwen, B. S. (2008). Central effects of stress hormones in health and disease: Understanding the protective and damaging effects of stress and stress mediators. *European Journal of Pharmacology, 583*(2-3), 174–185. DOI: 10.1016/j.ejphar.2007.11.071 PMID: 18282566

McGregor, D. (1960). *The human side of enterprise*. McGraw-Hill.

McKevitt, C., & Morgan, M. (1997). Illness doesn't belong to us. *Journal of the Royal Society of Medicine, 90*(9), 491–495. DOI: 10.1177/014107689709000907 PMID: 9370984

Meier, D. E. (2001). The inner life of physicians and care of the seriously ill. *Journal of the American Medical Association, 286*(23), 3007. DOI: 10.1001/jama.286.23.3007 PMID: 11743845

Meijman, T. F., & Mulder, G. (1998). Psychological aspects of workload. In Drenth, P. J., Thierry, H., & de Wolff, C. J. (Eds.), *Handbook of work and organizational psychology: Work psychology* (2nd ed., Vol. 2, pp. 5–33). Psychology Press.

Mendelsohn, D. (2022). Self in medicine: Determinants of physician well-being and future directions in improving wellness. *Medical Education, 56*(1), 48–55. DOI: 10.1111/medu.14671 PMID: 34559421

Mitra, L. G., Sharma, J., & Walia, H. S. (2024). Improving work–life balance and satisfaction to improve patient care. *Indian Journal of Critical Care Medicine : Peer-Reviewed, Official Publication of Indian Society of Critical Care Medicine, 28*(4), 326–328. DOI: 10.5005/jp-journals-10071-24689 PMID: 38585310

Montero-Marín, J. (2016). El síndrome de burnout y sus diferentes manifestaciones clínicas: Una propuesta para la intervención [The burnout syndrome and its different clinical manifestations: A proposal for intervention]. *Anestesia, Analgesia, Reanimación, 29*(1), 1–16.

Montero-Marín, J., Skapinakis, P., Araya, R., Gili, M., & García-Campayo, J. (2011). Towards a brief definition of burnout syndrome by subtypes: Development of the "Burnout Clinical Subtypes Questionnaire" (BCSQ-12). *Health and Quality of Life Outcomes, 9*(1), 74. DOI: 10.1186/1477-7525-9-74 PMID: 21933381

Neff, K. D. (2023). Self-compassion: Theory, method, research, and intervention. *Annual Review of Psychology, 74*(1), 193–218. DOI: 10.1146/annurev-psych-032420-031047 PMID: 35961039

O'Brien, N., Flott, K., Bray, O., Shaw, A., & Durkin, M. (2022). Implementation of initiatives designed to improve healthcare worker health and wellbeing during the COVID-19 pandemic: Comparative case studies from 13 healthcare provider organisations globally. *Globalization and Health, 18*(1), 24. Advance online publication. DOI: 10.1186/s12992-022-00818-4 PMID: 35193629

Ouliaris, C. (2019). The importance of self-awareness: Musings of a medical student. *Australasian Psychiatry, 27*(3), 267–269. DOI: 10.1177/1039856219839479 PMID: 30931586

Parks-Savage, A., Archer, L., Newton, H., Wheeler, E., & Huband, S. R. (2018). Prevention of medical errors and malpractice: Is creating resilience in physicians part of the answer? *International Journal of Law and Psychiatry*, *60*, 35–39. DOI: 10.1016/j.ijlp.2018.07.003 PMID: 30217328

Qamar, M. K., Sheikh, B. T., Kumar, R., & Armaghana, K. Q. (2024). Gender difference of burnout in physicians working in tertiary care hospital: A cross-sectional study. *Journal of the College of Physicians and Surgeons—Pakistan*, *34*(05), 620–622. DOI: 10.29271/jcpsp.2024.05.620 PMID: 38720228

Robinson, J. D., & Gottlieb, S. (1999). The new face of medical education. *Journal of the American Medical Association*, *281*(13), 1226. PMID: 10199435

Rodriquez, E. J., Kim, E. N., Sumner, A. E., Nápoles, A. M., & Pérez-Stable, E. J. (2019). Allostatic load: Importance, markers, and score determination in minority and disparity populations. *Journal of Urban Health*, *96*(S1), 3–11. DOI: 10.1007/s11524-019-00345-5 PMID: 30671711

Rotenstein, L., Harry, E., Wickner, P., Gupte, A., Neville, B. A., Lipsitz, S., Cullen, E., Rozenblum, R., Sequist, T. D., & Dudley, J. (2021). Contributors to gender differences in burnout and professional fulfillment: A survey of physician faculty. *Joint Commission Journal on Quality and Patient Safety*, *47*(11), 723–730. DOI: 10.1016/j.jcjq.2021.08.002 PMID: 34507905

Ryan, R. M., & Deci, E. L. (2020). Intrinsic and extrinsic motivation from a self-determination theory perspective: Definitions, theory, practices, and future directions. *Contemporary Educational Psychology*, *61*, 101860. Advance online publication. DOI: 10.1016/j.cedpsych.2020.101860

Sabo, B. M., & Vachon, M. L. S. (2011). Care of professional caregivers. In Davis, M. P., Feyer, P. C., Ortner, P., & Zimmermann, C. (Eds.), *Supportive oncology* (pp. 575–589). Elsevier Saunders., DOI: 10.1016/B978-1-4377-1015-1.00056-4

Salovey, P., & Mayer, J. D. (1990). Emotional intelligence. *Imagination, Cognition and Personality*, *9*(3), 185–211. DOI: 10.2190/DUGG-P24E-52WK-6CDG

Savickas, M. (2019). *Career construction theory: Life portraits of attachment, adaptability, and identity*. Mark L. Savickas.

Schaufeli, W. B., Desart, S., & De Witte, H. (2020). Burnout Assessment Tool (BAT)—Development, validity, and reliability. *International Journal of Environmental Research and Public Health*, *17*(24), 9495. Advance online publication. DOI: 10.3390/ijerph17249495 PMID: 33352940

Shanafelt, T. D., Boone, S., Tan, L., Dyrbye, L. N., Sotile, W., Satele, D., West, C. P., Sloan, J., & Oreskovich, M. R. (2012). Burnout and satisfaction with work-life balance among US physicians relative to the general US population. *Archives of Internal Medicine, 172*(18), 1377–1385. DOI: 10.1001/archinternmed.2012.3199 PMID: 22911330

Shirom, A., & Melamed, S. (2006). A comparison of the construct validity of two burnout measures in two groups of professionals. *International Journal of Stress Management, 13*(2), 176–200. DOI: 10.1037/1072-5245.13.2.176

Simone, S. D. (2015). Expectancy value theory: Motivating healthcare workers. *American International Journal of Contemporary Research, 5*(2), 19–23.

Sinsky, C. A., Trockel, M. T., Dyrbye, L. N., Wang, H., Carlasare, L. E., West, C. P., & Shanafelt, T. D. (2024). Vacation days taken, work during vacation, and burnout among US physicians. *JAMA Network Open, 7*(1), e2351635. Advance online publication. DOI: 10.1001/jamanetworkopen.2023.51635 PMID: 38214928

Sonnentag, S., & Kruel, U. (2006). Psychological detachment from work during off-job time: The role of job stressors, job involvement, and recovery-related self-efficacy. *European Journal of Work and Organizational Psychology, 15*(2), 197–217. DOI: 10.1080/13594320500513939

Sterling, P., & Eyer, J. (1988). Allostasis: A new paradigm to explain arousal pathology. In Fisher, S., & Reason, J. (Eds.), *Handbook of life stress, cognition and health* (pp. 629–649). John Wiley & Sons.

Strauss, K., Griffin, M. A., & Parker, S. K. (2012). Future work selves: How salient hoped-for identities motivate proactive career behaviors. *The Journal of Applied Psychology, 97*(3), 580–598. DOI: 10.1037/a0026423 PMID: 22122111

Temkin, S. M., Salles, A., Barr, E., Leggett, C. B., Reznick, J. S., & Wong, M. S. (2024). "Women's work": Gender and the physician workforce. *Social Science & Medicine, 351*, 116556. Advance online publication. DOI: 10.1016/j.socscimed.2023.116556 PMID: 38825379

Thomas, N. K. (2004). Issues in graduate medical education: Resident burnout. *Journal of the American Medical Association, 292*(23), 2880–2889. DOI: 10.1001/jama.292.23.2880 PMID: 15598920

Valley, M., & Stallones, L. (2018). A thematic analysis of health care workers' adoption of mindfulness practices. *Workplace Health & Safety, 66*(11), 538–544. DOI: 10.1177/2165079918771991 PMID: 29806801

Villagran, C. A., Dalmolin, G. de L., Barlem, E. L. D., Greco, P. B. T., Lanes, T. C., & Andolhe, R. (2023). Association between moral distress and burnout syndrome in university-hospital nurses. *Revista Latino-Americana de Enfermagem, 31*, Article e3747. https://doi.org/DOI: 10.1590/1518-8345.6071.3747

Vroom, V. H. (1964). *Work and motivation*. Wiley & Sons.

Wallace, J. E., Lemaire, J. B., & Ghali, W. A. (2009). Physician wellness: A missing quality indicator. *Lancet, 374*(9702), 1714–1721. DOI: 10.1016/S0140-6736(09)61424-0 PMID: 19914516

Wosny, M., Strasser, L. M., & Hastings, J. (2023). Experience of health care professionals using digital tools in the hospital: Qualitative systematic review. *JMIR Human Factors, 10*(1), e50357. Advance online publication. DOI: 10.2196/50357 PMID: 37847535

Wright, T. R. (2025). *An investigation into burnout in family physicians in low-and middle-income countries: A mixed methods study* (Publication No. 991004143194702986) [Doctoral dissertation, Keele University]. Keele Library. https://keele.primo.exlibrisgroup.com/permalink/44KLE_INST/8eg9a6/alma991004143194702986

Wrzesniewski, A., & Dutton, J. E. (2001). Crafting a job: Revisioning employees as active crafters of their work. *Academy of Management Review, 26*(2), 179–201. DOI: 10.2307/259118

Wrzesniewski, A., LoBuglio, N., Dutton, J. E., & Berg, J. M. (2013). Job crafting and cultivating positive meaning and identity in work. In Bakker, A. B. (Ed.), *Advances in positive organizational psychology* (Vol. 1, pp. 281–302). Emerald Group Publishing Limited., DOI: 10.1108/S2046-410X(2013)0000001015

Yarnell, L. M., Neff, K. D., Davidson, O. A., & Mullarkey, M. (2019). Gender differences in self-compassion: Examining the role of gender role orientation. *Mindfulness, 10*(6), 1136–1152. DOI: 10.1007/s12671-018-1066-1

Zakreski, E., & Pruessner, J. C. (2020). Psychophysiological models of stress. In Harkness, K. L., & Hayden, E. P. (Eds.), *The Oxford handbook of stress and mental health* (pp. 487–506). Oxford University Press., DOI: 10.1093/oxfordhb/9780190681777.013.23

Zhang, Z., Yu, X., & Liu, X. (2022). Do I decide my career? Linking career stress, career exploration, and future work self to career planning or indecision. *Frontiers in Psychology, 13*, 997984. Advance online publication. DOI: 10.3389/fpsyg.2022.997984 PMID: 36081730

KEY TERMS AND DEFINITIONS

Allostatic Avalanche: It denotes the cycle of worsening outcomes due to chronic stress leading to burnout syndrome.

Allostatic Load: It is the maintenance of normal physiology of the body by recalibration of responsive mechanisms to the cumulative burden of wear and tear as a result of environmental challenges encountered in daily life.

Burnout: Burnout is a condition characterized by physical and mental depletion, loss of idealism and a sense of inefficacy as a result of repeated or prolonged stress in any field of life.

Future Work Self: It is the vision of a worker that they imagine for themselves and represents the confidence that a person has in themselves to achieve their work-related goals and ambitions.

Healthcare Providers: The definition of healthcare providers is not only limited to doctors, physicians, or nurses but also includes dentists, therapists, midwives, paramedics, medical technical support staff and the outreach workers including emergency responders and health visitors.

Motivation: The intrinsic desire to initiate, execute and continue any action to achieve certain goals.

Self-Awareness: The capacity to understand one's own emotional states, capabilities and limitations is termed self-awareness.

Self-Compassion: Self-compassion is the aptitude of treating oneself with kindness in the wake of adverse events by acknowledging and accepting the human experience with mindfulness.

Work-Life Balance: A state of equilibrium between work and personal life activities achieved by an effective allocation of time, resources and attention to both aspects for better well-being and preventing burnout.

Chapter 5
Optimising Organisational Efficiency in Health Systems

Rohit Kumar
http://orcid.org/0009-0007-6292-7097
All India Institute of Medical Sciences, Delhi, India

Shameen Arif
http://orcid.org/0009-0009-3388-4168
Era's Lucknow Medical College and Hospital, India

ABSTRACT

Healthcare systems must continuously evolve to balance efficiency with holistic patient approach and workforce well-being. Proper resource allocation for wellness programs, mental health services, stress management, retreats, and support groups further strengthens workforce resilience and creates a safe space for addressing occupational stress. This chapter focuses on existing Healthcare Organisational cultures across varied settings, infrastructural differences, resources, tools, and the need to support HCWs. Collecting data and analysis from wellbeing surveys which plays a pivotal role in changing resource allocation, systems, workplace culture, implementing organisational changes, to reform and bring about changes into equity, gender inequality. Integrating these initiatives with Artificial Intelligence for automation and a systems thinking approach streamlines workflows, improving patient care and administrative efficiency. Also, highlights methods for aligning healthcare management with both operational efficiency and a compassionate, sustainable work culture.

DOI: 10.4018/979-8-2600-0582-8.ch005

INTRODUCTION

Healthcare workers face challenges impacting the overall efficiency of hospitals. This chapter will explain the root causes, their impact on the well-being of healthcare workers, organizational differences in global healthcare systems impacting well-being, and practical improvement solutions. This is simplified into 4 sections:

1. Streamlining Workflows to Reduce Administrative Burdens and Inefficiencies
2. Systems Thinking for Fostering Sustainable Improvements
3. Resource Allocation and Infrastructure Development
4. Organisational Factors Impacting Healthcare Provider Well-being and Data-Driven Insights

STREAMLINING WORKFLOWS TO REDUCE ADMINISTRATIVE BURDENS AND INEFFICIENCIES

There are numerous shortcomings in any healthcare organization. Some of the breakthrough events in the recent past have pushed organizations to have a deeper look at the ineffectiveness of existing systems. A collaborative approach is needed to address the shortcomings of health system organizations. Physicians enter the healthcare field with the intention of serving patients and enhancing the patient experience. However, providers are often swamped with administrative work like documenting patient records and treatment plans and facilitating multidisciplinary care, which requires extensive communication to ease continuity of quality care; coordinating referrals to specialists or external centers; ensuring proper transfer of medical records; navigating prescription refills while conveying the same to pharmacies; and navigating insurance claims and disputes. These tasks call for additional training and adaptations to stay updated with evolving healthcare codes and regulations. In health systems, *administrative burden* refers to the time and effort healthcare professionals dedicate to such administrative duties that divert their attention from direct patient care.

A survey from the Ontario College of Family Physicians found that physicians, on average, spend approximately 19.1 hours per week (40% of their time) on administrative tasks (Brown et al., 2025). Another survey conducted by The Harris Poll found that clinicians spend nearly 28 hours per week on administrative duties. The burden is even higher for medical office staff, who say they spend 34 hours per week on administrative tasks. Claims personnel spend 36 hours per week on such tasks, according to the report (Southwick, 2024).

Administrative procedures designed to govern and regulate treatment access in healthcare frequently overshadow the fundamental goal of patient care. Physicians, burdened by extensive paperwork and complex approval systems, struggle to deliver timely and effective treatment, severely compromising their potential. This situation extends beyond providers, creating a ripple effect that also impacts the patients who depend on them for essential medical services.

Drivers of administrative burden fell into three broad categories: health systems (documentation and patient records; billing, coding, and insurance interactions; referrals, prior authorization); technology (implementation of new health technology or platforms; telemedicine; Electronic Health Records [EHR]); and patient complexity (Storseth et al., 2025).

Some of the key administrative hazards contributing to inefficiencies are explained below:

Prior Authorization in Health Systems

One of the many pressing obstacles faced by both physicians and patients is the burden of prior authorization. Prior authorization requires healthcare providers to secure approval from a patient's health insurance company before delivering specific treatments, prescriptions, or procedures. While designed to control costs and ensure appropriate care, the procedure has evolved into a cumbersome administrative burden on medical professionals and their patients. The American Medical Association (AMA) in 2024 reported that 94% of physicians experience delays in patient care due to prior authorization processes, and 78% note that patients often abandon recommended treatments because of it (American Medical Association, 2024). These statistics highlight the urgency to address such administrative burdens not just as a clerical issue, but as a growing threat to timely care.

Technology as Both Driver and Solution

Technology has emerged as a paradoxical force contributing to administrative burdens. Digital tools such as e-consultation and referral platforms, EHR optimization, and patient monitoring platforms are often promoted as solutions to streamline workflows, reduce duplication, and enhance compliance. While these services are beneficial in theory, multiple studies show that they often increase workload due to poor usability and excessive documentation requirements. For example, EHR systems may require extensive training, demand excessive documentation, and create usability challenges that contribute to fragmented and inefficient work, ultimately increasing rather than decreasing physician workload. Kyle et al. (2025) conducted a scoping review of patient administrative burden and found that digital platforms designed to reduce compliance costs frequently became new sources of complexity and subsequent physician burnout. A 2023 analysis involving 1,052 ambulatory physicians reported that time spent on EHRs had increased to 5.5 hours per 8 scheduled patient hours, compared with 4.5 hours pre-COVID, with increased after-hours documentation demands, attributed to consecutive appointments and the expansion of telehealth (Holmgren et al., 2023). The study also noted that primary care clinicians spent nearly half of their working time, approximately 4.5 hours, on EHR-related tasks. Therefore, technology must be co-designed with clinicians and continuously optimized to ensure it alleviates rather than amplifies administrative strain.

Figure 1. shows physicians' routine tasks and responsibilities without artificial intelligence assistance, negatively impacting the real time spent with patients.

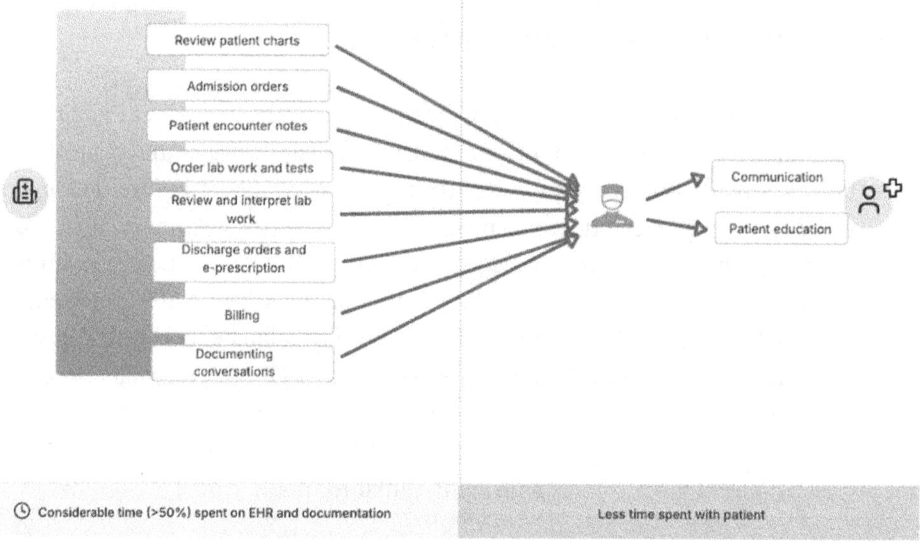

In response to these challenges, a large ambulatory network in the United States implemented a policy whereby 1 appointment slot per half-day was reserved for physicians to complete EHR-related tasks, such as messaging, prior authorizations, and prescription refills, undertaken at the physician's discretion (Kanaparthy et al., 2025). The initiative demonstrated that reserving structured time for EHR work significantly reduced after-hours and non-workday EHR use, without compromising institutional revenue.

Task Redistribution and Workforce Strategies

Another stream of literature highlights task shifting and redistribution as strategies to mitigate administrative burden. Interventions such as employing medical scribes, delegating administrative responsibilities to allied health professionals, or expanding administrative staff support may lessen the clerical load on physicians, allowing better focus towards direct patient care. Nonetheless, the review warns that redistribution may generate unintended inefficiencies, such as communication errors or increased operational costs (Storseth et al., 2025). The effectiveness of task shifting, therefore, depends on careful workflow integration and evaluation of system-wide impacts.

Patient complexity and Social Determinants of Health

Patient complexity, particularly among older adults, individuals with multiple co-morbidities, and those requiring intensive coordination, represents another significant driver of administrative workload. Collaborative, team-based care models distribute responsibilities across multidisciplinary teams and alleviate the administrative load on individual providers. Integrating social determinants of health (SDOH) and access to social support services can reduce fragmented care and improve equity and care quality. These approaches highlight that administrative burden is not solely a function of internal processes but also of broader patient needs. With less time for dedicated patient care, providers feel overwhelmed, ultimately leading to decreased efficiency, burnout, and low career satisfaction. Administrative burden is multifaceted and persistent, drains valuable time and resources, and shrinking this burden is a key point of focus for boosting patient care quality and provider well-being. Evidence suggests that interventions must be context-sensitive, co-designed with clinicians, and evaluated holistically to avoid unintended consequences. True progress lies not in isolated fixes but in system-level redesigns that balance efficiency, cost, and patient-centered care.

System Redesigns

Administrative waste refers to the unnecessary administrative expenses that show no meaningful contribution towards clinical care and outcomes. Many health sector experts attribute this to the system's intricate complexity, which affects not only professionals but also impacts patient experience. Operational inefficiencies, such as duplicated testing, process-related errors, and overuse of expensive resources, significantly amplify healthcare burdens. In a new study, Sahni et al. (2021) estimated that administrative spending was $950 billion in 2019, of which $265 billion could be saved by implementing appropriate interventions that reduce spending without negatively affecting patient care. The fee-for-service reimbursement model further exacerbates these challenges by incentivizing service volume rather than efficiency, as providers are compensated per intervention regardless of clinical necessity. Addressing these issues is a fundamental part of a patient-centered approach, as it has undesirable effects, including physician burnout surfacing as emotional exhaustion and a lowered sense of personal accomplishment; financial strain on the system, which drives up the overall expenditure, making it less affordable; an impact on healthcare businesses causing a reduced cost-benefit ratio; and finally, a decline in patient experience. Since patients are not immune to the consequences of administrative burdens, they may experience delays in care provision, find insurance requirements confusing, and feel frustrated by unnecessary paperwork, especially in times of distress. Those who have more complex health needs, are economically marginalized, and experience oppression, discrimination, or health injustices tend to face disproportionately high administrative burdens. In situations where administrative processes operate to reproduce structural inequities, this has been labelled administrative violence.

Understanding insurance requirements can be challenging and particularly more complicated for individuals facing obstacles like language barriers, cognitive impairments, or the added responsibilities of caregiving. Administrative inaccuracies, such as incomplete documentation, may lead to insurance denials, shifting the financial burden back onto troubled patients. It is therefore vital to tackle these administrative hurdles to preserve overall patient satisfaction.

Managing multiple workflows simultaneously constitutes case management, care coordination, patient engagement, remote monitoring, data analysis, staffing, scheduling, insurance, and billing. Conventional processes are time-consuming and often lack efficiency because they involve wearisome tasks like paper-based data entry, scheduling appointments, billing, and claims processing, which may introduce errors in workflows. This leads to unintended consequences such as misdiagnoses, over- or under-treatment, or medication errors, hindering coordinated care while also inflating administrative costs. Thus, management workflows at hospitals need to be simplified by removing such bottlenecks to ensure that operational efficiency is maximized whilst also reducing administrative burden.

Healthcare administrative waste, broadly representing spending by private payers, hospitals, and physician groups, can be cut through targeted interventions at 2 levels: organizational and industry.

Organizational-Level Interventions

At the organizational level, private payers, hospitals, and physician groups, together responsible for nearly two-thirds of U.S. administrative spending, have pursued targeted strategies to improve efficiency. For private payers, best-in-class claims processing emphasizes automation, accuracy, and efficiency, with leading examples showing that up to 95 percent of claims can be adjudicated without manual intervention. Fraud, waste, and abuse (FWA) still cost the government $60 billion a year, but real-time detection systems show promise (Shrank et al., 2019). Evidence suggests that scaling successful interventions, such as improving data quality and streamlining manual workflows, could reduce payer administrative spending by 20–25 percent, or $7–10 billion annually (Sahni, Gupta, Peterson, & Cutler, 2023).

Leading hospitals and physician groups are generally improving operational productivity in 5 ways: reducing denials and accounts receivable follow-up spending, eliminating manual work through digital workflows, automating documentation processes, improving clinical documentation accuracy, and streamlining financial clearance and prior authorization processes. Evidence from highly optimized revenue cycle operations suggests that extending these interventions to all hospitals and physician groups could reduce spending by 15% to 20%, or $15 billion to $20 billion annually (Sahni, Gupta, Peterson, & Cutler, 2023).

Industry-Level Interventions

Industry-level interventions generally play 2 types of roles: acceleration and augmentation of organizational-level interventions. One major proposal is the adoption of a centralized automated claims clearinghouse, which would standardize and automate financial transactions across providers. Smaller hospitals, physician groups, and smaller private payers currently face higher transaction costs due to limited resources, but a centralized system could lower costs to match those of larger organizations. Estimates suggest such standardization could reduce spending by 10–12 percent ($10–15 billion annually) (Sahni et al., 2021). Other industry-level strategies include standardizing medical policies for a subset of prior authorizations and streamlining physician licensure through a national provider directory. Simplifying prior authorization policies where clear evidence exists could reduce administrative spending by $1–3 billion annually and free up clinical staff time (Sahni et al., 2021). Similarly, standardizing physician licensure and creating a centralized directory could save $7–10 billion annually, with an additional $1–2 billion from directory efficiencies (Sahni, Gupta, Peterson, & Cutler, 2023).

Workflow Automations in Health Systems

Manual processes and conventional records can be burdensome to share or access patient information. Misplaced or lost patient records could result in missed opportunities for prompt interventions and negatively impact prognoses. Automation technologies for communication and scheduling, such as AI (Artificial Intelligence), integrating telehealth, automating Electronic Health Records (EHR) management, and machine learning, allow healthcare facilities to minimise manual interventions, reduce the time to process and stratify treatment regimens, maintain higher accuracy in processing data, and obtain faster results at lower costs. This streamlines patient record keeping, information, and enhanced communication between healthcare providers and provides valuable data for quality improvement and research.

This expanding reliance on automation explains why healthcare organizations are financially investing in automation. As per market researchers, the global healthcare automation market was estimated to be worth nearly $38 billion in 2024, and further projections stipulate that it will approach almost $63 billion by the end of 2030 (NetSuite, 2025). This represents the sector's confidence in the ability of automated systems to enhance the quality of healthcare for patients as well as providers.

The following summarises how workflow automation can be applied to healthcare management:

Disease Diagnosis and Treatment

Health systems globally generate excessive administrative workload and regulatory burdens in the form of massive volumes of clinical data that are overwhelming to review manually. One of the most cathartic contributions of healthcare automation lies in the ability of Artificial Intelligence (AI) to rapidly analyze and process this data with high precision and reduce subjectivity in interpretations and diagnoses. AI-powered automated systems can efficiently evaluate electronic health records (EHRs), laboratory results, and past treatment data to identify and detect patterns and anomalies that might be overlooked in heavy workload settings.

While radiologists play a crucial role in providing accurate imaging reports and strengthening communication between several medical specialists to culminate clinical decisions, AI enhances radiology accuracy through faster image analysis and report generation. It is known to improve scanning procedures and image clarity across diagnostic procedures like MRI, CT, and PET by reducing artifacts and upgrading resolution. These systems are trained to detect disease-specific patterns that tackle limitations of traditional reporting, such as fatigue and workload-induced errors. This advancement allows radiologists to focus on complex cases and deliver quick diagnoses, especially in high-stakes conditions where early intervention is ideal.

AI's capacity to analyze history and current patient data allows early detection of risk factors and the development of personalized treatment plans. In March 2024, the NHS (National Health Service) tested an AI tool, called Mia (Mammography Intelligence Assessment), conducted alongside NHS clinicians, to analyze the mammograms of over 10,000 women, which successfully identified tiny signs of breast cancer in 11 women that had been missed by doctors, as they were practically invisible to the human eye (Ng et al., 2023). Automated systems can objectively evaluate changes in tissue characteristics or tumor size, resulting in more reliable disease progression and monitoring.

This progression extends further into other healthcare fields like pathology, cardiology, genomics, drug discovery, and healthcare delivery and is gaining exponential recognition. This speeds up the diagnostic process and reduces human errors, ultimately redirecting providers' efforts towards patient care and reducing after-hours review time.

Treatment Personalization and Optimization

AI-powered algorithms can tailor treatment plans by analyzing and studying patient profiles with broad databases, including lifestyle factors, clinical history, real-time health conditions, and outcomes from similar cases. By leveraging such advanced technologies, it is possible to improve patient outcomes through personalized care, which helps achieve better survival rates with fewer adverse effects. A study was conducted in March 2025 to enhance oral cancer diagnostics using AI-based diagnostic models (Satheeskumar, 2025). The model had better sensitivity and specificity than standard diagnostic methods. The study concluded that patients following AI-curated treatment plans had a 20% higher survival rate than those receiving conventional care.

Additionally, automation tools allow for continuous monitoring of patients, both in the hospital and at home, through advances in smartwatches and other wearables. In a hospital setting, automated systems can examine the data that channels from a connected device, such as a patient monitor, and alert the care teams only when an intervention is required. This spares the team from sorting extensive data sets of normal vital signs to identify problematic ones, saving their time and energy and ultimately reducing fatigue.

Automated systems can help transform patient experience by managing administrative work such as scheduling appointments, bill payments, filling out intake forms, uploading electronic records, verifying insurance, and requesting referrals. Both the care process and administrative operations become more streamlined and efficient, and patients are less likely to miss appointments or have unmet healthcare needs. Clinicians, too, benefit from automated treatment protocols, freeing them from paperwork, resulting in improved patient care and job satisfaction.

Automated Drug Utilization Review (DUR) Checks

Automating prescription reviews adds a potent layer of clinical decision support that ultimately enhances the overall quality and safety of the healthcare experience. It alleviates cognitive fatigue in physicians and allows them to prioritize direct patient contact and focus on more complex clinical activities.

Once patient prescriptions are uploaded to an automated system by healthcare providers, AI-driven capabilities instantly analyze the new drug orders in conjunction with the patient's medical history, existing medication lists, documented allergies, and lab results. These swift reviews highlight potential risks like drug interactions, incorrect dosages, contraindications, and therapy duplications that might otherwise be overlooked during physical checks and audits, especially in busy or high-volume settings. Decision support for drug interactions alerts providers to a medication combination that could result in an unwanted pharmacologic effect. Some hospitals are also trying out robotic systems to dispense medications and even deliver them to patient rooms and nursing stations, which would help cut back on time spent fetching medications. A 2023 ICU study found that automated dispensing cabinets (ADCs) with DUR reduced prescription errors from 3.03 to 1.75 per 100,000 and dispensing errors from 3.87 to 0 per 100,000, freeing pharmacist time for reviews (Tu et al., 2023). By managing these complex reviews, automation tools reduce the mental effort clinicians expend into manually recalling client databases and drug information, enabling providers to devote more attention to meaningful communication, and also help manage the burnout associated with documentation tasks.

Prescription Refill Management

With an exponential population growth and more patients suffering from multiple comorbidities that require complex medication regimens, both patients and healthcare providers face increased challenges in coordinating complex treatments. Juggling frequent medication refills is not only physically exhausting for patients, especially those battling chronic diseases that necessitate regular treatment, but it also negatively impacts their mental health. Likewise, for healthcare providers, the incessant need to review and approve repetitive prescriptions hinders their workflow, causing cognitive fatigue over time.

Utilizing automation techniques to oversee drug refills empowers healthcare systems to expedite the prescription refill procedure while contributing to improved accuracy and transparency. When refill authorization requests are generated electronically and sent directly to prescribing healthcare providers (physicians, nursing staff, and pharmacists), possibilities of postponement stemming from manual communication, such as phone calls, fax exchanges, or paper records, are eliminated. Accelerated drug distribution and coordinated authorization reduce administrative burden and give patients reliable access to necessary treatments, overall improving both operational efficiency and health care standards. In turn, HCWs benefit from reduced administrative burden, which aids their mental well-being and emotional stability, allowing them to engage their energy in impactful patient care practices.

Advanced automations observe consistent refill patterns and medication adherence behaviors and automatically approve prescription drugs with an established refill history and regular schedules (e.g., diabetes medication every month; lithium for bipolar disorder patients). This bypasses the unnecessary manual reviews and redundant approvals, allowing pharmacies to process refills in a streamlined fashion. These systems, integrated with Electronic Health Records (EHRs), can cross-check refill requests to prevent conflict between prescriptions, which reduces the risk of adverse drug effects and promotes safe prescribing practices. For example, if a patient already taking aspirin has been prescribed an anticoagulant by the physician, the system will automatically alert for further review instead of auto-approving.

Providers can also see if patients refill prescriptions on time and comply with treatment. If not, providers can offer counselling sessions to discuss possible barriers or make adjustments to maintain adherence (e.g., reminder campaigns for diabetic patients; health education and targeted awareness for cardiovascular risk in patients aged 60+ with low statin adherence). This integration offers an uninterrupted workflow, allowing providers to focus on high-value tasks instead. It simplifies accreditation and quality assurance audits with the use of electronic refill authorizations, which guarantee highly detailed, time-stamped records of every refill, simplifying data retrieval in comparison to manual searches. Every authorization is automatically logged onto the system in chronological order, from physician approval to medication pickup. This feature not only cultivates a straightforward, transparent system but also maintains legal validity and data authenticity, thereby improving consistency in management.

Data Integration and Reporting

A health system catering to an immeasurably diseased population is constantly evolving regulatory standards and policies to ensure systematic workflow, which requires extensive documentation and records, resulting in data proliferation. Such clinical records might range from basic administrative documents (patient identification cards, driver's licenses, insurance cards, etc.) to prescriptions and radiology reports. Automation tools in modern healthcare settings can automatically scan, sort, organize, and classify clinical documents based on the information they contain. This makes it easier to use this structured data for analytics. These tools play a pivotal role by enabling seamless integration of data across various platforms such as Electronic Health Records (EHRs), Pharmacy Management Systems, Laboratory Information Systems (LIS), insurance portals, and billing software. Patient documents can be uploaded onto data extraction tools, which can take up information and details, recognize text, and map this data into appropriate fields in software, eliminating the need for manually entering data. A unified ecosystem is maintained using real-time exchange of patient data between different departments at the hospital, making updated information accessible to both administrative and clinical staff. Similarly, electronic intake forms are filled out online by patients themselves, helping to reduce errors and increase staff productivity.

For administrative staff, automation significantly reduces the burden of repetitive and time-consuming tasks. Automated appointment reminders (via SMS or email), AI-driven patient intake forms, and secure data-sharing protocols are replacing former means of communication like phone calls, faxing, and manual data entry. This shift not only boosts operational efficiency but also reduces burnout and workplace fatigue among HCWs. In the same way, for doctors and nurses, automation can help with writing notes by using tools like voice-to-text, ready-made templates, and smart Clinical Decision Support Systems (CDSS). This feature improves the overall experience for providers during the first steps of admitting a patient, which involves gathering a detailed history, doing a physical exam, and ordering necessary tests.

Automated systems create electronic discharge forms automatically (involving follow-up and recovery details), relieving discharge nurses and other staff to focus on more important details of post-stay care. With enhanced diagnostic accuracy and data-driven treatments, clinicians have more time to focus on what truly matters: building meaningful rapport with their patients and delivering the best care possible. Providing uninterrupted attention to the patients with less hurried consultations also allows the clinical staff to make more informed and conscious decisions. Ultimately, when both administrative and clinical teams are supported by automated systems, it creates a less stressful and more responsive work environment, nurturing the idea of patient and provider well-being. Smooth operations and limited wait times in clinics alleviate on-the-job stress, resulting in enhanced productivity and job satisfaction among healthcare providers. However, the real challenge lies in ensuring that these automation tools are integrated into a comprehensive framework that acknowledges the fact that health systems function as dynamic networks. To sustain the improvements achieved through automation and data integration, it becomes essential to adopt holistic perspectives that reinforce resilience and sustainability. This is achieved through adaptive strategies such as systems thinking.

SYSTEMS THINKING FOR FOSTERING SUSTAINABLE Improvements

Systems thinking (ST) is an integral approach that views a system with a holistic lens, examining various components within a system that are interconnected to each other, and their influence on one another in nonlinear ways. Specifically, it offers a clear perception by highlighting correlations and dependencies across different components of health systems.

Complex adaptive systems (CAS) are characterized by a vast network of innumerable and intricately interconnected components. These systems, with their dynamic and open nature, are constantly evolving in response to multiple internal and external interactions within and across the system, e.g., feedback loops, delays, and critical thresholds. This quality makes them inherently self-organizing. Health systems, with their holistic perspective, represent CAS, as they too have a myriad of interconnected components, i.e., healthcare providers, patients, policymakers, insurance agencies, infrastructure, patient behavior, and structures such as policies, histories, values, and norms that continuously change and adapt to changes (Thelen et al., 2023).

Figure 2. shows the six key characteristics of systems thinking as follows:

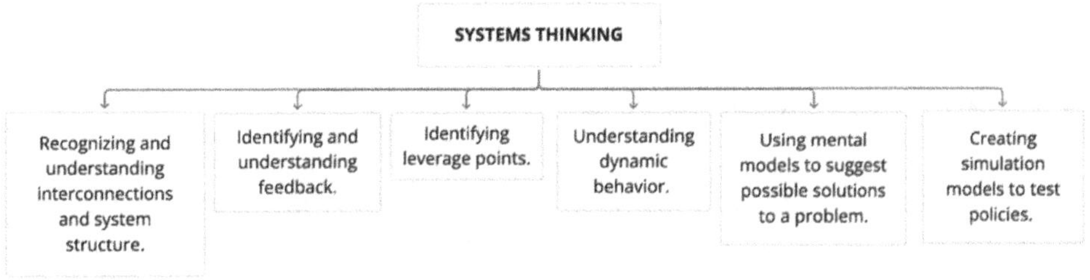

1) Recognizing and Understanding Interconnections and System Structure

The first step in shifting from standard linear thinking to ST involves *recognizing and understanding interconnections and system structure.* Mapping out the health system's processes and relationships helps figure out its operations and the bottlenecks and inefficiencies. This allows stakeholders in our system to set shared, mutual goals and acknowledge how the health system can operate as a cohesive unit to carry out effective health initiatives. These tasks can be accomplished using relevant ST tools, such as stakeholder analysis, process mapping, interviews, logic models, causal loop diagrams, and reflective practice.

2) Identifying and Understanding Feedback Within the System

The second ST characteristic involves *identifying and understanding feedback within the system*, especially since complex adaptive systems (CAS), such as health systems, are governed by feedback dynamics. Feedback loops, both positive and negative, create cause-and-effect relationships among various functional components within a workplace, which is essential for uncovering chains of causality within a health system. This characteristic builds on understanding how different elements influence each other over time and how certain interventions can indirectly tailor desired outcomes with their balancing or reinforcing properties. Thus, having an efficient feedback system in health actions enables providers to identify the changing needs in the system, allowing coherent interaction and logical communication. A useful example is that of a Markov model, which uses a probabilistic approach to represent systems, where at any given time, the future state depends on the current state and is independent of the sequence of events that occurred in the past. This logical interaction makes a system an autonomous system that is not influenced by an external agent and is useful in decision-making in distinct and stochastic environments, thereby helping the provider in making reliable choices based on current information.

3) Identifying Leverage Points

The third key feature is *identifying leverage points*, which are areas within a system where small adjustments can generate a significant impact. Identifying these points allows decision-makers to assign limited resources more efficiently and to prompt small changes in health systems that will yield major improvements in system performance. This can be achieved by using tools such as Scenario Planning, the Iceberg Tool, Decision Tree modelling, etc. Glenn *et al.* (2020) utilized qualitative data to develop a model of the overlooked tropical disease system with the aim of checking potential leverage points that could help in disease elimination. While prioritizing leverage points, one must consider the impact of intervening at each point, the feasibility of making those changes, and the cost versus the expected benefit. We can learn from successful examples where targeting leverage points, such as vaccination rates and disease surveillance, has helped improve public health systems. Additionally, changing information flows by increasing transparency or feedback can emerge as a strong leverage point. For instance, hospitals can increase transparency by providing physician star ratings and reviews from patients on their website. This action not only provides patients the relevant information to make informed choices but also motivates healthcare providers to focus on the quality of patient care delivered.

4) Understanding Dynamic Behaviour

Understanding dynamic behavior is a more advanced category of the Systems Thinking for Health Actions (STHA) framework. Health systems function as complex adaptive systems (CAS) that exhibit nonlinear properties and evolve. By studying feedback loops and such interconnected patterns between various system components, stakeholders can foresee and assess how a particular action or change in one component of the system may extend across and influence the entire system, often with effects that are unpredictable or do not appear immediately. This kind of envisionment allows for a more informed decision-making in an interconnected work environment, and can be achieved through systems thinking tools like behavior-over-time graphs, Innovation/change Management History, System Archetypes, etc.

Hospital-based interventions, which aim to reduce the incidence of catheter-associated urinary tract infections (CAUTIs), provide a well-established example. Hospitals often exercise policies to limit or discontinue urinary catheters early in order to prevent infections. Although the objective of such interventions is to reduce CAUTIs (which is a positive goal), it can cause an unfavorable increase in patient falls (a negative outcome). This increased risk can be attributed to the premature removal of urinary catheters, especially among the elderly or frail patient population, making them more susceptible to falls while attempting to walk towards the bathroom. Therefore, recognizing that these interventions can have inordinate results and carefully optimizing when and for whom they are implemented can help prevent undesirable consequences in the long run. This illustrates the significance of understanding the dynamic relationships within the healthcare system.

5) Using Mental Models to Suggest Possible Solutions to a Problem

Using models to suggest possible solutions to a problem is a useful strategy and refers to the use of visual depictions to demonstrate how feedback loops and other visual models (e.g., conceptual models, charts, graphs, and maps) accomplish the goals of a health system. These visual models do not show the exact way any system works in the real world but instead reflect how different stakeholders view a specific situation or obstacle. The process of generating systems models involves aligning stakeholder perceptions, where participants from diverse backgrounds and disciplines collaborate to define the problem, understand the impact of changes in one sector on another, and define its boundaries. These interactive visualization models unfold points of agreement and deviations, leading to better communication and conflict reduction by opening up a space for discussion and negotiating responsibilities. For example, hospitals and clinics use heatmaps to display areas experiencing high demand, such as excessive patient inflow and longer wait times, and staff distribution. Such information allows the administration to recognize backlogs and focus on streamlining workflow for smooth operational efficiency. During the COVID-19 pandemic, such live interactive maps offered real-time updates on active cases, outbreaks, and vaccination rates, helping health officials and the general population understand the spread and impact of the virus (Kamel Boulos & Geraghty, 2020).

6) Creating Simulation Models for Testing Policies

Lastly, *creating simulation models for testing policies* is a powerful way of translating detailed scientific discoveries and knowledge into simple, comprehensible outcomes. Current health technology assessment tools show finite usefulness in terms of the tangled functionality of health systems and are insufficient for working towards achieving "The Triple Aim." The Triple Aim of healthcare is a framework developed in 2007 by the Institute for Healthcare Improvement (IHI) and constitutes three main components that positively influence the health system's performance: (1) Population health, (2) Patient experience, (3) Cost per capita. Lacagnina (2018) suggested that this goal could be expanded as 'The Triple Aim Plus More' to additionally include the welfare of healthcare providers as well, especially with respect to constant stress at work, burnout, and increased suicidality. The application of ST simulation models is used to design and assess health system operations and estimate interventions needed to resolve inherent problems, if present. Mathematical representations (or formal models) are created based on processes and systems to test what- if' scenarios and their consequences over time. Such modeling helps in attaining an advanced understanding of a system and better communication between stakeholders and policymakers. Many developments in disease diagnosis and treatment plans implement unanticipated end results at multiple levels of a system. An approach that is implemented to ideally address challenges could create newer problems for providers as well as patients. By utilizing such models, decision makers can simulate how a certain policy change or intervention (e.g., a new treatment regimen or altering staff levels) can impact health services, thereby bridging the gap between theory and practice. It helps in extrapolating outcomes, both unintended and systemic loopholes. Relevant tools for testing policies include agent-based models, Scenario Planning Models, Systems Dynamics Models, etc. By promoting cross-functional collaboration and continuous feedback loops, systems thinking helps identify bottlenecks, integrate automation within a comprehensive framework, and streamline patient flow. This approach helps with provider well-being by lowering administrative overload, clarifying roles, improving coordination across departments, and mitigating burnout. This supports professional satisfaction and enhances the overall quality of care as clinicians gain more time for authentic patient interactions. Overall, incorporating systems thinking into hospital policy creates a culture of continuous improvement by shifting and realigning the form and function of a targeted system, thereby not only sustaining efficiency but also supporting the long-term sustainability of the health system and the well-being of its workforce.

RESOURCE ALLOCATION AND INFRASTRUCTURE DEVELOPMENT

Healthcare infrastructure should not be limited to having accessible physical structures or merely replicating existing institutions; it must be dynamic, adaptive to changing times and community needs, and robust enough to deliver patient care while optimizing workplace efficiency. Infrastructural challenges over the decades have been evolving. At first, attention was given to basic sanitation needs to resolve infectious disease burden, then to expanding the facilities to deliver effective care or patient care delivery with a structured insurance plan to have inclusive and broader reach, to now where digitally integrated infrastructure is a crucial component. These changes only highlight the pivotal role of innovation and building upon existing resources to deliver the unmet needs, which directly promotes provider well-being. For better understanding of resources and infrastructure, we need to understand the following:-

Variation in Global Healthcare Infrastructure
Changes in Healthcare and Infrastructure over time
Support Systems for Healthcare Workers
Vulnerable links like Underrepresented in Medicine (UiM) and Gender Equality
Challenges for Primary Care Providers
Work-life Balance, Violence and its Impact on Healthcare Workers
Role of Administrative Structure, Tools and Resources for Organisations
Managerial, Cultural, and Governance Structure: A Roadmap for Hospital Executives,
Quality Improvement Leads, and
Departmental Directors.

Variation in Global Healthcare Infrastructure

Both developed and developing healthcare systems have individual sets of limitations with unmet needs.

1. Developing countries face some of the infrastructural inadequacies, like sanitation, transportation, a lack of quality healthcare equipment, and accessibility in rural areas. Other aspects that remain unaddressed are limited budget allocation and substandard responsiveness to vulnerable groups like low-income and aged populations. Due to limited investment from policymakers, developing healthcare systems often fall short of quality essential and diagnostic equipment, causing overall resource scarcity and high-pressure working conditions for providers. Varied degrees of resource scarcity affect healthcare services and patient outcomes and it becomes worse during any public health crises, further amplifying job stress for healthcare workers. Still, in most of the developing healthcare settings, paper-based patient records are used. Resource allocation has shifted in recent times to balance socio-economic differences. Digital infrastructure is being promoted and used to bridge the healthcare gaps to run the system efficiently. In recent times, healthcare workers are being supported for training on digital systems and Electronic Health Records (EHRs), aiding coordinated care. Additionally, there is a greater emphasis on equality, as virtual care options like telemedicine provide increased flexibility for both providers and patients.
2. Developed countries allocate a relatively higher budget of about 10-13.5% of GDP to healthcare, but this spending has its limitations. Healthcare systems in developed countries mostly cater to specialty and acute healthcare rather than primary care or preventative medicine, which created a gap in the community and poorly managed chronic diseases. Initially, because of poor integration of digital systems, providers faced dissatisfaction and burnout. There has been adoption of electronic health records (EHRs), which has increased provider satisfaction, reduced delays, and replaced gruesome paper charts with digital patient data but has also introduced struggles related to user-friendliness and technical glitches. During the COVID-19 pandemic, major infrastructural shifts like telehealth expanded but there was still a divide between rural and marginalized communities. Also, with telehealth, it enables continuous patient monitoring and virtual follow-up. Current Western infrastructural challenges are quality facilities for the aging, cybersecurity threats, and a need for greener infrastructure.

How Have Healthcare and Infrastructure Changed Over Time?

Broadly, infrastructural investments for today and for the future depend on making it a priority amongst other elements of community welfare as well as planning, effective design, policies, budget allocation, and reforms even at the local level. If we compare the 2010s to the 2020s, earlier healthcare relied on electronic health records (EHRs) with challenging interoperability, stationary computers, or Computers on Wheels (COWs) for accessing clinical information. Lately, new and advanced AI-powered clinical decision support systems provide help at the point of care. EHRs are digitally integrated to schedule appointments and access real-time patient updates. Work efficiency and administrative support have also evolved. Providers used significant time with documentation and administrative tasks, which, because of AI-powered assistants, deal with routine tasks like managing scheduling and billing. Additionally, digital mobile devices have become ubiquitous for both patients and providers, aiding patient education and navigation support.

From a well-being perspective, earlier there was limited conversation about health and burnout among healthcare providers, and there were fewer workplace and systemic solutions for staff wellness. Additionally, integration of digital tools without proper training and simulation added stress. Now, virtual or hybrid work provides flexibility to healthcare staff. Provider support and well-being involve workplace systems, norms, administrative culture, and flexibility to work on systemic shortcomings and eventually policy initiatives.

Institutional support like implementing mental health, peer support networks or wellness counselling that allows addressing workplace, personal and financial challenges and addressing burnout and mental exhaustion enhance personal and workplace efficiency. There are research-backed interventions to support HCWs through mindfulness, gratitude, and positive psychology leading to more job satisfaction and reduced mental health struggles. Integrating mental and psychological health and workplace safety as core principles in the systemic policies helps with HCWs' well-being. Institutionalizing well-being support like counseling programs, employee assistance programs, and addressing and debriefing any distressing event provides reassurance to employees.

Support Systems for Healthcare Workers

Major drivers of overworked staff are chronically drained human resources, leading to unfair and unequal workloads and lengthy shifts, which promote an unhealthy workplace environment. Key changes to ensure adequate support for the HCWs:

1. Ensuring a systemic responsibility for sufficient staffing helps with fair workload, so workers have time and capacity to care for themselves and hence their patients. Keeping a monitoring system to reduce overcrowding and having an optimized workplace makes a significant difference.
2. Prioritizing work-life balance and ensuring personal time, including adequate sick leave, personal leave, parental leave, and scheduled time for personal appointments, should be included as protected time off to balance work and personal life for employees. Policies should also include regular research, audits, timely assessments, and adaptations, taking feedback from staff to implement continual improvements.
3. Cultural shifts are impactful in establishing a supportive and sustainable well-being for healthcare staff. A culture of collaboration and continuous learning effectively improves patient outcomes, in turn increasing professional satisfaction. Studies have shown benefits of post-shift clinical debriefing in strategizing patient safety that positively impact clinicians' well-being. Supportive leadership that models healthy practices with open communication and flexibility sets a tone to encourage the staff to do the same.
4. Providing professional development opportunities, like training, mentorship, and career advancement opportunities provides value and supports them professionally, which increases staff retention. Upskilling, providing financial incentives like sign-on bonuses, recognizing contributions, and loan waivers help with workforce retention. Policies to reform equity, pay gaps, and gender inequality need ongoing attention to build a supportive culture.

Underrepresented in Medicine (UiM) and Gender Equality

Feelings of workplace isolation, lack of inclusivity, or feeling unwelcome for authentic self-expression all negatively affect workplace culture. Allowing authentic self-expression enhances job satisfaction, fostering self-motivation, in turn for an energized workforce. Workplace representation is crucial to allow self-expressions to build trust amongst marginalized groups. Employees from underrepresented and marginalized backgrounds face isolation. Thus, having a culture of ease for authentic self-expression at work helps with a stronger sense of belonging. Employees who feel comfortable expressing themselves and have a safe place for self-expression are more likely to stay with the organization, increasing long-term engagement. When representation of marginalized groups is visible in the work culture and leadership, it shows prioritizing inclusion and diversity, which improves psychological safety and enhances collaboration and innovation.

Underrepresented in Medicine (UiM) face microaggressions, which affect the patient's care. Subtle verbal and nonverbal indignities and slurs make any workplace hostile. Having training and sensitization sessions to help HCWs recognize and respond to discrimination makes UiM feel empowered. Providing sponsorship and mentorship and advocating for UiM helps advance their career.

One of the Sustainable Development Goals (SDGs) is gender equality. Despite decades of advocating and promoting for gender equality and women's safety, there is still underrepresentation of women in leadership positions with limited infrastructure and support for their workplace safety. Committees dedicated to women's safety, which help with addressing workplace safety, reporting harassment, establishing Prevention of Sexual Harassment (PoSH Act), internal complaint units, and help-lines, are useful ways to keep these concerns in check.

Challenges for Primary Care Providers

Internationally educated health professionals and HCWs posted in rural settings require extra support as well as resources. Primary Care Workers (PCPs) are more vulnerable to workplace stress due to limited resources and inadequacies in structure and systemic aspects. Many PCPs face financial constraints, delayed penetration of updated technology, and limited supply, combined with a sense of time scarcity, which hampers quality care while also affecting personal life, causing more exhaustion and burnout. PCPs address complex social and behavioral needs, which further adds to their emotional burden. Added provider shortages in such regions increase the load on the available HCWs to bridge the gaps.

Certain systemic changes can help take some pressure off by having a buffer and protected time with no patient appointments, allowing PCPs to catch up on documentation, decompress, or take care of urgent tasks. Incorporating provider preferences for scheduling helps them adjust better to their personal commitments. Because of multidisciplinary care, there should be help with a seamless incorporation with public health and community organizations to effectively cater to medical, social, and economic needs to help PCPs. For seamless patient inflows, invest in modern clinic tools, training for digital and telehealth, check-in kiosks or tablets, and reduced wait times. Smarter data-driven changes help build new and effective infrastructure, and AI-assisted tools forecast patient surges and help allocate and optimize resources and staffing. Empowering PCPs with automated reminders for appointments helps reduce no-shows, and telehealth platforms help with increasing access with remote monitoring support and improved virtual care coordination. This has an impact on helping PCPs handle larger patient volumes without compromising on quality, helping retain providers, and improving job satisfaction, which in turn helps with scalability.

Violence and its Impact on Healthcare Workers

According to WHO, between 8% and 38% of health workers face physical violence at some point in their careers. This all can lead to serious physical injuries, depression, anxiety, and post-traumatic stress disorder (PTSD), causing higher absenteeism and further straining the system. There are numerous case studies across healthcare systems suggesting decreased motivation to work if the safety is compromised. There should be resources to manage violent patients and high-risk visitors. Enhancing security in high-risk areas and emergency rooms, implementing systems for reporting and tracking, and ensuring follow-up on incidents help build systemic trust. Training healthcare workers in techniques for de-escalation, recognizing warning signs, and equipping staff with panic buttons for a rapid response in emergencies.

Work-Life Balance

Across nations, healthcare systems have long, grueling hours with limited scope for work-life balance. Addressing staff shortages with specialized staffing services alleviates strain on existing staff. Having a flexible schedule, protected leave, or options of remote work provides more control over their time. Supporting the HCWs with childcare and family health benefits supports them during the crucial transition period of balancing work and supporting their families. Training the staff in effective time management, like prioritization and setting personal and professional boundaries, increases productivity, and fostering a culture of social events, meditation sessions, fitness initiatives, and access to wellness apps adds to the self-care and well-being of HCWs.

Tools and Resources for Organisations

The earliest digitalization included Electronic Health Records (EHRs) to help with concise and integrated patient information, data, and Personal Digital Assistants (PDAs) for assisting nurses and physicians with referencing drug information and clinical guidelines, which helped reduce errors. These tools have been improving, expanding, and becoming more sophisticated with multiple integrated advances like clinical decision support systems (CDSS) helping with important alerts for various crucial drug interactions, allergies, and abnormal lab values, increasing patient safety. EHR has been particularly advantageous in multi-specialized patient care to coordinate between providers, enhancing prompt care. Additionally, patient portals have empowered them to actively engage in patient care by retrieving online information of conditions, including lab results, medications, and patient summaries for record keeping. This has helped providers communicating with patients reach out about their concerns, fostering personalized patient care and improved physician-patient relationships. Autonomous Mobile Robots (AMRs) are helping providers in the hospitals with simplifying routine tasks and limiting human load. These robots help with cleaning, disinfection, etc., which frees up providers to have more time for other valuable duties. One of the main EHR concerns of these days is enhancing patient privacy and data protection. Over time, the introduction of telemedicine and remote patient consults helped bridge the gaps to cater to rural and underserved populations, helping relieve the burden on providers.

Role of Administrative Structure

Quality healthcare depends on systemic efficiency. A complex and inefficient administrative structure leads to poor and inadequate utilization of resources. A few of the components of effective healthcare infrastructure are access to care, equity for dispensing services, and equity for human resources, which in turn depend on administrative structure. Bureaucratic tasks like insurance, billing, claims processing, healthcare product design, sales, marketing, regulation, and accreditation of initiatives and maintenance of government and nongovernment resources cost money and time for patients and healthcare professionals. This complexity especially affects low-income people in accessing services and adds extra time and cost barriers. Low-income people with limited health literacy or social support face difficulty navigating insurance rules and accessing online services. In such cases, health navigators help with insurance and overall health services. Additionally, administrative work grows tedious when 'multiple players' contribute differently and have different payment modes; creating 'fragmented nodes' with complex compliance requirements leads to a waste of resources.

A few core components of health system functioning are governance, financing, inputs, and delivery of services. Currently, different healthcare systems are struggling with low public funding, irregularly distributed workers with issues with supply chain management, and misaligned objectives of federal and state resources. This creates duplicity in functioning across programs known as 'cross-programmatic inefficiencies.' Cross-Programmatic Efficiency Analysis (CPEA) is used by the WHO to assess different health programs like HIV, TB, malaria, and MCH. It analyzes the entire chain of resources as a unit and recommends reforms for efficiency and progress of Universal Health Coverage (UHC). Low-income healthcare systems need to prioritize limited resources. External funding flow motivates and amplifies the duplications within health programs, especially with their off-budget donors with off-cycle funding (Sparkes et al., 2024). These administrative inefficiencies lead to resource drain, and it's vital to fix them for provider well-being.

Managerial, Cultural, and Governance Structure

Healthcare is a High-Reliability Organization (HRO), a high-risk industry expected to have low rates of error despite hazardous work conditions. To ensure low errors, a culture of safety, resilience, learning, and adapting to new changes; cultural and behavioral shifts; prioritizing psychological safety; and ensuring continuous improvement are important. Learning from other HROs, implementing roles of debriefing, resource management, incident reporting, and propelling cultural changes helps reduce avoidable failures, reducing stress and burden on providers.

Improving governance starts with identifying high-waste workflows like rework loops, wait states, after-hour tasks, multistep documentation, and inefficient handoffs. Fixing them by employing SIPOC (Suppliers, Inputs, Process, Outputs, Customers) and failure-mode analysis that highlight systemic mismatches and role and decision conflicts. The structure of governance should be explicitly defined to increase accountability. The COO's role is to design the process and identify operational waste, the CMO maintains and improves clinical workflow structure and quality, the medical director is responsible for daily accountability for team management, and the chief digital officer ensures technological alignment with workflow. Having responsible governance establishes clear accountability and lessens ambiguity of roles and decisions.

Sustaining improvement comes from Learning Health Systems (LHS). It uses data, experience, and feedback from daily tasks to inform administrators and researchers to reduce repeated inefficiencies, which improves provider workload, reduces errors, and makes the system resilient. This can aid in rebuilding organizational trust, shared ownership, and accountability. Post the COVID-19 pandemic, some shifts in the framework were implemented. Certain reforms that helped implement staff well-being were 'Strategic Change Interventions,' which aligned system values with work values; appointing a chief wellness officer for stress management strategies; designing a wellness program; ensuring compassionate leadership; dedicating resources and funding for staff support; hiring adequate mental health professionals for staff mental health needs; scheduling flexibility for HCWs; implementing "Hear me" for staff to voice their stressors; and providing flexibility for administrative meetings to be hybrid or virtual. A cultural shift enables reducing stigma to voice out burnout and stressors and having peer support groups as buffers (Busis et al., 2025). Each of these interventions has significantly improved cultural shifts and staff well-being.

For Hospital Executives, Quality Improvement Leads, and Departmental Directors

Policy changes and initiatives, when inspired and implemented from existing effective high-performing systems, can be a guide for hospital executives, quality improvement leads, or departmental directors. To achieve an equitable healthcare infrastructure similar to that of high-performing countries, leaders should prioritize universal health coverage, eliminate cost barriers to ensure care accessibility, establish high-value services as primary care needs for all communities, and reduce discrimination. Time and effort are limited human resources, and addressing the administrative burdens of clinicians and patients encourages access to care. Healthcare demands are well distributed if social services investments are in place, which will improve nutrition, education, child care, workers' benefits, community safety, housing, and transport. Simplifying healthcare insurance and payment systems through standardization and regulations has shown improvement in countries like Norway, where copayments are standardized for all public sector clinicians. Smarter spending shows more promising changes than spending more. An essential minimum benefits package for all residents of the Netherlands, along with special services for sicker people to tackle discrimination and limits on cost sharing to control out-of-pocket expenses, has been quite effective (Mirror, 2021). Trying out policies that high-performing countries implement can address existing administrative ineffectiveness.

Investing in a culture of following standards, checklists, and effective routines makes processes uniform for patients, healthcare workers, and policymakers. Measuring clinicians' time to document per patient, data on adverse event rate per 1000 admissions after a redesign, and workforce resilience data with intent to leave, vacancy rate becomes a proxy of effectiveness. A simple time from a decision to action for basic imaging orders until completion would highlight bottlenecks that can be replicated in various other services. Checking incident reports related to workflow and measuring the outcomes after a reform helps track and improve solutions.

ORGANISATIONAL FACTORS IMPACTING HEALTHCARE PROVIDER WELL-BEING AND DATA-DRIVEN INSIGHTS

This chapter focuses on existing healthcare organizational cultures across varied settings, their infrastructural differences, and the need to support HCWs through their challenges. Multiple factors contribute to unhealthy healthcare workplace cultures and their overall impact on more vulnerable providers like Primary Care Providers (PCPs) and those who are Underrepresented in Medicine (UiM). It highlights the importance of collecting data and conducting analysis from well-being surveys, which play a pivotal role in changing resource allocation, systems, and workplace culture, as well as in implementing organizational changes to reform equity, address pay gaps, and reduce gender inequality. Proper resource allocation for wellness programs, mental health services, stress management workshops, retreats, and support groups further strengthens workforce resilience and creates a safe space for addressing occupational stress. This chapter highlights methods for aligning healthcare management with both operational efficiency and a compassionate, sustainable work culture.

The numbers involved drive policy and reforms in any workplace culture. Data analysis hints deeper into any organization to monitor and assess the existing workload, identify the gaps, and direct the redistribution of resources for optimal management. Because most systems have limited financial and systemic resources, data-driven practices help with meaningfully allocating budgets and prioritizing tasks with maximal outcomes. Data- and survey-driven insight into staffing ratios and their direct impact on their job satisfaction and well-being helps address the gaps and improve their workplace standards. These data-driven insights help identify what the patients need and where providers and stakeholders can fill in the gaps for overall improvement in delivering healthcare. To support the well-being of HCWs, data has played a pivotal role in changing systems, workplace culture, and general attitude. The way clinical and patient care is backed and practiced by evidence-based guidelines that help standardize the treatment, data analysis, and HCW surveys helps with evidence-based strategies for targeted interventions to support and deploy tools for providers' well-being.

For further clarity of the role of organizational factors and data insights on provider well-being, this section will explain data collection tools, well-being questionnaires, staffing ratio and its impact, and trends in resignation and quitting.

HCWs Data Collection Tools

The well-being of HCWs has been a concern nowadays. Additional changes or cultural shifts in the operational system, or mental health support for providers, were an outcome of data-backed changes. Wellbeing surveys, engagement surveys, teamwork readiness surveys, workforce analytics, feedback forms, clinical audits, and cross-sectional surveys are some of the ways to assemble data to get an insight into the reality of healthcare challenges and can be implemented for reliable changes. Some other wellness instruments that are relevant in clinical settings include the Lifestyle Assessment Questionnaire (LAQ), which is a questionnaire with a hundred items that focus on 10 wellness areas. The Optimal Living Profile (OLP) and the Five Factor Wellness Inventory (FFWEL) also assess perceived safety and perceived wellness, among others (Bart et al., 2018).

Mayo Clinic Screening Tool

Regular wellness screening tools like the Mayo Clinic screening employed a vast and anonymized data of HCWs to track burnout and depression, which helped organizations to actively identify vulnerable sections to intervene. The Well-Being Index, which was invented by the Mayo Clinic and is now used by thousands of healthcare organizations every day, helps with data-backed action plans. The reports generated from such data helped with assessing the trends, which pushed leadership to allocate resources and systemic and cultural changes. Multiple variables can be assessed that suggest HCWs' well-being, like job satisfaction, work-life balance, and workplace supportiveness.

CDC Developed NIOSH Workers Well-Being Questionnaires (NIOSH WellBQ)

These are questionnaires that are self-reported, providing insights into job satisfaction, stressfulness, resourcefulness, circumstances outside work, and perceived support at work. It measures workers' well-being not just at the place of work but with a holistic approach. Key aspects that are included are wage satisfaction, benefits satisfaction, supervisor support, coworker support, job security, and work-related positive and negative effects. Workplace policies and culture, schedule flexibility, work- and non-work-related conflicts, safety, discrimination, physical violence, bullying, amount of physical activity, mental stress, hours of sleep, and cognitive functioning. This particular system was based on numerous well-being scales from the past, which helped with the Pilot NIOSH WellBQ. These include the European Working Conditions Survey, Job Satisfaction Survey, Health and Work Performance Questionnaire, and Copenhagen Psychosocial Questionnaire–COPSOQ II. Because of its comprehensive nature, it has been used for policy and program design, evaluating shortcomings and gaps, and implementing data-backed changes. A recent study employed this tool to examine the disparities in well-being between clinicians in urban and rural areas. In 2022, 222 clinicians from one urban and three rural hospitals in North Carolina took part. The results showed that there is an urgent need for specific interventions that are appropriate for each setting. This tool highlighted issues such as higher job stress, lack of diversity, and workplace violence. Such studies help with effectively planning support strategies and policies for clinician well-being (Lee et al., 2025).

Another Canadian healthcare tool is the Caring for Healthcare Workers, which is an assessment tool that is evaluated by the Psychosocial Survey for Healthcare (PSH) and the Organizational Review for Healthcare (ORH). These two identify the psychological health and safety of the staff and help with identifying areas of improvement.

Staffing Ratio and its Impact

Appropriate staffing ratios are vital for the well-being of existing staff to distribute the work evenly and have a balanced schedule. It is crucial to regularly assess staff inadequacy and take appropriate action to meet the standard patient-to-physician and patient-to-nurse ratios. Plenty of studies and reviewers have drawn conclusions like when nursing care is rationed, the patient safety is also compromised and there is a higher incidence of falls, medication errors, pressure ulcers, infections, and readmissions. Higher nurse-to-patient ratios have been seen to directly reduce rates of readmission, and shorter stays improve overall quality of patient care, which in turn helps with staff job satisfaction and adequate work-life balance. Generally, hospitals adhere to the preset nurse-to-patient ratios like 1:4 or 1:5 on medical-surgical floors and 1:1 or 1:2 in intensive care units, 1:3 for emergency rooms, 1:4 for rehabilitation, 1:2 for labor and delivery and 1:3 for pediatrics. Lack of flexibility over scheduling has been seen to increase burnout, with standard shifts being 8, 10, or 12 hours, which makes staff locked into set times and days, offering limited room for work-life balance or addressing their personal emergent needs. Several models have shown promising nurse staffing, like adopting more flexible nurse shift patterns and schedules, which aren't traditional 8- or 12 hours of shifts and swapping them online gives some flexibility. It improves control of their time and boosts workplace engagement and retention. Another less physically taxing option is virtual or telehealth, where monitoring nurses have a vital role. Increased usage of mobile acuity assessment tools and wearables will help real-time visibility of patient needs to assign a better-fit nurse for the case.

As for doctor-to-patient ratios, Cuba has the highest, at around 9 doctors per 1,000 people in 2021, while Austria has 5.4 in 2024. The likelihood of making a medical error is 50% higher in doctors with high levels of burnout. Data from GPs in England suggested that 35% of GPs were intending to quit direct patient care in coming years. A similar survey from Scotland indicated that due to unmanaged stress and workload, 26% of GPs said they are unlikely to be working in general practice in coming times. Telehealth has a vital role in reducing some GPs' burden. In a survey by the Health Foundation analysis of the Commonwealth 2022, GPs from the UK make more remote consultations than other countries surveyed. In an average week, they reported that 40 percent of patient consults were in person, 55 percent by telephone, and 5 percent by video. GPs in Switzerland make up 88 percent of consultations in person, and in the US, 86 percent are conducted in person. There is a current trend of professionals pivoting, quitting, or HCWs going on strikes, and one study suggests the reasons are mostly staffing issues, not feeling valued at work, distress and overwork, supervisory burden, bullying, or issues with pay or pension.

Trend in Resignation and Quitting

According to the American Nurses Association, nurses are quitting due to increasingly unsustainable working conditions, which were amplified by COVID-19 responsibilities. A nationwide study at the time showed that 55% of healthcare workers feel burned out. About 18% of the newly licensed nurses quit during their first year. Younger nurses especially find it challenging, and in a survey, only 19% of nurses under 35 feel their organization cares about their well-being. Another major reason for quitting among nurses is that 89% of nurses feel that their organization is understaffed. In several Organisation for Economic Co-operation and Development (OECD) countries, nearly 20% of nurses were considering quitting as per 2021 surveys. This can be improved by recognizing and being valued by leadership, celebrating diversity and equality, having access to opportunities without disparities, and having an inclusive workplace where everyone feels heard, seen, and valued. According to the OECD, in the United States and the United Kingdom, burnout affects over one-third of the HCWs. Concise data from 10 OECD countries suggested that almost 40% of primary care doctors under age 55 report feeling burnt out, and more than 10% of them intend to stop seeing patients in the near future.

According to a pilot study conducted on 7,000 staff in 28 hospitals in mid-2021 by the National Healthcare Quality and Disparities Report, 34% of the workers experienced symptoms of burnout. One key factor for HCWs' burnout is their age and career demands. It was demonstrated by one study among community psychiatric nurses with bimodal peaks, one in their thirties and another in their fifties. The probable reasons are high expectations and heavy work demands from their supervisors. Because of issues with staff shortages and retention, international professionals are crucial to aid in improving and supporting healthcare organizations. Internationally trained HCWs make up a significant proportion of working professionals. Around 24% of doctors in the OECD countries are foreign-born and 19% foreign-trained, and 16% of nurses were foreign-born and 9% foreign-trained. Among doctors, a 2014 survey showed about 68% of family medicine physicians and 73% of internal medicine doctors would not choose the same specialty due to the burnout they feel. A review concluded that overall burnout in physicians was linked to a 4 times lower job satisfaction. This leads to increased regret about career choices and a decline in professionalism in the workplace. Among the specialties, emergency medicine physicians have the highest levels of burnout. A study from the US indicated that a 10 percent decrease in physician workload can reduce the odds of burnout by one-third (Harry et al., 2021).

Some of the data exists from developed nations, and many of the healthcare systems don't have a proper data inventory, especially for healthcare workers' safety and working conditions. One way to enhance healthcare worker safety and working conditions is to increase advocacy for leadership that prioritizes providers' well-being and to share data and resources from international platforms through collaboration. Global sharing of knowledge, experiences, case studies, and best practices can occur through platforms such as the OECD. Since not all countries have a standardized approach to measure HCWs' well-being, international survey tools from other nations can be used to benchmark and allow for international comparisons. For example, the SOPS Workforce Safety Supplement in the US, the NHS staff survey from the UK, the Employee Survey (WNE) from the Netherlands, Your Opinion Counts from Ireland, and the Be.well.pro survey from Belgium.

In conclusion, surveys and data create urgency for precise interventions and systemic changes. Workload, if distributed smartly and analytically, would optimize staff competencies. Ensuring reforms that rely on measuring and routinely monitoring workload, sentiments, communication, training needs, and resource allocation of HCWs and their well-being is crucial.

REFERENCES

American Medical Association. (2024, June 18). *AMA survey indicates prior authorization wreaks havoc on patient care.* https://www.ama-assn.org/press-center/ama-press-releases/ama-survey-indicates-prior-authorization-wreaks-havoc-patient-care (ama-assn.org)

Brown, J. B., Thorpe, C., Bal, S., George, C., Jan, S. H., Mathews, M., Premji, K., Ryan, B. L., & Terry, A. L. (2025). Burden of administrative responsibilities in primary care: Qualitative study. *Canadian Family Physician Médecin de Famille Canadien, 71*(6), e148–e153. DOI: 10.46747/cfp.7106e148 PMID: 40523739

. Busis, N. A., Alexander, C. M., Castner, J., Singer, S., Smith, C. D., Bernstein, C. A., … & the COVID-19 Working Group. (2025, April 7). *A path to improved health care worker well-being: Lessons from the COVID-19 pandemic.* NAM Perspectives. https://doi.org/ (PubMed)DOI: 10.31478/202504a

Holmgren, A. J., Thombley, R., Sinsky, C. A., & Adler-Milstein, J. (2023). Changes in physician electronic health record use with the expansion of telemedicine. *JAMA Internal Medicine, 183*(12), 1357–1365. DOI: 10.1001/jamainternmed.2023.5738 PMID: 37902737

Kamel Boulos, M. N., & Geraghty, E. M. (2020). Geographical tracking and mapping of coronavirus disease COVID-19/severe acute respiratory syndrome coronavirus 2 (SARS-CoV-2) epidemic and associated events around the world: How 21st century GIS technologies are supporting the global fight against outbreaks and epidemics. *International Journal of Health Geographics, 19*(1), 8. DOI: 10.1186/s12942-020-00202-8 PMID: 32160889

Kanaparthy, N. S., Holmgren, A. J., Sun, Y., Paek, H., Williams, B., McLean, R., Doolan, R., Goodman, K. E., Rotenstein, L., & Melnick, E. R. (2025). Protected time for electronic health record work and physician productivity. *JAMA Network Open, 8*(12), e2546550. DOI: 10.1001/jamanetworkopen.2025.46550 PMID: 41329489

Mirror. (2021). Mirror 2021: Reflecting Poorly: Health care in the U.S. Compared to Other High-Income Countries. National Library of Medicine. https://collections.nlm.nih.gov/catalog/nlm:nlmuid-9918300978506676-pdf

NetSuite. (2025, February 6). What is automation in healthcare? How does it help? *NetSuite.* https://www.netsuite.com/portal/resource/articles/erp/healthcare-automation.shtml (netsuite.com)

Ng, A. Y., Oberije, C. J. G., Ambrózay, É., Szabó, E., Serfőző, O., Karpati, E., Fox, G., Glocker, B., Morris, E. A., Forrai, G., & Kecskemethy, P. D. (2023). Prospective implementation of AI-assisted screen reading to improve early detection of breast cancer. *Nature Medicine*, *29*(12), 3044–3049. DOI: 10.1038/s41591-023-02625-9 PMID: 37973948

Sahni, N. R., Carrus, B., & Cutler, D. M. (2021, October 20). Administrative simplification: How to save a quarter-trillion dollars in US healthcare. McKinsey & Company. https://www.mckinsey.com/industries/healthcare/our-insights/administrative-simplification-how-to-save-a-quarter-trillion-dollars-in-us-healthcare

Sahni, N. R., Gupta, P., Peterson, M., & Cutler, D. M. (2023). Active steps to reduce administrative spending associated with financial transactions in US health care. *Health Affairs Scholar*, *1*(5), qxad053. Advance online publication. DOI: 10.1093/haschl/qxad053 PMID: 38756977

Sahni, N. R., Gupta, P., Peterson, M., & Cutler, D. M. (2023). Active steps to reduce administrative spending associated with financial transactions in US health care. *Health Affairs Scholar*, *1*(5), qxad053. Advance online publication. DOI: 10.1093/haschl/qxad053 PMID: 38756977

Satheeskumar, R. (2025). AI-driven diagnostics and personalized treatment planning in oral oncology: Innovations and future directions. [sciencedirect.com]. *Oral Oncology Reports*, *13*, 100704. DOI: 10.1016/j.oor.2024.100704

Shrank, W. H., Rogstad, T. L., & Parekh, N. (2019). Waste in the US health care system: Estimated costs and potential for savings. *Journal of the American Medical Association*, *322*(15), 1501–1509. DOI: 10.1001/jama.2019.13978 PMID: 31589283

Southwick, R. (2024, October 17). *Administrative work takes up bulk of week for clinicians, medical office staff: Poll. Chief Healthcare Executive*. https://www.chiefhealthcareexecutive.com/view/administrative-work-takes-up-bulk-of-week-for-clinicians-medical-office-staff-poll (chiefhealthcareexecutive.com)

Sparkes, S. P., Earle, A. J., & Kutzin, J. (2024). Cross-Programmatic Efficiency: The System is Greater Than the Sum of Its Programs. *Health Systems and Reform*, *10*(3), 2427715. Advance online publication. DOI: 10.1080/23288604.2024.2427715 PMID: 39666323

Storseth, O., McNeil, K., Grudniewicz, A., Correia, R. H., Gallant, F., Thelen, R., & Lavergne, M. R. (2025). Administrative burden in primary care: Critical review. *Canadian Family Physician Médecin de Famille Canadien*, *71*(6), 417–423. DOI: 10.46747/cfp.7106417 PMID: 40523738

Thelen, J., Sant Fruchtman, C., Bilal, M., Gabaake, K., Iqbal, S., Keakabetse, T., Kwamie, A., Mokalake, E., Mupara, L. M., Seitio-Kgokgwe, O., Zafar, S., & Cobos Muñoz, D. (2023). Development of the Systems Thinking for Health Actions framework: A literature review and a case study. *BMJ Global Health*, *8*(3), e010191. DOI: 10.1136/bmjgh-2022-010191 PMID: 36931663

Tu, H. N., Shan, T. H., Wu, Y. C., Shen, P. H., Wu, T. Y., Lin, W. L., Yang-Kao, Y. H., & Cheng, C. L. (2023). Reducing Medication Errors by Adopting Automatic Dispensing Cabinets in Critical Care Units. *Journal of Medical Systems*, *47*(1), 52. DOI: 10.1007/s10916-023-01953-0 PMID: 37103718

KEY TERMS AND DEFINITIONS

Clinical decision support systems (CDSS): CDSS helps healthcare professionals in making decisions, offering them a tool for improved medical care practices based on monitoring and management procedures.

Complex Adaptive Systems (CAS): A dynamic system with a large number of interacting elements that are constantly evolving and adapting to changes in the external environment and to internal conditions.

Electronic Health Records (EHRs): EHRs are digital platforms in clinical practice used to collect patients' clinical information related to their health status and represent a useful storage of real-world data.

Healthcare Workers (HCWs): HCW is defined as an individual engaged in activities aimed at enhancing health, such as physicians, nurses, pharmacists, and other professionals.

Internet of Medical Things (IoMT): It includes a collection of medical devices and applications that connect to healthcare information technology systems through online computer networks.

Organisation for Economic Co-operation and Development (OECD): It is a forum and knowledge hub for data, analysis, and best practices in public policy.

Systems Thinking (ST): ST is an integral approach that views a system with a holistic lens, examining how various components within a system are interconnected to each other, how they constantly interact, and how they influence one another in non-linear ways.

The Triple Aim Plus More: In addition to the Triple Aim, this includes a fourth component that emphasizes improving the lives of the providers, especially when it relates to areas of resilience, burnout, and suicide.

The Triple Aim: The triple aim describes an approach to optimize health system performance by focusing on improving patient experience (including the quality of care and patient satisfaction), improving the health of populations, and reducing the per capita cost of health care.

Underrepresented in Medicine (UiM): Association of American Medical Colleges (AAMC) defines UiM as racial and ethnic populations that are underrepresented in the medical profession relative to their numbers in the general population.

Chapter 6
Optimizing Organizational Efficiency: A Systems Based Approach to Healthcare Management

Muhammad Younus Ijaz
http://orcid.org/0000-0003-2104-112X
New Mowasat Hospital, Kuwait

ABSTRACT

In today's rapidly evolving healthcare landscape—marked by advancing healthcare technologies, increasing operational and regulatory demands, an overburdened workforce, high patient volumes, growing disease complexity, and rising patient expectations—organizations face mounting pressure to deliver high-quality care efficiently. A systems-based approach focuses on integrating the various components of healthcare delivery, including processes, technology, and human resources, to create a cohesive environment that promotes continuous improvement and patient-centered care. This chapter addresses these challenges by exploring how healthcare leaders and managers can apply the principles of systems thinking to diagnose inefficiencies and build adaptive, high-functioning organizations.

INTRODUCTION

Over the past 2 decades, many healthcare professionals have been transitioning to leadership or administrative roles. While my journey into this space was more incidental, there is a growing trend among clinicians and other allied healthcare professionals to pursue dual careers. This shift is mainly driven by the increasing complexity of healthcare systems, rising workforce burnout rates, fear of litigation

DOI: 10.4018/979-8-2600-0582-8.ch006

and recognition that leadership roles benefit from clinical insights (Parent & Parent, 2011). However, despite this shift, not all physicians transitioning to administrative positions have received formal or adequate training in managing healthcare systems. Additionally, the intensive short courses and diplomas often fall short in preparing professionals to navigate and influence such a complex and dynamic environment. Learning remains largely through lived experiences and a process of trial and error.

In conversation with clinical colleagues, I have noticed that even highly experienced professionals both practicing and non-practicing have limited understanding of how healthcare operates as a complex system. Understandably, their focus remains on direct clinical care i.e., at the patient level (Microsystem), which leaves them with little opportunities to engage with broader organizational and interconnected structures.

This chapter addresses challenges by exploring how healthcare leaders and managers can apply principles of systems thinking in diagnosing inefficiencies and in building adaptive, high-functioning organizations.

The Brewing Storm - "Why Now":

Is healthcare again late to the show as compared to other industries? The answer is No! In 1999, Institute of medicine (IOM) published, *"To err is human"* a landmark report catalyzing a movement towards patient safety, emphasizing the need to review the healthcare system as a whole (Institute of Medicine, 2000). Due to the dynamic nature of the healthcare industry, the progress even 25 years later has been gradual and is influenced by multiple factors.

Healthcare systems worldwide are experiencing unprecedented levels of burnout. This is no longer just an individual issue but more of a system failure. The increased migration of healthcare professionals in search of better opportunities has created an imbalance, especially in Low- and middle-income countries (LMICs). The consequences extend beyond the loss of experienced professionals and also affect newly graduated healthcare workers who often enter already strained systems. The ripple effect of such large-scale migrations not only affects healthcare systems but also impedes research and advancements in healthcare. Without an appreciation of how these systems influence one another, improvement efforts risk being fragmented, short-lived, or misaligned with the broader goals of the organization. To steer this complexity efficiently, a system-based approach is essential.

Systems Approach:

The origin of systems theory dates to the early 20th century, when Austrian biologist Ludwig von Bertalanffy challenged the reductionist approach that systems could be fully understood by analyzing their individual components in isolation. Instead, he argued that a system must be viewed as a whole, where the behavior and outcomes arise from the complex interactions and interdependencies among its parts (von Bertalanffy, 1968). His *General Systems Theory* laid the foundation for a holistic approach to understanding biological, organizational, and social systems. Deming, in his book *"The System of Profound Knowledge"*, defined system as a *"network of interdependent components that work together to accomplish some aim" (Deming, 1986).*

In healthcare, systems theory forms the foundation of modern quality and safety framework, such as SEIPS (Systems Engineering Initiative for Patient Safety) (see figure 1) These frameworks connect organizational inputs, processes, and outcomes to improve care reliability and resilience (Holden et al., 2013). The SEIPS framework is familiar to the healthcare audience as it resembles Donabedian's (1988) structure-process-outcome model of healthcare quality.

Figure 1. SEIPS 2.0 model explains how system inputs (people, technology, environment, tasks, organization) interact through processes (workflows, teamwork, communication) to produce outcomes (Patient outcomes, provider well-being, and system performance). The model also focuses on feedback loops and adaptability across the system.

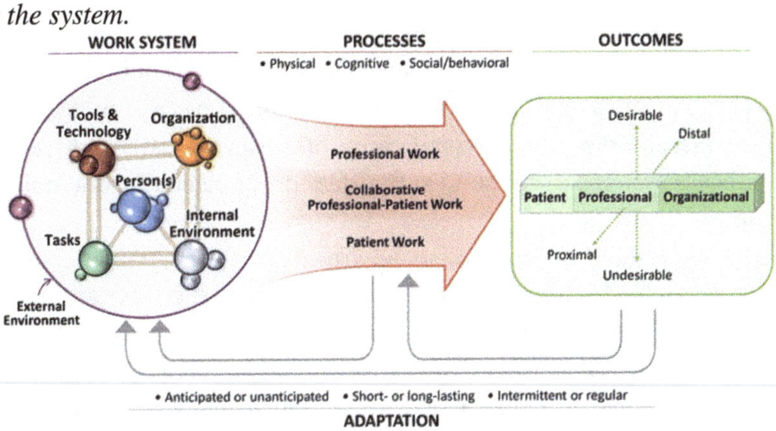

In today's rapidly evolving landscape, marked by complex healthcare technology, increasing operational and regulatory demands, an overburdened workforce, high patient volumes, disease complexity, and rising patient expectation, organizations face mounting pressure to deliver high-quality care efficiently. A systems-based approach focuses on integrating various components of healthcare delivery, including processes, technology, and human resources, to create a cohesive environment that promotes continuous improvement and patient-centered care.

Consider the analogy of Healthcare as a Car engine or a Car - Every part/player matters.

1. *The Car* (healthcare system) = Consider a vehicle like a healthcare system designed to move patients and the population forward. But it only functions when all parts (subsystems - or micro, meso and macrosystems) such as gears, brakes, dynamo and cooling fans work together just as in systems theory (Anderson, 2016)
2. *The Gears* (Subsystems / Departments) e.g. Emergency unit, Operating theater, Pharmacy and others. Each department has a different scope and function. Some gears would increase or control the torque of car; however, all are essential for the car's movement towards a common goal of the system. In healthcare different departments and specialties work together to achieve a common goal of providing safe , efficient and effective patient care. Any lapses, e.g. communication during handoffs may lead to patient harm
3. *The Driver* (Clinicians, Admins, Leadership), to be able to reach its destination that is, achieve goal of safer patient outcomes the driver needs to understand the system effectively. Even driving a luxury car with poor driving skills may result in a crash.

Just like in a car, every gear in healthcare – every department, every team must align and work smoothly together. Systems theory reminds us of that improvement of any kind cannot be achieved in isolation, it requires coordination, feedback and adaptability. Despite the growing availability of advanced tools and technology, many healthcare systems continue to suffer due to fragmentation and duplication of processes.

While we understand systems holistically from a healthcare staff perspective, it is crucial to also include how patients perceive and experience care at the center of these systems. For patients, healthcare is not merely a series of clinical events; it is more about the journey. A journey that begins with researching about the symptoms of a disease, navigating to choose a provider to transparency and communication, equity, trust and affordability.

Incorporating these patient-centered perspectives into systems thinking results in a more humane and effective healthcare delivery. As Dr. Donald Berwick stated in his call for "Patient centeredness," "*Quality care is not only about doing things right but also doing the right thing*s" (Berwick, 2009)

Levels Of Systems

To understand the dynamics of any system, it is vital to introduce some foundational concepts on which healthcare or any organization operates. These include levels such as (see figure 2):

1) Microsystems
2) Mesosystems and
3) Macrosystems.

At the center of all these levels outlined above is the patient, i.e. the focus of all the systems. Without this system-level understanding, well-intentioned improvement efforts risk being fragmented or unsustainable, even if the leaders are well-equipped to bring about changes.

Let us dive deeper to understand more about these fancy terminologies.

Microsystems are established *"As soon as a patient is in a relationship with a health care provider, and information about the patient and the patient's health needs is exchanged with the provider" (Nelson et al., 2011).* An example of the microsystem can be a patient's visit to a physician care provider, and care is delivered through direct interaction. On a broader scale, the operating theater is also an example where again the patient is at the center of the clinical microsystem (surgeons, technicians, scrub and circulating nurses) working together towards a shared aim.

Mesosystem: Multiple microsystems working together collaboratively to provide care to the population form a mesosystem. A patient's transition of care from the operating theater to the recovery room and finally back to the ward is a perfect example of the Mesosystem. Coordination and communication handoffs play a key role at this level.

Macrosystem: Macrosystems are broader structures and may include either the entire organizational i.e. Hospital level, or network of hospitals, or a regional healthcare system structure. Integrated healthcare delivery systems that combine to deliver care. The macrosystems provide governance, resources, and infrastructure across sub system (Nelson et al., 2011).

Healthcare cannot function as a collection of these layers working in isolation. All 3 layers (Micro, Meso, and Macro) systems must be interconnected; the challenge lies in integrating these layers to achieve smooth, continuous patient care and operational efficiency. A microsystem e.g. Surgical ward maybe highly efficient, but without coordination with the meso level (Pharmacy, Laboratory, Radiology) or macro level (Policy, Governance) the patient outcomes will be affected.

Without the interconnection between meso- and macro- systems, microsystems can still produce fair quality of work. However, within that work, various barriers may exist, e.g., fragmented information (such as lack of complete information on discharge summary), redundancy (for instance, same medication or lab test ordered by different physicians), resulting in a prolonged length of stay.

Aligned systems create better integration by establishing communication channels that allow for the voices (feedback) from the bottom level to reach the decision makers/organizational leaders. A key lesson that I learned from a course director (Dr. Anjala Tess at Harvard Medical School) was: *"Continue to include others' perspective to make your work stronger, especially those who are typically not allowed to be at the table with you". The insights from people who work behind scenes are often rich, offering unique experiences and viewpoints that others may not see or hear.*

Systems coordination should allow horizontal and vertical flow of information. e.g. The information flow of data, risk signals should flow from the bottom up, whereas decisions (priorities, resource allocations) should flow downwards. Dashboards should be shared at all levels with layered view for both operational and clinical teams.

Figure 2. Describes layers of a system, with microsystems at the center, connected with other layers of meso and macrosystem.

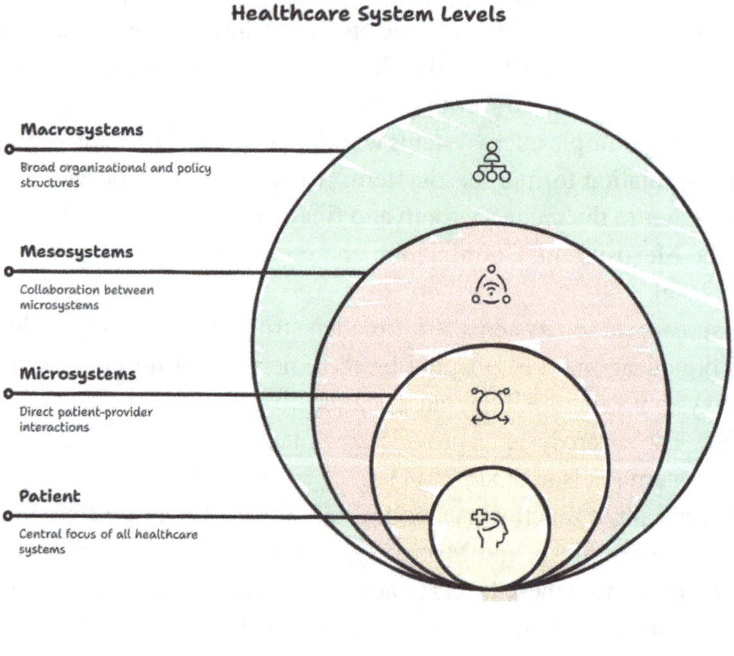

Underutilization Of the Systems Approach:

Compared to other industries, the healthcare industry has lagged in a adopting the systems approach. The understanding that hiring star doctors and nurses or, so to speak, good leadership may not necessarily produce the desired results, the system may function but may not always be efficient and effective.

Healthcare, because of its dynamic nature, has many variables that do not operate in isolation, and unpredictability is the norm. Unlike other industries where the output of, if not all, but most of the decisions can be predicted, even if results don't meet expectations, this may not always result in permanent harm or loss of life. While many variables require discussion, a few vital ones are listed below

1. *Patients and Families – The Core of the Healthcare System:* At the heart of the healthcare organization are the patients. Patients have unique anatomy, physiology, psychology, values, cultures, religious beliefs, age, and genetics. These factors, along with the comorbidities, play a role in shaping their trajectories.

Clinical outcomes of patients are rarely affected by a single factor in the patient's journey. Poor outcomes arise from lapses such as ineffective communication handoffs between teams, gaps and delays in care coordination, lack of automation in information systems, lack of resources and many other factors. Integrating digital health solutions and interoperable Electronic health records(EHRs), clinical decision supports systems (CDSS) can facilitate real time access to patient data, reducing the communication barriers, ultimately improving patient outcomes and operational efficiency. The rapid adoption of telemedicine during the pandemic has emerged as critical enabler for healthcare continuity for some nations (Keesara et al., 2020).

The quote by Edward Deming, "Every system is perfectly designed to produce the results it gets," means that if a patient experiences disrespect, confusion, or is overwhelmed, it is because the system allows that experience, whether intentional or not.

a) *Patient's Journey: A System of Gaps:* Consider a patient's journey from scheduling an appointment to receiving a diagnosis, undergoing treatment, and engaging in multiple follow-ups. At each stage/ level the patient participates with different teams, departments, paperwork and all this is done without a guide. The system could be more complicated and exhaustive if this was either a geriatric or patient with chronic disease. Even for less complex patients, the systems will have flaws in some way or another. This could range from language barriers, accessibility and other factors.

Various tools like process flows (e.g., Swimlane charts) and gap maps can be used to diagnose disconnects within the patient's journey. Unlike traditional audits detailing the gaps identified, these tools visualize the process and highlight the chasm across the system where the friction exists, care outcomes deteriorate, cost may rise as result of wastage and empathy erodes.

Let's take an example of a project (see Figure 3 – PDSA Cycle) to reduce 30-day readmission for patients with "X" condition by mapping the discharge to follow-up continuum (establishing scope & aim).

- Step One(Plan Phase): Identify the problem and define what we are trying to acheive. Make the aim SMART e.g., reducing 30days all cause readmission for patients with pneumonia in internal medicine ward by 20% by June 2026.
- Step Two: Assemble a multidisciplinary team of experts including patients, IT (Data requirements), case managers, nursing team, Pharmacist, Clinicians, Improvement or Quality department and a member from Operations team.
- Step Three: go to Gemba (the place where work happens) and understand the process by conducting interviews and direct observations.
- Step Four: Develop the process flow, detailing the touchpoints from admission, inpatient management, discharge planning, actual patient discharge, home transition, and ultimately the follow-ups.
- Step Five: Identify the gaps at all micro, meso, and macro levels by constructing fishbone or driver diagrams.
- Step Six: identify corrective actions and prioritize them on the impact-effort matrix. At all stages, there needs to be continuous discussion between all stakeholders, inviting them to share feedback on the current state and future corrective plans.
- Step Seven (Do Phase): Execute the change cycle and repeat again until aim is achieved.
- Step Eight (Study Phase): Monitor and evaluate results by reviewing the data collected during cycle of changes, compare outcomes with baseline data, identify what worked and what didn't.
- Step Nine(Act Phase): Standardize and sustain successful practice. If change leads to improvement, then adopt and standardize practice by changing policies and workflows. If not, adapt or discontinue.

Figure 3. PDSA – plan do study act cycle for improvement.

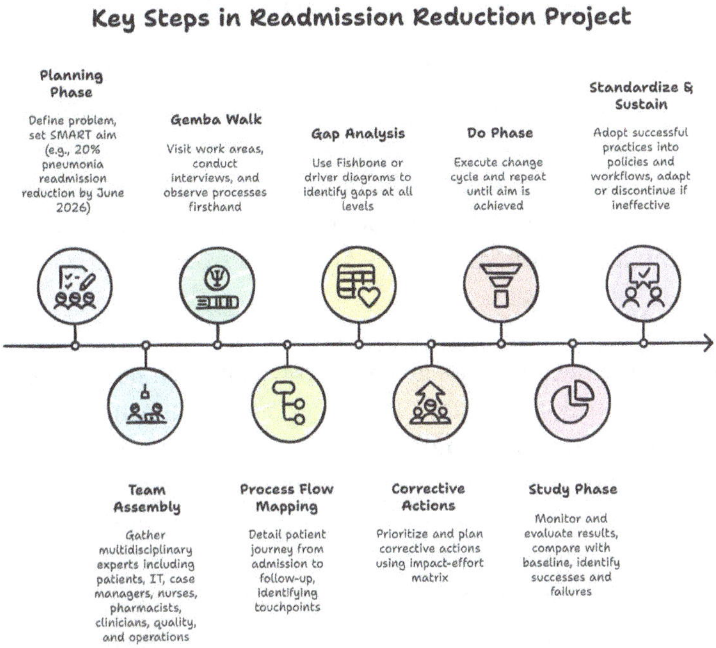

b) *Equity and Accessibility (The Invisible Barriers):* Equity and access refer to the differences in healthcare availability, quality, and outcomes experienced by various population groups. These inequalities are related to social, economic, and demographic factors.

Example: Population with low digital literacy may be locked out of telehealth platforms, designed without their needs in mind. Inhabitants of rural areas may have to drive for long hours to visit a specialist visit.

c) *Empathy and Transparency:* Empathy is about understanding people's emotions and feelings and is crucial for establishing a relationship of trust with patients. Studies have shown that empathy from care providers increases patients' compliance with the treatment plan and improves outcomes. Regrettably, many patients report a lack of empathy by healthcare providers (James A., 2023). Several factors may contribute to this issue, mostly attributed to system-related rather individual factors. These include high workloads, time constraints, staff shortages, performance pressures – all of which may eventually lead to burnout and fatigue (West et al., 2018)

Healthcare systems prioritize efficiency, documentation, and compliance with guidelines, protocols, pathways over human connection.

d) *Co-Creation (Human Centered Approach) to Healthcare:* In recent years, co-creation or Co-design in healthcare has gained prominence, it involves designing the systems and processes with the input of patients, families, and healthcare workers. It is not merely about conducting surveys or obtaining feedback to drive improvements, but creating partnerships with patients and families through a journey of mutual learning. The insights gained from the patient's experience add value to future care.

Instead of a top-down, traditional approach which often misses the distinction of the everyday clinical work and patient experience, a human centered approach invites frontliners, patients and families to work as team with policy makers, process improvement professionals, and managers to improve care pathways. This model fosters equity of voice and a deeper understanding of how care should be delivered. This model Fosters trust due to transparency and open sharing of information, shifting the focus towards continuity of care rather than few episodic encounters.

Some of the tools used to measure these outcomes include Patient reported outcome measures (PROMs) e.g. pain scales and functional status, and Patient reporting experience measures (PREMs) e.g. Clarity of discharge information.

A personal example from my experience comes from our Patient and Family Advisory Committee, where a patient advisory member suggested creating a checklist to help expectant mothers prepare for their hospital stay before delivery. The checklist included items like clothing and essential supplies that would be useful after birth. Simple yet thoughtful suggestions like these enhance the patient's experience and contribute to overall patient satisfaction.

2. *Communication And Handoffs: The "UHU Glue" Of Patient Safety:* To provide safe and good-quality care, effective communication is essential. Poor or missing communication can result in severe harm or even the death of a patient. Several factors can lead to gaps in communication, including (Joint Commission International, 2020)
    a) Poor handovers during care transitions between teams account for 67% of the medical errors (Maria Franco Vega et al., 2024), these handovers can occur between nurses, physicians or other clinical staff. Deficient communication can also arise during care transition between care units or as a result of inadequate discharge planning: For instance, Unclear instructions or use of complex clinical terminologies at the point of discharge can confuse patients. Because of these unclear instructions, there is a possibility that

the patient may be readmitted due to an inability to follow post-discharge instructions.

Recognizing these triggers proactively becomes the responsibility of administrative and safety teams, who must identify and mitigate them by implementing tools such as SBAR (Leonard et al., 2004) and I-PASS (Starmer et al., 2014), which encourage structured communication, eventually resulting in safer patient outcomes. A study performed by Starmer et al. 2014 showed a 23% decrease in medical error when compared to the pre-intervention phase; the rate of non-preventable adverse events had also dropped by 30%, upon use of structured communication tools. A caveat to the success of such a program is effective training and engagement of the involved groups (Clinical Staff).

b) Language Barriers: Due to the global migration of healthcare workers around the world, it has become vital to ensure that the staff members are well trained to speak and understand the local language and culture. Additionally, access to a list of interpreters within the hospital is crucial to ensure effective conversations not only within the outpatient clinic and inpatient wards but also inside the operating room (OR).

The example of a wrong procedure - Carpal tunnel release instead of a finger trigger release is a perfect example of how things can go wrong in even a closed system. In this case only the surgeon and the patient spoke Spanish, while the rest of the OR staff spoke English. The consent could not be interpreted by the OR team, who were not involved in the informed consent process. The time-out process was not performed as the circulating nurse misunderstood a conversation between patient and the operating physician in Spanish as a time-out. All of these factors combined to lead to an adverse patient event (Ring et al., 2010).

c) Cultural Barriers: Understanding and openly discussing the cultural barriers is critical to ensuring effective and efficient care. These Cultural barriers are not limited to those between patient and clinician but can exist among the clinical team members as well. Cultural barriers may include religious beliefs e.g. blood transfusions, organ donation, reproductive services or Gender roles and sensitivities such as being treated by a clinician or nurse of opposite gender.

3. *Working in Silos:* From my work in the Department of Quality systems, time and again, I have witnessed departments working in complete silos, with the sole aim of achieving their established goals, often with little or no communication and coordination with other departments. Each siloed system/group uses their own data without sharing information with other

units or even attempting to align efforts with others. This is quite like the metaphor "the right hand does not know what the left hand is doing"

Frequently occurring problems include cases where a patient might be visiting multiple physicians at a time, each of them focusing on their own speciality, often without having a multidisciplinary care plan/approach. These Silos can also exist in other areas, for instance pharmacist not involved in the discharge process of the patient.

4. *Resource Availability:* Healthcare is resource intensive. The survival of any establishment depends upon the constant supply of trained personnel, medical equipment and devices, and other consumables. The global shortage of healthcare workers, worsened by burnout, continues to strain the systems.

Material shortages, especially noticed during the COVID-19 pandemic, have set an example for the entire healthcare field of how paralyzed a system can become because of a shortage of supplies.

5. *Efficient Utilization: Doing More with Less:* This should not mean compromising care but doing better with smarter systems. However, more often than not, when not carefully planned, such initiatives often result in "doing the same with less," which may not be sustainable. Most of these initiatives are driven because of financial pressures or policy changes and have impacts on both patients (decline in quality of care) and healthcare workers, e.g. Staff burnout etc.
6. *External Influence on the Healthcare System:* in addition to the reasons stated above, many external forces influence healthcare outcomes and dictate how the care is delivered. Some of these include
   a) *Demographic Shifts:* The economic implication of population aging in developed and developing countries is redesigning service demand (World Health Organization, 2015). Chronic conditions such as diabetes, cardiovascular conditions, arthritis, and cognitive impairments are most common in the geriatric population. This trend highlights the growing need for:
      - Geriatric expertise
      - Long-term facilities (including palliative and end-of-life care).

Fertility rates are also on decline, leading to an imbalance of ratio between the younger working class and the aging population.

Healthcare systems will require greater investments in response to the population's needs. This includes expanded insurance coverage, workforce planning, constructing more facilities to cater to the population's needs, and staying aligned with technological advancements.

b) *Policy and Regulatory Shifts:*

These serve as the structural environment for healthcare delivery systems and define who receives care, how it is paid for, and the standards by which care is delivered, especially in low- and middle-income countries (LMICs). The forces behind these policy changes stem from political pressures, global health trends, or the latest scientific research and evidence. The key question is how these policymakers and system designers (change agents) position themselves in creating opportunities towards application of the systems approach from conceptualization to actual implementation.

In recent years, there has been an increasing shift from the fee-for-service model towards a value-based care model (Survey Results AHIP – Americas health insurance plans, 2024). Rather than paying providers based on volume (number of visits, surgeries performed, or tests done), healthcare systems are transitioning towards outcome-based care focusing on improved population health, reduced readmission, and chronic disease management.

Such policy changes and regulatory requirements require healthcare organizations to adapt at multiple levels by restructuring workflows and data systems, increasing collaboration, and introducing controls over expenditures. These changes reflect the classic systems approach, where a change in one component (policy) necessitates corresponding adjustments across the interconnected components of the system.

Policy changes have far broader implications beyond the clinical settings. Shifts in funding priorities can reshape research, innovation, and public health initiatives. At the patient level, variations in insurance coverage influence access to essential care. Many patients may even defer or forgo treatment due to financial barriers or inadequate insurance coverage. For instance, recent policy changes in the United States, have impacted research funding for institutions such as Centers for Disease Control and Prevention (CDC) . These changes risk not only slowing innovation in healthcare and technology but also placing a greater burden on the public, who will ultimately bear the consequences.

Healthcare insurance policies can play a major role in improving the disease burden on the population or intensifying it. For example, while exploring insurance coverage options for my parents, aged 65 and 67, I found that well-known providers declined coverage for those above 60 years of age. The few that did offer policies quoted premiums far beyond what most people can afford. This raises a fundamental question: who is responsible for identifying and bridging these systemic gaps in access and equity? Addressing such disparities requires not only regulatory reforms but also a system-oriented mindset that links policy, design, financial sustainability, and population health outcomes.

Challenges differ in high-income countries vs. low and middle-income countries (LMICs). In LMICs, governments choose to either implement incremental changes or choose major reforms across different components of health systems. Whatever the methodology adopted, systems thinking professionals need to translate the philosophy of systems approach towards a more practical implementation, such as having long-term strategic plans (3-5 years) for example, immunization plans and their uptake, financial projections of resources and funding gaps (Malik, 2015).

7. *Lack Of Standardization and Barriers To Personalization:*

Standardization streamlines the processes and reduces variation within complex systems. Personalization introduces flexibility to respond to individual needs, which is one of the main characteristics of an adaptive system.

When healthcare systems operate in silos, rely on inflexible protocols, or aim at excessive standardization, they lose the malleability required to manage complex processes, which can lead to fragmented care, poor clinical judgment, and adverse patient outcomes.

8. *Leadership In Navigating Complexities:* leadership is not just about having authority, but also about how leaders understand and influence various sub-systems across the organization. Effective Leadership is grounded in transparency of communication and collaborative approach, which directly enhances the organizational efficiency (see Figure 4). Leaders who advocate for open communication channels, facilitate psychological safety and encourage inter-professional collaboration that set an environment for where problems surface early and improvement actions can be implemented/accelerated.

Transformational and servant leadership styles have shown to strengthen teamwork, reduce medical errors, and improve staff engagement, all of which increase operational efficiency (West et al., 2018; Cummings et al., 2018). In a systems framework, communication acts as the connective tissue of efficiency, linking people, processes, and technology for reliable performance

Figure 4. Achieving organization excellence

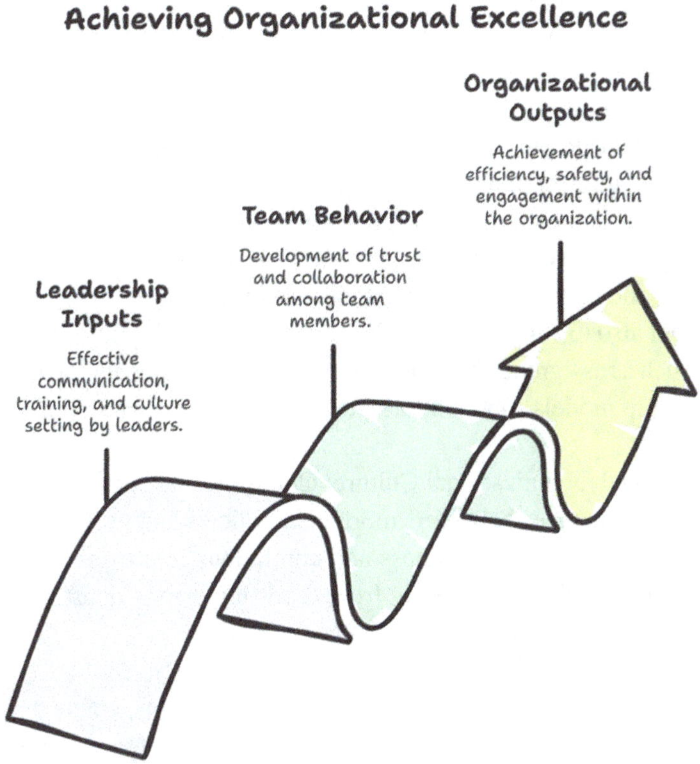

Despite growing recognition of a leader's importance, several barriers hinder the effectiveness of leadership and the promotion of a learning culture. These include

a. Fragmentation of leadership itself when operating in a siloed environment. Many leaders focus on short-term outcomes (budgets or targets) or metrics such as organizational scorecards. Failing to focus on the noise behind these sheets can reveal a bigger picture of departments and processes which do not work in a collaborative manner (Schein, 2010)

This begs the question: Are leaders trained to focus on subsystems? Leaders are expected to lead but often lack training in systems thinking, which is vital to understanding underlying issues, e.g., if the readmission rates are high, this could be a symptom of a larger problem. If waiting times have increased, what dynamics are at play that are leading to bottlenecks? How often do we see the leaders and C-Suites stepping down from their offices to sit with the teams from patient safety,

Improvement, and other clinical departments to review Root cause analysis (RCA) or driver diagram and PDSA cycles to work towards improvement?

A hierarchical and bureaucratic system in an organization limits decision-making and authority. This centralization delays the response required against fast-paced changing situations. Frontline providers and staff working in real-time operations are often excluded from vital discussions to improve services. Reliance is more towards filtered information received from managers.

Additionally, in a progressive organization, lapses such as lack or absence of staff training and development programs are problematic, as they may delay in identification and nurturing of future leaders. As the goal is not just to empower an individual but also to support growth by sharpening existing knowledge and skills. Strategies such as assigning champions and using change agents and using coaching or preceptorship models can facilitate raising the next generation of leaders.

b. Dysfunctional Organizational Culture: Culture is one of the "hidden operating systems.", influences behaviors more than policies and protocols. A culture of fear, blame discourages openness and continuous improvement. Staff may be discouraged implicitly or openly from reporting errors, questioning the status quo, or proposing new initiatives (Schein, 2010).

Such a culture is toxic to learning in larger organizations, where quick feedback and experimentation are critical. Disrespect between colleagues can further undermine collaborative approaches and hinder problem-solving.

Strategies that can bridge such gaps include establishing platforms where voice of employee can be heard (option of anonymous feedback), tiered daily huddles to maintain shared awareness, promote open dialogue and promote cross disciplinary communication.

c. Lack of psychological safety: The concept of psychological safety is still unfamiliar to many. I experienced this firsthand during a training session with our nursing team. At the end of the session, I opened the floor for questions – but to my surprise, there was complete silence. This felt odd, especially considering most of the staff were relatively young and typically more open to asking questions or speaking up.

Then it struck me: Perhaps my senior position and the fact that I worked in the Quality Department were inadvertently creating a barrier. The staff may have feared being judged, facing repercussions, or inviting negative consequences by speaking honestly. Realizing this, I paused and reassured them, saying, "Please feel free to share any suggestions or questions—this is an open meeting, and your voices truly matter in improving our systems."

That small gesture made a difference; if not all, a few staff members opened up and engaged in a meaningful dialogue. This highlights the importance of creating psychologically safe environments that invite feedback to improve systems.

When a leader steps in to address a situation, the choice of words used to raise questions should be very carefully thought through. E.g. Before assigning blame for any loss, event etc. One should be curious to know how the system failed rather than focusing on an individual.

9. *The role of Data and Measurement:* They say that data is the new "black gold". When properly analyzed and applied, it can influence decision-making, resource allocation, and systemic learning. From a systems theory perspective, data and measurement act as the nervous system of the healthcare organization assisting in converting gaps into actionable knowledge and ultimately resulting in practice change.

Barriers exist to effectively using data within a systems approach. Current data practices often reinforce fragmentation and reduce visibility across various parts of the systems/processes, negatively impacting decision-making. Some key failure modes are stated below

a) Information is often collected, analyzed, and stored in fragments across departments and service lines, due to this limited visibility of system-wide data, decision-making is affected (Senge, 1990). Clinical, operational, and patient experience data may exist isolated in departmental database. Without integrated insight, it isn't easy to translate this data into meaningful information that can guide to make useful decisions and improve outcomes. Example: Feedback surveys and patient complaint data collected by customer relations unit may indicate that patients are dissatisfied with long waiting time and delays in emergency room(ER). The operations team collects data on patient wait times in ER, while the physicians know that the patient's complaint often about the wait time but lack access to s daily or monthly reports reflecting how prolonged waits correlate with decreased census.

If all these 3 departments share information in a centralized manner, the intensity of the problem could be better understood, and corrective actions implemented. The ideal approach is to establish a multidisciplinary team (clinical, operational, customer relations) responsible for the change. This team should share the information in departmental meetings, identify gaps in the care process, implement the change actions and monitoring continuously.

b) Weak or Delayed Feedback loops: Most front-line service providers do not have access to the data produced by their work. In other cases, the data is collected but not interpreted in real time or shared meaningfully with those who can act on it. This lack of timely analysis and actionable feedback is a lost opportunity to improve systems. In most cases, errors or gaps reported through patient feedback remain as errors or inefficiencies in the system and persist unnoticed until the next event or until something significant occurs (Plsek & Greenhalgh, 2001) Automation of data collection process and live visualization of data to the frontliners can result in better understanding of how the process variates depending on the inputs, situations and dynamics.
c) Garbage in, Garbage out: From a systems lens, flawed data leads to misleading feedback, which can cause systemic dysfunction and misdirected improvement efforts.

When data improves system performance, it can also have unintended consequences. Anchoring onto specific metrics (e.g. time to discharge) can promote corner-cutting or neglect of certain unmeasured domains like empathy and communication. This phenomenon is called goal displacement, where measurement becomes the mission.

Maintaining a balance between quantitative and qualitative insights and incorporating patients' perspectives supports a more inclusive understanding of system performance. To move from analysis to sustained improvement, healthcare systems must anchor data utilization using structured framework that translate the insights into actionable tasks. Measurement frameworks such as Key Performance Measures (KPIs), Balance scorecards and Lean Six Sigma visualize data and assist in identifying areas for improvement, track trends over time and not as isolated events but as interdependent processes (Balancing measures).

A strong practice-based example comes from a project that I am currently engaged with the obstetrics and neonatology teams. The project monitors initiation of skin-skin contact post-delivery, time to ambulation post-delivery (for C-section patients) and incidence of nappy rashes in newborns. Each metric reflects a different subsystem but when reviewed together it reflects how these coordinated efforts are working towards improving patient outcomes.

Balance scorecards expand this concept and serve as a dashboard for the high-level management (Management, CEOs, and Board) showcasing progress on the organizational established priorities. Many people refer to Balance scorecards as "Christmas Trees" referring to the display of results or outcomes achieved versus not achieved. Meanwhile, *Lean Six Sigma* provides data-driven methods to identify variation, eliminate waste, and strengthen process reliability. When utilized appropriately, these frameworks reinforce the feedback loops essential to systems thinking.

10. *Staff Burnout:* While the term has gained much attention post COVID -19 pandemic, the progress towards decreasing burnout has been limited. When healthcare workers feel emotionally exhausted, detached from their work or their efforts are no longer meaningful or appreciated, these are the red flags that the system they are a part of is breaking down. This workplace stress leads to high staff turnover, reduced empathy, and medical errors (West et al., 2018).

Staff who are emotionally disengaged often are disconnected from making any improvement efforts, reporting any safety concerns; this undermines learning and adaptive capacity (National Academies of Sciences, Engineering, and Medicine; National Academy of Medicine; Committee on Systems Approaches to Improve Patient Care by Supporting Clinician Well-Being, 2019). Patients can sense this disconnect during rushed appointments. The loss of professional relationships can negatively influence patient clinical outcomes and satisfaction with care.

Contributing factors to burnout often originate within healthcare organizations and systems, including inefficient workflows, excessive administrative duties, work-life conflicts, limited physician autonomy in matters affecting their profession, insufficient organizational support structures, and unsupportive leadership culture (West et al., 2018). When identified,the response is frequently narrow scope, such as arranging yoga sessions recreational activities, which may not treat the root cause but the symptoms.

An organization may choose to implement performance measures to directly or indirectly evaluate if the workforce is experiencing burnout examples include absenteeism rate (sick leaves), high staff turnover rate, lack of engagement and many others. Various surveys like Maslach Burnout Inventor (MBI) or AHRQ patient safety culture survey – particularly its supplemental questions can assist in evaluating workforce fatigue.

System-level interventions that can be adopted to reduce burnout include optimizing workflows and eliminating waste. This can range from automating systems e.g. implementing electronic health records(EHRs), and incorporating the use of artificial intelligence or machine learning.

Workload management and staffing adequacy: Ensuring that staffing levels are adequate and skill mix match the work demands helps limit excessive overtime and role strain.

Team-based interventions; creating teams which have shared goals, promoting psychological safety, such as creating peer support mechanism as simple as psychological support committee. A study conducted in Australian public service (APS) showed strong teamwork and well-being policies significantly reduce the effect of stress on burnout (Saud & Rice, 2024).

Staff recognition, reward systems and career development opportunities: While resilience exists at an individual level, organizations can work on solutions such as peer mentorship program, continuing education opportunities, paid learning leave etc.

Leadership, teamwork and communication are the driving forces for efficient and happy workforce which eventually results in sustained organizational performance.

11. *Digitalization of Healthcare (Use of Information technology):* Digitalization of healthcare ensures a brighter future for healthcare; however, the implementation of these advanced technologies is not usually aligned with the systems thinking approach, in many cases, the interface design is not user friendly focusing more on completing the task than on supporting human factors and workflow efficiency.

The outcome of a poorly designed interface is usually user non-compliance, underutilizing of the full potential of the interface, cognitive overload, delays in workflow, at times even leading to longer wait times for patients (indirectly affecting patient satisfaction).This can also increase risk of error and contribute to staff burnout.

Despite the vast investment and advancement of IT health solutions, Electronic health records (EHRs) often do not communicate effectively across the different institutions or at times within the same hospital. This breaks the continuity of care due to fragmentation of information (difficulty in tracking the patient's journey), resulting in a lack of coordinated decision-making.

Another major challenge is for the patients. As explained earlier in the chapter, patients may face challenges in accessing digital health services, patient portals, and mobile health apps; these are only effective if patients have internet access and digital literacy,, 10% of the population in 65 years age group in the United States does not have internet (Pew Research Center, 2024). While accessibility is still there in the US, the 3rd World countries are lagging.

12. *Barriers To Resilience In Healthcare Systems: Resilience is defined as the process and outcome of successfully adapting to complex or challenging life experiences, especially through mental, emotional and behavioral flexibility and adjustment to external and internal demands (American Psychological Association, 2018).* However, resilience is just not “bouncing back”, it is about foreseeing, absorbing, adapting and evolving under stress. In healthcare, it refers to the ability to maintain safe (workforce sustainability, clinical reliability etc), effective, and patient-centered care when challenged with disruptions, be it a sudden patient surge, workforce shortage, or global pandemic (COVID-19).

> Though the terminology "Resilience" expresses itself in an aspirational tone, it faces the real world with limitations of fragmented systems, unbending hierarchies, lack of funding, and burnout.

The assumption of being prepared: Because the plans (Disaster management), protocols, and policies are well written on paper with a clear line of authority, they often fall during real-world situations. COVID-19 is one example that exposed how disaster management plans can fail in a dynamic situation. The ICUs are overwhelmed, there is a shortage of healthcare workers, burnout, supply shortages, etc (Legido-Quigley et al., 2020). Many hospitals maintain high goals for bed occupancy rates to maximize revenues, which makes sense financially. However, it leaves systems with little to no room to adapt in case epidemics, disasters, and mass casualties cause spikes.

The consequences are immense; the emergency department becomes overflooded with patients to the extent that patients receive care in hallways and corridors, not only compromising infection control practices but also patient privacy and clinical outcomes. Solutions for such events include pre-planning and infrastructure changes, including just-in-time convertible or extendible structures, oxygen, and a ventilation system (Hick et al., 2020).

Many organizations work towards proactively anticipating certain risks, this could be financial risks, structural risks, safety risks, daily operational risk. While the risks assessments are key to preparing, but how the risk analysis is done is the key. Does each risk identified consider the ever-evolving conditions of their surroundings e.g.

- External factors= apart from pandemics and epidemics, factors like Climate change (Tsunamis, Hot weather, drought, political impact (war zones), Supply chain management and Location e.g. distance from a chemical factory), policy changes e.g. insurance coverage for population.
- Internal factors such as structural aging, patient satisfaction, physician aging, cultural diversity, technological needs.

Once the annual risks assessment documentation is performed, the main actionable item is the continuous monitoring of all the prioritized list of risks identified and how effectively the mitigation plan is functioning. It is equally important to know if there are any learnings involved in the process from identification of the risk, to implementing the risk mitigation plan finally learnings if the mitigation plans have failed.

Systems Lens Must Become A Habit:

To truly transform healthcare, adopting systems lens must go beyond intellectual understanding and become an ingrained habit an automatic way of seeing, thinking, and acting among healthcare professionals and leaders. Systems thinking is fundamentally about recognizing complexity and interdependence, anticipating ripple effects rather than treating problems in isolation as is the case in healthcare, care is not intended to be delivered in isolated rooms. It is delivered through webs of relationships, communication / information flow, technologies, trust and beliefs and constraints. When any of these strands of a web breaks, the whole web breaks down and patients feel the tension as delays, confusion, cost or harm. Much of what we label as "Human error" or " Poor performance" at times is predictable output from the system's design.

Across the chapter we have repeatedly mentioned the patient's journey, navigating appointments, receiving education, transitions between care between units, accessibility and affordability of care, dignity and respect. Each touch point in patient experience is an interaction between 3 different layers of system. However, from the patient's perspective this is one continuous lived experience. What healthcare needs is humanization of care and redesigning system with lived experiences of patients with their input as advisory councils or a simple feedback loop. As saying goes "Nothing about us, without us" (Delbanco et al., 2001).

The outcomes produced by the relationship established above is measured through data, the nervous system of modern healthcare. But nerves and sensation are only useful if its connected and interpreted. Fragmented data storage, delays in reporting, lack of expertise in understanding of data may mask the red flags. Building an integrated network of system in healthcare translates to having limited set of meaningful but multi level measures, safety signals, workforce, well-beings, cost and patient reported outcomes and experiences. Feedback must be bidirectional (frontline to board and back).

And so, if data is the nervous system then culture and communication is the glue or the connective tissue of the organization. We have gone through various examples in the literature above, which shows how poor handoffs, language barriers, and siloed operations can lead to avoidable harm. Systems can be strengthened by having a standardized handover process (e.g. I-PASS, ISBAR, CUS). At my workplace, a list of interpreters is uploaded to eliminate language barriers – one of the perks of having a diversified cultural workforce. Additionally, if the staff feel psychologically safe in the work environment, they are more likely to share insights if they notice that something is not aligned with the best practices. Such conversations need to happen more frequently, for example in a recent meeting with the general surgery department, I brought up the time-out process in the OR could use some re-enforcement, since our audits show that not everyone is actively involved. Surprisingly, the feedback was that, the issue is with the anesthetist and not the surgeons. I realized this was the best moment to highlight the bigger picture; as its not about one team but the entire team involved. I then pointed out the nurses leading time-out often hesitate to call out those who are not joining, probably because they don't feel Psychologically safe, and empowered. They worry about the repercussions if they speak up.

Organization should stop talking burnout as a individualized employee issue, however it should be addressed symptom of a larger systemic issue which could range from lack of standardization of processes, administrative burden on physicians, poor work culture. Yoga alone may is not enough to relief stress and provide improvements in the well being, As this may not address the underlying root cause (Gupta, 2024).

Organization should strategize and ensure a balance between working towards standardizations of processes and personalization. Standardization of processes to reduce variation and improve efficiency by introducing checklists, bundles, protocols. These tools set a clear expectation and helps teams deliver a high quality of care (Research, 2023).

While standardization provides a useful framework, personalization based on patient preferences and cultural context is vital. Over standardization can limit clinical judgement and responsiveness to individual patient needs. Potentially worsening inequalities or causing confusion (Sinsky et al., 2021). I have firsthand seen how adapting practices in response to patient needs can lead to better outcomes, up until a few years ago, patients who required Radiological diagnostic tests had to move from the outpatient department (OPD) to inpatient department (IPD) building to get those tests done (This was done to centralize the departmental activities). Overtime, it became clear that this approach does not meet the patients' needs. As a result, a satellite U/S and Xray unit at the OPD was established itself.

This shift from a more standardized (centralized) approach to a more personalized approach not only improved patient satisfaction but also the capacity of the department to perform more tests and decreased waiting times.

Contrarily, there are circumstances when standardization is crucial to avoid patient harm. For instance, during a conversation with a clinician on Antibiotic prescribing practices and their compliance, I was informed that sometimes patients insist on receiving a specific type of antibiotic based on their previous positive experience. While patient preference is important, clinicians are required to keep a judicious balance in view of the resistance patterns, clinical guidelines, potential side effects, and other public health considerations. and so on – this necessary adherence to established guidelines can lead to patient dissatisfaction when their expectations are not met. This example highlights how, in certain cases, strict standardization is indispensable, even if it challenges personalized approaches because public safety and wider public health must take precedence.

Embedding habitual systems thinking requires sustained efforts in education and policy. Healthcare curricula increasingly should include system science and quality improvement methodologies which can bridge the chasm between the healthcare administrators and clinicians (Carayon et al., 2014). Policies promoting integrated care models, value-based purchasing, and transparent performance measurement creating incentives for organizations to prioritize systematic improvement rather than a fragmented approach. As Peter Senge (Senge, 1990). Highlighted in *The Fifth Discipline*, creating a learning organization capable of systemic transformation depends on cultivating collective understanding and a shared vision that permeates all levels of healthcare.

In conclusion, having a systems approach will transform healthcare delivery from reactive to proactive, coordinated and patient centered systems. It requires not only new knowledge but embedding new habits within the workforce, amongst team and the organization at large. With persistent commitment to this cultural shift, healthcare can evolve in to safe, more equitable and humanized system where the complexity of care I embraced and managed thoughtfully. Though the complexity of healthcare operation can be intimidating, however there are many leverage points for change. No single leader, technology or policy alone can "fix" it all. Progress appears when there is interdependence – inviting people who live through system – patient- front line staff into co designing the healthcare.

REFERENCES

AHIP, & the America's Health Insurance Plans. 2024 Survey results. https://www.ahip.org/news/articles/survey-shows-health-plans-are-expanding-value-based-arrangements-to-deliver-higher-quality-more-affordable-health-care

American Psychological Association. (2018). *APA dictionary of psychology*. Dictionary.apa.org;American Psychological Association. https://dictionary.apa.org/resilience

Anderson, B. R. (2016). Improving health care by embracing systems theory. *The Journal of Thoracic and Cardiovascular Surgery, 152*(2), 593–594. DOI: 10.1016/j.jtcvs.2016.03.029 PMID: 27113625

Berwick, D. M. (2009). What "Patient-Centered" Should Mean: Confessions Of An Extremist. *Health Affairs, 28*(Supplement 1), w555–w565. DOI: 10.1377/hlthaff.28.4.w555 PMID: 19454528

Carayon, P., Wetterneck, T. B., Rivera-Rodriguez, A. J., Hundt, A. S., Hoonakker, P., Holden, R., & Gurses, A. P. (2014). Human Factors Systems Approach to Healthcare Quality and Patient Safety. *Applied Ergonomics, 45*(1), 14–25. DOI: 10.1016/j.apergo.2013.04.023 PMID: 23845724

Delbanco, T., Berwick, D. M., Boufford, J. I., Edgman-Levitan, , Ollenschläger, G., Plamping, D., & Rockefeller, R. G. (2001). Healthcare in a land called PeoplePower: Nothing about me without me. *Health Expectations, 4*(3), 144–150. DOI: 10.1046/j.1369-6513.2001.00145.x PMID: 11493320

Deming, W. E. (1986). *Out of the crisis*. Mit Press.

Franco Vega, M. C., Ait Aiss, M., George, M., Day, L., Mbadugha, A., Owens, K., Sweeney, C., Chau, S., Escalante, C., & Bodurka, D. C.Maria Franco Vega. (2024). Enhancing implementation of the I-PASS handoff tool using a provider handoff task force at a Comprehensive Cancer Center. *Joint Commission Journal on Quality and Patient Safety, 50*(8), 560–568. Advance online publication. DOI: 10.1016/j.jcjq.2024.03.004 PMID: 38584053

Gupta, K. (2024). Evaluation of the Effectiveness of Yoga and Meditation in Alleviating Burnout Symptoms among Medical Student. *International Journal of Life Sciences (Amravati), 13*(12). Advance online publication. DOI: 10.69605/ijlbpr_13.12.2024.168

Hick, J. L., Hanfling, D., Wynia, M. K., & Pavia, A. T. (2020). Duty to plan: Health care, crisis standards of care, and novel coronavirus sars-cov-2. *NAM Perspectives*. Advance online publication. DOI: 10.31478/202003b PMID: 34532682

Holden, R. J., Carayon, P., Gurses, A. P., Hoonakker, P., Hundt, A. S., Ozok, A. A., & Rivera-Rodriguez, A. J. (2013, November). SEIPS 2.0: A Human Factors Framework for Studying and Improving the Work of Healthcare Professionals and Patients. *Ergonomics*, *56*(11), 1669–1686. DOI: 10.1080/00140139.2013.838643 PMID: 24088063

Institute of Medicine. (2000). *To err is human: Building a safer health system*. National Academies Press., DOI: 10.17226/9728

James, T. A. (2023, January 12). *Building Empathy into the Structure of Health Care | Harvard Medical School Professional, Corporate, and Continuing Education*. Https://Learn.hms.harvard.edu/Insights/All-Insights/Building-Empathy-Structure-Health-Care. https://learn.hms.harvard.edu/insights/all-insights/building-empathy-structure-health-care

Joint Commission International. (2020). *Communicating Clearly and Effectively to Patients How to Overcome Common Communication Challenges in Health Care*. https://store.jointcommissioninternational.org/assets/3/7/jci-wp-communicating-clearly-final_(1).pdf

Keesara, S., Jonas, A., & Schulman, K. (2020). Covid-19 and Health Care's Digital Revolution. *The New England Journal of Medicine*, *382*(23). Advance online publication. DOI: 10.1056/NEJMp2005835 PMID: 32240581

Legido-Quigley, H., Asgari, N., Teo, Y. Y., Leung, G. M., Oshitani, H., Fukuda, K., Cook, A. R., Hsu, L. Y., Shibuya, K., & Heymann, D. (2020). Are high-performing health systems resilient against the COVID-19 epidemic? *Lancet*, *395*(10227), 848–850. DOI: 10.1016/S0140-6736(20)30551-1 PMID: 32151326

Leonard, M.. (2004, October 1). The Human Factor: The Critical Importance of Effective Teamwork and Communication in Providing Safe Care. *Quality & Safety in Health Care*, *13*(1, suppl_1), 85–90. qualitysafety.bmj.com/content/13/suppl_1/i85. DOI: 10.1136/qshc.2004.010033 PMID: 15465961

Malik, A. U. (2015, March 19). Application of Systems Thinking in Health: Opportunities for Translating Theory into Practice Comment on "Constraints to Applying Systems Thinking Concepts in Health Systems: A Regional Perspective from Surveying Stakeholders in Eastern Mediterranean Countries.". *International Journal of Health Policy and Management*, *4*(8), 537–539. Retrieved August 21, 2018, from. DOI: 10.15171/ijhpm.2015.69 PMID: 26340394

National Academies of Sciences, Engineering, and Medicine; National Academy of Medicine; Committee on Systems Approaches to Improve Patient Care by Supporting Clinician Well-Being. (2019). Taking Action Against Clinician Burnout: A Systems Approach to Professional Well-Being. In *PubMed*. National Academies Press (US). https://pubmed.ncbi.nlm.nih.gov/31940160/

Nelson, E. C., Batalden, P. B., & Godfrey, M. M. (2011). *Quality By Design*. John Wiley & Sons.

Parent, A., & Parent, A. (2011, November 2). *Physician Executive Career Options Abound - NEJM CareerCenter Resources*. NEJM CareerCenter Resources. https://resources.nejmcareercenter.org/article/physician-executive-career-options-abound

Pew Research Center. (2024, November 13). Internet/Broadband Fact Sheet. Pew Research Center: Internet, Science & Tech; Pew Research Center. https://www.pewresearch.org/internet/fact-sheet/internet-broadband/

Plsek, P. E., & Greenhalgh, T. (2001). Complexity science: The challenge of complexity in health care. *BMJ (Clinical Research Ed.)*, *323*(7313), 625–628. DOI: 10.1136/bmj.323.7313.625 PMID: 11557716

Research, T. (2023, September 27). *How Healthcare Standardization Helps Improve Patient Safety*. Think Research Canada. https://www.thinkresearch.com/ca/2023/09/27/how-healthcare-standardization-helps-improve-patient-safety/

Ring, D. C., Herndon, J. H., & Meyer, G. S. (2010). Case 34-2010. *The New England Journal of Medicine*, *363*(20), 1950–1957. DOI: 10.1056/NEJMcpc1007085 PMID: 21067387

Saud, J., & Rice, J. (2024). Stress, Teamwork, and Wellbeing Policies: A Synergistic Approach to Reducing Burnout in Public Sector Organizations. *Administrative Sciences*, *14*(12), 319. DOI: 10.3390/admsci14120319

Schein, E. H. (2010). *Organizational Culture and Leadership (4th ed.). San Francisco, CA Jossey-Bass. - References - Scientific Research Publishing*. Www.scirp.org. https://www.scirp.org/reference/ReferencesPapers?ReferenceID=1848176

. Reference: Schein, E. H. (2010). *Organizational Culture and Leadership*

Senge, P. M. (1990). *The Fifth Discipline*. Broadway Business.

Sinsky, C. A., Bavafa, H., Roberts, R. G., & Beasley, J. W. (2021). Standardization vs Customization: Finding the Right Balance. *Annals of Family Medicine*, *19*(2), 171–177. DOI: 10.1370/afm.2654 PMID: 33685879

Starmer, A. J., Spector, N. D., Srivastava, R., West, D. C., Rosenbluth, G., Allen, A. D., Noble, E. L., Tse, L. L., Dalal, A. K., Keohane, C. A., Lipsitz, S. R., Rothschild, J. M., Wien, M. F., Yoon, C. S., Zigmont, K. R., Wilson, K. M., O'Toole, J. K., Solan, L. G., Aylor, M., & Landrigan, C. P. (2014, November 6). Changes in Medical Errors after Implementation of a Handoff Program. *The New England Journal of Medicine, 371*(19), 1803–1812. www.nejm.org/doi/10.1056/NEJMsa1405556?url_ver=Z39.88-2003&rfr_id=ori:rid:crossref.org&rfr_dat=cr_pub%20%200www.ncbi.nlm.nih.gov. DOI: 10.1056/NEJMsa1405556 PMID: 25372088

Von Bertalanffy, L. (1968). *Von Bertalanffy, L. (1968). General System Theory Foundations, Development. New York George Braziller. - References - Scientific Research Publishing*. Www.scirp.org. https://www.scirp.org/reference/referencespapers?referenceid=2040488

West, C. P., Dyrbye, L. N., & Shanafelt, T. D. (2018). Physician burnout: Contributors, consequences and solutions. *Journal of Internal Medicine, 283*(6), 516–529. DOI: 10.1111/joim.12752 PMID: 29505159

World Health Organization. (2015). *World report on ageing and health*. World Health Organization. https://www.who.int/publications/i/item/9789241565042

Chapter 7

Organizational Culture and the Quality of Work Life of Healthcare Providers in Pakistan: A Systems-Based Perspective

Arfa Masihuddin
http://orcid.org/0009-0006-4697-6318
Rufayda, Karachi, Pakistan

Waqas Hameed
Aga Khan University, Pakistan

Mohammad Asim
Aga Khan University, Pakistan

Syed Mairaj Shah
Aga Khan University, Pakistan

ABSTRACT

This chapter examines the perception of quality of work life (QWL) among healthcare providers in private-sector tertiary care hospitals in Karachi, Pakistan. The research involved 42 healthcare providers from three hospitals, using in-depth interviews. The findings revealed that QWL is a combination of a well-paying job, a good work-life balance, a comfortable working environment, supportive leadership, and family support. Organizational factors affecting QWL include fair monetary compensation, increased workload, lack of infrastructure, decision-making autonomy, and feedback from leadership. Emotional and practical support from colleagues

DOI: 10.4018/979-8-2600-0582-8.ch007

significantly influences QWL by mitigating workplace stress. Family expectations were recognized as a factor influencing QWL, as healthcare providers frequently encounter challenges in fulfilling unrealistic demands. Initiatives to improve QWL include introducing confidential mental health services, support facilities, and personal development skills. The results are shown using the 5Ss framework: Self, Society, State, Systems, and Spirituality. Key themes include workload and burnout, leadership behavior, infrastructure gaps, peer and familial support, and a lack of recognition. The chapter proposes human-centered and policy-driven interventions to improve QWL in resource-constrained healthcare settings. Healthcare organizations should establish wellness committees to promote a positive work culture and improve QWL.

ELEVATING THE DISCUSSION: WHY HEALTHCARE WORKFORCE WELL-BEING MATTERS

Quality of work life (QWL) refers to the quality of time healthcare providers (HCPs) spend at work. It is a multidimensional concept that includes job satisfaction, pay, relationships with colleagues, and overall well-being. QWL also reflects the ability of employees to influence decisions, participate openly, and align their work with organizational goals, factors linked to higher satisfaction and lower burnout. A positive QWL not only supports individual health and performance but also enhances retention, reduces turnover, and strengthens organizational stability.

Healthcare professionals, particularly doctors and nurses, form the backbone of health systems. Yet the high stress of their roles, compounded by organizational pressures, often compromises their QWL, harming both providers and the quality of care. As Randy Pausch aptly said, "*Put on your own oxygen mask before assisting others.*" Prioritizing QWL is, thus, essential for effective leadership, workforce sustainability, and safe, high-quality patient care.

Most research on QWL has been conducted in Western contexts using quantitative tools, leaving a gap in understanding within Pakistani healthcare organizations. This chapter addresses that gap by exploring physicians' lived experiences across specialties and settings. Understanding these perspectives can help identify factors that shape QWL and guide human-centered design approaches, where providers themselves contribute to solutions. Such approaches can inform sustainable policies that foster innovation, efficiency, and staff well-being, ultimately improving patient outcomes and system performance.

The study that forms the basis of this chapter was, therefore, a first step toward building evidence-based interventions that enhance the QWL of healthcare providers, laying the foundation for future research on its role in patient-centered care.

QUALITY OF WORK LIFE: A STRATEGIC PERSPECTIVE

The term "quality of life" (QoL) carries more complexity than it first appears. While it often evokes positive ideals of how we want to live, its meaning varies greatly from person to person, making it difficult to define (Edlund & Tancredi, 1985). Its roots, however, lie in the World Health Organization's (WHO) definition of health as "a state of complete physical, mental, and social well-being, and not merely the absence of disease and infirmity" (Post, 2014). Building on this, the WHO defines QoL as an individual's perception of their place in life in relation to expectations, goals, concerns, and standards (World Health Organization, 2012). This definition has been widely used in the social and health sciences to shape policies that recognize health as only one aspect of QoL (Post, 2014). QoL is understood as a multidimensional concept that reflects social, emotional, and physical well-being, functional competence, daily activities, and economic stability, all within the context of culture, traditions, religion, personal preferences, and life goals (Diener & Suh, 1997; Cella, 1994). Scholars have approached the study of QoL in three ways: by identifying attributes of a good life through social or philosophical systems, by evaluating how well individuals can fulfill their desires with available resources, and by measuring subjective well-being through experiences of happiness and contentment (Diener & Suh, 1997). In recent decades, the concept has been associated with humanistic and environmental values, which were frequently neglected in industrialized societies that emphasized technology, industry, and economic productivity (Walton, 1973).

The term "quality of work life" (QWL) extends the idea of quality of life into the workplace (Easton & Van Laar, 2013). It has been described as a value-based approach that seeks to improve both employees' well-being and organizational effectiveness (Economics Discussion, n.d.). Definitions differ: some focus on job satisfaction, pay, relationships with coworkers, and overall well-being (Elizur & Shye, 1990), while others focus on employees' ability to affect decisions and take part in open communication that is in line with the goals of the organization (Gomathi & Swapna, 2012). Walton identified eight key factors that contribute to QWL: fair compensation, safe working conditions, social integration, work-life balance, opportunities for development and career growth, constitutionalism, and the social significance of work (Golovina, Kuchina, & Serova, 2019). In essence, it reflects how individuals feel about all aspects of work, including financial benefits, job security, working conditions, organizational culture, and the meaning of work in their lives (Khajehnasiri et al., 2021).

Research from various countries and professions indicates that Quality of Work Life (QWL) is affected by multiple factors, such as turnover intentions, equitable employment opportunities, job enrichment, supervision, work content, job security, and the organizational environment. In fact, organizational environment has been identified as one of the strongest predictors of QWL, second only to income (Akter et al., 2018). While early models sought universal criteria, more recent work recognizes that QWL can vary across organizations, professions, and employee groups (Easton & Van Laar, 2018).

UNDERSTANDING QUALITY OF WORK LIFE IN HEALTHCARE SETTINGS

Work is a central part of life, providing not only income for physical and psychological needs but also intangible benefits such as value, competence, and confidence. At the same time, it is a major source of stress (Horst et al., 2014). Since people now spend more than a third of their lives in the workplace, its influence on overall well-being is profound.

The concept of quality of work life (QWL) first emerged during the 1960s and 1970s at an International Labor Relations conference (Hian & Einstein, 1990). Over time, it has gained importance due to rising business demands and evolving family structures (Taher, 2013). With more households relying on two incomes and both men and women balancing professional and domestic responsibilities, concern for employees' QWL has increased, leading to a need to support their well-being (Beh & Idris, 2006).

QWL programs aim to enhance quality of life by providing adequate resources, reducing conflict between personal and professional roles, strengthening role identity, lowering stress, and increasing the sense of worth attached to work (Dhamija, Gupta, & Bag, 2019). In today's globalized economy, driven by information technology and the growth of the services sector, employees are recognized as an organization's most valuable asset (Afroz, 2017).

Healthcare is an important part of society, and there are systems in place to make sure everyone has access to it and to meet the needs of the population (Thulth & Sayej, 2015). These systems encompass the diagnosis, treatment, and prevention of illness, injury, and disability, delivered through primary, secondary, and tertiary care as well as public health. Healthcare professionals (HPs), especially doctors and nurses, play a central role in strengthening these systems and ensuring equitable access to care (Atun, 2004; Afroz, 2017). The contribution of high-performing physicians, in particular, is indispensable for the sustainable development of any nation's healthcare sector (Akhtar & Qureshi, 2019).

Quality of work life (QWL) has been shown to correlate negatively with job stress and positively with job satisfaction (Aruldoss, Kowalski, & Parayitam, 2021). Despite their achievements in fulfilling their demanding roles, HPs often experience compromised QWL due to stress and organizational pressures, which in turn affects their health and performance (Starfield & Shi, 2004; WHO, 2001; Van Laar et al., 2007). To provide effective healthcare, the workforce must itself be empowered. As Randy Pausch noted, "*Put on your own oxygen mask before assisting others.*" QWL in healthcare is therefore not only an issue of individual well-being but also one of systemic importance, shaping governance, workforce stability, and service delivery (Brock,2 1993; WHO, 2010). By influencing burnout, stress levels, and job satisfaction, QWL directly impacts patient safety, care quality, and outcomes.

Evidence shows that improving QWL benefits institutions, providers, and patients alike. High QWL is associated with greater productivity, lower costs, stronger organizational commitment, and higher patient satisfaction (Vagharseyyedin et al., 2011). Issues of staff development and well-being are now recognized as central to healthcare organizations' performance and integral to the broader quality movement (Moradi et al., 2014). Researchers have also linked better patient care to a supportive work environment (Akter et al., 2018).

Improving QWL is essential for recruiting and retaining skilled staff. Motivated and capable employees are the foundation of effective service provision, and their development requires not only resources but also strong leadership (Kelbiso et al., 2017). Strengthening QWL therefore advances three fundamental pillars of the WHO health system framework: service delivery, leadership and governance, and the health workforce (WHO, 2010).

HOW DO ORGANIZATIONAL FACTORS AFFECT QWL IN HEALTHCARE ORGANIZATIONS?

Organizational factors define the environment in which healthcare workers perform their duties, directly influencing both their performance and patient outcomes. These include leadership and governance, availability of resources, workload, night shifts, opportunities for education and training, and managerial support. Together, such elements shape patient satisfaction, organizational mission, and the broader healthcare context (Thulth & Sayej, 2015).

Improvement in QWL has been linked to fostering a humanized work environment (Srivastava & Kanpur, 2014). Such an environment avoids excessive negative conditions or undue stress that harm workers' dignity or threaten their well-being. Work should not impair one's ability to function as a citizen, spouse, or parent but instead contribute to broader social advancement (Srivastava & Kanpur, 2014).

Positive organizational conditions—such as low levels of stress, supportive supervisors, role clarity, constructive feedback, opportunities for growth, and fair compensation—are strongly associated with higher QWL (Vagharseyyedin et al., 2011). For

For example, nurses report improved QWL when their achievements are recognized, when they are given autonomy, adequate staffing, and supportive working conditions (Hemanathan, Sreelekha, & Golda, 2017). Research indicates that building effective relationships between leaders, managers, and employees not only enhances QWL but also reduces vocational burnout (Brunetto & Farr-Wharton, 2006).

When these factors are absent, employees face excessive stress that can lead to burnout—a condition characterized by emotional exhaustion, depersonalization, and reduced personal accomplishment (Schaufeli, Bakker, & Sixma, 2011). Burnout has been described as a public health crisis with serious consequences for healthcare providers, patients, and organizations (West, Dyrbye, & Shanafelt, 2018). High workload, inefficient practices, administrative burdens, work–home conflict, lack of control over decisions, and poor organizational support have all been identified as key drivers (West et al., 2018). For nurses in particular, leadership style, decision-making latitude, salary and benefits, relationships with colleagues, and workload are major predictors of QWL (Vagharseyyedin et al., 2011). Staff development and well-being are therefore essential aspects of organizational performance and of the wider quality movement in healthcare (Moradi et al., 2014).

Leadership plays a decisive role. A failure to provide organizational support and cultivate a climate of teamwork leads to diminished QWL and greater risk of burnout (Rider et al., 2018). Humanism in healthcare management extends beyond patient care to include compassion for healthcare workers themselves and their families (Kilpatrick, 2009). Studies have shown that lack of organizational support is associated with increased medical errors, prescribing mistakes, and dispensing errors, which harm both patients and providers by worsening emotional strain (Carayon et al., 2014; Dyrbye et al., 2013; Abd Elwahab & Doherty, 2014; Iqbal, 2021; Tawfik et al., 2018; Panagioti et al., 2018; Shanafelt et al., 2016). This creates a cycle of burnout: as errors increase, job dissatisfaction rises, public confidence in healthcare declines, and the burden of disease grows. Overworked staff must then handle worsening crises, which further erodes their QWL (Liang et al., 2015).

Breaking this cycle requires a shift toward humanistic healthcare environments. Organizations must support healthcare professionals not only as providers but also as individuals with social and personal needs. Empowering workers to care for themselves enables them to care more effectively for patients (Kilpatrick, 2009). Ultimately, strengthening organizational pillars that sustain QWL enhances health, provides social and financial security, and contributes to the broader determinants of quality of life (Atun, Berman, & Hsiao, 2009).

HOW ARE BURNOUT AND QWL RELATED?

The excessive stress caused by organizational factors often culminates in *burnout*, a condition characterized by emotional exhaustion, depersonalization, and a diminished sense of personal accomplishment (Panagioti et al., 2018; Shanafelt et al., 2016). Burnout is now widely recognized as a long-term condition and a public health crisis with serious consequences for healthcare professionals, patients, and healthcare systems alike (Liang et al., 2015).

A range of factors drive this epidemic, including heavy workloads, inefficient work practices, administrative burdens, conflicts between work and home, lack of autonomy, insufficient organizational support, and leadership deficiencies (Liang et al., 2015). These challenges contribute not only to burnout but also to associated mental health conditions such as depression, anxiety, emotional exhaustion, and even suicidal ideation (Atun, Berman, & Hsiao, 2009; Nicholls, 2019; Shanafelt et al., 2002; Asante et al., 2019).

The downstream effects are severe. Mental health issues among healthcare providers often manifest as reduced productivity, lower quality of care, substance abuse, alcohol misuse, physical illness, and an overall decline in quality of life (Willard-Grace et al., 2019; Parikh et al., 2020; Bragard, Dupuis, & Fleet, 2015; van der Wal, Wallage, & Bucx, 2018; Linzer et al., 2016). Numerous studies consistently highlight how burnout and vocational stress directly undermine QWL (Nicholls, 2019; Shanafelt et al., 2002; Asante et al., 2019; Deckard, Meterko, & Field, 1994).

Data from global research paints a troubling picture: between 10–20% of physicians report clinical depression, nearly half are burnt out, and a majority are dissatisfied with their work–life balance, often citing fatigue and poor quality of life as major concerns (Dyrbye et al., 2013). These outcomes translate into absenteeism, staff turnover, aggression, hostility, and decreased productivity, all of which threaten the quality of healthcare services (Mosadeghrad, Ferlie, & Rosenberg, 2011).

Specialty-specific studies further highlight the scale of the problem. For instance, a U.S. study found that 55% of radiologists identified burnout as a "very significant problem," with 71% attributing it primarily to organizational factors and 36% to personal factors (Parikh et al., 2020). Similarly, emergency medicine physicians and anesthesiologists report disproportionately high levels of stress and burnout due to intense work environments, which points to the importance of policies that account for both organizational and personal determinants (Bragard et al., 2015; van der Wal et al., 2018).

Workplace setting also plays a role. Physicians in public hospitals often report higher levels of emotional exhaustion and depersonalization than their counterparts in private facilities, who benefit from comparatively stronger organizational infrastructures (Miranda-Ackerman et al., 2019; Rojas, Seghieri, & Nuti, 2014). A study at Tehran University of Medical Sciences revealed widespread dissatisfaction among hospital staff regarding QWL (Saraji & Dargahi, 2006). Nursing professionals, in particular, face unique challenges such as compassion fatigue, heavy workloads, and shift-based schedules, all of which significantly reduce their QWL (Ruiz-Fernández, Pérez-García, & Ortega-Galán, 2020; Moradi et al., 2014). Dissatisfaction rates among nurses are strikingly high: 52.4% in Saudi Arabia and 70.8% in Iran, particularly among those in primary health care units (Kelbiso et al., 2017). Factors such as long hours, poor work–life balance, inadequate break times, delayed promotions, and insufficient training opportunities all contribute to this dissatisfaction.

Interestingly, regional differences exist. A study in Karachi, Pakistan, found that private-sector healthcare workers reported higher stress levels and poorer QWL compared to those in public institutions (Zehra, Ather, & Zehra, 2017). This discrepancy may be linked to the differing patient populations each sector serves: public hospitals are often overburdened by lower-income groups, while private hospitals cater to smaller, more financially stable populations (Villa & Kane, 2013). However, the bulk of existing research is Western and largely quantitative, leaving a significant gap in context-specific insights for Pakistani healthcare organizations.

ADDRESSING CHALLENGES: PRACTICAL STRATEGIES FOR ENHANCING QUALITY OF WORK LIFE

As a precursor to changes in practice structures, investigations that have sought to identify these aspects provide insights and recommendations for managing them effectively. One study examining humanistic organizational factors influencing practicing physicians suggested several ways to improve QWL and reduce burnout, including supportive leadership and role modeling, recruiting a workforce whose values align with the organization, creating facilitative practice structures, and organizing wellness activities for physicians and their families (Rider et al., 2018). Results from a national survey on work life and wellness among American internists similarly recommended workflow redesigns involving scribes and support staff, better management of indirect care time, attention to work–home balance, encouragement of part-time practice, promotion of exercise and workplace wellness programs, and regular evaluation of stress and burnout to guide local wellness initiatives (Linzer et al., 2016). A survey conducted at Tehran University of Medical Sciences (TUMS) advocated for more training and education for hospital managers on QWL-related issues (Saraji & Dargahi, 2006). Kelly, Lefton, & Fischer (2019) urge nurse leaders at all levels to address burnout risks through individual and organizational resilience initiatives. When seeking to enhance the work engagement of new nurses, career identity and burnout within the broader QWL framework must also be considered

(Sun et al., 2022). Similarly, improving hospital work environments has been shown to reduce burnout and turnover among nurses while increasing patient satisfaction (Vahey et al., 2004). Other studies recommend strategies to address and improve working conditions, including reducing workplace stress, workload, and conflict, while promoting coping mechanisms for challenging environments (Khaghanizadeh, Ebadi, & Rahmani, 2008).

Although not all of these strategies may be directly applicable or sustainable in a lower-middle-income country such as Pakistan, the evidence emphasizes the value of identifying and understanding these factors. Adaptation and improvisation of such approaches, such as offering flexible promotion opportunities for doctors (Akhtar & Qureshi, 2019), remain viable for improving the quality of life of Pakistani healthcare professionals.

ORGANIZATIONAL THEORIES AND QWL

Organizational theories play a crucial role in shaping the quality of work life (QWL) within a workplace. The modern theory of organization emphasizes flexibility, adaptability, and innovation, contributing to a work environment that fosters continuous improvement and employee engagement (Morgan, 1986). This approach aligns with QWL principles by promoting a dynamic and responsive organizational culture. Motivation theories, such as Maslow's Hierarchy of Needs and Herzberg's Two-Factor Theory highlight the significance of recognizing individual needs and providing intrinsic motivation for employees. A study (Herzberg, 1968) found that factors like achievement, recognition, and the nature of the work itself have a profound impact on job satisfaction and, consequently, QWL. Open Systems Theory views organizations as interconnected entities interacting with their external environment. This perspective underscores the importance of adapting to external changes for organizational success, thereby influencing the overall work experience (Katz & Kahn, 2015). In integrating these theories, organizations can enhance QWL by fostering a supportive, motivating, and adaptable workplace culture.

The 5Ss Framework

The chapter adopts the 5Ss framework—Self, Society, State, Systems, and Spirituality—to analyze the findings. This lens enables a nuanced interpretation of individual, interpersonal, organizational, and policy-level influences on QWL.

Why This Study Matters

Quality of Work Life (QWL) programs improve overall quality of life by equipping employees with adequate resources to meet role identity expectations, reducing role conflict between personal and professional domains, strengthening multiple role identities, lowering role demands, relieving stress, and enhancing the perceived worth of their roles (Dhamija et al., 2019). While existing literature highlights the importance of QWL in healthcare and the factors influencing it, there is a lack of research from lower-middle-income countries. Most evaluations of healthcare professionals' QWL in South Asia rely on Western-based models that overlook the local cultural, organizational, and environmental contexts, even though cultural variation is a recognized determinant of QWL (Easton & Van Laar, 2018).

Cross-cultural research demonstrates that while stress and strain are universally linked, their sources differ across settings. In the United States, job overload and lack of autonomy were the main stressors, whereas for Indian workers, role ambiguity was most significant (Easton & Van Laar, 2018). Taiwanese studies highlighted poor managerial recognition and unclear managerial roles, while in the UK, interpersonal relationships, organizational climate, and personal responsibility were primary stress factors (Easton & Van Laar, 2018). These findings suggest that although the underlying dimensions of QWL may be broadly consistent, the critical components and their relative importance vary across cultures. Further cross-cultural research is needed to refine universal QWL measures or develop culture-specific tools.

In Pakistan, literature on QWL remains scarce. A population-based study assessing general quality of life revealed poor outcomes across diverse socio-demographic groups, with age, socioeconomic status, and rural residence predicting lower QoL, while higher social capital improved outcomes (Lodhi et al., 2019). This landmark study emphasizes the urgent need for regular QoL monitoring; however, it did not address QWL specifically. Consequently, there is extremely limited research on the QWL of Pakistani healthcare professionals (HCPs).

This chapter addresses this gap by examining whether organizational factors uniquely influence the QWL of HCPs in Pakistan within the context of local cultural and institutional structures. By filling this void in the literature, the chapter aims to contribute evidence that can inform policies to improve QWL for Pakistani healthcare professionals.

The study for this chapter included physicians, surgeons, and nurses of all cadres from all major clinical departments, including internal medicine, surgery, and obstetrics and gynecology, hence, giving a balanced representation of the physician workforce to assess the different kinds of issues faced by each cadre and to establish generalizability of the findings.

As a subtheme of QoL, the QWL of HCPs in light of profession-specific organizational culture and environmental factors was necessary (Brock, 1993). It was evident that healthcare providers' roles and functions in the workplace were constantly changing. An up-to-date review of the QWL literature for HCPs revealed potentially novel perspectives. There was evidence indicating that assessing the QWL of employees and disentangling the factors contributing to its deterioration bore fruitful results in terms of employee well-being, improved productivity, and financial sustainability (Easton & Van Laar, 2013). High-performing physicians played an essential role in a nation's healthcare industry, directly influencing that nation's sustainable development (Akhtar & Qureshi, 2019). The direct impact of this QWL was on the health workforce, which was responsible for service delivery to the population through patient care. The culture, leadership, and governance of the organization were also determinants of the effectiveness of the health workforce and the ensuing service delivery (World Health Organization, 2010). This, in turn, determined the strength of the health system (World Health Organization, 2010). As a result, it was critical to highlight the factors that influenced their QWL, particularly the organizational factors. Hence, the need arose to conduct studies designed to identify key organizational factors that would help in formulating sustainable approaches to improve the QWL and, consequently, the performance of Pakistani physicians (Akhtar & Qureshi, 2019). The chapter serves as a stepping stone to achieving similar outcomes by developing interventions based on its findings, laying the groundwork for future research into how the quality of work life affected patient-centered care and the interventions that could be implemented to favor it.

In light of the 5Ss, the chapter advocates for integrative interventions that address both structural and human dimensions of work. For instance, embedding wellness programs and employee support structures (Systems), fostering peer and family-inclusive policies (Society), and enabling reflective practice and spiritual support at work (Spirituality) can enhance resilience and engagement.

CONCEPTUAL FRAMEWORK

A previous study published by Afroz, Saman (Afroz, 2017) developed a conceptual model for the QWL. Published in India, the model is based along the same social and cultural settings as our study and hence, provided the relevant context necessary to carry out this study. It used the Pareto analysis to explore existing literature to identify 13 major factors of QWL out of a set of 27 factors. For the purpose of our chapter, the conceptual model was adapted using two other studies (Charles, Kathiravan, & Velaudham, 2016), (Mosteller & Falotico-Taylor, 1989) to make a comprehensive framework that covered all the relevant organizational characteristics that determine the QWL for an employee.

(Figure 01)

Research Objectives

1. To understand the perception of and self-evaluation of the quality of the work life of healthcare providers, including physicians, surgeons, and nurses in private-sector tertiary care hospitals in Karachi, Pakistan.
2. To identify the organizational factors influencing the quality of work life of healthcare providers in private-sector tertiary care hospitals in Karachi, Pakistan.

Methodological Approach: Capturing the Voices of Healthcare Professionals

Study Design: Qualitative exploratory design with in-depth interviews.

Study Duration: July 20 to September 1, 2023.

Study Setting: Three accessible private hospitals. Convenience sampling was done, including participants who met practical criteria such as accessibility, proximity, availability, or willingness to participate (Etikan, Musa, & Alkassim, 2016).

Eligibility Criteria: Currently employed physicians, surgeons, and nurses from the departments of internal medicine, general surgery, and obstetrics and gynecology (OBGYN) at selected private tertiary care hospitals in Karachi, Pakistan. The participants were required to have been working at the selected hospitals for more than three months.

Sample Size: A total of 42 participants were interviewed. These included one HOD, one consultant, one final-year resident, one HN, and one practicing nurse each from the departments of internal medicine, general surgery, and OBGYN from each of the selected hospitals. This range was considered until theoretical saturation was achieved and no new themes emerged. Figure 2 shows the number of interviews conducted at each department of the selected hospitals.

Sampling Technique: After obtaining approval from the Ethical Review Committee at Aga Khan Hospital, permission was sought from the relevant departments of the selected hospitals. Following departmental approval, lists of consultants, final-year residents, and nurses from the departments of internal medicine, surgery, and obstetrics and gynecology (OBGYN) were obtained. Participants were then shortlisted using non-probability, convenience sampling based on the predetermined eligibility and exclusion criteria for each hospital and department (Figure 2).

Data collection tools/instruments: Data collection was conducted using a single, uniform semi-structured interview guide to carry out in-depth interviews with all targeted participants. The interview guide was developed following an extensive literature review and was informed by previous qualitative research as well as the conceptual framework of this study (Dhamija et al., 2019; Tempski et al., 2012; Ghazanfar, Iqbal, & Naseem, 2018; The WHOQOL Group, 1998).

The questions were designed around themes identified in the literature, allowing the exploration of relationships between different factors influencing quality of work life (QWL).

The guide included open-ended questions that explored work-related QWL, its modifying factors, and coping strategies. Participants were asked questions such as, "*What is your understanding of quality of life and quality of work life?*"; "*How would you describe your own quality of work life?*"; "*Which organizational factors increase or decrease your quality of work life?*"; "*What coping strategies do you use to improve your quality of work life?*"; and "*What recommendations would you suggest at the organizational level to improve quality of work life?*" To minimize courtesy bias and concerns regarding confidentiality when discussing unsatisfactory organizational policies, individual interviews were conducted rather than focus group discussions. This approach also allowed the inclusion of healthcare providers with diverse experiences, providing flexibility and a broader understanding of the complexities surrounding QWL. All data were anonymized prior to analysis. Only the principal investigator had access to the dataset which were securely stored in password-protected systems.

Data Analysis: A framework analysis approach (Smith & Firth, 2011) guided by the study's conceptual framework was employed to analyze the qualitative data. Audio-recorded interviews were transcribed verbatim and reviewed multiple times for familiarization. Initial coding was undertaken to identify recurring patterns related to quality of work life and organizational culture. Codes were subsequently grouped into themes and sub-themes aligned with the research objectives. The final themes were reviewed collaboratively by the research team to ensure coherence and analytical rigor (Asim et al., 2023). Representative excerpts were selected to illustrate each theme.

Rigor and trustworthiness: Methodological rigor and trustworthiness were ensured through peer debriefing, respondent triangulation, and transparent documentation of the analytic process. Participants were recruited from multiple professional cadres and departments to ensure diversity of perspectives. Data collection continued until thematic saturation was achieved. Regular review meetings with the research committee strengthened analytical objectivity and minimized researcher bias. All interviews were conducted with strict adherence to confidentiality and ethical standards.

Ethical Considerations

Aga Khan University's Ethics Review Committee (ERC) and the Department of Community Health Sciences' (CHS) Departmental Research Committee (DRC) approvals were taken prior to the data collection.

All communication about the study was honest and open. Inaccurate information of any kind, as well as biased reporting of primary data findings, was avoided. The privacy and respect of research subjects was prioritized. Prior to the study, the full consent of all participants was obtained. Their confidentiality was adequately protected and anonymity of research participants and organizations was ensured.

FINDINGS AT A GLANCE: KEY INSIGHTS FROM THE FIELD

This section provides a description of the key characteristics of the study participants. The research objectives correspond to Themes 1 and 2 of the results section. In presenting the findings, the term "majority" refers to approximately more than 50% of participants, "some" refers to 20% to 40% of participants, and "few" refers to 10% or less. Relevant participants' quotes are presented under the themes to which they correspond, illustrating the perspectives and experiences discussed in the study.

Key Characteristics of Study Participants

A total of 42 healthcare providers were included in the analysis. Table 2 shows the characteristics of the participants. The mean age of the participants was 41.2 (±5.9) years. More than half were females with 11 males. 36 participants were married and 6 were unmarried, with 32 financially supporting their families. 10 respondents were the head nurses, followed by 9 final year residents, 8 nurses, 8 consultants, and 7 heads of departments. A total of 15 respondents were from the OBGYN department, with 14 respondents from GS, and 13 from IM. Table 2 organizes the key characteristics of the study participants.

Table 2. Characteristics of study participants

Characteristics	n (%)
Sex	
Females	31 (74)
Males	11 (26)
Age in years	

continued on following page

Table 2. Continued

Characteristics	n (%)
20 - 31 years	6 (14)
32 - 43 years	20 (48)
44 - 55years	10 (24)
56 years and above	6 (14)
Marital status	
Married	36 (86)
Unmarried	6 (14)
Financially supporting	
Yes	32 (76)
No	10 (24)
Cadres	
Head of department	7 (17)
Consultant	8 (19)
Final year resident	9 (21)
Head nurse	10 (24)
Nurse	8 (19)
Departments	
General surgery	14 (33)
Internal medicine	13 (31)
Gynecology and obstetrics	15 (36)

The qualitative comparison of QWL across cadres found residents and nurses to be highly dissatisfied with their QWL. The main study findings are organized into three main themes: perceived notion and self-evaluation of current state of quality of work life; organizational factors affecting quality of work life; and enhancing quality of work life: current practices and future recommendations. Contrasting views of the different cadres and departments were also provided, where necessary.

Leadership, Workload, and Organizational Culture: Drivers of Workforce Satisfaction

Theme 1: Perceived Notion and Self-Evaluation of Current State of Quality of Work Life

A key factor affecting the quality of work life (QWL) reported by participants was workload and work-life balance. The majority highlighted that manageable workloads, flexible working hours, and employee retention strategies reduce stress and burnout, increasing job satisfaction. Residents and nurses were identified as the most overworked due to long hours and staff shortages, resulting in lower QWL. Participants emphasized that sufficient rest prevents errors, enhances concentration, and supports patient care.

"One is long work hours... if a lot of stress is being given, then a person cannot work...if the workload is a lot; headcount is less and work is more, then it creates a problem and we don't enjoy working." (Male, surgery nurse)

Respectful behavior from seniors and organizational leadership emerged as another major factor. Participants reported that recognition, support, and respectful communication boost morale and performance, whereas scolding or insults in front of colleagues or patients negatively impact both staff well-being and patient compliance. A balanced approach that enforces rules while maintaining respect was seen as critical to sustaining QWL.

"But it is not supportive of them when they scold and insult us in front of patients or colleagues. How will the patients listen to us then?" (Female, internal medicine resident)

A stress-free workplace was consistently emphasized, particularly by residents and nurses, who experience high levels of work-related stress. Bullying and unsupportive environments were highlighted as major barriers to job satisfaction and mental well-being. The presence of supportive colleagues and a collaborative environment was considered essential to reduce burnout and improve QWL.

"During the initial days of my training, I faced a lot of bullying... I was under too much stress. I didn't want to go to the psychiatrist here because I did not want to risk my job if the management found out I said something." (Female, internal medicine resident)

Fair compensation was identified as crucial for motivation, retention, and job satisfaction. Disparities in pay across specialties and cadres, especially in relation to workload and inflation, were reported to negatively impact QWL. Participants noted that inequitable remuneration contributed to job dissatisfaction and prompted considerations of leaving for better opportunities.

"Even though our working hours are the same, maybe more, and more unpredictable, but our pay is lesser than other surgical specialties...it is because the admin thinks that OBGYNs are easily available so if one leaves, they can get another one easily." (Female, OBGYN HOD)

Family support was also highlighted as a significant factor influencing QWL. Participants emphasized that understanding from family members regarding demanding schedules and missed personal commitments helps reduce stress, prevent burnout, and enhance overall well-being. Unrealistic family expectations were seen as a source of additional stress, impacting the ability of HCPs to maintain work-life balance.

"*...family should also understand the demands of this profession and know that it is normal to miss occasions and not being able to give 100% time at home... their unrealistic expectations can make it difficult to cope so quality of work life is affected.*" *(Female, internal medicine resident)*

Table 3 summarizes the theme, sub-themes, and categories that reflect the perceptions and self-evaluation of QWL among physicians, surgeons, and nurses in private-sector tertiary care hospitals in Karachi, Pakistan.

Table 3. Objectives, themes, sub-themes, categories

Objective 1: To understand the perception of and self-evaluation of the quality of the work life of healthcare providers, including physicians, surgeons, and nurses in private-sector tertiary care hospitals in Karachi, Pakistan.		
Themes	Sub-themes	Summary
Theme 1: Perceived notion and self-evaluation of current state of quality of work life	1.1. Adequate Workload and work-life balance	Adequate workload reduces the chances of burnout, increases job satisfaction and quality of patient care. Sufficient time off needed to maintain adequate work-life balance. Residents and nurses were found to be the most overworked and were least satisfied with their QWL.
	1.2. Respectful behaviour of seniors	Respectful work environment was found to boost morale and work performance, increase employee retention, and improved QWL.
	1.3. Stress free workplace	Stress-free workplace was found to be associated with increased job satisfaction and performance, and a decreased risk of medical errors that resulted in lower burnout rates and improved QWL. Residents and nurses reported workplace stress as a key factor in decreasing their QWL.
	1.4. Fair compensation	Adequate monetary compensation contributed to financial stability, making employees feel valued for their expertise and work, enhancing their QWL.
	1.5. Support from family	Families' emotional and practical support with the daily household and personal responsibilities makes it easier for HCPs to cope with the demands of their profession, increasing their QWL. All cadres and departments unanimously agreed to lack family support adversely affecting their QWL.

Theme 2: Organizational Factors Affecting Quality of Work Life

Organizational leadership and governance emerged as a key factor influencing QWL. Participants across all cadres emphasized the importance of policies and leadership behaviors that prioritize employee well-being, support decision-making, and promote growth. Heads of departments and consultants highlighted that supportive leadership allows them to focus on patient care and leadership responsibilities rather than navigating bureaucratic hurdles, excessive paperwork, or rigid procedures, which contribute to frustration and low QWL. For final-year residents, supportive leadership translates into effective training, mentoring, and a respectful work environment. Head nurses and nurses reported that leadership policies that recognize and support their roles enhance job satisfaction and overall QWL. Lack of professional respect and mentorship was consistently identified as a barrier.

"It is important for our boss to be cooperative and understanding. When they are demotivating and strict or when they bully us in front of juniors, it gives us a lot of stress...before having training sessions for us, they should have sessions with the management to teach them why to be good with us." (Female, internal medicine resident)

Workplace environment, including workload, infrastructure, and amenities, was another critical factor. Heads of departments and consultants reported that access to well-equipped offices allows better management of research and administrative tasks, enhancing productivity and QWL. Residents and nurses emphasized the need for safe transport, break areas, clean restrooms, aesthetic surroundings, daycare and breastfeeding facilities, support staff, and subsidized medical services. Participants noted that the availability of such facilities reduces stress, conveys organizational support, and strengthens their sense of value.

"There should be a safe transport facility for employees...once they took our phones on gunpoint when we were on the way." (Female, surgery head nurse)

"There should be a daycare for working women...there is even no room for breastfeeding mothers or storage facility for the breast milk...in a hospital at least it should be there." (Female, surgery head nurse)

Workplace autonomy was highlighted as essential for empowerment and efficient decision-making. Lack of control and bureaucratic obstacles were reported to cause frustration and reduce QWL, especially among residents and nurses burdened with administrative tasks.

"There are too many red-tapes to get anything done...even if I have to get a new shelf in my office, there are too many emails that need to be generated so for other bigger decisions, the bureaucracy gets too frustrating." (Male, surgery HOD)

Feedback, recognition, and appreciation also significantly influence QWL. Heads of departments and consultants reported that recognition for research and leadership motivates them, while residents, head nurses, and nurses feel more satisfied when acknowledged for dedication and performance. Patient appreciation also enhances morale and reinforces the value of their work. However, participants observed that certain recognition programs, like "employee of the month," primarily focus on nursing staff, potentially causing other cadres to feel neglected.

"The negative ones [feedback] are definitely discussed but good ones should also be. Sometimes when patients appreciate us, it makes us happy...we feel like we did something good and it is encouraging." (Male, surgery head nurse)

Relationships and peer support emerged as another critical factor affecting QWL. Positive collaboration, practical assistance, and emotional support from colleagues help alleviate stress and foster a sense of belonging. Challenges such as after-hours work calls were highlighted as breaches of work-life boundaries, negatively affecting QWL.

"Sometimes the work gets too much when we receive calls at home...It can be frustrating." (Female, internal medicine nurse)

Table 4 summarizes the organizational factors affecting QWL and highlights differences in perceptions across cadres and departments.

Table 4. Summary of objectives, themes, sub-themes, categories of the organizational factors affecting QWL od HCPs

Objective 2. To identify the organizational factors influencing the quality of work life of healthcare providers in private-sector tertiary care hospitals in Karachi, Pakistan.			
Themes	**Sub-themes**	**Categories**	**Summary**
Theme 2: Organisational factors effecting quality of work life	2.1. Organisational leadership and governance systems	Employee centric policies	There is a need for policies and behaviours within the organization that are designed to prioritize the QWL of employees, boost their morale, and promote their overall growth. Majority of the HCPs across all cadres and specialties listed this factor as significantly affecting their QWL.
	2.2. Workplace environment	Work load; infrastructure; employee amenities	Lack of safe transport facilities, limited space for breaks, and the need for a day care centre, breastfeeding rooms, along safe and subsidized transport, and medical facilities was reported to have an impact on HCPs' QWL. HCPs across all cadres and departments agreed to this.
	2.3. Control at workplace	Decision making autonomy	Lack of decision-making autonomy causes HCPs to feel restricted in the course of actions available to them, upsetting the desired outcomes, and leading to frustration and inefficiencies that negatively impacts their QWL. HODs, consultants, and head nurses expressed a desire to have more autonomy to improve their QWL.
	2.4. Feedback, recognition, and appreciation	Appreciation and reward for good performers; patient appreciation and prayers	Having mechanisms in place to acknowledge and reward good performance boosts motivation and job satisfaction, improving QWL. This was a general consensus across all cadres and departments interviewed.
	2.5. Relationships and peer-support	Support from colleagues both instrumental and emotional etc.	Practical and emotional support from colleagues was reported to have alleviated stress and positively impacted the QWL of HCPs. Cadres like those of residents and nurses who had longer working hours ranked this as an important factor.

The Role of Support Systems: Colleagues, Families, and Institutional Policies

Theme 3: Enhancing quality of work life: current practices and future recommendations

Based on participant responses, several current practices within healthcare organizations were found to influence the QWL of healthcare providers. Analysis of these practices has informed recommendations for future initiatives aimed at enhancing QWL, using a human-centered approach to ensure that interventions address the specific needs of HCPs.

Workplace Amenities

While most workplaces offered some level of amenities, participants consistently reported that these were either insufficient or below standard. Safe and subsidized transport was highlighted as a critical need, particularly by residents, head nurses, and nurses, to ensure security during commutes. Female staff emphasized the absence of breastfeeding facilities and daycare services, which increased stress for young working mothers returning from maternity leave. Participants noted that the lack of these facilities prevented them from fully focusing on work, thereby negatively impacting their QWL.

"...there should be a safe transport facility for employees..." (Female, surgery head nurse)

"There should be a daycare for working women...there is even no room for breastfeeding mothers or storage facility for the breast milk...in a hospital at least it should be there." (Female, surgery head nurse)

Medical facilities provided to employees were also reported as inconsistent. Some organizations offered coverage only for employees, their spouses, and children, while others extended benefits to parents or not at all, creating disparities that contributed to dissatisfaction and variable QWL.

"Subsidized medical facilities should be offered for parents also...it will facilitate those who are not married or don't have kids." (Female, OBGYN HOD)

The availability of break areas and refreshments was noted as inadequate, particularly in operating rooms, and the physical work environment, including cleanliness and aesthetic surroundings, was reported to affect morale and overall QWL.

"...there's no staff room to take a break because of no space...there is no tea or water available in the theatre..." (Female, internal medicine resident)

"It's depressing in a way because there is garbage all around the building, no greenery." (Female, OBGYN nurse)

Employee Wellness Programs

The study highlighted a general absence of structured employee wellness programs tailored to the needs of HCPs within the context of their demanding work schedules and sociocultural environment. Participants expressed a strong desire for such programs and emphasized the importance of locally adapted policies rather than importing practices from other contexts.

"This isn't considered important enough. I think if you give priority to something then you make policies for it too...Why do you import the processes and policies, why don't you develop your own because you have an entirely different community and social structure?" (Female, OBGYN HOD)

Personal Development

Participants recommended programs supporting personal development alongside professional skills. Education on interpersonal skills, conflict management, financial management, and emotional regulation was identified as essential for developing coping strategies to manage professional challenges. Some respondents suggested introducing such training at the undergraduate level to better prepare future HCPs for the demands of their professions, ultimately improving QWL.

"...there are no such courses or workshops on life skills like communication, conflict management...only on leadership and time management. They should be there..." (Female, surgery nurse)

"At an undergrad level it might help depending on the maturity level of people." (Male, general surgery HOD)

Regular QWL Assessments and Mental Health Support

Participants unanimously supported the idea of regular assessments, surveys, and feedback mechanisms as the first step toward improving QWL. They emphasized that the effectiveness of such initiatives depends on feasible implementation and tangible outcomes.

"It's a good interview and such interviews should take place...if we have given feedback, there should be some implementation on it." (Male, surgery HOD)

The lack of accessible and confidential mental health services emerged as a significant concern. Some HCPs were unaware of existing resources, while others hesitated to use them due to privacy concerns. The absence of safe avenues for mental health support and burnout management was reported to negatively affect QWL. Participants recommended mobile applications, helplines, and confidential support mechanisms that are accessible without adding to work demands. Some also suggested the introduction of mental health leave to allow time for recovery and improved productivity.

"...I didn't want to go to the psychiatrist here because I did not want to risk my job if the management found out I said something." (Female, internal medicine resident)

"There is an app for everything now so maybe have one for us...It should be anonymous so we can talk freely." (Female, OBGYN nurse)

"Mental health leaves should be given just like sick leaves...they will help us..." (Male, surgery resident)

Overall, participants highlighted that addressing gaps in workplace amenities, wellness programs, personal development, and mental health support is essential for improving the QWL of HCPs. Implementing these recommendations in ways that consider local social and cultural contexts can ensure meaningful and sustainable improvements.

Table 5 below shows a summary of the current practices relevant to the state of QWL.

Table 5. Current practices

Themes	Sub-themes	Summary
Theme 3: Enhancing quality of work life: current practices and future recommendations	3.1. Work place amenities	Majority of the HCPs across all cadres and specialties reported having a severe lack of supportive facilities and workplace amenities that adversely affected their QWL.
	3.1. Employee wellness programmes (like retreats, support groups, mental health support)	Study participants across all cadres and departments reported an absence of any kind of wellness programs, emphasizing on an urgent need to be able to improve their QWL.
	3.2. Personal development	The absence of any personal development sessions to empower HCPs with coping skills to mitigate burnout and improve QWL was highlighted across all cadres and departments.
	3.3. Regular QWL assessments and burnout surveys to promote mental health services	Some organizations offer mental health services but the main hurdle towards availing them has been ease of access, availability of time, and privacy concerns.
		While no such assessments are currently held, all the participants endorsed the need for having them regularly as the first step towards improving their QWL.

IMPLICATIONS FOR PRACTICE AND POLICY

Theme 1 explored healthcare providers' perceptions of their quality of work life. Adequate workload, particularly for final-year residents and nurses, was identified as critical in reducing stress and burnout while enhancing job satisfaction with potential positive effects on patient care. Respectful behavior from leaders, stress-free workplaces, fair compensation, and family support, especially for female healthcare providers, emerged as key contributors to overall quality of work life. The findings indicate that residents and nurses reported the highest levels of dissatisfaction with their work-life quality.

Theme 2 focused on organizational factors influencing quality of work life. Supportive leadership and governance systems were highlighted as crucial for effective decision-making, staff morale, and overall work satisfaction. Workplace environment, autonomy in decision-making, regular feedback, recognition, and peer support were identified as essential elements that foster a positive and productive work atmosphere.

Theme 3 examined current organizational practices and proposed recommendations to improve quality of work life. Participants emphasized inadequacies in workplace amenities, the absence of tailored wellness programs and mental health services, and the need for personal development initiatives. Regular quality of work life assessments and feasible implementation strategies were also prioritized. These findings highlight the importance of adopting a human-centered approach to address the unique needs of healthcare professionals.

There is notable overlap among the themes, sub-themes, and categories. For example, aspects of the workplace environment such as workload, infrastructure, and employee amenities appear in both Theme 1 and Theme 2. This overlap reflects the interconnected nature of the factors influencing quality of work life and illustrates the multifaceted challenges faced by healthcare providers. The themes complement each other and suggest that interventions to enhance quality of work life should consider the interaction between organizational policies, leadership behaviors, workplace resources, and opportunities for personal development. For clarity, overlapping features have been grouped under relevant subheadings in this discussion.

Organizational Leadership and Governance Systems

Our study highlighted that disrespectful behavior from senior colleagues and organizational leadership, such as being shouted at, scolded, or mocked in front of juniors, patients, or attendants, was detrimental to the morale and self-esteem of healthcare providers. Working in an already demanding and emotionally charged profession, participants reported that such behavior contributed to stress, anxiety, and emotional exhaustion, which could negatively affect mental health and reduce the quality of patient care. For final-year residents, supportive leadership was defined as effective training, mentoring, and a nurturing work environment that treated them with respect and dignity. This reinforces that disrespectful behavior from leadership adversely affects the quality of the work life of healthcare providers. Previous research has similarly highlighted that bullying at work has a significant negative impact on employee well-being and health (Dehue et al., 2012). Conversely, transformational and positive leadership styles that mitigate disrespectful behavior and promote collaboration foster a supportive culture, contributing to employee well-being and overall job satisfaction (Dewi, Supriadi, & Iswanto, 2022). Comparative studies have also shown that higher levels of leadership support are associated with lower burnout among physicians, underlining the role of leadership in promoting overall well-being (Maslach, 2003).

The study also emphasized the importance of employee-centric policies designed to prioritize well-being and quality of work life, boost morale, and support professional growth. Participants across all cadres and specialties reported that the absence of such policies, including flexible work hours, wellness programs, professional development opportunities, and systems for recognition and feedback, decreased their quality of work life and expressed a desire for their implementation. Head nurses and nurses indicated that employee-centered policies enhanced their job satisfaction, while heads of departments and consultants noted that supportive work environments enabled efficient decision-making, timely action based on data, optimized resource use, and clear responsibilities. This allowed them to focus on This focus on leadership and patient care was more beneficial than dealing with bureaucratic hurdles like excessive paperwork, rigid procedures, or red tape, which caused significant frustration and led to a lower quality of work life. For final-year residents, supportive leadership again translated into respectful and effective mentoring and training. Existing literature supports these findings, showing that transparent, employee-centered policies combined with leadership that prioritizes employee wellness can reduce burnout and promote better quality of work life among healthcare providers (Shanafelt et al., 2012; Puni & Hilton, 2020).

Workplace Environment

The quality of work life of healthcare providers is strongly influenced by the workplace environment, encompassing workload, infrastructure, and employee amenities. Participants emphasized that these factors also contribute to workplace stress. Excessive workload, particularly affecting medical residents and nurses, occurs when a limited number of staff work long hours with minimal rest. This can lead to burnout, characterized by physical and mental exhaustion. High staff turnover further disrupts patient care, increasing the burden on remaining staff and negatively impacting both patient outcomes and the QWL of healthcare providers. Similar findings have been reported in Western healthcare settings, where increased workload was linked to physician burnout, high stress levels, and reduced QWL (Shanafelt et al., 2012). Our study reinforces the importance of adequate work-life balance as a preventive factor against burnout and a contributor to better QWL (West et al., 2009).

The absence of essential amenities such as comfortable workspaces, accessible refreshments, medical facilities for employees and their families, safe transport, daycare centers, and breastfeeding rooms for new mothers emerged as additional barriers to QWL. Participants indicated that the lack of these facilities detracts from work focus and contributes to poor work experiences. A supportive work environment that addresses workload, infrastructure, and employee amenities is critical for enabling healthcare providers to deliver quality patient care while maintaining their own well-being. These findings align with research demonstrating that well-equipped, supportive work environments positively affect physician well-being and patient care (Kelly et al., 2020; Vahey et al., 2004).

Participants also identified workplace stress as a persistent challenge, arising from patient care demands, high workloads, insufficient infrastructure, urgent clinical decisions, exposure to human suffering, bullying, and administrative burdens. Chronic stress can lead to emotional and physical exhaustion, impacting personal relationships and reducing the ability to provide compassionate care. Our findings emphasize the importance of maintaining a stress-free workplace, consistent with studies linking supportive work environments to reduced burnout and improved well-being (Shanafelt et al., 2012; Stimpfel, Rosen, & McHugh, 2014).

The study emphasized the necessity for customized wellness programs to assist healthcare providers in coping with the emotional and physical challenges of their profession. Participants recommended initiatives such as stress-reduction activities, mental health support, and personal development courses to maintain QWL. The lack of easily available mental health resources makes people feel alone, stressed, and burned out. Similar trends have been observed in the United States, where inadequate mental health support negatively affected QWL (Shanafelt et al., 2016).

Prior studies provide evidence to support these recommendations. Wellness toolkits, including designated wellness champions, biannual burnout assessments, educational sessions, support activities, and mentorship, have been shown to mitigate burnout and enhance QWL (Eckleberry-Hunt et al., 2009). Programs that teach interpersonal skills, conflict management, and emotional regulation can further strengthen healthcare providers' coping abilities and improve overall quality of work life (West et al., 2016).

Fair Compensation

Adequate monetary compensation emerged as a key determinant of quality of work life for healthcare providers. Participants highlighted disparities across departments, with OBGYN staff reporting lower pay compared to other surgical specialties based on the perception that they are easily replaceable. Lack of uniform pay scales across cadres led some HCPs to seek employment elsewhere, reflecting poor QWL in their current organizations. When remuneration aligns with responsibilities and workload, HCPs feel respected and valued for their expertise and dedication. Fair compensation positively influences motivation, job satisfaction, professional fulfillment, and overall QWL. It also addresses financial stressors such as student loans and inflation, allowing HCPs to focus on their work and reduce the risk of burnout (Koinis et al., 2015).

Support From Family

Family support was identified as a major contributor to QWL, particularly for female HCPs. Many participants reported challenges balancing work and family obligations due to demanding and unpredictable schedules. Unrealistic expectations from family members intensified stress, feelings of guilt, and isolation, negatively impacting job focus and the quality of patient care. Studies support the role of family support in enhancing resilience and mental well-being among healthcare providers (Andlib et al., 2022).

Control at Workplace

Decision-making autonomy emerged as an important factor affecting QWL. HCPs emphasized that having the freedom to exercise professional judgment and have their input respected in patient care and administrative processes reduces stress, increases job satisfaction, and fosters a sense of empowerment. Conversely, restricted autonomy can result in frustration, low morale, and decreased QWL, consistent with previous research linking professional autonomy to reduced burnout (Kelly et al., 2020).

Feedback, Recognition, and Appreciation

Acknowledgment of HCPs' efforts, both from organizational leadership and through patient feedback, was reported as essential to motivation and job satisfaction. Lack of recognition can lead to feelings of undervaluation, whereas positive feedback contributes to a supportive work environment, mitigates burnout, and enhances QWL (Maslach, 2003).

Relationships and Peer Support

Support from colleagues, both practical and emotional, was consistently highlighted as improving QWL. Assistance with work responsibilities, knowledge sharing, and fostering a friendly and collaborative environment reduce stress and create a sense of belonging among HCPs (Stimpfel, Rosen, & McHugh, 2014).

Regular QWL Assessments and Burnout Surveys

Participants emphasized the importance of regular QWL assessments and burnout surveys as a mechanism to understand challenges, address needs, and implement meaningful changes. Such initiatives allow organizations to monitor employee well-being and foster a supportive work environment, aligning with findings from Australia highlighting the value of systematic assessments in improving QWL (Dewa et al., 2014).

KEY FINDINGS MAPPED TO THE 5SS FRAMEWORK

1. Self: Burnout, Stress, and Mental Health

Healthcare providers reported high levels of stress and exhaustion due to extended work hours, insufficient breaks, and emotional fatigue. Residents and nurses were especially vulnerable to burnout. Many expressed fear of seeking mental health support due to confidentiality concerns.

Illustrative Quote: “I haven’t taken an off in one year... I feel like if I don’t take a break now, I will reach burnout.” (OBGYN Consultant)

2. Society: Familial Expectations and Peer Support

Family support served as a buffer against occupational stress, particularly for female HCPs. However, unrealistic familial expectations about time and availability often contributed to stress. Peer support, when available, helped mitigate isolation and emotional burden.

3. State: Policy and Regulatory Gaps

Respondents highlighted the absence of standardized pay structures, lack of institutional mental health services, and the need for regulatory frameworks that protect HCPs' well-being. Participants called for national policies on workload regulation and institutional wellness.

4. Systems: Organizational Culture and Leadership

Leadership style, workplace respect, autonomy in decision-making, and recognition were pivotal to how HCPs perceived their QWL. Disrespectful behavior from seniors, lack of feedback, and punitive workplace environments were commonly cited issues.

Illustrative Quote: "It is not supportive when they scold us in front of patients... How will the patients listen to us then?" (Internal Medicine Resident)

Infrastructure constraints such as the absence of amenities (e.g., childcare, transport, breastfeeding rooms) further exacerbated dissatisfaction.

5. Spirituality: Meaning, Purpose, and Values in Work

Several HCPs noted that their sense of purpose in caregiving, spiritual beliefs, and professional ethics helped them cope. However, the lack of a compassionate organizational climate often challenged these internal motivators.

PRACTICAL IMPLICATIONS FOR SYSTEMS STRENGTHENING, POLICY TRANSLATION, AND WORKFORCE WELL-BEING

The findings of this study demonstrate that the quality of work life (QWL) of healthcare providers is shaped by a complex interplay of leadership behaviors, organizational systems, workplace infrastructure, policy environments, and socio-familial contexts. These findings necessitate coordinated systems-level reforms, regulatory policy translation, and human-centered organizational transformation grounded in the 5Ss framework.

Systems-Level Implications

Healthcare organizations must institutionalize *transformational and respectful leadership practices* through mandatory leadership development programs for consultants, heads of departments, and nurse managers. Zero-tolerance policies for workplace bullying, humiliation, and public shaming should be enforced through confidential reporting and disciplinary systems. Structured *mentorship programs for residents and nurses* should be embedded within clinical departments to ensure psychological safety and professional growth.

Workforce protection requires the implementation of *safe staffing ratios, duty-hour regulation, and rotation-based workload redistribution* to prevent chronic fatigue and burnout. Workplace infrastructure must be reframed as a *patient safety and workforce sustainability priority*, requiring the provision of essential amenities such as rest areas, breastfeeding rooms, daycare facilities, safe transport, and subsidized healthcare services for employees and their families.

Mental health support systems should be formally integrated into hospital operations through *confidential in-house or outsourced psychological services*, supported by trained wellness champions in each department. Additionally, institutions must establish structured *performance feedback and recognition systems* to enhance employee motivation, retention, and organizational commitment.

Policy Translation Implications

At the regulatory level, the findings support the urgent need for *national workforce protection policies* that regulate workload, mandate rest hours, and ensure standardized, equitable pay structures across specialties and cadres. Gender-sensitive wage audits and institutional protections for maternity and caregiving responsibilities are essential to address disparities faced by female healthcare providers.

Mental health access should be protected through *legal safeguards that prevent professional repercussions for seeking psychological care*, supported by institutional mandates for confidential counseling services. Furthermore, *family-friendly employment policies*, including flexible scheduling, return-to-work transition support, and institutional childcare, should be formally integrated into hospital licensing and accreditation requirements.

To ensure accountability and evidence-based reform, *mandatory periodic QWL and burnout assessments* should be institutionalized at provincial and national levels for benchmarking, workforce planning, and leadership performance evaluation.

5Ss-Based Human-Centered Recommendations

At the level of **Self**, institutions must implement routine mental health screenings, emotional regulation training, and structured coping-skills programs. Under *Society*, family sensitization initiatives and structured peer-support groups are necessary to alleviate psychosocial stress, particularly for women healthcare providers. At the level of *State*, standardized workforce protection policies, legal safeguards against harassment, and national mental health access frameworks must be enforced. The **Systems** domain requires leadership accountability for psychological safety, infrastructure enhancement, and governance reform. Finally, under *Spirituality*, healthcare organizations must cultivate reflective spaces, narrative medicine, and ethical dialogue forums to sustain meaning, purpose, and compassionate care.

Collectively, these implications emphasize that burnout is a systems failure rather than an individual deficiency, and that sustainable improvements in QWL demand synchronized interventions across leadership, governance, infrastructure, policy frameworks, and humanistic organizational values.

Policy Recommendations

1. *National Duty-Hour Regulation* for residents and nurses
2. *Standardized Pay Scales* across cadres and specialties
3. *Mandatory Confidential Mental Health Services* in all tertiary hospitals
4. *Gender-Sensitive HR Policies* (flexibility, childcare, maternity reintegration)
5. *Legal Protection from Workplace Harassment and Bullying*
6. *Mandatory Annual QWL & Burnout Surveillance*

Expected Impact

- Reduced burnout and workforce attrition
- Improved patient safety and provider performance
- Enhanced gender equity in healthcare employment
- Strengthened national health system resilience

CONCLUSION: BUILDING SUSTAINABLE HEALTHCARE ENVIRONMENTS

Our study concluded that healthcare providers in tertiary care hospitals across Karachi perceived their quality of work life to be shaped by workload and work-life balance, respect and support from seniors and organizational leadership, the presence of a stress-free workplace, fair monetary compensation, and family support. The qualitative comparison across cadres indicated that residents and nurses experience the highest levels of dissatisfaction with their QWL.

A distinct finding highlighted the dual impact of family expectations and support, particularly for female HCPs. Unrealistic expectations can increase stress, whereas understanding and practical support from family contribute to resilience and coping. Organizational policies should therefore include family-friendly initiatives, such as flexible schedules and communication channels, to help female providers manage both professional and personal demands.

The study also emphasized the role of cultural and organizational contexts in shaping QWL, highlighting the importance of context-specific interventions. Key organizational factors influencing QWL included leadership and governance, workplace environment, decision-making autonomy, feedback and recognition, and peer support.

Based on these findings, the chapter concludes that interventions to improve QWL should focus on creating a supportive workplace, fostering organizational leadership that prioritizes employee well-being, and providing amenities such as safe and subsidized transport, well-equipped common rooms, daycare centers, breastfeeding facilities, aesthetic surroundings, and subsidized medical services for families. Tailored wellness programs, personal development training in emotional regulation, conflict and financial management, and confidential mental health support were also identified as essential. Regular QWL assessments and burnout surveys were recognized as critical first steps toward monitoring and enhancing the well-being of healthcare providers.

REFERENCES

Abd Elwahab, S., & Doherty, E. (2014). What about doctors? The impact of medical errors. *The Surgeon, 12*(6), 297–300. DOI: 10.1016/j.surge.2014.06.004

Afroz, S. (2017). Quality of work life: A conceptual model. [AEBM]. *Advances in Economics and Business Management, 4*(8), 570–578.

Afroz, S. (2017). Quality of work life: A conceptual model. [AEBM]. *Advances in Economics and Business Management, 4*(8), 570–578.

Akhtar, M., & Qureshi, Q. A. (2019). Impacts of QWL (promotion & work environment) on doctors' performance in public sector hospitals of Pakistan. *International Transaction Journal of Engineering, Management, &. Applied Sciences & Technologies, 11*(5), 1–9.

Akter, N., Akkadechanunt, T., Chontawan, R., & Klunklin, A. (2018). Factors predicting quality of work life among nurses in tertiary-level hospitals, Bangladesh. *International Nursing Review, 65*(2), 182–189. DOI: 10.1111/inr.12401

Andlib, S., Inayat, S., Azhar, K., & Aziz, F. (2022). Burnout and psychological distress among Pakistani nurses providing care to COVID-19 patients: A cross-sectional study. *International Nursing Review, 69*(4), 529–537. DOI: 10.1111/inr.12750

Aruldoss, A., Kowalski, K. B., & Parayitam, S. (2021). The relationship between quality of work life and work-life balance: Mediating role of job stress, job satisfaction and job commitment. *Journal of Advances in Management Research, 18*(1), 36–62. DOI: 10.1108/JAMR-05-2020-0082

Asante, J. O., Li, M., Liao, J., Huang, Y. X., & Hao, Y. T. (2019). The relationship between psychosocial risk factors, burnout and quality of life among primary healthcare workers in rural Guangdong province: A cross-sectional study. *BMC Health Services Research, 19*(1), 447. DOI: 10.1186/s12913-019-4278-8

Asim, M., Hameed, W., Khan, B., Saleem, S., & Avan, B. I. (2023). Applying the COM-B model to understand the drivers of mistreatment during childbirth: A qualitative enquiry among maternity care staff. *Global Health, Science and Practice, 11*(2), e2200434. DOI: 10.9745/GHSP-D-22-00267

Atun, R. A., Berman, P., & Hsiao, W. C. (2009). Building on health systems frameworks for developing a common approach to health systems strengthening. *Unpublished manuscript*, 1–35.

Beh, L.-S., & Idris, K. (2006). An analysis of quality of work life (QWL) and career-related variables. *American Journal of Applied Sciences, 3*(12), 2151–2159. DOI: 10.3844/ajassp.2006.2151.2159

Beh, L.-S., & Idris, K. (2006). An analysis of quality of work life (QWL) and career-related variables. *American Journal of Applied Sciences, 3*(12), 2151–2159. DOI: 10.3844/ajassp.2006.2151.2159

Bragard, I., Dupuis, G., & Fleet, R. (2015). Quality of work life, burnout, and stress in emergency department physicians: A qualitative review. *European Journal of Emergency Medicine, 22*(4), 227–234. DOI: 10.1097/MEJ.0000000000000194

Brunetto, Y., & Farr-Wharton, R. (2006). The importance of effective organisational relationships for nurses: A social capital perspective. *International Journal of Human Resources Development and Management, 6*(2–4), 232–247. DOI: 10.1504/IJHRDM.2006.010397

Carayon, P., Wetterneck, T. B., Rivera-Rodriguez, A. J., Hundt, A. S., Hoonakker, P., Holden, R., & Gurses, A. P. (2014). Human factors systems approach to healthcare quality and patient safety. *Applied Ergonomics, 45*(1), 14–25. DOI: 10.1016/j.apergo.2013.04.023

Cella, D. F. (1994). Quality of life: Concepts and definition. *Journal of Pain and Symptom Management, 9*(3), 186–192. DOI: 10.1016/0885-3924(94)90129-5

Charles, J. V., Kathiravan, C., & Velaudham, C. (2016). Customer satisfaction towards C-segment cars in Chennai City. *International Journal of Management and Social Sciences, 4*(4), 412–423.

Deckard, G., Meterko, M., & Field, D. (1994). Physician burnout: An examination of personal, professional, and organizational relationships. *Medical Care, 32*(7), 745–754. DOI: 10.1097/00005650-199407000-00007

Dehue, F., Bolman, C., Völlink, T., & Pouwelse, M. (2012). Coping with bullying at work and health related problems. *International Journal of Stress Management, 19*(2), 111–131. DOI: 10.1037/a0028969

Dewa, C. S., Loong, D., Bonato, S., Thanh, N. X., & Jacobs, P. (2014). How does burnout affect physician productivity? A systematic literature review. *BMC Health Services Research, 14*(1), 325. DOI: 10.1186/1472-6963-14-325

Dewi, D. Y., Supriadi, Y. N., & Iswanto, A. H. (2022). The effect of transformational leadership, quality of work-life on organizational citizenship behavior with organizational commitment mediation. *Journal of Social Sciences, 3*(5), 865–878. DOI: 10.46799/jss.v3i5.259

Dhamija, P., Gupta, S., & Bag, S. (2019). Measuring of job satisfaction: The use of quality of work life factors. *Benchmarking*, *26*(3), 871–892. DOI: 10.1108/BIJ-06-2018-0155

Dhamija, P., Gupta, S., & Bag, S. (2019). Measuring of job satisfaction: The use of quality of work life factors. *Benchmarking*, *26*(3), 871–892. DOI: 10.1108/BIJ-06-2018-0155

Diener, E., & Suh, E. (1997). Measuring quality of life: Economic, social, and subjective indicators. *Social Indicators Research*, *40*(1–2), 189–216. DOI: 10.1023/A:1006859511756

Dyrbye, L. N., Satele, D., Sloan, J., & Shanafelt, T. D. (2013). Utility of a brief screening tool to identify physicians in distress. *Journal of General Internal Medicine*, *28*(3), 421–427. DOI: 10.1007/s11606-012-2252-9

Easton, S., & Van Laar, D. (2013). QoWL (Quality of Working Life) – What, how, and why? *Psychological Research*, *3*(10), 596–605.

Easton, S., & Van Laar, D. (2018). Reconciling organizational stress, cultural differences and quality of working life. *Indian Journal of Career and Livelihood Planning*, *7*(1), 27–38.

Eckleberry-Hunt, J., Van Dyke, A., Lick, D., & Tucciarone, J. (2009). Changing the conversation from burnout to wellness: Physician well-being in residency training programs. *Journal of Graduate Medical Education*, *1*(2), 225–230. DOI: 10.4300/JGME-D-09-00026.1

Edlund, M., & Tancredi, L. R. (1985). Quality of life: An ideological critique. *Perspectives in Biology and Medicine*, *28*(4), 591–607. DOI: 10.1353/pbm.1985.0034

Elizur, D., & Shye, S. (1990). Quality of work life and its relation to quality of life. *Applied Psychology*, *39*(3), 275–291. DOI: 10.1111/j.1464-0597.1990.tb01054.x

Etikan, I., Musa, S. A., & Alkassim, R. S. (2016). Comparison of convenience sampling and purposive sampling. *American Journal of Theoretical and Applied Statistics*, *5*(1), 1–4. DOI: 10.11648/j.ajtas.20160501.11

Ghazanfar, H., Iqbal, S., & Naseem, S. (2018). Quality of life of post-graduate medical students working in private and public hospitals in Punjab as measured by WHOQOL-BREF questionnaire. *JPMA. The Journal of the Pakistan Medical Association*, *68*(6), 908–913.

Golovina, S. Y., Kuchina, Y. A., & Serova, A. (2019). Increasing the quality of working life: Modern labor legislation's strategic task. *Public Policy and Administration, 18*(3), 7–14. DOI: 10.5755/j01.ppaa.18.3.24266

Gomathi, S., & Swapna, M. (2012). A study on impact of job satisfaction on quality of work life: With special reference to IT professionals in Bangalore city. *Journal of Management and Science, 2*(1), 1–12.

Hemanathan, R., Sreelekha, P. P., & Golda, M. (2017). Quality of work life among nurses in a tertiary care hospital. *Health Care, 5*, 1–8.

Herzberg, F. (1968). One more time: How do you motivate employees? *Harvard Business Review*.

Hian, C. C., & Einstein, W. O. (1990). Quality of work life (QWL): What can unions do? *S.A.M. Advanced Management Journal, 55*(2), 17–22.

Hian, C. C., & Einstein, W. O. (1990). Quality of work life (QWL): What can Unions Do? *S.A.M. Advanced Management Journal, 55*(2), 17–22.

Horst, D. J., Broday, E. E., Bondarick, R., Serpe, L. F., & Pilatti, L. A. (2014). Quality of working life and productivity: An overview of the conceptual framework. *International Journal of Managerial Studies and Research, 2*(5), 87–98.

Iqbal, M. S. (2021). Health-related quality of life among healthcare providers in Pakistan. *Journal of Pharmacy & Bioallied Sciences, 13*(1), 31–38. DOI: 10.4103/jpbs.JPBS_265_20

Katz, D., & Kahn, R. (2015). The social psychology of organizations. In *Organizational Behavior 2* (pp. 152–168). Routledge.

Kelbiso, L., Belay, A., & Woldie, M. (2017). Determinants of quality of work life among nurses working in Hawassa town public health facilities, South Ethiopia: A cross-sectional study. *Nursing Research and Practice, 5181676*, 1–11. Advance online publication. DOI: 10.1155/2017/5181676

Kelly, L. A., Lefton, C., & Fischer, S. A. (2019). Nurse leader burnout, satisfaction, and work-life balance. *The Journal of Nursing Administration, 49*(9), 404–410. DOI: 10.1097/NNA.0000000000000784

Kelly, M., Soles, R., Garcia, E., & Kundu, I. (2020). Job stress, burnout, work-life balance, well-being, and job satisfaction among pathology residents and fellows. *American Journal of Clinical Pathology, 153*(4), 449–469. DOI: 10.1093/ajcp/aqaa013

Khaghanizadeh, M., Ebadi, A., & Rahmani, M. (2008). The study of relationship between job stress and quality of work life of nurses in military hospitals. *Journal Mil Med, 10*(3), 175–184.

Khajehnasiri, F., Foroushani, A. R., Kashani, B. F., & Kassiri, N. (2021). Evaluation of the quality of working life and its effective factors in employed nurses of Tehran University of Medical Sciences hospitals. *Journal of Education and Health Promotion, 10*(1), 160. DOI: 10.4103/jehp.jehp_790_20

Kilpatrick, A. O. (2009). The health care leader as humanist. *Journal of Health and Human Services Administration, 32*(4), 451–465. DOI: 10.1177/107937390903100405

Koinis, A., Giannou, V., Drantaki, V., Angelaina, S., Stratou, E., & Saridi, M. (2015). The impact of healthcare workers job environment on their mental-emotional health. Coping strategies: The case of a local general hospital. *Health Psychology Research, 3*(1), 1984. DOI: 10.4081/hpr.2015.1984

Liang, Y., Wang, H., & Tao, X. (2015). Quality of life of young clinical doctors in public hospitals in China's developed cities as measured by the Nottingham Health Profile (NHP). *International Journal for Equity in Health, 14*(1), 1–2. DOI: 10.1186/s12939-015-0199-2

Linzer, M., Poplau, S., Babbott, S., Collins, T., Guzman-Corrales, L., Menk, J., Murphy, M. L., & Ovington, K. (2016). Worklife and wellness in academic general internal medicine: Results from a national survey. *Journal of General Internal Medicine, 31*(9), 1004–1010. DOI: 10.1007/s11606-016-3720-4

Lodhi, F. S., Montazeri, A., Nedjat, S., Mahmoodi, M., Farooq, U., Yaseri, M., Kasaeian, A., & Holakouie-Naieni, K. (2019). Assessing the quality of life among Pakistani general population and their associated factors by using the World Health Organization's quality of life instrument (WHOQOL-BREF): A population based cross-sectional study. *Health and Quality of Life Outcomes, 17*(1), 1–17. DOI: 10.1186/s12955-018-1065-x

Maslach, C. (2003). Job burnout: New directions in research and intervention. *Current Directions in Psychological Science, 12*(5), 189–192. DOI: 10.1111/1467-8721.01258

Miranda-Ackerman, R. C., Barbosa-Camacho, F. J., Sander-Möller, M. J., Buenrostro-Jiménez, A. D., Mares-País, R., Cortes-Flores, A. O., Morgan-Villela, G., Zuloaga-Fernández del Valle, C. J., Solano-Genesta, M., Fuentes-Orozco, C., Cervantes-Cardona, G. A., Cervantes-Guevara, G., & González-Ojeda, A. (2019). Burnout syndrome prevalence during internship in public and private hospitals: A survey study in Mexico. *Medical Education Online, 24*(1), 1593785. DOI: 10.1080/10872981.2019.1593785

Moradi, T., Maghaminejad, F., & Azizi-Fini, I. (2014). Quality of working life of nurses and its related factors. *Nursing and Midwifery Studies, 3*(2), e19450. DOI: 10.5812/nms.19450

Morgan, G. (1986). *Images of organization*. Sage Publications.

Mosadeghrad, A. M., Ferlie, E., & Rosenberg, D. (2011). A study of relationship between job stress, quality of working life and turnover intention among hospital employees. *Health Services Management Research, 24*(4), 170–181. DOI: 10.1258/hsmr.2011.011009

Mosteller, F., & Falotico-Taylor, J. (1989). *Quality of life and technology assessment*. National Academy Press.

Nicholls, M. (2019). *Cardiologists and the burnout scenario*. Oxford University Press. DOI: 10.1093/eurheartj/ehy788

Panagioti, M., Geraghty, K., Johnson, J., Zhou, A., Panagopoulou, E., & Chew-Graham, C.. (2018). Association between physician burnout and patient safety, professionalism, and patient satisfaction: A systematic review and meta-analysis. *JAMA Internal Medicine, 178*(10), 1317–1331. DOI: 10.1001/jamainternmed.2018.3713

Parikh, J. R., Wolfman, D., Bender, C. E., & Arleo, E. (2020). Radiologist burnout according to surveyed radiology practice leaders. *Journal of the American College of Radiology, 17*(1), 78–81. DOI: 10.1016/j.jacr.2019.07.008

Post, M. (2014). Definitions of quality of life: What has happened and how to move on. *Topics in Spinal Cord Injury Rehabilitation, 20*(3), 167–180. DOI: 10.1310/sci2003-167

Puni, A., & Hilton, S. K. (2020). Dimensions of authentic leadership and patient care quality. *Leadership in Health Services (Bradford, England), 33*(4), 441–456. DOI: 10.1108/LHS-11-2019-0071

Rider, E. A., Gilligan, M. C., Osterberg, L. G., Litzelman, D. K., Plews-Ogan, M., Weil, A. B., Dunne, D. W., Hafler, J. P., May, N. B., Derse, A. R., Frankel, R. M., & Branch, W. T.Jr. (2018). Healthcare at the crossroads: The need to shape an organizational culture of humanistic teaching and practice. *Journal of General Internal Medicine, 33*(7), 1092–1099. DOI: 10.1007/s11606-018-4470-2

Rojas, D., Seghieri, C., & Nuti, S. (2014). Organizational climate: Comparing private and public hospitals within professional roles. *Suma De Negocios, 5*(SPE11), 10–14. https://doi.org/DOI: 10.1016/S2215-910X(14)70003-3

Ruiz-Fernández, M. D., Pérez-García, E., & Ortega-Galán, Á. M. (2020). Quality of life in nursing professionals: Burnout, fatigue, and compassion satisfaction. *International Journal of Environmental Research and Public Health*, *17*(4), 1253. DOI: 10.3390/ijerph17041253

Saraji, G. N., & Dargahi, H. (2006). Study of quality of work life (QWL). *Iranian Journal of Public Health*, *35*(4), 8–14.

Schaufeli, W. B., Bakker, A. B., & Sixma, H. J. (2011). Stability and change in burnout: A 10-year follow-up study among primary care physicians. *Journal of Occupational and Organizational Psychology*, *84*(2), 248–267. DOI: 10.1111/j.2044-8325.2010.02013.x

Shanafelt, T. D., Boone, S., Tan, L., Dyrbye, L. N., Sotile, W., Satele, D., West, C. P., Sloan, J., & Oreskovich, M. R. (2012). Burnout and satisfaction with work-life balance among US physicians relative to the general US population. *Archives of Internal Medicine*, *172*(18), 1377–1385. DOI: 10.1001/archinternmed.2012.3199

Shanafelt, T. D., Bradley, K. A., Wipf, J. E., & Back, A. L. (2002). Burnout and self-reported patient care in an internal medicine residency program. *Annals of Internal Medicine*, *136*(5), 358–367. DOI: 10.7326/0003-4819-136-5-200203050-00008

Shanafelt, T. D., Mungo, M., Schmitgen, J., Storz, K. A., Reeves, D., Hayes, S. N., Sloan, J. A., Swensen, S. J., & Buskirk, S. J. (2016). Longitudinal study evaluating the association between physician burnout and changes in professional work effort. *Mayo Clinic Proceedings*, *91*(4), 422–431. DOI: 10.1016/j.mayocp.2016.02.001

Smith, J., & Firth, J. (2011). Qualitative data analysis: The framework approach. *Nurse Researcher*, *18*(2), 52–62. DOI: 10.7748/nr2011.01.18.2.52.c8284

Srivastava, S., & Kanpur, R. (2014). A study on quality of work life: Key elements and its implications. *IOSR Journal of Business and Management*, *16*(3), 54–59. DOI: 10.9790/487X-16315459

Starfield, B., & Shi, L. (2004). The medical home, access to care, and insurance: A review of evidence. *Pediatrics*, *113*(Supplement 4), 1493–1498. DOI: 10.1542/peds.113.S4.1493

Stimpfel, A. W., Rosen, J. E., & McHugh, M. D. (2014). Understanding the role of the professional practice environment on quality of care in Magnet® and non-Magnet hospitals. *The Journal of Nursing Administration*, *44*(1), 10–16. DOI: 10.1097/NNA.0000000000000015

Sun, B., Fu, L., Yan, C., Wang, Y., & Fan, L. (2022). Quality of work life and work engagement among nurses with standardised training: The mediating role of burnout and career identity. *Nurse Education in Practice*, *58*, 103276. DOI: 10.1016/j.nepr.2021.103276

Taher, A. (2013). Variations of quality of work life of academic professionals in Bangladesh: A discriminant analysis. *European Journal of Training and Development*, *37*(6), 580–595. DOI: 10.1108/EJTD-05-2013-0060

Taher, A. (2013). Variations of quality of work life of academic professionals in Bangladesh: A discriminant analysis. *European Journal of Training and Development*, *37*(6), 580–595. DOI: 10.1108/EJTD-05-2013-0060

Tawfik, D. S., Profit, J., Morgenthaler, T. I., Satele, D. V., Sinsky, C. A., Dyrbye, L. N., Tutty, M. A., West, C. P., & Shanafelt, T. D. (2018). Physician burnout, well-being, and work unit safety grades in relationship to reported medical errors. *Mayo Clinic Proceedings*, *93*(11), 1571–1580. DOI: 10.1016/j.mayocp.2018.05.014

Tempski, P., Barros, B., Paro, H. B., Enns, S. C., Martins, M. A., & Schraiber, L. B. (2012). What do medical students think about their quality of life? A qualitative study. *BMC Medical Education*, *12*(1), 106. DOI: 10.1186/1472-6920-12-106

Thulth, A. S., & Sayej, S. (2015). Selected organizational factors affecting performance of professional nurses in North West Bank governmental hospitals. *Journal of Education and Practice*, *6*(7), 100–110.

Thulth, A. S., & Sayej, S. (2015). Selected organizational factors affecting performance of professional nurses in North West Bank governmental hospitals. *Journal of Education and Practice*, *6*(7), 100–110.

Vagharseyyedin, S. A., Vanaki, Z., & Mohammadi, E. (2011). The nature of nursing quality of work life: An integrative review of literature. *Western Journal of Nursing Research*, *33*(6), 786–804. DOI: 10.1177/0193945910378855

Vahey, D. C., Aiken, L. H., Sloane, D. M., Clarke, S. P., & Vargas, D. (2004). Nurse burnout and patient satisfaction. *Medical Care*, *42*(2, Suppl), II57–II66. DOI: 10.1097/01.mlr.0000109126.50398.5a

Vahey, D. C., Aiken, L. H., Sloane, D. M., Clarke, S. P., & Vargas, D. (2004). Nurse burnout and patient satisfaction. *Medical Care*, *42*(2, Suppl), II57–II66. DOI: 10.1097/01.mlr.0000109126.50398.5a

van der Wal, R. A., Wallage, J., & Bucx, M. J. (2018). Occupational stress, burnout and personality in anesthesiologists. *Current Opinion in Anaesthesiology*, *31*(3), 351–356. DOI: 10.1097/ACO.0000000000000587

Van Laar, D., Edwards, J. A., & Easton, S. (2007). The work-related quality of life scale for healthcare workers. *Journal of Advanced Nursing*, *60*(3), 325–333. DOI: 10.1111/j.1365-2648.2007.04409.x

Villa, S., & Kane, N. (2013). Assessing the impact of privatizing public hospitals in three American states: Implications for universal health coverage. *Value in Health*, *16*(1), S24–S33. DOI: 10.1016/j.jval.2012.10.003

Walton, R. E. (1973). Quality of working life: What is it? *Sloan Management Review*, *15*(1), 11–21.

West, C. P., Dyrbye, L. N., & Shanafelt, T. D. (2018). Physician burnout: Contributors, consequences and solutions. *Journal of Internal Medicine*, *283*(6), 516–529. DOI: 10.1111/joim.12752

West, C. P., Dyrbye, L. N., Erwin, P. J., & Shanafelt, T. D. (2016). Interventions to prevent and reduce physician burnout: A systematic review and meta-analysis. *Lancet*, *388*(10057), 2272–2281. DOI: 10.1016/S0140-6736(16)31279-X

West, C. P., Tan, A. D., Habermann, T. M., Sloan, J. A., & Shanafelt, T. D. (2009). Association of resident fatigue and distress with perceived medical errors. *Journal of the American Medical Association*, *302*(12), 1294–1300. DOI: 10.1001/jama.2009.1389

WHOQOL Group. (1998). Development of the World Health Organization WHOQOL-BREF quality of life assessment. *Psychological Medicine*, *28*(3), 551–558. DOI: 10.1017/S0033291798006667

Willard-Grace, R., Knox, M., Huang, B., Hammer, H., Kivlahan, C., & Grumbach, K. (2019). Burnout and health care workforce turnover. *Annals of Family Medicine*, *17*(1), 36–41. DOI: 10.1370/afm.2338

Zehra, S. Z., Ather, M., & Zehra, B. (2017). A correlation between workplace stress and organizational commitment: Doctors' response from public and private hospitals in Karachi, Pakistan. *International Journal of Academic Research in Business & Social Sciences*, *7*(6), 636–648. DOI: 10.6007/IJARBSS/v7-i6/3022

Chapter 8
Policy as a Catalyst for Shaping Organisational Culture, Ethics, and Safety in Healthcare:
Aligning Culture in Healthcare Organizations

Tahirah Atif
http://orcid.org/0009-0000-3859-9686
IOBM, Pakistan

ABSTRACT

Effective policies for healthcare providers health are mandatory for maintaining perfect workflow and their safety in workplace. Policies bring about workload management, supportive environment, fair reward system and a healthy culture of organisation. Governance brings about structure, transparency and accountability from workers and fosters collaboration among stakeholders. Thus, policies shape the environment of an organisation and governance runs the organisation flawlessly. This chapter will explore the critical role of policy in shaping organisational culture, beginning with theoretical underpinnings of culture and governance. It will examine how policies serve as ethical and legal anchors in clinical practice and explore their role in promoting accountability and safety. Finally, it will examine regulatory frameworks that reinforce patient safety and support continuous improvement. Each section integrates real-life examples and case studies to provide a practical understanding of policy's transformative potential in healthcare

DOI: 10.4018/979-8-2600-0582-8.ch008

1. INTRODUCTION: POLICY AS A CULTURAL CATALYST IN HEALTHCARE

Organizational culture is an important factor that influences the behavior, attitudes, and outcomes within healthcare systems. Defined as the shared values, beliefs, and norms that influence how work is performed and how people interact (Schein, 2010), organizational culture determines not only the efficiency of care delivery but also the ethical standards and legal compliance of clinical and administrative practices. In such complex environments, policy serves as a primary tool for shaping and sustaining a culture that prioritizes safety, accountability, and well-being for both patients and providers.

Policies are more than bureaucratic requirements; they are instruments that codify institutional values, guide behavior, and structure decision-making. When crafted effectively, policies help integrate ethical principles into daily routines and align clinical practices with legal standards. In doing so, they foster environments characterized by trust, transparency, and mutual respect. This chapter argues that policy is not only a mechanism for control and compliance but also a catalyst for cultivating organizational culture in healthcare settings.

Policy in Context: Why It Matters

Policy provides much-needed structure and guidance in healthcare, where life-and-death decisions occur daily. For instance, we design infection control protocols, medication administration policies, and documentation procedures to minimize errors and ensure consistent, high-quality care. Even well-trained professionals can be unsure of what to do if there aren't clear policies in place. These issues can lead to inconsistent care, a higher risk of harm, and possible legal problems (Gostin et al., 2020).

The COVID-19 pandemic brought home the value of responsive, ethically grounded, and transparent policies. During the height of the crisis, healthcare systems around the world scrambled to create or modify policies around triage, use of personal protective equipment (PPE), staff deployment, and telehealth. These policies, while often developed under pressure, were critical in coordinating large-scale responses, protecting healthcare workers, and maintaining patient care standards (Rosenbaum, 2020). The pandemic also showed how policy affects culture: institutions with clear, caring policies were more likely to keep staff morale high, encourage teamwork across disciplines, and create a safe space for people to talk about their feelings.

Bridging Ethical and Legal Mandates

At its best, policy bridges the ethical ideals of healthcare with the legal realities that define professional accountability. Ethical frameworks such as principlism Autonomy, beneficence, non-maleficence, and justice guide moral reasoning in clinical practice, but policies make these principles operational (Beauchamp & Childress, 2019). For example, policies governing informed consent are rooted in respect for patient autonomy, ensuring that individuals receive the information they need to make decisions about their care. Similarly, mandatory reporting policies for adverse events are grounded in ethical imperatives for transparency and justice.

Legal compliance is another key dimension. Regulatory mandates—such as those set by the Health Insurance Portability and Accountability Act (HIPAA) in the United States or the Care Quality Commission (CQC) in the United Kingdom—require that healthcare organizations implement specific policies to safeguard patient information, maintain accurate records, and ensure staff competence (Annas, 2011). Non-compliance not only exposes institutions to penalties but also erodes public trust. Thus, the development and enforcement of policy are essential to ethical integrity and legal accountability in healthcare.

Organizational Culture and the Policy Feedback Loop

Policy both shapes and reflects organizational culture. Schein (2010) posits that leaders systematically reinforce culture by rewarding, punishing, or modeling certain behaviors. In healthcare organizations, policies signal what behaviors are valued and expected. For example, when a hospital develops a zero-tolerance policy for workplace bullying and actively enforces it, the action sends a message about the institution's commitment to respect and inclusivity. Conversely, the absence of such policies—or the failure to enforce them—can normalize toxic behaviors and perpetuate unsafe working conditions.

The relationship between policy and culture is iterative. As culture evolves, it may challenge existing policies, prompting review and revision. Policies must therefore be dynamic, adapting to changes in clinical knowledge, societal values, and workforce expectations. Organizations have revised policies to ensure staff training, adapt environments to minimize re-traumatization, and support staff resilience as awareness of psychological trauma has increased. These policies, in turn, reinforce a culture of empathy, safety, and healing (Harris & Fallot, 2001).

Real-Life Example: The Role of Policy in Preventing Medical Errors

A powerful example of how policy shapes culture is the adoption of surgical safety checklists. Inspired by aviation protocols, the World Health Organization (WHO) introduced a 19-item surgical safety checklist aimed at reducing preventable errors during surgery. Institutions that adopted this policy reported significant declines in postoperative complications and mortality (Haynes et al., 2009). More importantly, the checklist helped foster a team-based culture where communication, mutual respect, and accountability became the norm. Surgeons, nurses, and anesthesiologists began each procedure with a shared understanding of patient needs, risks, and roles—an outcome enabled by policy and sustained by cultural change.

2. THEORETICAL FOUNDATIONS: UNDERSTANDING ORGANIZATIONAL CULTURE AND POLICY

The effectiveness of healthcare delivery is inextricably linked to the underlying culture of the organizations that provide it. Organizational culture not only shapes how healthcare professionals interact with one another and with patients, but it also guides decision-making, defines ethical boundaries, and influences how institutions respond to crises. To comprehend the influence of policy on the formation and maintenance of organizational culture, it is imperative to initially analyze fundamental theories of organizational behavior, the function of leadership, and the ethical principles that inform healthcare policy formulation.

2.1 Defining Organizational Culture in Healthcare

Organizational culture is often described as "the way things are done around here," but this simplification belies the complexity of the concept. Edgar Schein (2010), a foundational theorist in organizational psychology, defined organizational culture as a pattern of shared basic assumptions learned by a group as it solves its problems of external adaptation and internal integration. New members are taught that these are the right ways to see, think, and feel about those problems.

Schein's model identifies three levels of culture:

1. **Artifacts**: The visible and tangible elements of culture, such as language, dress code, policies, and procedures.
2. **Espoused Values**: The stated beliefs and values that an organization claims to uphold, such as patient-centered care or professionalism.

3. **Basic Underlying Assumptions**: Deeply ingrained beliefs that are often unconscious but guide behavior and perceptions.

In healthcare, these layers of culture manifest in myriad ways. For instance, the presence of protocols for hand hygiene represents an artifact; the institution's stated commitment to safety reflects an espoused value; and the belief that all patients deserve equitable treatment might be a basic underlying assumption. Policy, in this context, serves as a mechanism to translate values and assumptions into observable and actionable artifacts.

2.2 Policy as a Cultural Artifact and Shaping Mechanism

Policies act as both a mirror and a mold of organizational culture. They reflect existing values while also shaping future behaviors. In this dual role, policies become critical tools for organizational leaders seeking to reinforce desired cultural attributes or correct harmful patterns. For example, a policy mandating diversity training may reflect an espoused value of inclusion, but its implementation also aims to mold a culture of equity and respect.

Moreover, policies can institutionalize ethical standards and legal norms, making them accessible and enforceable in everyday practice. This codification is especially important in complex healthcare environments, where staff operate under high stress and time pressure. Well-designed policies reduce ambiguity, guide decision-making, and foster consistency in care delivery—key indicators of a strong, positive culture (Scott et al., 2003).

Policies are not static; they evolve in response to internal assessments, external regulations, and cultural shifts. Consider the growing recognition of the need for psychological safety in healthcare teams. Historically, many organizations lacked policies addressing workplace bullying or whistleblower protections. However, as research has highlighted the negative impacts of hostile work environments on staff retention and patient safety (Edmondson, 1999), institutions have increasingly adopted policies that promote respectful communication and protect staff who report concerns.

2.3 Leadership and Cultural Transmission through Policy

Organizational leaders are at the forefront of creating and sustaining culture through the strategic use of policy. According to Schein (2010), leaders influence culture by:

- What they pay attention to, measure, and control

- How they respond to critical incidents
- How they allocate resources
- Their modeling of behavior
- How they enforce policies and procedures

When leaders visibly prioritize staff well-being—through policies that support work-life balance or flexible scheduling, for instance—they signal to employees that their well-being is integral to the organization's mission. Conversely, when punitive or outdated policies persist without revision, it may suggest that the organization is resistant to change or unsupportive of its workforce.

Healthcare organizations that have successfully shifted their cultures often begin by revisiting and revising key policies. The Cleveland Clinic, for example, underwent a cultural transformation by developing a comprehensive set of policies and practices centered on patient experience and employee engagement. The clinic was able to change its culture to one of empathy, accountability, and continuous improvement by aligning its strategic priorities with policy changes. These changes included open performance reviews, cross-disciplinary teamwork projects, and structured listening sessions (Merlino, 2014).

2.4 Ethical Foundations of Healthcare Policy

Healthcare deeply intertwines ethics and culture. Policies, to be legitimate and effective, must be grounded in robust ethical frameworks. Several key approaches inform ethical decision-making in healthcare settings:

Principalism

Developed by Beauchamp and Childress (2019), the principlist approach emphasizes four main principles:

1. *Autonomy*—Respecting the patient's right to make informed decisions
2. *Beneficence*—Promoting the patient's well-being
3. *Non-maleficence*—Avoiding harm
4. *Justice*—Ensuring fair and equitable treatment

Policies that enforce informed consent, for example, operationalize the principle of autonomy. Triage policies in emergency departments, which prioritize treatment based on medical need, reflect the principle of justice.

Deontology

Rooted in the philosophy of Immanuel Kant, deontological ethics emphasize duty and rules over outcomes. In healthcare, this perspective supports policies that uphold rights and duties, such as confidentiality or the prohibition against euthanasia in certain jurisdictions, regardless of potential benefits.

Utilitarianism

Utilitarian ethics, articulated by philosophers like Bentham and Mill, prioritize outcomes and the greatest good for the highest number. Public health policies, such as vaccination mandates or quarantine regulations, are often justified using utilitarian reasoning, particularly during infectious disease outbreaks.

Each ethical framework provides a different lens for evaluating policy. A balanced policy approach in healthcare typically integrates aspects of all three, ensuring that policies are morally defensible, practically feasible, and culturally sensitive.

2.5 The Role of Professional Codes and Institutional Ethics

Professional codes and institutional ethics committees, in addition to philosophical ethics, shape healthcare policy. Professional associations such as the American Nurses Association (ANA) and the American Medical Association (AMA) offer codes of ethics that guide the development of institutional policies. These documents articulate professional values and can serve as benchmarks for evaluating whether a policy is ethically sound.

Institutional ethics committees play a critical role in reviewing complex or controversial policy proposals. Their involvement ensures that diverse perspectives—including those of clinicians, patients, legal advisors, and ethicists—are considered in the policy-making process (McCormick et al., 2012). These committees also help create an environment where people can think, be open, and learn.

3. POLICIES AS INSTRUMENTS OF ETHICAL AND LEGAL INTEGRITY

Policies in healthcare do more than set rules—they institutionalize core ethical principles and ensure compliance with the legal frameworks that govern clinical and organizational conduct. In high-stakes environments like hospitals, clinics, and long-term care facilities, policies serve as a foundation for ethical consistency, operational clarity, and legal accountability. By translating broad ethical ideals into concrete behavioral expectations and by aligning those expectations with statutory and regulatory requirements, policies play a critical role in maintaining organizational integrity.

This section examines how policies integrate ethical frameworks, enforce legal compliance, and foster environments of trust, fairness, and responsibility. Real-life cases and institutional practices demonstrate how the ethical-legal foundation of policy drives decision-making, improves care delivery, and safeguards patients and providers alike.

3.1 Legal Compliance: Policies as Risk Management Tools

In addition to ethical considerations, healthcare policies ensure compliance with national and international laws. Legal frameworks govern virtually all aspects of healthcare, from patient privacy to professional licensure, workplace safety, and anti-discrimination protections. Failure to comply can result in fines, loss of accreditation, legal liability, and reputational damage.

Patient Privacy and Confidentiality

A key legal area where policy is essential is *patient privacy*. The Health Insurance Portability and Accountability Act (HIPAA) in the United States, for example, mandates strict standards for how patient data is collected, stored, and shared. Organizations must have full privacy and data security policies that include training for employees, access controls, procedures for responding to breaches, and regular audits (Annas, 2011).

A widely cited breach occurred in 2018 when a large U.S. hospital faced federal penalties after several staff members accessed a celebrity's medical records without authorization. The investigation revealed that while HIPAA policies were in place, they were not enforced effectively, highlighting the importance of both robust policy content and strong implementation practices (Office for Civil Rights, 2018).

Informed Consent and Legal Liability

Informed consent is not only an ethical obligation—it is a legal requirement. In many jurisdictions, failure to obtain informed consent constitutes negligence and can expose providers and institutions to legal action. Policies that standardize the informed consent process protect both patients and organizations by making sure that all the paperwork is in order, that patients know what their options are, and that staff follow the same steps every time (Joffe et al., 2001).

Workplace Safety and Employment Law

Legal compliance also extends to *workplace safety* and employment practices. Laws such as the Occupational Safety and Health Act (OSHA) in the United States, or similar regulations globally, require healthcare employers to provide safe working environments. Policies that require the use of personal protective equipment (PPE), control exposure to infectious agents, or deal with violence at work are both legal and moral requirements (NIOSH, 2016).

3.2 Policy Failures and Ethical-Legal Consequences

Poorly designed, outdated, or inconsistently enforced policies can result in ethical lapses and legal violations. The Mid Staffordshire NHS Foundation Trust scandal in the United Kingdom is a well-known example. Between 2005 and 2009, systemic failures in policy implementation and enforcement contributed to hundreds of preventable patient deaths. Investigations revealed that cost-cutting policies, inadequate staffing levels, and poor incident reporting mechanisms undermined patient care and organizational accountability (Francis, 2013).

This case illustrates how misaligned or negligent policy frameworks can foster toxic cultures where ethical standards are compromised, legal obligations are ignored, and patients suffer the consequences. Conversely, timely policy reform—particularly when driven by ethical reflection and legal rigor—can prevent such failures.

3.3 Policies that Support Transparency and Accountability

Strong policies support transparency and accountability by establishing clear expectations, decision-making processes, and avenues for recourse. Two types of policies are particularly important:

Error Disclosure Policies

Policies that require the disclosure of medical errors to patients and families are essential to ethical integrity. These policies often include guidelines for apology, documentation, follow-up, and compensation when appropriate. Institutions that use open disclosure practices usually have fewer malpractice lawsuits and happier patients (Gallagher et al., 2007).

For example, the University of Michigan Health System implemented a disclosure-and-offer model that included training, proactive communication, and early resolution processes. Within three years, the system saw a significant reduction in legal claims and total liability costs (Kachalia et al., 2010).

Whistleblower Protections

Ethical and legal integrity also depend on policies that protect employees who report wrongdoing. Whistleblower policies ensure that individuals can raise concerns about unsafe practices, fraud, or abuse without fear of retaliation. Such policies are mandated by laws like the False Claims Act in the U.S. and are essential for maintaining ethical vigilance and organizational accountability (Lewis, 2011).

3.4 Integrating Policy Across Clinical and Administrative Domains

To be effective, ethical, and legal, policies must be integrated across both *clinical* and *administrative* operations. This includes:

- Clinical procedures (e.g., surgical checklists, infection control)
- Human resources (e.g., anti-discrimination policies, staff credentialing)
- Governance (e.g., board conduct, leadership accountability)
- IT systems (e.g., cybersecurity, electronic health record access)

Cross-functional policy design ensures consistency and helps break down silos that can lead to fragmentation of care and governance failures. Integrated policies promote whole-system learning and cultivate a shared commitment to ethical practice across all roles.

3.5 Real-Life Case: Ethical and Legal Alignment in Policy

One prominent example of effective ethical-legal alignment in policy is the Veterans Health Administration (VHA)'s implementation of its National Center for Ethics in Health Care. In the early 2000s, the VHA launched an IntegratedEthics program to embed ethical decision-making into every level of its operations. Policies were developed to:

- Ensure informed consent and advance care planning
- Create ethical leadership standards
- Guide resource allocation fairly
- Develop ethics consultation services

Evaluations showed improvements in staff confidence when handling ethical dilemmas, better compliance with consent laws, and higher patient satisfaction

(Foglia et al., 2009). This program demonstrates how policies can both reflect and promote ethical and legal excellence in large healthcare systems.

4. CREATING A CULTURE OF ACCOUNTABILITY AND SAFETY THROUGH POLICY

Patient safety and organizational accountability are inseparable goals in healthcare. A culture that prioritizes safety fosters continuous improvement, encourages open communication, and minimizes harm, while a culture of accountability ensures that responsibilities are clear, actions are transparent, and learning is integrated into practice. Central to achieving both outcomes is effective policy: codified guidance that not only mandates safe behaviors but also embeds safety and responsibility into the organizational DNA.

This section explores how healthcare organizations develop and enforce policies that build a culture of accountability and safety. Drawing on the principles of high-reliability organizations (HROs), it presents key policy domains such as incident reporting, standardization, and team communication. Real-world examples illustrate how thoughtfully designed policies reduce errors, improve staff engagement, and elevate patient outcomes.

4.1 High Reliability in Healthcare: The Role of Policy

High-reliability organizations—such as those in aviation or nuclear energy—operate in complex, high-risk environments yet manage to avoid catastrophic failures through meticulous attention to safety, learning, and resilience. These organizations share characteristics that healthcare institutions increasingly strive to emulate: preoccupation with failure, deference to expertise, reluctance to simplify, sensitivity to operations, and commitment to resilience (Weick & Sutcliffe, 2007).

Policies in high-reliability healthcare systems are not merely regulatory checklists—they are active instruments to create situational awareness, empower frontline staff, and reinforce consistent behaviors under pressure. For example, policies on emergency protocols or handoff communications are designed to reduce variability, support cognitive aids (such as checklists), and institutionalize team-based responses to crises.

Healthcare systems that model HRO principles use policy not only as a tool of control but also as a catalyst for shared accountability, where safety is everyone's responsibility (Chassin & Loeb, 2013).

4.2 Building a Just Culture Through Policy

A foundational concept in creating safety-focused environments is the *just culture* model. In contrast to punitive models, a just culture recognizes that most healthcare errors stem from system flaws rather than individual negligence. This model encourages staff to report errors and near-misses without fear of retaliation, while still holding individuals accountable for reckless or intentional behavior (Marx, 2001).

Policy is essential in operationalizing a just culture. Key features of just culture policies include:

- Definitions of blameworthy vs. non-blameworthy actions
- Clear guidelines for incident investigation
- Emphasis on systems improvement rather than individual punishment
- Pathways for reporting and debriefing

Example: Cincinnati Children's Hospital implemented a just culture framework by developing a policy that defined behavior categories (human error, at-risk behavior, reckless behavior) and aligned responses accordingly. The policy emphasized coaching, systems fixes, and only rare disciplinary action. As a result, staff reporting increased, and adverse events declined (Muething et al., 2012).

4.3 Standardization and Safety Protocol

Standardization through policy reduces clinical variation—a major contributor to medical errors. Policies that mandate the use of *evidence-based protocols*, checklists, and time-outs help prevent omissions, miscommunication, and procedural risks.

One of the most successful safety interventions is the *World Health Organization's Surgical Safety Checklist*, which standardizes three critical phases of surgery: sign-in, time-out, and sign-out. A multicenter study found that implementation of the checklist reduced postoperative complications by 36% and mortality by 47% (Haynes et al., 2009).

Policies built around standardization have been particularly impactful in areas such as

- Central line insertion (to prevent bloodstream infections)
- Medication reconciliation
- Falls prevention
- Antimicrobial stewardship

Case in point: At Johns Hopkins Hospital, a checklist-based policy for central line insertions, paired with a safety culture campaign, led to a 66% reduction in bloodstream infections across intensive care units (Pronovost et al., 2006). The policy required not only the use of a checklist but also empowered nurses to stop the procedure if protocols were not followed—reinforcing shared accountability.

4.4 Incident Reporting Policies and Learning Systems

Robust incident reporting systems—supported by clear policy—are essential for identifying risks, understanding system vulnerabilities, and initiating change. A key characteristic of learning organizations is their ability to transform adverse events into opportunities for improvement.

Effective incident reporting policies typically include:

- Confidentiality assurances
- Defined processes for review and root cause analysis (RCA)
- Feedback loops to communicate outcomes and lessons learned
- Support for second victims (staff involved in adverse events)

However, policies must go beyond reporting to ensure *actionable learning.* Without follow-up, staff may disengage or lose trust in the process.

Example: The NHS National Reporting and Learning System (NRLS) is one of the world's largest patient safety incident databases. Policies require organizations to report specific types of incidents (e.g., never events), and the system uses this data to issue national safety alerts and identify trends (Vincent, 2010). Despite challenges, NRLS has led to significant learning in areas such as opioid safety and wrong-site surgery.

4.5 Team Communication and Psychological Safety

Safety and accountability also depend on effective *interprofessional communication*, especially during high-risk interactions like handoffs, team huddles, and emergencies. Policies that support structured communication tools—such as *SBAR* (Situation, Background, Assessment, Recommendation) and *TeamSTEPPS* (Team Strategies and Tools to Enhance Performance and Patient Safety)—help standardize communication, clarify roles, and reduce errors due to misunderstandings.

Policies that require daily huddles, safety briefings, or post-event debriefings contribute to a culture of *psychological safety*, where staff feel comfortable speaking up with concerns, questions, or ideas (Edmondson, 1999). Psychological safety is strongly correlated with error reporting, learning behavior, and patient safety outcomes.

Real-world example: Kaiser Permanente Northern California adopted a policy requiring preoperative huddles using structured templates. This initiative led to improved team cohesion, fewer interruptions, and reductions in surgical complications (Mukamel et al., 2015).

4.6 Transparency and Public Accountability

Healthcare policies increasingly promote *external accountability* by requiring public reporting of safety and quality metrics. These include infection rates, hospital readmissions, and patient satisfaction scores. Transparency policies, enforced by regulators or accreditation bodies, aim to:

- Inform patient choice
- Encourage institutional benchmarking
- Drive quality improvement

While some clinicians express concern that public reporting may encourage gaming or data manipulation, studies suggest that well-structured transparency policies can incentivize real improvement (Berwick, 2009). Transparency also aligns with ethical principles of justice and respect for persons by giving patients access to information that affects their care.

5. STATE AND ORGANIZATIONAL POLICIES TO SUPPORT PROVIDER WELL-BEING

A well-being-centered healthcare environment is not merely a "nice-to-have"; it is a fundamental component of safe, high-quality patient care. The prevalence of burnout, moral distress, and mental health challenges among healthcare providers is well-documented, and these conditions directly affect job satisfaction, retention, and, most importantly, patient outcomes (Shanafelt et al., 2017; West et al., 2018). Effective policies at both state and organizational levels can address systemic stressors, promote balance, and build resilience, creating a virtuous cycle where provider well-being and patient safety reinforce one another.

5.1 The Challenge of Burnout and Moral Distress

Burnout—characterized by emotional exhaustion, depersonalization, and reduced personal accomplishment—is a serious concern across professional groups. Studies suggest that 30–60% of physicians and nurses experience symptoms of burnout during their careers (Shanafelt et al., 2017). Burnout contributes to decreased empathy, higher rates of medical errors, physician turnover, and compromised patient care (Dyrbye et al., 2017). Moral distress—arising when clinicians feel unable to act according to their ethical beliefs due to system-level constraints—further deepens this well-being crisis (Epstein & Hamric, 2009).

A holistic policy approach is necessary to address burnout and moral distress. Such policies involve institutional recognition of these issues, systematic monitoring, and proactive intervention strategies.

5.2 State-Level Mandates: Staffing Ratios and Leave Policies

Nurse-to-Patient Ratios

State legislation on staffing ratios has been among the most impactful tools in reducing burnout and improving safety. California's landmark law (AB 394), implemented in 2004, mandates specific nurse-to-patient ratios in acute care settings, such as 1:5 in general medical-surgical units and 1:2 in intensive care (Aiken et al., 2010). Research shows that this policy has led to:

- Lower nurse burnout and job dissatisfaction
- Reduced patient mortality and failure-to-rescue events
- Improved nurse retention rates (Aiken et al., 2010; Mark et al., 2013)

By prescribing safe staffing levels, the legislation operationalizes the ethical principles of beneficence and non-maleficence—not just toward patients, but also toward the workforce.

Paid Leave and Mental Health Support

Some jurisdictions have introduced policies supporting mental health and work-life balance for providers. For example, Oregon recently enacted laws ensuring paid sick leave for all workers, including healthcare staff, allowing them to address their own health needs without financial penalty. Similarly, some states mandate employee assistance programs (EAPs) for healthcare organizations, offering confidential counselling, stress management resources, and referral pathways (National Academy of Medicine, 2020).

5.3 Organizational Policies: Creating Supportive Work Environments

While state mandates are essential, much of the responsibility for provider well-being lies with organizational leadership. Key policy areas include:

Wellness Programs and Protected Time

Effective policies establish protected time for well-being activities. The Cleveland Clinic, for instance, introduced "Recharge Rooms"—quiet spaces for mental rest—alongside policy directives allowing employees to take short wellness breaks without fear of reprisal (Trockel et al., 2018). Other organizations include access to mindfulness training, peer support groups, and resilience workshops as part of formal well-being policies.

Flexible Scheduling and Workload Control

Policies that enable flexible scheduling—for example, part-time options, job-sharing, compressed workweeks, and predictable block time—reduce work-life conflict, a known contributor to burnout (Shanafelt & Noseworthy, 2017). Furthermore, workload policies that limit mandatory overtime and allow self-scheduling empower staff to manage stress proactively.

Peer Support and Debriefing After Critical Events

Healthcare organizations are increasingly adopting policies to provide structured peer support after adverse events, sometimes referred to as "second victim" programs. The University of Missouri Health System, for example, implemented a peer response program that trains colleagues to provide emotional support, guidance, and resources in the aftermath of errors or traumatic incidents (Schwartz Center, 2020).

5.4 Impact on Patient Care and Organizational Outcomes

Research consistently supports the connection between provider well-being and patient outcomes. In a systematic review, West et al. (2018) found that compared to less burned-out colleagues, physicians experiencing burnout were twice as likely to report major medical errors, and nurses reported increased patient falls and infections.

Conversely, organizational well-being policies are linked to retention, morale, and safety. Aiken et al. (2002) demonstrated that hospitals with better staffing and supportive work environments had lower nurse burnout, reduced staff turnover, and improved patient satisfaction. Health systems with formal counselor programs and wellness policies also see reduced provider sick leave and higher engagement scores.

5.5 Real-Life Case: Implementing Provider Well-being Policies

Case Study: Mayo Clinic's Physician Well-Being Program

The Mayo Clinic responded to rising burnout by launching a comprehensive Well-Being Index (WBI) and related policies. The WBI is a validated, anonymous tool clinicians complete periodically. Policies mandate follow-up support for respondents indicating distress. The organization also enacts support for workload balancing, resilience training, and administrative burden reduction. Over five years, the program correlated with stable low burnout rates and increased professional fulfillment (Shanafelt et al., 2020).

Case Study: Stanford Health Care's Fatigue Mitigation Policies

Stanford Health Care implemented policies to limit resident physician work hours, enforce mandatory rest periods between shifts, and provide wellness resources. These policies emerged from data showing that fatigue-related errors were significantly higher when residents worked over 80 hours per week. After policy implementation, fatigue indicators decreased, resident well-being improved, and performance metrics—such as chart completion rates—saw measurable improvement (Lockley et al., 2007).

6. REGULATORY FRAMEWORKS AND CONTINUOUS IMPROVEMENT

External regulatory frameworks and continuous quality improvement mechanisms serve as essential complements to internal policies in healthcare. These frameworks define minimum standards, enforce accountability, and stimulate organizational learning pathways. Through accreditation, compliance checks, and data-driven reviews, regulatory oversight supports transparent governance and incentivizes improvements. In this section, we explore how healthcare organizations leverage regulatory tools—from national accreditation programs to international standards—to enhance safety, quality, and leadership performance.

6.1 Key Regulatory Bodies and Accreditation Organizations

Healthcare systems operate within a landscape rich in regulatory oversight. Major entities include:

- *Joint Commission (TJC)*—In the U.S., TJC accreditation is a hallmark of quality. TJC standards address patient safety, infection control, governance, and staff competency (The Joint Commission, 2023).
- *Centers for Medicare & Medicaid Services (CMS)*—Through conditions of participation, CMS sets requirements for hospitals to receive federal funding.
- *Occupational Safety and Health Administration (OSHA)*—OSHA enforces workplace safety and hazard protocols.
- *International Organization for Standardization (ISO)*—Standards like ISO 9001 (quality management) and ISO 45001 (occupational health & safety) provide frameworks for global consistency.

These bodies utilize site surveys, performance indicators, and corrective action plans to ensure compliance. Regular re-accreditation cycles compel institutions to maintain continuous readiness and embed learning in the organizational fabric.

6.2 Accreditation as Cultural Driver

Accreditation does more than satisfy external mandates—it drives cultural transformation by setting performance benchmarks and fostering collective responsibility. The accreditation process unfolds in cycles of self-assessment, external evaluation, and corrective action—a structure mirroring the Plan–Do–Check–Act (PDCA) model (Deming, 1986).

When healthcare leaders dedicate resources to achieving accreditation, they signal organizational values that prioritize quality, transparency, and patient safety. Staff engagement in preparatory work—such as policy review, mock surveys, and interdisciplinary committees—enhances ownership and embeds quality-focused mindsets (Greenfield & Braithwaite, 2008).

6.3 Quality Metrics and Reporting Requirements

Regulatory frameworks increasingly mandate *public reporting* of core quality metrics, such as surgical mortality, readmission rates, and infection incidents. CMS's

Hospital Compare and other private reporting platforms incentivize continuous improvement by enabling benchmarking and accountability (CMS, 2023).

Internally, organizations develop dashboards that track metrics like central line-associated bloodstream infection (CLABSI) rates, medication errors, and patient satisfaction. Policies that require data transparency and multidisciplinary review ensure that metrics inform decision-making and corrective actions—not merely serve as compliance checkboxes.

6.4 Feedback Loops and Continuous Learning

Continuous improvement is central to quality frameworks like the *IHI Model for Improvement* and ISO's quality principles. These models stress the importance of using data to find gaps, try out small changes, and learn quickly.

Policies that institutionalize regular *after-action reviews*, morbidity & mortality (M&M) conferences, and quality improvement (QI) committees promote a culture where mistakes are learning opportunities. Organizations such as Intermountain Healthcare use embedded QI teams to review cases, measure change impact, and scale successful interventions organization-wide (Spath, 2013).

A strong feedback loop requires structural supports: centralized analytics, leadership sponsorship, and protected time. Policies that ensure teams can dedicate time to QI activities—without disrupting patient services—align operational workflows with strategic goals.

6.5 Regulatory Enforcement and Organizational Response

When regulatory reviews identify deficits, organizations must develop *corrective action plans (CAPs)* to rectify issues. Effective policies specify roles, timelines, metrics, and escalation channels within CAP frameworks.

For instance, after CMS identified clinical deficiencies at a hospital, the institution enacted a policy tasking a multidisciplinary committee to update protocols, deliver staff training, and report progress monthly to the board. The visible ownership of CAPs reinforces a culture of accountability and learning.

6.6 Case Study: The Magnet Recognition Program®

The Magnet Recognition Program®, led by the American Nurses Credentialing Center, evaluates nursing excellence across domains such as leadership, professional development, structural empowerment, and exemplary care (ANCC, 2024). Organizations pursuing Magnet status implement a suite of policies: shared governance councils, data-based staffing, nurse-led QI projects, and leadership mentoring structures.

Achieving Magnet certification signals a culture that values clinical excellence, interdisciplinary collaboration, and continual advancement. Studies demonstrate that Magnet hospitals exhibit better nurse satisfaction, lower turnover, and improved patient outcomes compared to non-Magnet peers (Patrician et al., 2019).

6.7 International Standards: ISO 9001 and ISO 45001

While U.S.-based frameworks dominate domestically, *ISO standards* offer universal mechanisms for governance and safety. ISO 9001 (quality management) and ISO 45001 (occupational health & safety) require organizations to implement system-wide processes: risk assessments, stakeholder engagement, resource allocation, and leadership commitment.

For example, a tertiary hospital in Singapore adopted ISO 9001 to structure its quality programs. The hospital experienced reductions in procedural errors and increased compliance with international best practices (Chin et al., 2017). Integration with internal policies ensured long-term sustainability, transcending the accreditation cycle.

7. INTEGRATED CASE STUDY: POLICY-DRIVEN TRANSFORMATION IN A HEALTHCARE ORGANIZATION

7.1 Introduction

Understanding how policy translates into practice requires more than theoretical discussion—it requires insight into real-world implementation. In this section, we conduct an in-depth analysis of *Virginia Mason Medical Center (VMMC)* in Seattle, a health system widely recognized for its innovative application of lean principles, patient-first philosophy, and data-driven governance. The changes that have happened at VMMC over the past 20 years show how structured, ethical, and constantly updated policy can be the key to cultural change, operational excellence, and long-term safety outcomes.

Virginia Mason's journey is not just a story of quality improvement; it is a case study in the deliberate use of policy to shape professional behavior, align strategic intent with ethical obligations, and balance provider well-being with clinical accountability.

7.2 Historical Context and Crisis as Catalyst

Virginia Mason experienced a pivotal moment in 2001. A series of preventable adverse events—including the high-profile death of a patient due to a misadministered medication—served as a wake-up call for institutional leadership (Kenney, 2011). Internally, employees said they felt overwhelmed, unsupported, and cut off from the organization's larger goals. Externally, the institution risked reputational damage and regulatory scrutiny.

These conditions reflect a common theme in healthcare: cultural inertia can persist until a crisis forces change. However, what differentiates VMMC is the leadership's response—a strategic, policy-centered transformation rather than short-term remediation.

7.3 Strategic Pivot: Policy as Moral and Operational Anchor

Instead of simply introducing new procedures, Virginia Mason redefined its organizational DNA. The hospital's executive team established a foundational policy principle: *"The patient comes first."* This was not a branding exercise; it was institutionalized in policy documents, governance structures, performance evaluations, and budgeting priorities.

This guiding principle had both *ethical* and *operational* implications:

- *Ethically*, it aligned with principles of beneficence and respect for autonomy.
- *Operationally*, it justified investment in patient safety technologies, frontline empowerment, and care redesign—even when such actions did not yield immediate financial return.

For instance, VMMC adopted the *Virginia Mason Production System (VMPS)*, a healthcare-adapted version of the Toyota Production System. This lean model emphasizes respect for people, elimination of waste, and standardization of high-risk processes. Unlike many hospitals that implement lean superficially, VMMC rewrote internal policies to institutionalize lean as a core operating system (Spear, 2005).

7.4 Transformative Policies and Frameworks

7.4.1 Safety Protocol Standardization

One of the first policy interventions was the standardization of clinical procedures. High-risk processes—such as central line insertion, blood transfusions, and chemotherapy administration—were redesigned using standardized bundles.

Policy features included:

- Clear protocol checklists tied to mandatory EHR fields
- Real-time compliance monitoring with public scorecards
- Mandatory error reporting within 24 hours of deviation

Compliance was not optional; deviation required written justification and review by a clinical governance board. This formalized accountability while encouraging learning over punishment.

7.4.2 Just Culture and Non-Punitive Reporting

A cornerstone of the transformation was the introduction of a *Just Culture Policy*. Unlike traditional punitive approaches, this policy created a framework to differentiate between:

- Human error (console and support)
- At-risk behavior (coach and redesign systems)
- Reckless behavior (discipline appropriately)

Staff were trained in the Just Culture algorithm, and event debriefs became routine. A crucial element was transparency: aggregated safety data and learning summaries were shared across departments to reinforce collective ownership (Marx, 2001).

7.5 Empowering the Workforce: Policies for Well-being and Autonomy

7.5.1 Daily Management Systems and Shared Governance

Every clinical unit was required to conduct *Daily Management System (DMS)* meetings—short, structured huddles where staff reviewed safety concerns, near misses, and quality indicators. Policies required attendance, and senior leaders were expected to do weekly walkthroughs and show support in person.

Additionally, shared governance councils were formalized, giving nurses and allied health professionals direct input into policy development. By codifying these participatory structures, Virginia Mason reinforced psychological safety and intrinsic motivation (Shanafelt & Noseworthy, 2017).

7.5.2 Policies for Burnout Mitigation and Support

Recognizing that provider well-being was essential to quality care, VMMC introduced policies such as

- *Peer support debriefs* after critical incidents, led by trained facilitators
- *Protected mental health days* and flexible shift-swapping systems
- *Leadership development programs* for frontline staff to improve career satisfaction

Importantly, provider burnout rates became a *quality indicator* tracked on the institutional dashboard. Department heads were held accountable for improvements, incentivizing long-term cultural investment.

7.6 External Alignment: Regulatory Standards and Strategic Accreditation

Rather than viewing regulatory compliance as burdensome, VMMC used it as a catalyst for improvement. The organization seamlessly integrated *Joint Commission standards*, *CMS reporting metrics*, and *IHI campaign goals* into its operational policies.

Examples include:

- *Real-time infection dashboards* that fed into CMS public reporting and internal QI teams
- *CLABSI bundle compliance policies* that mirrored Joint Commission NPSGs
- *Annual RCA policy review cycles* aligned with accreditation timelines

By embedding these external standards into internal governance, VMMC created a system where compliance was not episodic but embedded in culture.

7.7 Measurable Outcomes: Sustained Excellence Through Policy

Virginia Mason's commitment to policy-guided transformation yielded impressive and sustained results, as shown in table 1:

Table 1. Virginia's Results

Domain	Impact
Patient Safety	74% reduction in ADEs (Kenney, 2011); zero-harm units established
Provider Satisfaction	Sustained increase in engagement scores; burnout decreased by 25%
Regulatory Performance	Exceeded Joint Commission benchmarks five years consecutively
Financial Sustainability	Operational efficiency increased, reduced length of stay and cost per case
Patient-Centered Metrics	Press Ganey scores in the top 10% nationally for patient satisfaction

These metrics did not result from isolated initiatives—they were the result of coherent, well-designed, and ethically grounded policy architecture.

7.8 Cultural Indicators: Signs of Deep Change

Beyond metrics, indicators of cultural transformation included:

- *Visible psychological safety*—Staff openly discussed errors and near misses in meetings. —Staff
- *Flattened hierarchies*—junior nurses and aides routinely contributed to policy reviews.
- *Narrative ownership*—"The "patient comes first" was cited by staff at all levels, unprompted.

Such depth of alignment between stated values and lived practice is rare—and highly dependent on continuous policy reinforcement, leadership modeling, and frontline empowerment.

7.9 Transferability and Lessons for Other Systems

While some may argue that VMMC's transformation was context-specific, key elements mentioned in table 2 are generalizable:

Table 2. Key Elements

Principle	Transferable Policy Strategy
Values-driven care	Anchor all policies in clear, ethical organizational values
Frontline empowerment	Codify staff participation in governance and improvement structures
Data transparency	Publicly report outcomes; share failures as opportunities
Integrated compliance	Harmonize internal policies with regulatory frameworks
Well-being as strategic priority	Track burnout as a key performance indicator; build support into policy

By viewing policy not just as compliance but as cultural infrastructure, other organizations can use similar methods to align their workforce, elevate safety, and transform outcomes.

8. GHANA HEALTH SERVICE / SELECTED GHANAIAN HOSPITALS (2021–2022)

- In 2022 a national cross-sectional study assessed patient safety in 27 hospitals across Ghana. Using the World Health Organization (WHO) Patient Safety Long Form, the study found an overall patient safety "score" of ~ 85%. "Knowledge and learning in patient safety" was the strongest domain (97%), while areas like safety surveillance, funding for patient safety, and systemic safety partnerships fared worse. Less than half (≈ 42%) of hospitals had a dedicated budget for patient-safety activities.
- A follow-up (2024) facility-level study at one hospital (in Ghana) found *poor compliance* (≈ 29.2%) with safety-culture protocols and a high prevalence of adverse events, highlighting persistent gaps between "policy/knowledge" and implementation on the ground.
- Qualitative work from 2023–2024 among frontline staff in some regional hospitals shows awareness of patient safety culture is "average," and many feel safety depends heavily on individual practices rather than systemic safeguards.

Why this matters (as an LMIC "policy-driven culture" example):

- The Ghanaian work demonstrates an explicit attempt to *evaluate* patient safety across multiple hospitals using a structured framework (WHO tools).
- By doing so, it lays the groundwork for a *national patient safety policy* (since the 2015 draft) to be finalized and implemented—a policy-level ambition rooted in data, not just ad hoc efforts.

- At the same time, the 2024 compliance data remind us that *policy or assessment ≠ perfect practice*—culture, resources, and implementation remain key constraints.

8.1 Ministry of Health, Timor-Leste / National-level Strengthening (2020–2023)

- During the COVID-19 pandemic and beyond, Timor-Leste invested in strengthening its health system—expanding diagnostic lab capacity, building clinical care capacity, and improving emergency preparedness and health governance. This was part of its broader long-term strategic plan under the Second National Health Sector Strategic Plan (Timor-Leste) 2020-2030 (NHSSP II).
- As part of reorganizing its health services, the country renewed its commitment to infection prevention and control (IPC), surveillance, and resilience—thus embedding patient-safety-related policies into broader health system reform rather than treating them as optional add-ons.
- In parallel, the government updated its antimicrobial-resistance containment plan (National Action Plan for Antimicrobial Resistance Containment 2022–2026), emphasizing infection control, stewardship, and cross-sectoral governance—policies with direct implications for patient safety and ethical usage of medications.

Why this matters:

- This is a *system-wide, cross-sector policy effort*—not just hospital-level—which strengthens infrastructure, governance, surveillance, and safety preparedness, aligning with global standards for resilient health systems.
- The Timor-Leste example shows that even small LMICs—under resource constraints—can embed safety, surveillance, ethics (e.g., antimicrobial stewardship), and preparedness into national health policy, improving baseline resilience and capacity.

8.3 What These Examples Show—and What They Don't

These cases reveal several realities for LMICs striving toward policy-driven culture, patient safety, and governance:

- **Strength through assessment and policy ambition:** The Ghanaian study demonstrates that data-driven assessments can build the foundation for national-level policy and resource allocation. Without initial measurement and baseline assessment, reforms are unlikely to be prioritized.

- **Implementation gaps remain large:** Even when policy or assessment exists, actual compliance—especially around safety culture, consistent protocols, and dedicated funding—is still spotty (as shown in the Ghana 2024 study).
- **Systemic vs. institutional scale:** While LMICs like Timor-Leste pursue national-level reforms (governance, surveillance, IPC, antimicrobial stewardship), that doesn't always translate into consistent, frontline hospital practice—especially in smaller or rural facilities.
- **Resource constraints & sustainability challenges:** Dedicated budgets, staff training, and infrastructure upgrades are often limited or temporary (e.g., during COVID-19), which makes sustaining gains over time difficult.

What remains largely missing—and what ought to be a target—is a comprehensive, *integrated "culture overhaul"* (communication norms, patient-centered care, empathy, staff well-being, ethics committees, and shared decision-making). The existing LMIC examples often focus on safety, IPC, governance—but less on humanistic care or staff psychological safety (as in the original high-resource model)

REFERENCES

Aiken, L. H., Clarke, S. P., Sloane, D. M., Sochalski, J., & Silber, J. H. (2002). Hospital nurse staffing and patient mortality, nurse burnout, and job dissatisfaction. *Journal of the American Medical Association, 288*(16), 1987–1993. DOI: 10.1001/jama.288.16.1987 PMID: 12387650

Aiken, L. H., Sloane, D., Cimiotti, J., Clarke, S., Flynn, L., Seago, J., Spetz, J., & Smith, H. (2010). Implications of the California nurse staffing mandate for other states. *Health Services Research, 45*(4), 904–921. DOI: 10.1111/j.1475-6773.2010.01114.x PMID: 20403061

American Nurses Credentialing Center (ANCC). (2024). *Magnet Recognition Program® standards*. ANCC.

Annas, G. J. (2011). *The rights of patients: The authoritative ACLU guide to the rights of patients* (3rd ed.). New York University Press.

Beauchamp, T. L., & Childress, J. F. (2019). *Principles of biomedical ethics* (8th ed.). Oxford University Press.

Berwick, D. M. (2009). What 'patient-centered' should mean: Confessions of an extremist. *Health Affairs, 28*(4, Supplement 1), w555–w565. DOI: 10.1377/hlthaff.28.4.w555 PMID: 19454528

Centers for Medicare & Medicaid Services (CMS). (2023). *Hospital Compare*. U.S. Department of Health & Human Services.

Chassin, M. R., & Loeb, J. M. (2013). High-reliability health care: Getting there from here. *The Milbank Quarterly, 91*(3), 459–490. DOI: 10.1111/1468-0009.12023 PMID: 24028696

Chin, C.-L., Goh, J., & Lim, S. (2017). ISO 9001 certification and its impact on hospitals: A case study from Singapore. *International Journal of Health Care Quality Assurance, 30*(5), 453–467. DOI: 10.1108/IJHCQA-02-2016-0022

Cleveland Clinic. (2021). *Annual Caregiver Experience Report*. Cleveland Clinic Press.

Deming, W. E. (1986). *Out of the crisis*. MIT Press.

Dyrbye, L. N., West, C. P., Satele, D., Boone, S., Tan, L., Sloan, J., & Shanafelt, T. D. (2017). Burnout among US medical students, residents, and early-career physicians relative to the general US population. *Academic Medicine, 89*(3), 443–451. DOI: 10.1097/ACM.0000000000000134 PMID: 24448053

Edmondson, A. (1999). Psychological safety and learning behavior in work teams. *Administrative Science Quarterly*, *44*(2), 350–383. DOI: 10.2307/2666999

Epstein, E. G., & Hamric, A. B. (2009). Moral distress, moral residue, and the crescendo effect. *The Journal of Clinical Ethics*, *20*(4), 330–342. DOI: 10.1086/JCE200920406 PMID: 20120853

Foglia, M. B., Fox, E., Chanko, B. L., & Bottrell, M. M. (2009). Ethics and the healthcare organization: Strategy, leadership, and accountability. *Public Administration Review*, *69*(6), 1067–1075. DOI: 10.1111/j.1540-6210.2009.02045.x

Francis, R. (2013). *Report of the Mid Staffordshire NHS Foundation Trust public inquiry*. The Stationery Office.

Gallagher, T. H., Waterman, A. D., Ebers, A. G., Fraser, V. J., & Levinson, W. (2007). Patients' and physicians' attitudes regarding the disclosure of medical errors. *Journal of the American Medical Association*, *289*(8), 1001–1007. DOI: 10.1001/jama.289.8.1001 PMID: 12597752

Gostin, L. O., Wiley, L. F., & Frieden, T. R. (2020). *Public health law: Power, duty, restraint* (3rd ed.). University of California Press.

Greenfield, D., & Braithwaite, J. (2008). Health sector accreditation research: A systematic review. *International Journal for Quality in Health Care : Journal of the International Society for Quality in Health Care*, *20*(3), 172–183. DOI: 10.1093/intqhc/mzn005 PMID: 18339666

Harris, M., & Fallot, R. D. (2001). *Using trauma theory to design service systems*. Jossey-Bass.

Haynes, A. B., Weiser, T. G., Berry, W. R., Lipsitz, S. R., Breizat, A. H. S., Dellinger, E. P., & Gawande, A. A. (2009). They developed a surgical safety checklist aimed at reducing morbidity and mortality in a global population. *The New England Journal of Medicine*, *360*(5), 491–499. DOI: 10.1056/NEJMsa0810119 PMID: 19144931

Lockley, S. W., Landrigan, C. P., Barger, L. K., Czeisler, C. A., & Rothschild, J. M. (2007). Effects of reducing interns' weekly work hours on sleep and attentional failures. *PLoS Medicine*, *4*(12), e262. DOI: 10.1371/journal.pmed.0040262

Mark, B. A., Harless, D. W., McCue, M., & Xu, Y. (2013). Effects of state minimum staffing legislation on hospital nurse staffing and patient outcomes: A synthesis of evidence from California's staffing mandate. *Nursing Research*, *62*(2), 79–92. DOI: 10.1097/NNR.0b013e318286566b

Marx, D. (2001). *Patient safety and the "just culture": A primer for health care executives*. Columbia University.

McCormick, T. R., Min, D., & Rosenblatt, D. E. (2012). Ethics committees and consultation. In Field, M. J., & Behrman, R. E. (Eds.), *When children die: Improving palliative and end-of-life care for children and their families* (pp. 201–228). National Academies Press.

Merlino, J. (2014). *Service fanatics: How to build superior patient experience the Cleveland Clinic way*. McGraw-Hill Education.

Merlino, J. (2014). *Service fanatics: How to build superior patient experience the Cleveland Clinic way*. McGraw Hill Education.

Muething, S. E., Goudie, A., Schoettker, P. J., Donnelly, L. F., Goodfriend, M. A., Bracke, T. M., Brady, P. W., Wheeler, D. S., Anderson, J. M., & Kotagal, U. R. (2012). Quality improvement initiative to reduce serious safety events and improve patient safety culture. *Pediatrics*, *130*(2), e423–e431. DOI: 10.1542/peds.2011-3566 PMID: 22802607

National Academy of Medicine. (2020). *Taking action against clinician burnout: A systems approach to professional well-being*. National Academies Press.

Patrician, P. A., Shang, J., & Lake, E. T. (2019). The Magnet recognition program: Nursing excellence and implications for care outcomes. *The Journal of Nursing Administration*, *49*(10), 511–518. DOI: 10.1097/NNA.0000000000000789

Pronovost, P., Needham, D., Berenholtz, S., Sinopoli, D., Chu, H., Cosgrove, S., Sexton, B., Hyzy, R., Welsh, R., Roth, G., Bander, J., Kepros, J., & Goeschel, C. (2006). An intervention to decrease catheter-related bloodstream infections in the ICU. *The New England Journal of Medicine*, *355*(26), 2725–2732. DOI: 10.1056/NEJMoa061115 PMID: 17192537

Rosenbaum, L. (2020). Facing Covid-19 in Italy—Ethics, logistics, and therapeutics on the epidemic's front line. *The New England Journal of Medicine*, *382*(20), 1873–1875. DOI: 10.1056/NEJMp2005492 PMID: 32187459

Schein, E. H. (2010). *Organizational culture and leadership* (4th ed.). Jossey-Bass.

Schwartz Center. (2020). *Peer support program: A model for second victim recovery*. The Schwartz Center for Compassionate Healthcare. Retrieved from https://www.theschwartzcenter.org

Scott, T., Mannion, R., Davies, H., & Marshall, M. (2003). The quantitative measurement of organizational culture in health care: A review of the available instruments. *Health Services Research*, *38*(3), 923–945. DOI: 10.1111/1475-6773.00154 PMID: 12822919

Shanafelt, T. D., & Noseworthy, J. H. (2017). Executive leadership and physician well-being: Nine organizational strategies to promote engagement and reduce burnout. *Mayo Clinic Proceedings*, *92*(1), 129–146. DOI: 10.1016/j.mayocp.2016.10.004 PMID: 27871627

Shanafelt, T. D., West, C. P., & Satele, D.. (2017). Burnout and satisfaction with work-life balance among US physicians relative to the general US population. *PeerJ*, *5*, e3246. DOI: 10.7717/peerj.3246

Shanafelt, T. D., West, C. P., Sloan, J. A., Novotny, P. J., Poland, G. A., Menaker, R., & Swartz, H. A. (2020). Changes in burnout and professional satisfaction with an innovative physician well-being program: Mayo Clinic 2015–2019. *Mayo Clinic Proceedings*, *95*(12), 2590–2603. DOI: 10.1016/j.mayocp.2020.06.010

Spath, P. (2013). *Introduction to healthcare quality management* (2nd ed.). Health Administration Press.

The Joint Commission. (2023). *Comprehensive accreditation manual for hospitals*. The Joint Commission.

Vincent, C. (2010). *Patient safety* (2nd ed.). Wiley-Blackwell. DOI: 10.1002/9781444323856

Weick, K. E., & Sutcliffe, K. M. (2007). *Managing the unexpected: Resilient performance in an age of uncertainty* (2nd ed.). Jossey-Bass.

West, C. P., Dyrbye, L. N., & Shanafelt, T. D. (2018). Physician burnout: Contributors, consequences, and solutions. *Journal of Internal Medicine*, *283*(6), 516–529. DOI: 10.1111/joim.12752 PMID: 29505159

Chapter 9

G.R.A.S.P. Model: Impact on Well-Being of Healthcare Providers

Minhaj A. Qidwai
http://orcid.org/0009-0003-0770-481X
Al-Kawthar University, Karachi, Pakistan

Tehrim Toqir
http://orcid.org/0009-0006-7027-077X
Ziauddin Medical University, Pakistan

ABSTRACT

Measuring impact of an organisation need studying the inputs required for the desired outcome and the impact. If the desired outcomes are not met, the inputs are re-assessed and reprocessed. Till we do not achieve the desired outcomes, the cycle of input, process, output, and outcome is continued. Therefore, healthcare managers and leaders need to understand the input variables effecting the Eco system of the organisation and its culture for the desired impact. Thus, the need of a model comprising of the input factors to be processed for the desired output, outcome and impact. G.R.AS.P. model comprising of the key variables of Governance, Resource Allocation, Accountability, Sustainability and Profitability is presented as a concept for impacting the organisational culture. The organisational Eco system, thus can impact on the well-being of the healthcare providers. Thus, the need to create an organisational culture to have an impact on the well-being of healthcare providers, enabling them to produce the desired results.

DOI: 10.4018/979-8-2600-0582-8.ch009

INTRODUCTION

Human capital is the most critical component of organizations, serving as their economic engine. The employees play a vital role in gaining a competitive advantage for the organization. Their quality, competence, capability, and ability are decisive in its performance.

The health of the organization depends upon the environment within and outside and is deeply rooted in the satisfaction, engagement, and performance of employees. Their well-being influences productivity, innovation, and profits, resulting in a thriving economy and societal culture. Studies have shown that employee satisfaction and engagement enhance both individual and organizational outcomes, fostering resilience and sustainable growth (Bakker et al., 2023; Oswald, Proto, & Sgroi, 2023). A healthy organizational culture—characterized by psychological safety, ethical leadership, and supportive work environments—acts as a microcosm of societal well-being (Salas-Vallina, Alegre, & Fernández, 2021; Cooper & Cartwright, 2022). In line with the World Health Organization's framework for healthy workplaces, which emphasizes that nurturing organizational well-being contributes not only to improved workforce performance but also to broader social stability and health equity (WHO, 2020; Kim & Wang, 2022). Thus, fostering an organizational culture significantly impacts employee well-being, which is not only a corporate responsibility but also a societal imperative, linking workplace well-being to the overall happiness and functionality of nations (Helliwell, Layard, & Sachs, 2024)[7].

To remain healthy, an organization must adopt structural measures like institutionalizing good governance and accountability and developing performance indicators. Market research should be conducted to identify the key customers and competitors for sustainability. Governance is a set of individual and institutional, public and private actions for planning joint administration of affairs and a continuous process of creating understanding between different and conflicting interests (WHO 2021, OECD 2023). Empirical research substantiates that effectively governed institutions exhibit enhanced operational efficiency, employee satisfaction, and stakeholder trust, thereby directly fostering organizational health (Panda & Patnaik, 2021; Abdullah & Ashraf, 2022)[11].

Good governance is incomplete without incorporating elements such as accountability, a participatory approach, the rule of law, foresight ability, democratic practices, and civil liberties.

Accountability is one of the primary objectives and components considered by policymakers and health systems managers. The World Health Organization (WHO 2022)[12] framework for evaluating health system performance revolves around health, responsiveness, and financial fairness as the primary objectives of any health system. Today, accountability has gained increasing importance and it is a systemic concept.

Outcomes or benefits for customers are designed to provide adequate recognition and an appropriate response to their reasonable expectations.

HUMAN WELLNESS MANAGEMENT AND THE 5SS'

The outcomes for employees are geared towards health status with well-being as the impact. However, it depends upon the management of various dimensions of human wellness at the outset. Ensuring the well-being of the healthcare providers (HCPs) is the key to impacting the organizational performance and profitability. The various human wellness dimensions form the inputs processed for the desired output, outcome, and impact, resulting in well-being. As per WHO (2008), wellness is "the optimal state of health of individuals and groups." On the other hand, well-being refers to the comprehensive state of being healthy, happy, and fulfilled. Organizational leadership needs to ensure the well-being of their employees and devise a plan for Human Wellness Management (Fig. 1).

Figure 1.

As per Figure 1, wellness for health needs inputs from various dimensions to be processed to ensure ease with healthy status as an outcome and well-being as the desired impact. Thus, wellness is "an active process through which people become aware of, and make choices toward, a more successful existence." The various wellness dimensions revolve around the

The 5Ss of Dr. Minhaj Qidwai

- The *Self*: The individual is the hub of functionality. We must prioritize self-reflectivity.

- The *Society*: The environment and people are the hub of community activities that revolve around individuals (self).
- The *State*: The laws, policies, rules & regulations for self-implementation.
- The *Systems*: Backbone of functioning for people, organizations, and institutions. For operation, a system needs resources focused on their effective and efficient use for quality service delivery.
- The *Spirituality*: Self-awareness—to discover the meaning of self-existence. It is crucial to extend love to everyone through compassionate and ethical actions.

Figure 2.

The various dimensions (Fig. 2) can be categorized according to the 5Ss (Self, Society, State, Systems, and Spirituality) as follows:

A. Self-Health: Physical, Intellectual, Emotional, Occupational, Financial, Vocational, and Economical Health.
B. Systems Health: Quality Service Delivery, Human Resources, Information System (Digital Health/AI), Access to Health and Medicines, Financial Health, Leadership, and Governance.
C. State Health: Economy, Environment, Health Security, Laws, Policies, Rules & Regulations.
D. Social Health: Societal and Environmental Health.
E. Spiritual Health: Finding meaning of "self" existence and transcendence.

Out of all the dimensions, there are 8 core dimensions (Swarbrick, M. 2023). These dimensions are mapped as per the 5S philosophy mentioned earlier.

Figure 3.

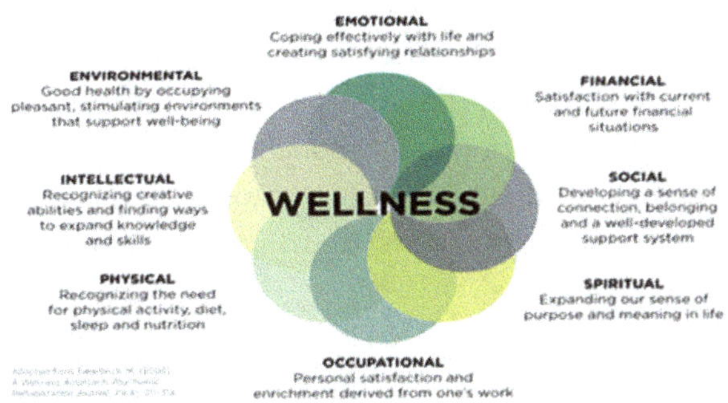

Based on the above table (1) and Fig. 3, it is apparent that the organizational leadership and the Human Resource department play a vital role in ensuring the well-being of employees and the organization. Furthermore, mapping the wellness dimensions against the 5Ss gives empirical evidence of the role they can play in elucidating their role in nailing down the organizational inputs required for Human Wellness Management to have an impact on their well-being.

Organizational leadership and the human resource department play a vital and synergistic role in ensuring the well-being of both employees and the organization. Effective leadership establishes vision, trust, and psychological safety, while Human Resource Management (HRM) operationalizes these values through supportive policies, fair practices, and employee development initiatives. Empirical research demonstrates that transformational and participative leadership styles foster engagement, job satisfaction, and overall psychological well-being among staff (Zheng, Diaz, & Zhu, 2022; Kelloway, Nielsen, & Dimoff, 2023). Similarly, strategic HRM practices—such as wellness programs, equitable workload management, and continuous feedback—are associated with reduced burnout and improved organizational resilience (Guest, 2017; Harney & Collings, 2021). The integration of leadership and HRM under a wellness-oriented governance framework not only enhances employee morale but also drives productivity, innovation, and institutional sustainability (Peccei & Van De Voorde, 2019; WHO, 2020). Consequently, leadership and HR departments function as dual custodians of organizational health, ensuring that individual and institutional well-being remain aligned and mutually reinforcing.

Spiritual development is usually considered the role of self. However, considering an organization, it is the role of the leadership and HRM to foster spiritually awakened employees who know the mission, vision, and core values of the organization for building a covalent bond with the organization.

Thus, it is evident that various factors contribute to developing a culture within an organization that ensures the well-being of healthcare providers. An organization's potential for performance can be maximized when leadership and HRM ensure that inputs from various dimensions are effectively integrated within the organization. With this complex nature of inputs through the wellness dimensions and the organization's inputs, the dynamics of organizational culture and employee well-being need a model comprising the input factors to be processed for the desired output of ease of functioning for a healthy outcome of the organization with employee well-being as the ultimate impact.

G.R.A.S.P. (GOVERNANCE, RESEARCH, ACCOUNTABILITY, SUSTAINABILITY, AND PERFORMANCE LEADING TO PROFITABILITY), AN INTEGRATED MODEL BY DR. MINHAJ QIDWAI.

The G.R.A.S.P. model is being presented for organizational performance enhancement, profitability, and ensuring the well-being of the Healthcare Providers (HCPs). As described by the Johns Hopkins Medicine study by Mathews et al. (2016), the four components—governance, accountability, reporting of consolidated quality performance statements, and auditing—form a performance management system for prioritizing safety and quality improvements:

- **Governance:** Oversight is provided by a board committee that reviews goals, strategy, and performance.
- **Accountability:** An accountability plan includes escalating levels of review for missed performance targets.
- **Reporting of consolidated quality performance statements:** Consolidated statements inform leadership about key quality and safety issues.
- **Auditing:** This component ensures the accuracy and completeness of quality measure reporting by evaluating data processes

The model proposed by Mathews et al. (2016) lacked essential components necessary for conducting research on data generation for management, ensuring organizational sustainability, and achieving profitability. Considering the importance of these factors and a lacuna towards developing a sustainable organizational culture leading to enhanced performance and profitability led to the conceiving of the G.R.A.S.P. model. This model connects the wellness dimensions at one end and the well-being of the HCPs at the other end for developing a sustainable organizational culture leading to enhanced performance and profitability.

Conceptual Framework Linking the G.R.A.S.P. Model to Organizational Outcomes and Healthcare Provider Well-Being

Conceptual framework illustrating how Dr. Minhaj Qidwai's G.R.A.S.P. model (Fig. 4)—comprising governance, research, accountability, sustainability, and performance improvement—links the wellness dimensions at one end, with the key role played by leadership and human resources for evolving a positive organizational culture, operational systems, and resource resilience, focusing on the ultimate impact on the well-being of employees and healthcare workers. These linked systemic processes lead to improved organizational outcomes, enhanced provider well-being, improved performance with feedback loops reinforcing continuous learning, profitability, and sustainability.

Figure 4.

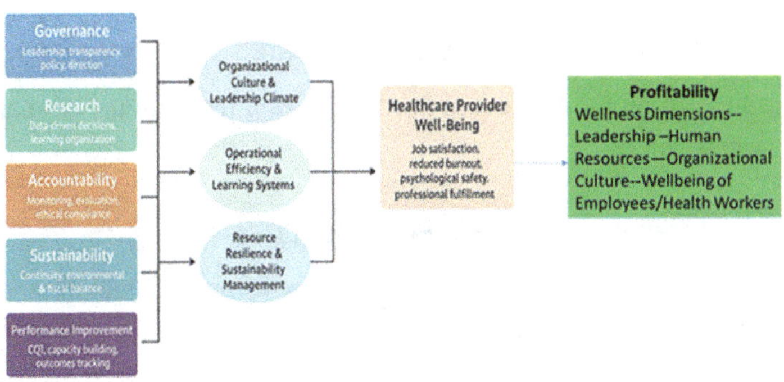

This diagram illustrates how the G.R.A.S.P. model of Dr. Minhaj Qidwai functions as a systemic and iterative process within healthcare organizations.

A. Input Layer – G.R.A.S.P. Components

Five vertically aligned boxes on the left side (Table 1):

Table 1.

Component	Core Function	Example Keywords
Governance (G)	Vision, leadership, strategic alignment, ethical oversight	Leadership, transparency, policy, direction
Research (R)	Evidence generation, innovation, feedback loops	Data-driven decisions, learning organization
Accountability (A)	Measurement, responsibility, reporting, integrity	Monitoring, evaluation, ethical compliance
Sustainability (S)	Resource optimization, long-term planning, resilience	Continuity, environmental & fiscal balance
Performance Improvement (P)	Continuous quality cycles, benchmarking, learning	CQI, capacity building, outcomes tracking

B. Process Layer – Integrative Organizational Mechanisms

Arrows from each G.R.A.S.P. element converge into three interconnected ovals or nodes at the center, representing core organizational mechanisms:

1. Organizational Culture & Leadership Climate

Driven mainly by governance and accountability, it promotes ethical behavior, trust, and empowerment.

2. Operational Efficiency & Learning Systems

Supported by research and performance improvement, it ensures adaptability, data-driven decision-making, and innovation.

3. Resource Resilience & Sustainability Management

Anchored in Sustainability and Governance
It prioritizes stable financing, infrastructure, and the well-being of the workforce.

C. Outputs

Arrows from the three mechanisms move rightward into a box titled "Organizational Outputs," containing sub-elements such as:

- Improved service quality and safety
- Higher patient satisfaction
- Enhanced productivity and efficiency
- Ethical, transparent operations

- Stronger institutional resilience

D. Outcome – Provider Well-Being

From the Organizational Output box, arrows point toward an end-stage box of Healthcare Provider Well-Being

- o Job satisfaction
- o Reduced burnout
- o Psychological safety
- o Professional fulfillment

E. Feedback Loops

From the outcomes a feedback loop is directed back to the inputs. This is required to revisit the inputs and processes if the outcomes are not as expected, symbolizing continuous learning and adaptive change.

The 5S is considered an integral part of the G.R.A.S.P. model. They impact the entire organization. Self is the focus of the inputs. Society, state, systems, and spirituality are involved in the processes for the outcomes and the impact. If the outcomes are not as expected, the inputs are revisited for process improvement.

EXPLANATION OF THE COMPONENTS OF THE G.R.A.S.P. MODEL:

Figure 5. Connecting the 5Ss' with the G.R.A.S.P. model

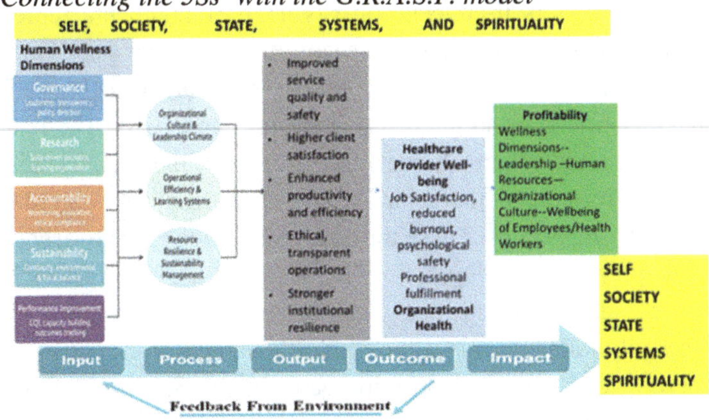

With the above (Fig. 5), it is evident that the G.R.A.S.P. model needs to be studied in terms of its individual factors influencing the entire model as proposed by Dr. Minhaj Qidwai's (Governance, Resources, Accountability, Sustainability, and Profitability) model.

Governance

As per the Merriam-Webster dictionary, governance is defined as an act or process of governing or overseeing the control and direction of something (such as a country or an organization). However, considering the healthcare organization, as per WHO[24]

- Health systems governance refers to the processes, structures, and institutions that are in place to oversee and manage the healthcare system.
- Effective health systems governance is essential for ensuring that healthcare services are accessible, equitable, efficient, affordable, and of high quality for all.
- Moreover, health systems governance plays a crucial role in promoting equity and social justice in healthcare.

Considering the 5Ss (Self, System, State, Society, and Spirituality) approach, the governance of an organization will depend upon the ingredients of this model (Fig. 5).

a. *Self:* Self-governance plays an important role in shaping one's future. The self-concept occupies a central role in psychological theory, partly because of its relevance to ensuing cognitive, motivational, affective, and behavioral processes (Alicke, Dunning, & Krueger, 2005; Ellemers & Haslam, 2012; Leary & Tangney, 2012)[25]. The self-concept consists of three fundamental representations: the individual self, the relational self, and the collective self. The individual self reflects a person's subjective uniqueness—characteristics such as traits and behaviors, hobbies and interests, aspirations and goals. The relational self reflects dyadic bonds or attachments (e.g., romantic liaisons, friendships). The collective self reflects membership in, as well as similarity and identification with, valued social groups. These three representations are governed by certain factors that play a role in regulating SELF (Fig. 6). These factors include the environment, identification, regulation, protection, development, fulfillment, empowerment, wellness, and wellbeing. Self-awareness makes a person aware of his strengths, weaknesses, opportunities, and threats. Self-regulation is required for building controls.

Figure 6. Factors Governing Self

We must evaluate our actions and focus on positive outcomes and performance. Therefore, self-regulation can be described as the process by which we seek to control or alter our thoughts, feelings, behaviors, and urges. The elements of self-regulation include self-control, self-efficacy, goal orientation, and the types of goals one may want to achieve. Self-regulation is influenced by personality, society, motivational factors, and task design or rewards. The most important plan will be around self-development. There are five SPECS to focus on self-development: spiritual, physical, emotional, cognitive, and social.

Spiritual Development

Questioning our inner selves about the meaning of our existence is the beginning of spiritual development. Spirituality is a relationship to a superior one. When we focus on our spiritual development, it is like working on creating a deeper connection with the world around us.

Physical Development

For managing wellness and well-being, our own physical development, and keeping healthy and fit in life, it is important. Regular physical check-ups, appropriate diet, exercise, adequate sleep, and relaxation are important for health. We need to handle the other priority wellness dimensions, which include occupational, emotional, intellectual, spiritual, financial, environmental, and social aspects.

Emotional Development

According to the American Psychological Association (APA), emotion is defined as "a complex reaction pattern, involving experiential, behavioral, and physiological elements." Alternatively, it can be described as a strong feeling that leads to an action, which is derived from an individual's circumstances, mood, or relationships with others. An individual needs to build on his/her emotional experiences, learning from them, reacting, and considering the relationship with others.

Cognitive Development

Cognition refers to the conscious intellectual activities of the brain, including mental processes. Cognitive skills are the essential qualities the brain utilizes to think, listen, learn, understand, justify, question, and pay close attention.

Social Development

The development of social skills is essential, as they are reflected in our day-to-day life. Social development helps people work on their social tendencies.

On the path of self-development, the next factor is self-fulfillment, which is the ability of a person to make themselves happy by meeting their goals. Self-fulfillment is a personal concept that is different for everyone. Another factor that facilitates self-development is self-empowerment. Self-empowerment is the act of making intentional, conscious efforts to take responsibility and reasonable control of your own life. Above all, one needs to care for his self-protection. This is a behavior or coping tool employed when a part of us doesn't feel that it can manage or navigate a solution. Self-protection fosters a risk-avoidant orientation and is often contrasted with self-enhancement.

System Governance: Clinical Governance

Clinical Governance is "a framework through which HCOs are accountable for continually improving the quality of their services and safeguarding high standards of care…." Clinical governance is an overarching term that encompasses a range of activities in which clinicians should become involved to maintain and improve the quality of the care they provide to patients and to ensure full accountability of the system to patients. There are seven foundational pillars for clinical governance (Fig. 7). These 7 pillars of clinical governance form the foundation of this framework.

Figure 7.

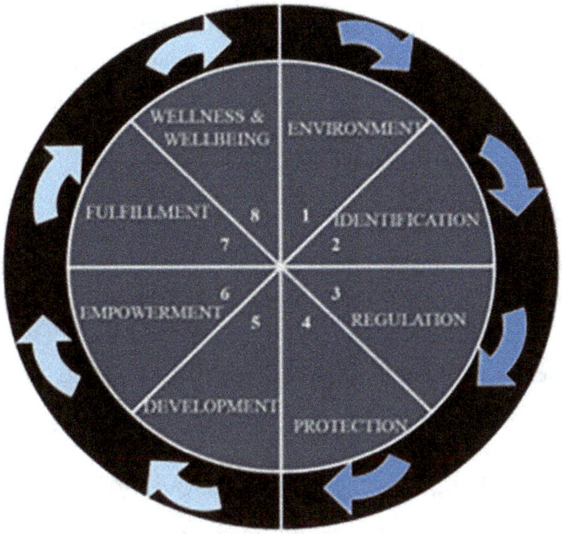

Pillar 1: Patient-Centered Care

This is the cornerstone of clinical governance. It emphasizes the importance of involving patients, families, and the community/public (when needed) in decision-making processes, respecting their preferences, and promoting effective communication between healthcare providers and patients.

Pillar 2: Clinical Effectiveness

This is focused on providing evidence-based care that leads to positive outcomes. This phase involves applying best practices, tracking treatment results, and continuously evaluating clinical processes.

Pillar 3: Patient Safety

It is a top priority for an HCOS and highlights the importance of creating a safe environment for the well-being of both patients and healthcare providers. This involves implementing robust reporting systems for adverse events, conducting regular risk assessments, and adhering to safety protocols. Ensure an organizational culture of transparency and accountability, which is crucial for preventing errors and ensuring patient safety.

Pillar 4: Leadership

Strong leadership is essential for the success of clinical governance within any organization. This pillar focuses on establishing clear lines of responsibility, promoting leadership development, and ensuring that the HCOS' structure supports the delivery of high-quality care.

Pillar 5: Information Management

Effective management of information is critical for providing quality care and improving healthcare. This involves implementing a robust health management information system to collect, analyze, and disseminate data relevant to patient care. Accurate and timely information enables organizational healthcare providers to make informed decisions, track performance, and identify areas for improvement.

Pillar 6: Capacity Building (Human Capital Development)

Ongoing capacity building and continuous medical education programs for the development of healthcare professionals are central to clinical governance. Training and development are essential considering the dynamic nature of healthcare and the need for continued learning to stay ahead of changes in healthcare. Continuous learning ensures that organizational providers are equipped with the knowledge and skills necessary to deliver high-quality, up-to-date care.

Pillar 7: Performance and Monitoring

Key Performance Indicators are essential for ensuring that employees are on track with their performance in service delivery related to clinical governance. This involves establishing mechanisms for performance monitoring and quality and improvement. Regular audits, reviews, and evaluations allow HCOs to assess their performance against established standards.

The 7 pillars of clinical governance form a comprehensive framework that guides healthcare HCOs towards excellence in clinical care. By focusing on patient-centered care, clinical effectiveness, patient safety, leadership, information management, capacity building, and performance monitoring, the healthcare providers can create an organizational environment that fosters innovation, quality and improvement, and high-quality care. An organization with such an ecosystem fosters the culture of well-being for individuals and patients alike (Fig. 8).

Figure 8.

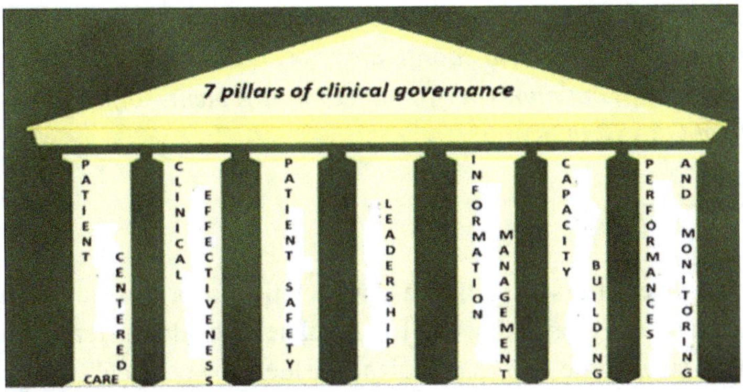

The seven pillars of clinical governance ensure stakeholder engagement, leading to inclusivity in decision-making; development of a health system resulting in quality of care, patient safety, and client satisfaction; and an environment for continuous professional development, ensuring employee well-being. The seven pillars are governed by accountability and transparency. These seven pillars interact with each other, with the leadership playing a key role in shaping humane policies and providing a learning and sharing environment within the organization, therefore having an impact on the well-being of healthcare providers, improving quality of care and patient safety.

Systems and e-Governance:

In the digital era, several healthcare organizations (HCOs) have adopted the concept of e-governance. However, there is a need for a comprehensive taxonomy for governance domains to better guide digital health governance enhancements in low-middle-income country settings (Gotsadze et al., 2024).

The WHO's Global Strategy on Digital Health 2020–2025 focuses on strengthening governance for digital health at global, regional, and national levels through the creation of sustainable and robust governance structures and building the capacity for digital health at global and national levels. Governance for digital health aims to strengthen the capabilities and skills needed for countries to promote, innovate, and scale up digital health technologies.

> *"Digital governance is now recognized as a core health-systems function: countries that define operational governance domains, assign institutional responsibilities, and invest in interoperability show better capacity to use data for accountability and planning. Considering the GRASP model, they link research (data) and accountability (transparency) with governance and sustainability—*

showing how digital stewardship enables measurement and long-term viability. Sri Lanka's primary health care (PHC) system demonstrated resilience during the COVID-19 pandemic via coordinated governance, data use, accountability mechanisms, and continuous performance improvement—offering a South Asian example of GRASP in action.

State Governance:

State governance offers insights into how societies are organized and managed. It involves the study of systems that control, regulate, and administer various aspects of life within a state. State governance also considers the political structures, power and authority, resource distribution, and citizen interaction.

- **Political Structures:** The organization of governments and institutions that formulate and enforce rules and policies.
- **Power and Authority:** The legitimate use of power in a society to influence or regulate actions and behaviors.
- **Resource Distribution:** The allocation and regulation of resources through governmental systems.
- **Citizen Interaction:** The ways in which individuals and groups engage with state mechanisms.

From a healthcare organizational perspective:

- **Political Structures:** Individuals from various cadres, special interests, and ethnicities form the core of the political structure within an organization. However, one important factor that is often overlooked is the role of professional bureaucracy, particularly that of healthcare providers. These include the technicians, paramedics, service delivery staff, and consultants. However, different departments also form the center of power and political structure, like administration or finance, etc. Individuals within the organization create their own groups based on their affiliations, ethnicity, interests, and preferences regarding governments and institutions that establish and enforce rules and policies.
- **Power and Authority:** Power is an entity's or individual's ability to control or direct others and take control of their behavior. Authority is influence that is predicated on perceived legitimacy and refers to the legal and formal rights to give commands and make decisions. The "power" in healthcare organizations refers to the ability of the leader to use his/her authority to take the necessary steps to have the others act in a certain way or agree on something.

Leadership with power often results in those beneath you agreeing with what you've said as a healthcare leader, despite potentially not believing in the same thing. Individuals may only agree with the leader due to the fear or worry of the rejection consequences. This type of leadership can limit honest collaboration due to the lack of an inclusive approach to addressing issues.

- **Resource Distribution:** Financial management and resource distribution with equity and equality are the essence of resource distribution within a healthcare organization. Adequate allocation of resources for employees' capacity building, health insurance, and the provision of quality materials serves as an incentive, promoting their well-being within the organization.
- **Citizen Interaction:** From an organizational perspective, the term "citizens" refers to the employees within the organization. Employee interaction is an HR term that primarily refers to the study and description of interpersonal relationships among employees, including their peers (colleagues and co-workers) and managers; thus, interaction can be horizontal (how workers relate to each other) or vertical (how workers relate to their supervisors/managers). Quality of employee interactions may have both negative and positive effects on employee attitudes, productivity, performance, etc. In other words, employee interactions influence the employee's motivation, enthusiasm, opinion about his or her mission in the organization, etc.

Corporate Governance

State governance influences the shaping of corporate governance structures. The state's rules, regulations, and policies influence corporate governance. Adopting a corporate governance structure, HCOs can develop a structure focused on ethical practices, ethical business development, employee well-being, quality of service delivery and patient safety.

The Principles of Corporate Governance

There can be many governing principles guiding a company, as its founders and directors believe make sense. However, there are several that are common across companies and industries.

Fairness

The board of directors must treat shareholders, employees, vendors, and communities fairly and with equal consideration.

Transparency

The board should provide timely, accurate, and clear information about such things as:

- Financial performance
- Conflicts of interest
- Risks to shareholders and other stakeholders

Risk Management

The board and management must determine risks of all kinds and how to best control them. They must act on those recommendations to manage risks and inform all relevant parties about the existence and status of risks.

Responsibility

The board is responsible for the oversight of corporate matters and management activities. It must be aware of and support the successful, ongoing performance of the company. Part of its responsibility is to recruit and hire a chief executive officer. It must act in the best interests of a company and its investors.

Accountability

The board must explain the purpose of a company's activities and the results of its conduct. Its leadership is accountable for the assessment of a company's capacity, potential, and performance. It must communicate issues of importance to shareholders.

Corporate Governance and Healthcare Organizations

Healthcare organizations need to align themselves with the rules, regulations, and procedures adopted for corporate governance. However, it depends on its leadership to follow them and adopt an organizational culture coherent with the laid-down principles of corporate governance. This will have a positive impact on the well-being of healthcare providers.

Societal Governance:

Social-political or interactive governing is an arrangement in which public as well as private people aim at solving societal problems or creating societal opportunities, aim at the care for the societal institutions within which these governing activities take place, and phrase the principles according to which these activities are carried out. The term "governance" denotes conceptual or theoretical ideas about such governing activities.

The Societal Governance is an interconnected systems approach between policy makers, people and providers (Fig. 9) When considering societal governance in terms of healthcare organizations, the healthcare providers and their rating in the society impact not only their functioning but also the functioning of healthcare establishments.

Figure 9.

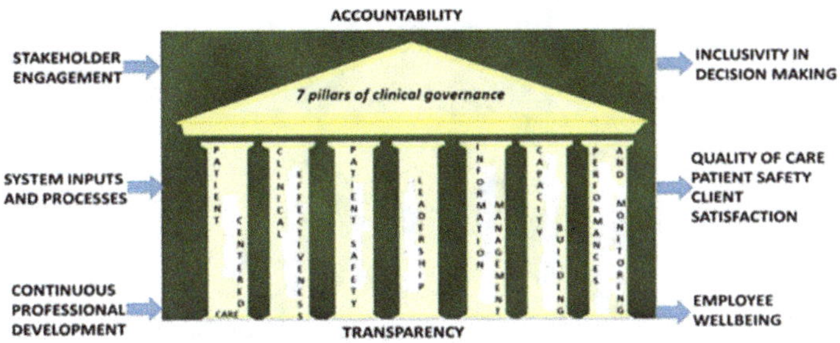

Societal governing strengths require people, money, and wisdom, all shared to work together to support progress. The funding typically originates from the public, individuals, and private entities through their corporate social responsibility initiatives. High-net-worth individuals not only contribute financially, but also people in general fulfill their societal responsibilities as a moral and ethical obligation by working and cooperating with others and organizations for the benefit of the community.

SPIRITUALITY—SPIRITUAL GOVERNANCE

For understanding spiritual governance, we first need to understand the difference between the soul and spirit[34]. A soul is the "life principle" of a body. While plants, animals, and anything living contain a soul, the human soul is unique. It has not only vegetative powers (as plants have) and sensitive powers (as animals have) but also rational powers. It is this rational power that separates us from other living beings in this world.

> *"Soul" provides life to a body. "Spirit," when contrasted with "soul," simply means those aspects of human life and activity that open the soul toward the supernatural life of grace.*

Spirit is within self, while soul comprises *mind*, *will*, and *emotions*, giving rise to the development of personality. We function through our body (Fig. 10). Therefore, we have a material part, our *body*, and an immaterial part, *soul* and *spirit*. Therefore, a human is tripartite. It's in our *spirit* that drives our body. At its deepest level, our spirit gives us meaning and purpose, enabling us to love one another. Our well-being and growth are dependent on our spiritual health. The connection between the spirit, the soul, and the body is complex. Our beliefs and attitudes play a major role in our thinking patterns. The day-to-day thinking will impact our emotions and feelings. Such thinking will have a major impact on our behaviors.

Figure 10.

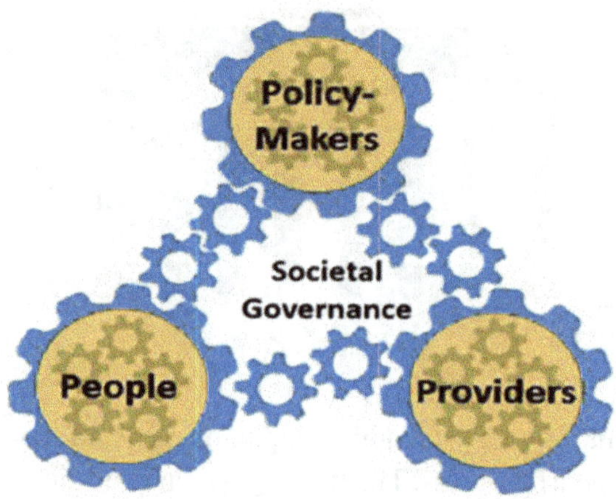

Developing spirituality needs general considerations, including developing mindfulness and better cognition of the stressors with the subconscious values and feelings impacting our will for making choices and decisions in life. The healthier the spirit, the better our well-being (Fig. 11).

Figure 11.

The Self is responsible for his own spiritual governance. The personality needs connectedness with others to feel their emotions and provide them a personal touch.

Our faith and hope in ourselves, family, friends, and loved ones gives us strength for self-governance. Therefore, self-governance is directly proportional to spiritual governance. With spiritual awareness of having love for all, one gains strength and peace. Once a person is detached with worldly matters, his quest is towards transcendence and self-transcendence. He is on a quest to find the meaning of his existence and to plan his path towards this goal (Fig. 12).

Figure 12.

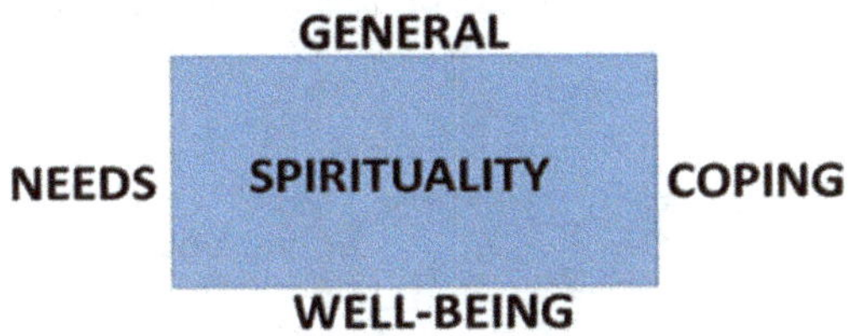

Spiritual governance revolves around spirit, spirituality, and the development of spiritual well-being. Helping others to cope with their stressor, creating a love bond when one extends hand towards others with reciprocity, responsiveness, safeguarding the covenants and the relationship, understanding emotions and feelings, giving sense of ownership to others and acknowledging them for their work,

Thus, spiritual governance is the controlling factor for the path to traverse spirituality. This leads to an insightful relationship with both self and others, a strong personal value system, the discovery of self transcendence, and a meaningful purpose in one's life (Fig. 13).

Figure 13.

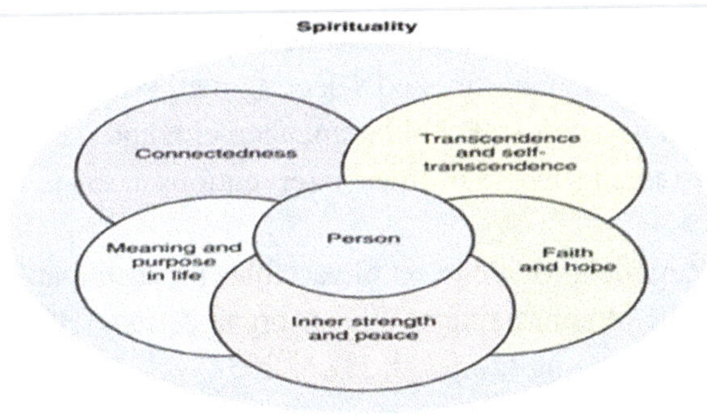

Governance and HCOs'

The 5Ss model of governance includes self-governance, systems governance (clinical governance), state governance (corporate governance), societal governance, and spiritual governance. When applying the themes of governance to HCOs, inclusive governance could involve the engagement of a board, committees, medical and nursing staff, and a community representative. Commitment to accountability for clinical, financial, social, and political matters across the board will ensure transparency. This accountability needs to be planned with an established reporting line.

While ensuring an independent governance can be established, choose either a decentralized, autonomous, or hybrid governance model (Fig. 14).

Figure 14.

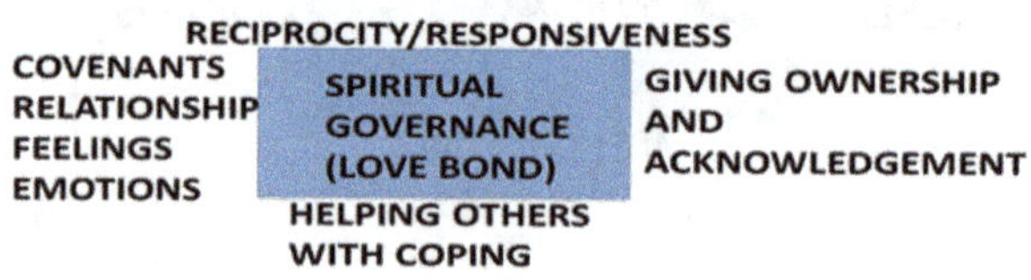

Considering the G.R.A.S.P. model, governance and sustainable leadership are in direct relationship with increasing the workers' subjective well-being and performance enhancement. Schreier's hypothesis suggests that sustainable performance of healthcare systems (SPHS) and change interventions require continued financial support for a long period of time instead of the usual grant period of 3–5 years. Further, it is proposed that sustainability should be assessed at least 1 year after the implementation of an intervention. The changes might require a longer time to create an impact. Conducting longer-term sustainability assessments ensures that the reforms have been fully institutionalized and provides a comprehensive picture of whether practices and policies have been maintained and adapted.

While considering sustainability assessments for SPHS, it requires planning that includes defining sustainability and selecting methods, approaches, and timeframes to measure outcomes, stakeholder engagement, and partnership, as well as funding for the sustained success of these interventions to ensure long-lasting and meaningful impact.

The G.R.A.S.P. model provides a set of variables for sustainable performance of health systems (SPHS), emphasizing healthcare organizations (HCOs) and healthcare providers' (HCPs) well-being *(Zurynski et al., 2022).*

R-research-R.E.S.T. Model of Dr. Minhaj Qidwai

Research is an essential feature in reaching new ideas, self and organizational evaluation, program evaluation, gathering data for improving quality of service delivery, etc. The goal of medical research is to improve patient care. Basic science research aims to elucidate the underlying biological mechanisms of health and disease. Clinical research aims to determine the best treatment of a given disease by comparing therapies. Health Services Research (HSR) examines patients in a broader context that includes the physician, the hospital, and the health care system at large. Health services research examines how people get access to health care, how much it costs, and what happens to patients as a result of this care. The main goals of HSR are to identify the most effective ways to organize, manage, finance, and deliver high-quality care, reduce medical errors, and improve patient safety.

Data is required for managing the organization's business health, quality improvement, and employee well-being. Incorporating research to ensure the organization's health and the well-being of employees is essential. In addition, education and capacity building serve as incentives for the employees. Research will also be required to study the functioning of health systems for process improvement that will have an impact on the quality of services and the well-being of employees and healthcare providers. Building the capacity of employees without letting them use it through training and job rotation for their skills development is mandatory. Therefore, the R.E.S.T. (Research, Education, Systems, and Training) model of Dr. Minhaj Qidwai can be adopted. This tool has been used effectively in curriculum development and in promoting mental health in organizations. It has provided a platform for organizations to present and discuss their research findings, education on health systems, and encouragement of training and capacity building. It can be adopted as a comprehensive model for HCOs, ensuring the well-being of employees and healthcare providers.

Research:

a.It enables employees to learn the fundamentals of research in general and conduct market research.

b. Undertake evidence-based research on areas related to organizational management.

Education:

a. Enabling the employees in capacity building and self-development.
b. Keeping employees retained with their well-being ensured.

Systems:

a. Enable the HCOS to adopt a systems-based approach towards its management.
b. Working on the seven pillars of clinical governance and adopting state and corporate governance features.

Training:

a. To apply learned concepts for improving quality of services and patient safety.
b. Job rotation will enhance employee satisfaction.

Along with research, innovation is essential for an organization to find out its niche and areas for growth.

Innovation in healthcare refers to "those changes that help healthcare practitioners focus on the patient by helping healthcare professionals work smarter, faster, better, and more cost-effectively." However, when these are employee-driven innovations (EDI), they leverage the role of "employees close to where services are delivered," create context, and deploy mechanisms in health organizations that can be described as "frontline staff-led" and "open and collaborative." While entrepreneurial doctors have historically driven clinical and technological innovations, EDI concentrates on the role of a broader set of health professionals, health workers, and managers of health organizations that deliver care in shaping health innovations. These innovators are often referred to as "front-line innovators," "healthcare insiders," or "street-level bureaucrats." They play a crucial role in the healthcare sector and their involvement in the innovation processes of health organizations can positively impact the quality of healthcare.

WHO's strategic goals also highlight its aims to improve measurement and monitoring of and research on the application of digital health in the health sector. The research agenda should meet the need to improve and disseminate evidence and information on the use of digital health at all levels. Research and evaluation of digital health outcomes and impacts are essential to support its safe implementation, establish and promote accountability, and justify the financial investment.

A-Accountability

Accountability can be described as the quality or state of being accountable. The term “accountable” refers to being subject to giving an account, while “answerable” means being capable of being accounted for. An accountant is the one that gives an account or is accountable.

Acceptability is a part of excellent governance. ‘Governance’[41] is the process of decision-making and the process by which decisions are implemented (or not implemented). Effective governance has 8 major characteristics. ‘ Effective governance is participatory, consensus-oriented, accountable, transparent, responsive, effective and efficient, equitable and inclusive, and adheres to the rule of law (Fig. 15).

Figure 15. Principles of Good Governance by United Nations

Governance Themes	Subthemes
Inclusive governance	Hospital board (of trustee, governance, or director)
	Committees
	Medical staff
	Nurse representative
	Community representative
Commitment to accountability	clinical accountability
	Financial accountability
	Social and Political accountability
Planning for accountability	Accountability plan
	Clear report line
Independent governance	Decentralized
	Autonomous
	Hybrid governance

Accountability in good governance aims towards betterment of people, and this cannot take place without the government being accountable to the people. The public and institutional stakeholders should hold governmental institutions, private sectors, and civil society organizations accountable. Governance in health is a cross-cutting theme, intimately connected with issues surrounding accountability. In the context of strengthening health systems, governance is an integral component of the overall health system. Despite consensus on the importance of leadership and governance in improving health outcomes, they remain inadequately monitored and evaluated.

The HCOS’s internal environment has various independent specialists, such as physicians, nurses, paramedics, financial managers, and management professionals, who communicate and make them accountable for achieving hospital goals. Considering a typical Health Service Delivery Program, there could be five components of accountability:

a. Legal: planning, contracting, and budgeting;
b. Financial: tracking and reporting on fund allocations, funds disbursement, and ethical use of resources;

c. Professional: promotes service delivery according to legal, ethical, and professional standards;
d. Political: governments fulfill public trust, represent the public's interest, and respond to societal needs and concerns; and
e. Public: Engaging the public at all levels and establishing appropriate structures to facilitate information flow between decision-makers and various forms of public involvement.

Considering the 5Ss for accountability, we have:

Self: Self-Accountability
System: Clinical Audits
State: Financial Audits
Society: Societal audit and feedback on quality of service
Spirituality: Spiritual accountability is an audit of one's own self in terms of "willingness to explain actions, to answer for one's life, and to supply the reason why."

Therefore, accountability applies to everyone in the organization for their actions. It impacts the well-being of healthcare providers. Those responsible for developing an organizational culture need to be accountable for their actions toward ensuring the well-being of employees and healthcare providers.

S-Sustainability

Sustainability refers to the ability to maintain or support a process continuously over time. In business and policy contexts, sustainability seeks to prevent the depletion of natural or physical resources so that they will remain available for the long term. Sustainability is used for programs, initiatives, and actions aimed at the preservation of a particular resource. The Global Sustainable Development Goals are intertwined around the 5Ps': People, Planet, Prosperity, Peace, and Partnerships. By 2030, we aim to achieve these 17 goals. During the evaluation period, the next targets will be determined, along with an assessment of their potential to contribute to sustainable development on a global scale. However, considering the 5S philosophy, sustainability can be applied to the entire spectrum of activities.

- Sustaining Self within the surrounding environment requires personal perseverance and coping skills to deal with the situations. It needs understanding for the prudent use of wisdom for decision-making.

- Sustaining System: Improving health system outcomes while minimizing negative impacts on the environment within and outside and ensuring the well-being of individuals.
- Sustaining State: Four distinct areas to sustain the State functions include human, social, economic, and environmental factors—known as the four pillars of sustainability. The state also needs to focus on the four aspects of sustainability, namely, awareness about state policies, actions towards the betterment of society, universal accountability and Transparency and affordability of services for its people.
- Sustaining Society: Societal sustenance will depend upon the communal living of individuals. Individuals participate in community activities, ensure cleanliness, care for each other, and share cultural values.
- Sustaining Spirituality: This needs efforts to understand the Self, the Spirit within, and working towards the ultimate of self-actualization and transcendence.

Sustainability in HCOs'

What is sustainability in health care? In health care, sustainability refers to the integration of environmental stewardship, social equity, and fiduciary responsibility to support healthy, equitable, and resilient environments and communities over time. Four principles of sustainable clinical practice need to be practiced: prevention, patient self-care, quality service delivery, optimizing resources, and conserving energy. Clinical perspective means allocating resources appropriately (both human and material) and considering the health and wellbeing of staff.

Sustainability and Organizational Culture

A "sustainable healthcare organizational culture" is a workplace environment within an HCOS that actively promotes and integrates environmentally conscious practices, resource efficiency, and patient-centered care, where all staff members are empowered and encouraged to contribute to minimizing the healthcare system's ecological footprint while maintaining high-quality patient outcomes; it emphasizes values like collaboration, continuous improvement, and a commitment to long-term sustainability. Key elements of a sustainable healthcare organizational culture:

- Environmental awareness:

Staff are educated about the environmental impact of healthcare operations, including waste management, energy consumption, and resource usage, and are encouraged to identify areas for improvement.

- Patient-centered sustainability:

Incorporating patient education and engagement in sustainable healthcare practices, like promoting healthy lifestyle choices and reducing unnecessary tests or procedures.

- Leadership commitment:

Visible leadership support for sustainability initiatives, setting clear goals, and allocating resources to implement sustainable practices.

- Collaboration and teamwork:

Encourage cross-disciplinary collaboration to identify and implement sustainable solutions across various departments.

- Continuous improvement mindset:

Fostering a culture where staff actively seek ways to optimize processes and reduce waste, using data-driven approaches to track progress.

- Employee engagement:

Providing opportunities for staff to participate in sustainability initiatives, recognizing and rewarding contributions towards environmental goals.

Examples of sustainable healthcare practices that contribute to a sustainable culture:

- **Waste reduction:**

Implementing strategies to minimize medical waste generation and promoting recycling and proper disposal procedures are examples of sustainable healthcare practices that contribute to a sustainable culture.

- **Energy efficiency:**

Optimizing building energy usage through energy-efficient equipment, lighting systems, and building design.

- **Sustainable procurement:**

Prioritizing purchasing environmentally friendly products and supplies.

- Green transportation:

Encouraging staff to use public transportation, carpooling, or electric vehicles

- Clinical practice optimization:

Implementing evidence-based practices to reduce unnecessary tests, treatments, and resource utilization.

Benefits of a sustainable healthcare organizational culture:

- Reduced environmental impact:

It helps to mitigate climate change by reducing the ecological footprint of healthcare.

- Cost savings:

Optimizing resource usage can lead to cost reductions within the healthcare facility.

- Improved staff morale:

Employees feel empowered and engaged when they can contribute to environmental sustainability.

- Enhanced community health:

Promoting healthy lifestyle choices and environmental awareness can positively impact the overall health of the community.

Organizational sustainability is fostered by commitment to making an organization sustainable by everyone in the organization. It resonates with their personal values, showing a deeper connection with the organizational goals and objectives.

Sustainable organizations, through their cultures, impact the well-being of employees and healthcare providers.

P-Performance for Profitability

The performance of an organization is dependent upon the functioning of its Human Resources Department (HRD). Human capital development is the key function of the HRD. Developing and implementing knowledge-based learning and building the ability and skill base of the employees are the key functions of the learning and development aspect of HRD. Although motivation is considered as an internal factor, it also depends on the leadership to ensure the HCPs are motivated and provided with opportunities to participate and perform for HCOs' development and enhanced performance (Fig. 16).

Figure 16. AMO framework (Appelbaum et al., 2000; Kellner et al., 2019)[46]

Healthcare organizations, being involved in the delivery of non-tangible services, evaluate their performance based on the quality of their service delivery and the satisfaction of their clients. Quality is a continuous process of improvement. It has a major influence on service delivery, client safety, and satisfaction.

Factors influencing the quality of healthcare[47]:

Three factors that affect the quality-of-service delivery revolve around patient, provider, and environment.

Table 2.

Category	Themes
Patient related factors	Patient socio-demographic variables
	Patient cooperation
	Type of patient illness

continued on following page

Table 2. Continued

Category	Themes
Provider-related factors	Provider socio-demographic variables
	Provider competency
	Provider motivation and satisfaction
Environmental factors	Healthcare system
	Resources and facilities
	Leadership and management
	Collaboration and partnership development

a. **Patient-Related Factors:** These include their socio-demographic variables, including income, family size, education level, access to healthcare services, etc. Additionally, the cooperation of the patient, their family, and the community within the healthcare establishment's catchment area plays a crucial role. The type of patient illness is another parameter that will affect the quality of service delivery. Is the illness treatable? Is it acute or chronic? What is the financial impact of illness on the patient?
b. **Provider-Related Factors:** The HCP's sociodemographic variables, including his education, training, specialty, location of practice, mindset, character, and personality, will affect the quality of service delivery. Providers' personal and family problems and their mental presence impact their behavior and the quality of services provided to patients. Another factor is the provider's competency in his area of specialty, coupled with various variables like professionalism, altruism, and extending respect and dignity to the client. The healthcare professional does develop excellent rapport with their clients through reliability and intelligence in practice. However, the key factor is communication that builds bridges with the client, family, and community. The quality of healthcare services depends on the provider's knowledge and technical skills. The provider gains this knowledge as part of his development process. The acquired knowledge enables a person to effectively apply it in practice. Repeated use of the abilities makes one skilled to perform that activity. Further study and experience make one competent for that activity. Providers' job satisfaction is crucial in delivering high-quality services to patients.

HCPs identified nine organizational factors they believed influence their motivation and consequently job satisfaction (Fig. 17). These include pay, working environment, managerial leadership, organizational policies, co-workers, recognition, job security, job identity, and chances for promotion. The common reason for employee dissatisfaction is usually the insufficient and unfair pay and benefits. Employees usually leave as soon as they discover a secure and well-paid job. Ensuring well-being and providing job security to the employee is the most important factor for employee motivation.

Figure 17.

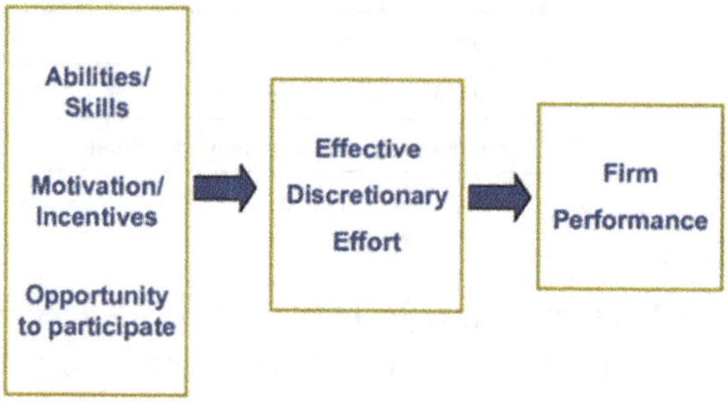

Environmental Factors

Table 3.

Environmental factors	Healthcare system
	Resources and facilities
	Leadership and management
	Collaboration and partnership development

Healthcare System

Healthcare systems are essentially the social systems (in the attitudes, perceptions, motivations, and expectations of human beings). The goals of the health systems can revolve around prolonging life with quality and preventing premature death; minimizing departures from physiological or functional norms by focusing attention on precursors of illness; minimizing discomfort and disability; promoting high-level "wellness" or satisfaction with the environment; extending resistance to ill health by building immunity; and increasing opportunities for consumers to participate in health matters.

The components of healthcare systems consist of several interrelated subsystems. Each of these subsystems has a purpose, which, if attained, aids the larger system in reaching its overall goals.

If the goal is set to ensure patient safety, then the actors within the system will be the patient and the family members, while the subsystem will include the patient, nurse, physician, healthcare delivery system, allied healthcare professionals, insurance agency, and the hospital.

The other systems affecting the system will be the industrial system and the educational system, while the society and the social system will be the supra system surrounded by the environment surrounding them. To consider the environment adequately, an organization must operate as an open system.

Therefore, the health system should deal with health in the context of complete well-being, not only for the community but also for the healthcare providers mainly involved in the healthcare service delivery. This ensures the well-being of both the community and healthcare workers (Fig. 18).

Figure 18.

As a part of Health System Strategies[6], WHO defines health systems to comprise service delivery, healthcare workforce, medical products and technology, finance, information, leadership, and governance (Fig. 19).

Figure 19.

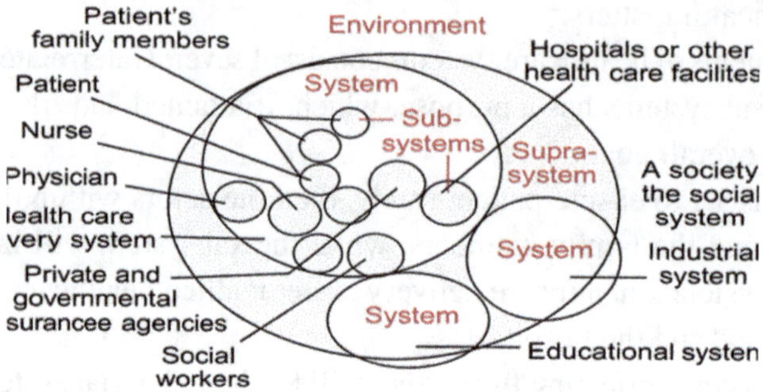

As per the above framework, the following are the factors essential for these components (Table 4):

Table 5.

Components	Administration and Management Issues
Leadership and Governance	Accountability, Resources, Health Transition, Bio-terrorism, Pandemic, Strategic Planning
Service Delivery	Purchasing of services, Quality, Diversity and Community Behavior, Effective and Efficient, Equitable and Fair, Social Morbidity - HIV…
Health Workforce	Motivation/Rewards, Accountability, Capacity Building…
Information	Management Information System, Patient Centered…
Healthcare Products and Technology	Social Morbidity - HIV, Drugs, Digital Health…
Financing	Pooling of Resources, Risk Pooling, Purchasing

Over the years, healthcare service delivery has gone through a transition. Following is a comparison between the old and new views (Fig. 20):

Figure 20.

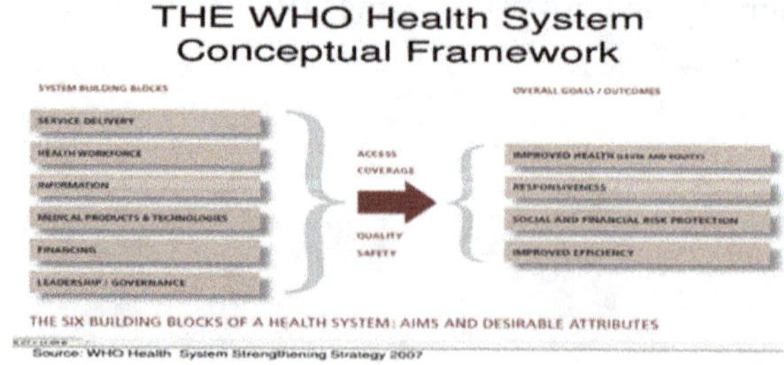

The transformation in the health service delivery brings challenges for management. The business orientation of healthcare brings nine external forces and the challenges that may have implications for the management (20):

- FINANCIAL INCENTIVES: These are important for the workforce. We must link these to the employees' performance indicators.
- PERFORMANCE ACCOUNTABILITY: The performance of all individuals needs to be linked with the Key Performance Indicators to facilitate accountability.
- TECHNOLOGY ADVANCES: The health staff need to keep up with the latest information in terms of therapies and patient management and cognizance of the ethical issues in patient management.
- AGING AND CHRONIC ILLNESS: Health promotion and disease prevention activities need to be planned at all levels of care. Special geriatric care and home healthcare also need consideration.
- ETHNIC & CULTURAL DIVERSITY: For the health planners establishing systems, ethnic and cultural diversity must be considered with universal policies for the community.
- SUPPLY & EDUCATION OF PROFESSIONALS: Human resources in managing healthcare are usually scarce and always in demand. The challenge is their retention and keeping them motivated.
- SOCIAL MORBIDITY (AIDS, DRUGS): Society-related behavioral issues harming the health of an individual result in social morbidity. Strategies need to be adopted in coping with them.
- INFORMATION COMMUNICATION TECHNOLOGY (ICT): With the advent of social media, ensuring privacy has become challenging. Strict rules need to be implemented to ensure confidentiality.
- GLOBALIZATION AND ECONOMY: Social media has brought globalization to the doorstep of organizations. Keeping pace with globalization and the economy, new alliances, networking, and strong marketing need to be undertaken for survival.

The above nine factors also bring challenges for the management. Following is a summary of the management implications while considering these external forces (Fig. 21):

Figure 21.

The development of health systems is essential, and the key is quality service delivery for performance enhancement, leading to profitability. However, profitability comes when the employees are satisfied.

Performance also needs resources and capital for profitability. The types of capital available[49] within an HCOS include leadership, social, cultural, human, and physical (Fig. 22).

Figure 22.

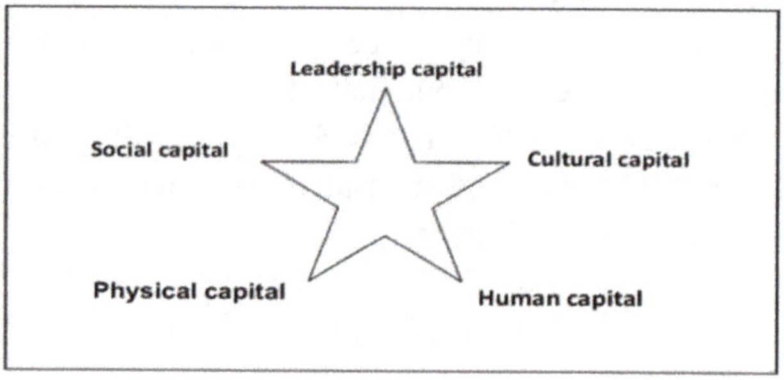

Physical capital refers to any non-human asset used in rendering quality services. To provide high-quality services, we need high-quality resources. Healthcare HCOs should provide their staff with the resources and support they need to deliver high-quality services.

Human capital refers to the skills, experience, and knowledge gained by an employee to perform the job well. The quantity and quality of healthcare providers affect the quality of services. High-quality providers are critical to producing high-quality outcomes. Healthcare managers should have distinctive approaches for the attraction and the retention of qualified employees that are able to deliver the highest-quality care.

Social capital is about one's responsibility and accountability to society and human beings. It consists of the norms, obligations, and trust embedded in social relations, which enable participants to act together more effectively and to pursue shared objectives. Accountability, coupled with transparent information, helps improve social capital. Professionals must be accountable to those they serve for the quality of care delivered. Delivering high-quality healthcare services is a corporate social responsibility of a healthcare organization (HCOS).

Cultural capital comprises the social assets of a person (education, intellect, style of speech, style of dress, etc.) that promote social mobility in a society. Pierre Bourdieu and Jean-Claude Passeron coined and defined the term *"cultural capital"* in the essay "Cultural Reproduction and Social Reproduction" (1977). Cultural capital functions as a social relation within an economy of practices (i.e., a system of exchange) and includes the accumulated cultural knowledge that confers social status and power. Therefore, the cultural capital comprises the material and symbolic goods, without distinction, that society considers rare and worth seeking.

There are three types of cultural capital: (i) *embodied capital*, (ii) *objectified capital*, and (iii) *institutionalized capital.*

Embodied cultural capital comprises the knowledge that is consciously acquired and passively inherited by socialization to culture and tradition. *Linguistic cultural capital* is the mastery of language and its relations. The embodied cultural capital, which is a person's means of communication and self-presentation, is acquired from the national culture.

Objectified cultural capital comprises the person's property (e.g., a work of art, scientific instruments, etc.) that can be transmitted for economic profit (buying and selling) and for symbolically conveying the possession of cultural capital facilitated by owning such things.

Institutionalized cultural capital comprises an institution's formal recognition of a person's cultural capital, usually academic credentials or professional qualifications. The greatest social role of institutionalized cultural capital is in the labor market (a job), wherein it allows the expression of the person's array of cultural capital as qualitative and quantitative measurements (which are compared against the measures of cultural capital of other people).

Leadership capital is the leader's ability to direct an HCOS forward in a positive direction. It is important that managers develop their leadership skills and demonstrate their commitment to quality by establishing a shared vision and setting a clear direction for the HCOS'. Managers should transform their HCOS''s value system and ultimately the HCOS' culture, policies, and structure in order to meet the needs of their employees and customers.

To summarize, performance of an organization can only bring profitability if the leadership and HRD focus on the human wellness dimensions at one end, building a positive organizational culture and ensuring the well-being of employees. Performance can only be enhanced when the employees are appropriately incentivized, there is no burnout, the shifts and working hours are planned in a humane manner and motivation is at its peak. A positive organizational culture serves as the foundation for human development. Spiritual development of employees in terms of ingraining of the mission, vision, and core values is essential so they are well aligned with the leadership.

SUMMARY

The G.R.A.S.P. model is a unique approach to implement in HCOS for reshaping the organizational culture to impact the well-being of employees and healthcare providers. Following are the *G.R.A.S.P. Model-Summarized Thematic Statements*:

- *Governance & leadership* shape institutional priorities and staff morale (affecting retention and quality).
- *Research, education, systems, and training (R.E.S.T.), with knowledge, abilities, and skills translation,* enable adaptive performance improvement and context-specific solutions.
- *Accountability mechanisms* (financial, clinical, and managerial) mediate governance effects on outcomes and public trust.
- *Sustainability* integrates fiscal and human-resource planning to maintain long-term service delivery and workforce well-being.
- *Performance and bringing Profitability* is the bottom line for all the organizations, which cannot be achieved without ensuring the well-being of HCPs.

From these themes we derive four practical hypotheses for empirical testing (e.g., strong governance predicts higher staff well-being mediated by accountability; investment in embedded research increases service quality when paired with performance improvement cycles). This frames the GRASP model for future empirical work.

Summary of Dovetailing of G.R.A.S.P. with the 5Ss' model

Intersection of Dr. Minhaj Qidwai's 5Ss Model (Self, Society, State, Systems, and Spirituality) with the *G.R.A.S.P. Model (Governance, Research, Accountability, Sustainability, and Profitability/Performance Improvement)*—forming a comprehensive wellness and organizational excellence framework:

Intersectional Framework: 5Ss × G.R.A.S.P.

5S Dimension	Corresponding G.R.A.S.P. Element	Integration Insight
Self	**Accountability**	Personal responsibility and ethical conduct form the foundation of both wellness and professional integrity. Individual accountability ensures that self-management and reflective practice contribute to overall system performance.
Society	**Sustainability**	Social wellness and community engagement promote long-term social sustainability. Collaborative societal action strengthens collective health outcomes and ensures enduring social impact.
State	**Governance**	The role of state institutions aligns with governance—policy-making, leadership, and regulatory oversight. Strong governance ensures that public health, education, and wellness initiatives are systematically implemented.
Systems	**Research & Performance Improvement**	Systems are the operational structures that rely on data, innovation, and research. Continuous learning, evidence-based improvement, and feedback loops strengthen organizational and health systems.
Spirituality	**Profitability (Reframed as Purposeful Performance)**	Spirituality brings meaning and moral direction to work, transforming profit into purpose. Ethical profit and value-driven performance complete the human-centered cycle of wellness and productivity.

Holistic Intersectional Insight

At the *core intersection* lies *Human Wellness Management (HWM)*—a paradigm uniting ethical governance, evidence-based practice, responsible leadership, sustainable development, and spiritual alignment.

This integrated framework ensures:

- *Governance with empathy*
- *Research with human purpose*
- *Accountability with integrity*
- *Sustainability with societal impact*
- *Performance with spiritual balance*

To summarize: L*eadership and governance shape organizational culture, which mediates staff engagement, psychological safety, and burnout. The transformational leadership practices are associated with higher staff motivation and lower stress, suggesting a direct pathway from Governance Organizational Climate Provider Well-being."*

The G.R.A.S.P. model adopted with an integrated approach of 5Ss is a new and unique concept. It can be tested by the organizations for its implementation by the

HCOs to maximize their performance, profitability, and organizational growth while ensuring the well-being of HCPs.

REFERENCES

Abdullah, H., & Ashraf, M. (2022). Institutional governance and organizational effectiveness in public health institutions of developing countries. *Journal of Health Management, 24*(4), 561–576. DOI: 10.1177/09720634221110364

Appelbaum, E., Bailey, T., Berg, P., & Kalleberg, A. (2000). *Manufacturing advantage: Why high-performance work systems pay off.* Cornell University Press.

Bakker, A. B., Demerouti, E., & Sanz-Vergel, A. (2023). Job demands–resources theory: Ten years later. *Annual Review of Organizational Psychology and Organizational Behavior, 10*(1), 25–53. DOI: 10.1146/annurev-orgpsych-120920-053933

Cooper, C. L., & Cartwright, S. (2022). Organizational health and well-being: A core issue for 21st-century organizations. *Journal of Organizational Effectiveness: People and Performance, 9*(1), 7–24. DOI: 10.1108/JOEPP-08-2021-0214

Cooper, C. L., & Cartwright, S. (2022). Organizational health and well-being. *Journal of Organizational Effectiveness, 9*(1), 7–24.

Gotsadze, G., Zoidze A, Gabunia T, Chin B. (2024). Advancing governance for digital transformation in health: Insights from Georgia's experience. *Advance online publication.* https://pubmed.ncbi.nlm.nih.gov/39353684/https://www.who.int/docs/default-source/documents/gs4dhdaa2a9f352b0445bafbc79ca799dce4d.pd

Gotsadze, G., Chikovani, I., & Kapanadze, S.. (2024). Advancing governance for digital transformation in health: Insights from Georgia's experience. *BMJ Global Health, 9*(10), e015589. Advance online publication. DOI: 10.1136/bmjgh-2024-015589 PMID: 39353684

Guest, D. E. (2017). Human resource management and employee well-being: Towards a new analytic framework. *Human Resource Management Journal, 27*(1), 22–38. DOI: 10.1111/1748-8583.12139

Guest, D. E. (2017). HRM and employee well-being. *Human Resource Management Journal, 27*(1), 22–38. DOI: 10.1111/1748-8583.12139

Harney, B., & Collings, D. G. (2021). Navigating the shifting landscape of HRM and employee well-being: Challenges and opportunities. *Human Resource Management Review, 31*(4), 100812. DOI: 10.1016/j.hrmr.2021.100824

Harney, B., & Collings, D. G. (2021). HRM and employee well-being challenges. *Human Resource Management Review, 31*(4), 100812.

Helliwell, J. F., Layard, R., & Sachs, J. (Eds.). (2024). *World Happiness Report 2024*. Sustainable Development Solutions Network.

Helliwell, J. F., Layard, R., & Sachs, J. (Eds.). (2024). *World happiness report 2024*. Sustainable Development Solutions Network.

Kellner, A., Townsend, K., Wilkinson, A., & Lawrence, S. A. (2019). Performance management and the AMO framework. *Human Resource Management Journal, 29*(4), 597–613. DOI: 10.1111/1748-8583.12238

Kelloway, E. K., Nielsen, K., & Dimoff, J. K. (2023). Leading healthy workplaces: The roles of leadership and human resource management. *Journal of Occupational Health Psychology, 28*(1), 1–14. DOI: 10.1037/ocp0000334 PMID: 36480367

Kim, T. Y., & Wang, J. (2022). Healthy organizations, healthy society: The mediating role of organizational citizenship and employee satisfaction. *International Journal of Environmental Research and Public Health, 19*(16), 9954. DOI: 10.3390/ijerph19169954 PMID: 36011590

Kim, T. Y., & Wang, J. (2022). Healthy organizations and society. *International Journal of Environmental Research and Public Health, 19*(16), 9954. PMID: 36011590

Mathews, S. C., Demski, R., & Pronovost, P. J. (2016). Management's discussion and analysis: A tool for advancing quality and safety. *Health Care, 4*(3), 129–131. DOI: 10.1016/j.hjdsi.2016.02.006 PMID: 27637813

Merriam-Webster. (n.d.). *Governance*. In *Merriam-Webster.com dictionary*. https://www.merriam-webster.com/dictionary/governance

Mukinda, F. K., Van Belle, S., & Schneider, H. (2020). Accountability experiences of frontline health managers. *International Journal for Equity in Health, 19*(1), 110. DOI: 10.1186/s12939-020-01229-w PMID: 32611355

Organisation for Economic Co-operation and Development. (2023). *Public sector governance and organizational resilience*. Organisation for Economic Co-operation and Development.

Organisation for Economic Co-operation and Development. (2023). *Public sector governance and organizational resilience*. OECD Publishing.

Oswald, A. J., Proto, E., & Sgroi, D. (2023). Happiness and productivity revisited. *Journal of Economic Behavior & Organization, 209*, 105–120. DOI: 10.1016/j.jebo.2023.03.004

Panda, S., & Patnaik, B. (2021). Corporate governance and organizational performance: A systematic review. *The International Journal of Organizational Analysis*, *29*(3), 897–915. DOI: 10.1108/IJOA-03-2020-2092

Peccei, R., & Van De Voorde, K. (2019). The application of the mutual gains model in HRM–well-being–performance research. *Human Resource Management Journal*, *29*(3), 539–563. DOI: 10.1111/1748-8583.12254

Peccei, R., & Van De Voorde, K. (2019). Mutual gains model in HRM–well-being research. *Human Resource Management Journal*, *29*(3), 539–563. DOI: 10.1111/1748-8583.12254

Salas-Vallina, A., Alegre, J., & Fernández, R. (2021). Organizational learning capability and organizational health: The role of employee well-being and engagement. *Personnel Review*, *50*(5), 1233–1250. DOI: 10.1108/PR-07-2019-0391

Salas-Vallina, A., Alegre, J., & Fernández, R. (2021). Organizational learning and health. *Personnel Review*, *50*(5), 1233–1250.

Sedikides, C., Gaertner, L., Luke, M. A., O'Mara, E. M., & Gebauer, J. E. (2013). Self-potency hierarchy. In Vol. 48, pp. 235–295). Advances in Experimental Social Psychology. Academic Press.

Swarbrick, M. (2023). *The evolution of the wellness model* [Unpublished manuscript]. Collaborative Support Programs of New Jersey.

Swarbrick, M. (2023). *The evolution of the wellness model* [Unpublished manuscript]. Collaborative Support Programs of New Jersey.

World Health Organization. (2020). *Healthy workplaces: A model for action*. World Health Organization.

World Health Organization. (2020). *Healthy workplaces: A model for action*. World Health Organization.

World Health Organization. (2020). *Global strategy on digital health 2020–2025*. World Health Organization.

World Health Organization. (2021). *Global report on effective access to assistive technology: Governance for health systems strengthening*. World Health Organization.

World Health Organization. (2022). *Health system performance assessment: A framework for policy analysis*. World Health Organization.

Zheng, X., Diaz, I., & Zhu, W. (2022). Transformational leadership and employee well-being: The mediating role of trust and work engagement. *Journal of Business Research*, *139*, 744–754. DOI: 10.1016/j.jbusres.2021.10.047

Zurynski, Y., Herkes-Deane, J., & Holt, J.. (2022). Sustainability of health system improvement interventions: A systematic review. *BMJ Open*, *12*(5), e059207. DOI: 10.1136/bmjopen-2021-059207 PMID: 35613812

Chapter 10
Spirituality:
Cultivating Meaning and Compassion in Healthcare

Sadaf Naveed
http://orcid.org/0009-0009-8915-0921
Tabba Heart Institute, Pakistan

Memona Guldost Khan
http://orcid.org/0009-0006-5822-1262
Saifee Hospital, Pakistan

ABSTRACT

This chapter examines the integration of spirituality into healthcare, emphasizing its role as foundational component of holistic patient care and staff well being. Utilizing five dimensional framework Self, Society, State, Systems and Spirituality, discussion highlights how spiritual awareness aids healthcare providers in managing emotional burdens, moral distress and burnout. The chapter presents real world applications including leadership practices, institutional rituals and chaplaincy models from global healthcare organizations. Challenges such as secular resistance and cultural pluralism are addressed with strategies proposed for developing inclusive policies and support systems. Evaluation tools for assessing the impact of spiritual care on patient outcomes and organizational sustainability are also discussed. Ultimately the chapter advocates for recognizing spirituality as central to creating healing environments that honor the whole person urging healthcare leaders and policymakers to embed spiritual considerations into their systems as a public good and clinical necessity.

DOI: 10.4018/979-8-2600-0582-8.ch010

1. INTRODUCTION

1.1 Defining Spirituality and Its Relevance in Healthcare

Spirituality, though intangible and deeply personal, is fundamental to the human experience. It encompasses the pursuit of meaning, purpose, transcendence, and a sense of connectedness—whether to others, nature, a higher power, or the inner self (Puchalski et al., 2009). Unlike religion, which may involve institutional doctrines and rituals, spirituality is broader and often independent of formal belief systems. It may be expressed through ethical living, compassionate service, artistic creation, or silent reflection.

In healthcare, spirituality is increasingly recognized as an essential component of holistic well-being. Illness, suffering, and loss often provoke existential reflection, raising questions about life's purpose, fairness, mortality, and identity (Sulmasy, 2006). For many patients, spiritual beliefs influence health decisions, coping behaviors, and overall quality of life. Addressing spiritual concerns such as fear of death, loss of control, or existential despair can relieve emotional suffering, improve satisfaction, and foster hope (Koenig, 2012).

For healthcare providers, spirituality plays an equally vital role. The demands of caregiving—exposure to trauma, moral distress, high workloads, and emotional labor—can erode motivation and increase burnout. Spirituality supports moral clarity, emotional resilience, and professional integrity, offering an inner compass to navigate complex ethical terrain (Delaney, 2005). Whether through prayer, meditation, gratitude, or acts of service, spiritual practices help providers sustain empathy and reconnect with their purpose.

Moreover, the COVID-19 pandemic underscored the fragility of life and systems alike. Healthcare professionals found themselves physically exhausted and spiritually depleted, grappling with death, uncertainty, and injustice. This collective trauma renewed attention to the importance of spiritual care—not only for patients, but for the caregivers themselves (Berlinger et al., 2017).

Spirituality also humanizes the medical system. In an era dominated by protocols, electronic health records, and performance metrics, spirituality re-centers care around relationships, values, and presence. It restores the healing intention behind medicine, reminding providers that technical skill alone does not suffice. True healing engages the body, mind, and spirit in unison.

1.2 Spirituality as a Catalyst for Resilience and Well-Being

In high-stress clinical environments, spiritual resilience becomes a survival tool. Healthcare workers often carry silent burdens—unresolved grief, moral injury, or emotional depletion. Spiritual practices, such as reflection, prayer, mindfulness, or storytelling, offer safe spaces to process and heal. Evidence shows that spiritual engagement is associated with lower burnout, greater empathy, and improved team cohesion (Pargament, 2007; Krasner et al., 2009).

Spirituality also enhances purpose, which buffers against disengagement. Providers who see their work as meaningful—aligned with their values—are more motivated, patient-centered, and ethically responsive (Milliman et al., 2003). Work becomes a vocation rather than a job, a service rather than a transaction.

Furthermore, workplace spiritual culture fosters psychological safety, mutual respect, and openness. Teams that reflect on shared values, express gratitude, and honor moral experiences are more likely to sustain compassion under pressure.

1.3 Chapter Objectives and Structure

This chapter aims to achieve the following:

- Define and differentiate spirituality within the context of healthcare
- Present a five-dimensional model that situates spirituality within personal, social, systemic, and institutional realities
- Explore how spirituality supports coping, resilience, and ethical clarity
- Provide evidence-based strategies for integrating spirituality into care, leadership, and workplace well-being
- Offer real-world examples, case narratives, and actionable tools for implementation

2. THE ROLE OF SPIRITUALITY IN COPING AND RESILIENCE

2.1 Understanding the Emotional Burden of Healthcare Work

Healthcare is more than a profession—it is a vocation that requires immense emotional investment, ethical commitment, and physical endurance. For those who serve in this field, the daily exposure to suffering, death, and moral dilemmas can create an emotional toll that, if left unaddressed, evolves into psychological distress and burnout. This burden is not often overtly discussed, but its presence is deeply felt and enduring. Shanafelt et al. (2012) describe this phenomenon as the "hidden grief" of caregiving—accumulated sorrow that lingers in the background of clinical routines and decisions.

Unlike singular traumatic events, this type of grief is incremental, deeply embedded in the routine of caregiving. It seeps into the psyche of healthcare workers through repeated exposure to trauma, patient deaths, and the perceived failure to provide optimal care in resource-constrained environments. Over time, it distorts not just emotional wellbeing but the professional identity and spiritual grounding of the provider. Frontline caregivers, such as nurses, physicians, paramedics, and therapists, are particularly susceptible due to their proximity to intense human suffering and life-and-death decision-making.

The demanding nature of healthcare work—marked by long shifts, night duties, emergency calls, and administrative burdens—leaves little room for emotional recuperation. Furthermore, ethical dilemmas such as being forced to prioritize patients due to lack of beds, or witnessing suffering without being able to alleviate it fully, add to a growing sense of helplessness. These situations often create moral distress, defined as the psychological discomfort that arises when one knows the right thing to do but is unable to act due to external constraints (Epstein & Hamric, 2009).

If persistent, moral distress can culminate into moral injury, a deeper psychological rupture that threatens the provider's sense of morality, dignity, and professional purpose. Moral injury involves a betrayal of one's own ethical values and is often experienced in silence. Without structured support systems, these inner wounds remain unresolved, leading to emotional disengagement, increased absenteeism, or eventual departure from the profession.

In such emotionally saturated contexts, spirituality emerges as an essential lens for meaning-making. It allows healthcare providers to interpret suffering not as futile pain, but as part of a larger, meaningful journey. Spiritual frameworks, whether religious or secular, help restore inner coherence, reaffirm personal values, and renew the sense of calling that often motivated professionals to enter healthcare in the first place.

2.2 Common Stressors and Burnout in Healthcare

Burnout in healthcare is not a transient phenomenon but a systemic issue that undermines both personal and institutional resilience. The World Health Organization (2019) categorizes burnout as an occupational syndrome characterized by chronic workplace stress that has not been successfully managed. It manifests in three primary dimensions:

1. *Emotional exhaustion* – A state of being emotionally overextended and drained by one's work.
2. *Depersonalization* – Developing a detached, impersonal, or negative attitude towards patients and coworkers.
3. *Reduced personal accomplishment* – A diminished sense of professional efficacy and fulfillment.

Burnout arises from an interplay of multiple stressors that affect healthcare professionals at all levels. High patient-to-provider ratios, limited breaks, administrative overload, and lack of autonomy are common contributors. Time pressure diminishes the ability to offer compassionate care and erodes the depth of patient-provider relationships, while administrative expectations often overshadow the clinical and emotional aspects of care.

Additionally, ethical tensions exacerbate this stress. Providers frequently encounter situations where they must act contrary to their moral compass—for instance, resuscitating terminal patients when palliative care would be more appropriate. These ethically dissonant experiences contribute to a sense of disillusionment and can lead to moral disengagement.

A significant yet overlooked contributor to burnout is the loss of meaning. When providers are distanced from the human aspect of caregiving—when checklists, metrics, and protocols replace conversations, empathy, and presence—they begin to lose the very purpose that once energized their work. Isolation, too, plays a critical role. In many hospital settings, emotional processing or peer support mechanisms are lacking, leaving staff to absorb and carry their burdens alone.

The ripple effects of burnout are profound. Studies have consistently linked healthcare provider burnout with lower patient satisfaction scores, decreased adherence to safety protocols, increased rates of medical errors, and even malpractice claims (Shanafelt et al., 2012). Institutions that ignore the emotional and spiritual well-being of their workforce face not only human costs but organizational inefficiencies.

2.3 How Spirituality Supports Coping and Emotional Resilience

Amidst these multifaceted stressors, spirituality offers a holistic approach to coping that transcends traditional psychological tools. Unlike cognitive strategies that focus purely on thought patterns, spirituality taps into deeper reservoirs of purpose, meaning, and interconnectedness. It empowers providers to navigate adversity without losing their sense of self or compassion.

Key roles of spirituality in promoting resilience include:

- *Meaning-making*: Spirituality helps providers assign value to suffering. Rather than being viewed as senseless, suffering becomes a path to greater understanding, empathy, or humility.
- *Moral grounding*: In the face of ethical ambiguity, spiritual values serve as an internal compass that preserves integrity and guides compassionate action.
- *Emotional regulation*: Spiritual practices such as prayer, deep breathing, mindfulness, and silent reflection support emotional stability and prevent reactive or impulsive behavior.

- *Transcendence*: Spirituality offers a sense of connection to something greater—be it God, community, or universal compassion—helping providers rise above the immediacy of their stressors.

Research by Pargament (2007) shows that individuals who engage in spiritual coping strategies—such as positive religious reframing, seeking divine support, or spiritual journaling—exhibit greater resilience in the aftermath of trauma. Koenig et al. (2012) also found that spiritually engaged providers reported stronger adaptive capacity, better interpersonal relationships, and greater endurance in emotionally demanding roles.

Unlike external motivators such as pay or promotions, spirituality nurtures intrinsic motivation—reaffirming the provider's calling and sustaining them through difficult periods. This internal renewal fosters not just survival, but personal growth and transformation.

2.4 Types of Spirituality and Their Impact

Spirituality is not monolithic. Its expression varies across cultures, belief systems, and individual preferences. Understanding these variations enables institutions to support diverse spiritual needs without imposing uniform practices.

2.4.1 Religious Spirituality

For many providers, religious affiliation is an essential source of comfort, ethical guidance, and community support. Practices like daily prayer, reading sacred scriptures, or attending services foster a sense of divine companionship and meaning. These rituals help anchor the provider in a moral universe where their caregiving efforts are divinely sanctioned and supported.

Moreover, belonging to a religious community can serve as a critical buffer against loneliness and isolation. Shared beliefs and collective rituals reinforce solidarity, making it easier for individuals to face challenges with hope and courage (Pargament, 2007).

2.4.2 Secular or Humanistic Spirituality

Not all healthcare workers identify with organized religion. Many find spiritual solace in human connection, ethical living, artistic expression, or mindfulness-based practices. For them, spirituality is about being present, compassionate, and aligned with their values.

Practices like meditation, yoga, gratitude journaling, and acts of kindness foster inner clarity and emotional balance. Milliman et al. (2003) emphasize that such humanistic expressions of spirituality enhance workplace engagement, reduce stress, and encourage ethical decision-making even in secular environments.

2.4.3 Ecospirituality

A growing number of providers find spiritual renewal in nature. Ecospirituality refers to a sense of sacredness embedded in the natural world. Activities such as walking in green spaces, gardening, observing wildlife, or engaging in environmental advocacy help healthcare workers reconnect to life's larger rhythms.

Benefiel (2005) notes that ecospiritual practices reduce physiological stress markers such as cortisol and blood pressure, while simultaneously instilling a sense of humility, stewardship, and gratitude. In the context of high-tech, fast-paced hospital environments, such natural pauses become vital for emotional recalibration.

2.5 Lived Experiences: Personal Practices of Spiritual Coping

While spirituality is often discussed in terms of belief systems or institutional rituals, its most enduring expressions are found in the lived experiences of individual healthcare providers. In the midst of high-pressure environments, many caregivers cultivate small, personal practices that restore their inner balance and renew their emotional capacity. These spiritual acts are often quiet, individualized, and informal—but their impact is profound.

For instance:

- A pediatric oncology nurse who has witnessed the prolonged suffering of terminally ill children finds healing in writing a personalized note of blessing for each child discharged from the unit.
- An anesthesiologist who often operates in life-threatening scenarios has developed the habit of silently reciting a mantra just before administering anesthesia.
- A midwife working in remote communities maintains a handwritten journal in which she records her reflections after every childbirth.
- A hospital chaplain, dealing with grief-stricken families and spiritually distressed staff, begins each day with a five-minute ritual involving deep breathing, a reading from a sacred text, and the lighting of a candle.

- An emergency nurse has a ritual of touching the photograph of her late mentor in moments of chaos.

Such lived experiences demonstrate that spiritual coping does not always require formal religion or elaborate frameworks. It is often rooted in intentional actions that carry symbolic meaning for the individual. These habits are deeply embedded in daily work, acting as emotional reset buttons that prevent cumulative grief from becoming pathological distress.

Moreover, these practices are not only restorative but also formative—shaping the kind of caregiver the individual becomes over time. They promote emotional presence, ethical clarity, and sustained empathy. When encouraged and respected by healthcare institutions, these personal rituals can foster a culture of psychological safety and spiritual nourishment.

2.6 Scientific Evidence: Spirituality as a Determinant of Mental Health and Resilience

In recent decades, the intersection between spirituality and mental health has been rigorously explored across disciplines ranging from psychology and neuroscience to healthcare management and organizational behavior. The overwhelming consensus is that spirituality plays a pivotal role in protecting emotional well-being, especially in high-stress professions such as healthcare.

A landmark study by Koenig et al. (2001) found that healthcare workers who scored high on spiritual engagement scales reported significantly lower levels of anxiety, depression, substance misuse, and work-related dissatisfaction.

Building on this, Pargament (2007) introduced the distinction between positive and negative spiritual coping:

- Positive coping includes seeking spiritual support, finding benevolent meaning in adversity, and using faith to guide ethical decisions.
- Negative coping involves spiritual guilt, feelings of abandonment by the divine, or interpreting illness as punishment.

In terms of practical application, Krasner et al. (2009) conducted an intervention involving an 8-week mindfulness-based stress reduction (MBSR) program with primary care physicians. Participants reported reduced burnout, improved emotional regulation, and more meaningful patient interactions.

Newberg and Waldman (2009) employed functional MRI technology to study the brains of individuals engaged in spiritual practices. They found that such practices activated regions of the brain responsible for empathy, emotional regulation, memory processing, and stress resilience.

Smith et al. (2021), in a meta-analysis, examined the effectiveness of meaning-centered interventions in healthcare providers. These included gratitude exercises, expressive writing, awe experiences, and reflective storytelling. Across both religious and non-religious populations, these interventions improved psychological well-being, reduced absenteeism, and increased professional satisfaction.

Beyond individual-level benefits, organizations that integrate spirituality into their workforce wellness strategies have reported tangible improvements in team morale, patient satisfaction scores, and staff retention.

3. INTEGRATING SPIRITUALITY INTO ORGANIZATIONAL CULTURE

3.1 Cultivating Ethical and Compassionate Care Through Spiritual Values

Healthcare institutions operate not only as technical hubs for clinical intervention but as moral ecosystems where profound human experiences of vulnerability, hope, fear, and healing are constantly unfolding. In such an environment, ethical practice and compassion are not just procedural requirements but spiritual imperatives. Values such as integrity, humility, justice, empathy, and respect are deeply rooted in both spiritual traditions and universal human ethics. These values are foundational to fostering trust and dignity in patient care (Sulmasy, 2006).

Spirituality in this context transcends religious dogma—it is about recognizing and responding to the human need for meaning, connection, and inner peace. When caregivers respond to suffering, not merely by managing symptoms but by acknowledging the emotional, psychological, and existential distress accompanying illness, they practice care that is both technical and transcendent. This dual response forms the ethical heart of compassionate care.

Institutionalizing these spiritual values into policy, training, and culture provides staff with a moral compass that guides decision-making even under duress. Daily micro-actions such as how patients are greeted, how bad news is delivered, or how care is extended to the dying reflect an institution's spiritual character. For instance, ensuring that a patient is addressed by name, that their beliefs are respected during procedures, and that family members are emotionally supported—these acts form the sacred rituals of everyday care.

Moreover, the incorporation of spiritual values fosters moral coherence among staff. They begin to see themselves not merely as individual professionals but as part of a collective mission rooted in human dignity and healing. This shared sense of purpose reduces moral distress, enhances job satisfaction, and builds psychological safety in the workplace. According to Puchalski et al. (2009), clinicians who operate within systems that prioritize spirituality and compassion report increased empathy, job satisfaction, and patient connection.

Furthermore, patients perceive care as more holistic and trustworthy when delivered in environments that honor their spiritual and emotional needs. This, in turn, contributes to improved health outcomes and satisfaction scores. Thus, spiritual values are not ancillary but central to achieving high-quality, ethical healthcare. As the late Dr. Edmund Pellegrino noted,

"The act of healing is not just a technical skill but a moral and spiritual vocation."

Healthcare must transition from a model that prizes efficiency alone to one that is meaning-driven. Such a transformation becomes possible only when spirituality is woven into the operational fabric—not as an optional feature, but as a core organizational identity.

3.2 The Role of Spirituality in Leadership and Workplace Culture

Leadership in healthcare extends far beyond budgeting and performance indicators—it establishes the emotional and ethical climate in which care is delivered. When leaders embody spiritual values, they shape a culture of authenticity, humility, compassion, and connectedness. These values not only enhance team morale and collaboration but serve as a buffer against cynicism, stress, and moral injury.

Spiritual leadership, as articulated by Fry (2003), involves creating a vision based on altruistic love, instilling a sense of meaning and purpose, and fostering hope and faith in the workplace. Leaders with a spiritual compass do not merely set strategic goals—they inspire others to see their work as a sacred calling, tied to the well-being of patients, families, and society.

In practical terms, spiritually grounded leaders engage in deep listening, model reflective practice, and invite feedback with openness. They are not afraid to show vulnerability, admit uncertainty, or prioritize ethics over expediency. For example, a spiritually aware leader may open departmental meetings with a short reflection, a moment of silence for a departed patient, or a story of compassion from the ward—symbolic acts that reinforce moral intention.

Additional strategies to embed spiritual leadership include:

- *Value-anchored communication*: Aligning institutional messaging with principles of healing, justice, service, and community.

- *Reflective rituals*: Starting staff meetings with affirmations, gratitude rounds, or ethical storytelling to foster presence and mindfulness.
- *Mentorship with meaning*: Encouraging senior staff to coach others not only in skills but in values, helping them navigate the moral complexities of care.
- *Healing initiatives*: Creating spaces for grief circles, post-trauma debriefings, or staff retreats to address emotional burdens collectively.

The presence of such leadership fosters emotional safety. Reave (2005) found that spiritual leadership correlates with higher employee well-being, trust in leadership, reduced turnover, and increased organizational commitment. In environments where spiritual leadership is present, staff feel seen, supported, and valued—not just as workers, but as whole human beings.

In times of crisis—such as pandemics, public health emergencies, or institutional transitions—spiritual leaders act as emotional anchors. They offer clarity, connection, and hope amid chaos. They reaffirm that healthcare is not just a profession, but a form of service that links science with soul, and management with meaning.

3.3 Case Examples of Organizational Spiritual Integration

Globally, a number of institutions have taken proactive steps to embed spirituality into their systems—demonstrating that spiritual integration is not only possible but deeply transformative.

Cleveland Clinic (USA)

Cleveland Clinic's model of integrated spiritual care is one of the most comprehensive globally. Its Department of Spiritual Care employs board-certified chaplains who support patients, families, and staff across religious and spiritual backgrounds. The clinic also features dedicated meditation and reflection spaces, "healing gardens," and "Compassion Circles" that allow caregivers to process emotional fatigue. Leadership at Cleveland Clinic endorses the belief that healing involves mind, body, and spirit—a stance reflected in caregiver training programs and the institution's core mission.

Aga Khan University Hospital (Pakistan)

Aga Khan University Hospital (AKUH) exemplifies the integration of ethical, spiritual, and humanistic care within an academic medical center in a Muslim-majority country. Grounded in the ethical framework of the Aga Khan Development Network (AKDN), the hospital emphasizes pluralism, dignity, and service as guiding values. While not overtly religious in institutional practice, AKUH embraces a spiritually-informed culture of care that honors compassion, humility, and ethical decision-making across all levels of operation.

The hospital offers regular ethics rounds, patient-centered workshops, and reflective practice sessions for clinical staff. End-of-life care protocols encourage clinicians to engage with families on spiritual needs, honoring faith-based preferences and providing space for prayers, rituals, and family presence. Chaplaincy-style spiritual support is informally available through trained social workers and nurse leaders who are taught to recognize and respond to patients' spiritual cues with empathy and cultural sensitivity.

AKUH's nursing and leadership development programs integrate reflective exercises and mentorship rooted in moral clarity, ethical leadership, and respect for diversity—offering future caregivers a spiritual lens on professional identity formation. This model demonstrates how spirituality can be woven into institutional life without overt religiosity—emphasizing values-based leadership, ethical practice, and culturally sensitive care delivery in a tertiary academic setting.

NHS Trusts (United Kingdom)

Several NHS Trusts have institutionalized spiritual care through "Values in Practice" workshops, interfaith chaplaincy models, and inclusive prayer rooms. For example, the Royal Free London NHS Foundation Trust incorporates spiritual care metrics into its staff well-being and quality improvement programs. Staff are encouraged to express their values during team meetings, and chaplains participate in end-of-life care discussions and bereavement services, reinforcing the spiritual dimension of holistic care.

These examples reveal that spiritual integration is not a luxury—it is a necessity that enhances not only patient care but institutional resilience, inclusivity, and trust. They prove that when healthcare systems prioritize meaning, purpose, and compassion, both patients and providers thrive.

3.4 Navigating Challenges in Spiritual Integration

While the benefits of spiritual integration are widely acknowledged, its execution is often hindered by practical and philosophical challenges. Understanding and addressing these barriers is essential for developing sustainable, inclusive models of spiritual care.

1. Skepticism and Secular Resistance

Many healthcare systems, especially in secular or heavily bureaucratized contexts, regard spirituality with caution. This skepticism is rooted in biomedicine's emphasis on objectivity, standardization, and empirical data. As a result, spiritual practices may be dismissed as unscientific or relegated to the margins of care (Delaney, 2005).

To counteract this, institutions must present spirituality as evidence-based and outcome-enhancing. Research now confirms that spiritual well-being correlates with improved immune response, reduced anxiety, better pain management, and increased satisfaction (Koenig et al., 2012). Framing spiritual care as a health-promoting intervention, grounded in psychological and physiological research, helps reframe its relevance in clinical terms.

2. Religious Diversity and Inclusivity

Modern healthcare teams and patient populations reflect a rich diversity of faiths, cultures, and spiritual identities. Without intentional inclusivity, spiritual programs may inadvertently marginalize non-religious or minority voices.

Therefore, spiritual integration must be pluralistic:

- Appoint interfaith chaplains and culturally competent care providers.
- Avoid prescriptive religious language in organizational communication.
- Design sacred spaces that are neutral, open, and adaptable.
- Honor staff and patient preferences for silence, ritual, or shared expression.

Inclusivity ensures that all individuals—regardless of belief—feel spiritually safe, respected, and seen.

3. Unclear Professional Boundaries

Many clinicians fear overstepping boundaries when discussing spirituality. Without training, they may avoid spiritual conversations or refer too late, missing opportunities to support patients in distress.

Institutions must provide:

- Training on spiritual assessments like FICA (Faith, Importance, Community, Address) or HOPE (Hope, Organized religion, Personal spirituality, Effects on care).
- Ethical guidance on maintaining professional boundaries while offering emotional presence.

- Clear referral systems to chaplains or spiritual counselors.

With appropriate frameworks, clinicians become empowered to integrate spirituality into care without fear or confusion.

4. Resource Constraints and Competing Priorities

In underfunded health systems, spiritual care is often overlooked in favor of measurable, revenue-generating services. Chaplaincy departments may lack personnel, and leadership may deprioritize spiritual programs.

To counter this:

- Position spiritual care as essential to well-being, quality, and retention.
- Use ROI arguments to show reduced burnout, fewer absenteeism days, and improved patient outcomes.
- Include spiritual metrics in quality dashboards and satisfaction surveys.
- Secure dedicated funding for chaplaincy, spiritual training, and healing spaces.

Sustainability depends on recognizing spiritual care as a strategic investment—not a soft cost.

4. HOLISTIC CARE: ADDRESSING PHYSICAL, MENTAL, SOCIAL, AND SPIRITUAL NEEDS

Holistic care represents a shift in healthcare philosophy—one that acknowledges the intricate interplay between the physical, psychological, social, and spiritual dimensions of the human experience. Rooted in a humanistic worldview, holistic care resists the fragmentation of modern biomedicine by restoring dignity, empathy, and meaning to the clinical encounter. It recognizes that patients are not just passive recipients of treatment but whole beings with stories, beliefs, emotions, and aspirations that shape how they experience illness and healing.

The need for holistic care has never been more urgent. In an era marked by high patient loads, technological complexity, and emotional burnout among healthcare workers, holistic models offer a way to reconnect with the core purpose of healing. These models address not only the symptoms of disease but also the root causes of suffering, promoting well-being through integration rather than isolation. By honoring the full person—body, mind, community, and spirit—holistic care becomes a practice of presence, compassion, and ethical stewardship.

This section explores the conceptual foundations and operational strategies of holistic care, with a focus on spiritual well-being as a core pillar of healing. Drawing from global best practices, clinical research, and culturally inclusive approaches, we examine how integrated care models enhance outcomes, empower patients, and support sustainable caregiving environments.

4.1 The Interconnection of Well-being Dimensions

Human beings are biologically intricate and existentially complex. The reductionist lens of traditional medicine—focused largely on biological pathology—often fails to address the lived realities of individuals navigating illness. Holistic care fills this gap by offering a model that recognizes how disruptions in one domain of health (e.g., physical pain) often reverberate across others (e.g., mental anguish or spiritual despair).

Research in psychoneuroimmunology underscores this interconnection, demonstrating that emotional trauma, chronic stress, and unresolved spiritual conflicts can impair immune functioning, exacerbate symptoms, and delay recovery (Segerstrom & Miller, 2004). Patients with chronic illness frequently report existential suffering—grappling with questions of identity, loss, meaning, and control. If left unaddressed, these experiences can become barriers to healing, adherence, and coping.

Puchalski et al. (2009) found that patients with unmet spiritual needs were more likely to report dissatisfaction with care and lower emotional well-being. Conversely, spiritual support was associated with increased resilience, better coping mechanisms, and improved quality of life—even in the face of terminal illness. The simple act of being invited to share one's values, fears, or beliefs fosters connection and therapeutic trust.

This understanding also applies to the social domain. Individuals embedded in supportive social environments—where they feel seen, heard, and held—tend to experience faster recoveries and more favorable outcomes. Family caregivers who feel emotionally supported are more equipped to manage stress, make informed decisions, and offer comfort to their loved ones (Given et al., 2001). Holistic care models that include families and communities in the care process create a wider circle of healing.

The World Health Organization (2006) has long emphasized that health is not merely the absence of disease but a state of complete physical, mental, and social well-being. More recently, spiritual well-being has been proposed as a fourth domain critical to whole-person health. This broader definition challenges healthcare systems to expand their goals—from fixing illness to fostering meaning, purpose, and coherence.

For example, a patient with terminal cancer may not experience a biological "cure," but can still achieve healing—through spiritual peace, restored relationships, or a sense of legacy. Similarly, a patient with chronic illness may find strength in faith, hope, and narrative, thereby improving their outlook and engagement with treatment.

The integration of spirituality is particularly vital in palliative and end-of-life care, where physical interventions often give way to emotional, social, and existential support. Koenig (2012) notes that attention to spiritual needs in these settings not only improves symptom management but also strengthens the emotional well-being of families facing grief and uncertainty.

In this view, healing becomes a multidimensional process—a reweaving of disrupted threads into a coherent whole. Holistic care reclaims this ancient and essential understanding of health.

4.2 Practical Approaches for Spiritual Care in Clinical Settings

While the theory of holistic care is widely accepted, its implementation requires deliberate practice, training, and cultural sensitivity. The following approaches offer a blueprint for integrating spiritual care into everyday clinical work:

Recognizing and Respecting Diverse Spiritual Beliefs

Spirituality is not a one-size-fits-all experience. For some, it is grounded in organized religion; for others, it emerges through nature, music, meditation, or personal values. Some patients may reject traditional spirituality entirely yet still seek existential clarity or connection. Effective care therefore begins with curiosity and humility.

Open-ended, non-judgmental questions can provide powerful entry points into a patient's inner world:

- "What gives your life meaning?"
- "Are there beliefs or practices that help you cope with illness?"
- "Is there anything you would like us to know about your spiritual background?"

These questions convey presence and respect, even when patients decline to engage further. They also serve as ethical touchpoints, allowing clinicians to tailor treatment plans in ways that honor the patient's worldview.

In pluralistic healthcare environments, cultural competence is essential. Clinicians must be prepared to navigate religious diversity without imposing assumptions. This includes understanding key faith-based practices (e.g., prayer times, dietary restrictions, rituals around birth or death), being aware of one's own biases, and referring to chaplains or spiritual care professionals when needed.

Training Healthcare Providers in Spiritual Communication

Despite the recognized importance of spiritual care, many healthcare professionals report feeling unprepared to engage in such conversations. Medical education tends to prioritize technical proficiency over reflective capacity, leaving gaps in interpersonal and existential care.

To address this, institutions can embed spiritual care modules into undergraduate and postgraduate curricula. Key competencies include:

- Recognizing signs of spiritual distress (e.g., hopelessness, fear of death, isolation)
- Using validated tools like the FICA (Faith, Importance, Community, Address) or HOPE models
- Distinguishing between spiritual support and religious counseling
- Knowing when and how to involve chaplains or culturally appropriate resources

Simulation-based learning, role-playing, and reflective journaling can help clinicians develop the empathy and confidence needed for spiritual care. Even brief interventions—such as acknowledging a patient's fear, offering a moment of silence, or listening without interruption—can have profound effects on trust and emotional safety.

Best Practices in Holistic Care Delivery

Numerous institutions have pioneered models of holistic care that embed spiritual well-being into their service delivery:

1. Integrative Medicine Clinics

These centers offer a blend of biomedical and complementary therapies—such as guided imagery, acupuncture, yoga, art therapy, and narrative healing. The aim is not only to reduce symptoms but to restore balance and agency. Patients are encouraged to explore emotional and spiritual resources as part of their healing plan.

2. Palliative and Hospice Units

In palliative settings, spiritual care is often a core component of interdisciplinary rounds. Teams that include chaplains, social workers, and psychologists address existential suffering, unresolved grief, and anticipatory loss. Techniques like legacy-building, life review, and storytelling help patients make peace with their journey.

3. Sacred and Reflective Spaces

Hospitals with interfaith chapels, healing gardens, and meditation rooms create environments that support stillness and reflection. These spaces offer comfort to patients and families during times of uncertainty, and serve as restorative zones for staff as well.

4. Narrative Medicine Programs

By inviting patients to share their life stories—through interviews, journals, or artwork—clinicians gain insight into the personal and spiritual meanings behind illness. This helps humanize care and ensures that medical decisions align with patient values.

5. Spiritual Rounds and Reflections

Some organizations incorporate moments of spiritual reflection into staff huddles or team debriefings. This may include reading a poem, offering a gratitude circle, or acknowledging an act of compassion. These practices build emotional resilience and moral connection among teams.

4.3 Organizational Strategies for Embedding Holistic Care

To make holistic care sustainable, institutions must integrate it into policies, leadership models, and evaluation systems. This requires moving beyond isolated programs to system-wide culture change.

Leadership Commitment

Leaders who embody holistic values—such as humility, compassion, and integrity—model the importance of whole-person care. Their support legitimizes spiritual care as an organizational priority rather than a peripheral service.

Policy Integration

Spiritual assessments should be incorporated into patient intake processes, palliative protocols, and care planning templates. Standards for chaplaincy services, culturally sensitive care, and staff well-being should be written into institutional guidelines.

Training and Development

Mandatory training on spiritual communication, cultural humility, and reflective practice can enhance staff confidence and competence. Chaplaincy services should be adequately staffed and included in team consultations and ethics committees.

Measurement and Evaluation

Outcomes related to holistic care can be tracked through patient satisfaction surveys, spiritual distress screenings, and chaplaincy utilization rates. Institutions can also evaluate staff well-being metrics—such as burnout, absenteeism, and retention—as indirect indicators of a compassionate workplace culture.

4.4 The Impact of Holistic Care on Patients and Providers

Holistic care transforms not only how care is delivered—but how it is experienced. For patients, it provides a sense of being fully seen and respected. They are treated not as problems to solve but as persons to accompany—on a journey that is as emotional and spiritual as it is physical.

For providers, holistic care reduces the sense of moral fragmentation that often accompanies high-stress environments. It reconnects them to their purpose, strengthens team cohesion, and builds emotional resilience. Clinicians who engage in reflective practice and spiritual inquiry often report greater job satisfaction and lower compassion fatigue (Rushton et al., 2015).

Moreover, holistic care aligns healthcare with broader ethical goals: justice, equity, and human dignity. By addressing the whole person, it supports marginalized communities whose spiritual needs may be overlooked or misunderstood. It promotes equity not just in access to treatment—but in the quality of presence, listening, and support.

5. STRATEGIES FOR INTEGRATING SPIRITUALITY INTO HEALTHCARE

While the value of spirituality in patient and staff well-being is increasingly acknowledged, it must be systematically and sustainably integrated into the infrastructure of healthcare delivery. This requires deliberate action on multiple fronts: policy formulation, workforce engagement, resource allocation, and continuous evaluation. Spirituality should be seen not as an auxiliary aspect of care, but as a core dimension that informs ethical practice, nurtures emotional resilience, and enriches patient-provider relationships. The following strategies provide a framework for how institutions can create enduring cultures of spiritual care.

To move from vision to action, healthcare institutions must operationalize spiritual care across all levels—policy, practice, leadership, training, and evaluation. These strategies should reflect the complexity of healthcare systems and the diversity of spiritual expressions among staff and patients alike. By embedding spirituality into the clinical, administrative, and cultural frameworks of institutions, we ensure its relevance, sustainability, and inclusivity.

5.1 Developing Institutional Policies on Spiritual Support

Policy serves as the foundation for consistency, accountability, and institutional commitment. By formally recognizing spiritual care in organizational policies, healthcare systems signal its legitimacy, importance, and role in the healing process. Policies must ensure that spiritual care is a standard part of care delivery rather than an optional add-on.

Key policy elements should include:

- Integrating spiritual history-taking into patient admission protocols using structured tools such as FICA or HOPE.
- Documenting spiritual distress alongside physical and emotional pain in electronic health records.
- Defining professional roles and referral processes for spiritual care providers, including pathways for interprofessional collaboration.
- Respecting religious and cultural diversity, with clear guidelines for accommodating various spiritual practices during hospitalization (e.g., dietary preferences, ritual objects, prayer times).
- Ensuring equal access to spiritual care services for patients, families, and staff across units and shifts.

Institutional policies must be inclusive, reflect ethical neutrality, and protect against religious coercion. They should also outline patient rights concerning spiritual care, empowering individuals to make informed choices about how their values are supported during treatment.

Effective integration begins with policy. Institutions must articulate a formal commitment to recognizing and supporting the spiritual dimension of care. This includes:

- Including spiritual assessment as part of standard patient intake processes.
- Recognizing spiritual distress as a clinical concern, particularly in palliative and chronic care.
- Mandating referral pathways to chaplains or spiritual care providers.
- Providing protected spaces for reflection, prayer, and ritual.
- Ensuring that spiritual support is available for both patients and staff.

Policies must be inclusive, allowing for pluralism and avoiding any bias toward a particular faith or tradition. Institutional mission statements can explicitly recognize holistic care, including spiritual well-being, as part of the organization's ethical commitment.

5.2 Chaplaincy, Multifaith, and Peer-Support Programs

Chaplains are essential members of the healthcare team. They provide nonjudgmental support, facilitate rituals, and assist with existential questions and ethical dilemmas. To ensure chaplaincy effectiveness:

- Hospitals should maintain staffing benchmarks (e.g., one chaplain per 50–75 patients).
- Chaplains should be board-certified, trained in trauma-informed care, grief counseling, and cultural humility.
- Chaplains must be visible, accessible, and embedded in daily clinical practice, especially in palliative care, ICUs, oncology, and behavioral health units.

A multifaith model of chaplaincy ensures that diverse spiritual worldviews are acknowledged and supported. This can be facilitated by:

- Interfaith chaplaincy teams representing major belief systems and secular perspectives.
- Training modules on global spirituality to prepare chaplains for culturally appropriate responses.

- Collaboration with community religious leaders when needed, especially during end-of-life situations or complex ethical cases.

In parallel, peer-led programs—such as resilience circles, caregiver support groups, or spiritually reflective huddles—complement formal chaplaincy services. These initiatives normalize emotional sharing and create psychologically safe spaces for staff to process the spiritual dimensions of their work.

Chaplains are trained professionals who provide spiritual and emotional support in diverse clinical contexts. Hospitals should:

- Maintain adequate chaplain-to-patient ratios.
- Offer interfaith or multifaith chaplaincy models based on community demographics.
- Integrate chaplains into multidisciplinary rounds, especially in oncology, palliative care, mental health, and ICU units.

In addition to chaplains, peer-support networks can foster spiritual connection through storytelling circles, reflective listening groups, or support groups grounded in shared values. These programs enhance team morale and reduce burnout.

5.3 Building Workplace Spirituality through Practices and Routines

Organizational culture is shaped not only by policies but by the rituals, language, and norms that guide everyday behavior. To make spirituality part of healthcare's daily rhythm, leaders must create intentional spaces for reflection, gratitude, and emotional connection.

Examples of spiritual workplace practices include:

- The Pause: A moment of silence observed by the care team after a patient dies, honoring their life and the efforts of the staff.
- Gratitude boards: Interactive displays where patients, families, and staff can leave notes of appreciation.
- Reflective practice rounds: Dedicated team sessions where clinicians share emotionally impactful experiences, guided by trained facilitators.
- Ritualized transitions: Marking retirements, leadership changes, or ward milestones with ethically resonant ceremonies that foster continuity and purpose.

Staff well-being initiatives grounded in spirituality also include:

- Mindfulness and meditation rooms open 24/7
- Bi-weekly "spiritual resilience workshops" on themes like forgiveness, purpose, and empathy
- Staff storytelling platforms to celebrate moments of moral courage, compassion, and healing

When spiritual care is normalized in the culture of a workplace, staff report feeling more connected, fulfilled, and resilient in their roles.

Spiritual care integration goes beyond formal services—it involves cultivating a work environment where meaning, presence, and values are part of the culture. This includes:

- Hosting "pause practices" after patient deaths to honor life and acknowledge grief.
- Creating rituals such as gratitude walls, team reflections, and legacy storytelling.
- Offering staff training in mindfulness, emotional regulation, and compassionate presence.
- Recognizing acts of moral courage or compassionate care in performance reviews or team debriefs.

When staff are invited to reflect on their purpose and spiritual identity, they are more likely to act with empathy and resilience. Workplace spirituality builds moral stamina—crucial in high-stress healthcare environments.

5.4 Measuring Impact and Ensuring Sustainability

The integration of spirituality into healthcare must go beyond philosophical support—it must be demonstrable, measurable, and adaptable. In the increasingly evidence-driven world of healthcare, spiritual care must meet the same standards of accountability and performance as clinical interventions. Measuring its impact is crucial for gaining institutional legitimacy, securing resources, and maintaining alignment with strategic goals. Moreover, data-driven evaluation provides clarity on what works, for whom, and under what conditions—making it possible to replicate and scale successful initiatives.

5.4.1 Importance of Measurement in Spiritual Care

Healthcare administrators and policymakers rely on outcome metrics to make decisions about funding, staffing, and program sustainability. Without concrete evidence, spiritual care programs risk being seen as non-essential or expendable during budget cuts. Measuring spiritual care, therefore, is not a symbolic exercise—it is a strategic imperative.

The act of measurement also reinforces organizational learning and innovation. It helps teams identify gaps in access, effectiveness, and staff engagement. Institutions can then use this feedback to continuously improve the relevance, reach, and cultural sensitivity of their spiritual care initiatives.

5.4.2 Core Dimensions of Evaluation

To provide a robust picture of spiritual care's impact, evaluation must encompass four key dimensions: clinical outcomes, patient-reported experiences, staff well-being metrics, and process-level indicators.

a) Clinical Outcomes

There is growing evidence that spiritual care positively affects medical outcomes—particularly in patients facing chronic illness, terminal diagnoses, or complex medical decisions. Healthcare providers who address spiritual needs have been shown to influence:

- **Length of stay**: Spiritual care, especially in palliative settings, can help patients make informed decisions that reduce unnecessary interventions and expedite discharge planning.
- **Pain and symptom management**: Spiritual distress can exacerbate perceptions of pain and fatigue. Addressing these concerns can improve patient-reported symptom control.
- **Palliative care utilization**: Early spiritual care is associated with higher rates of hospice enrollment and lower use of aggressive end-of-life treatments.
- **Advance care planning**: Patients who receive spiritual support are more likely to engage in meaningful conversations about treatment preferences, code status, and goals of care.

Clinical data should be tracked through existing hospital quality systems, with chaplain consultations or spiritual documentation linked to relevant health outcomes. Collaboration with palliative care teams can enhance data triangulation.

b) Patient-Reported Measures

To accurately assess patient spiritual needs and monitor the impact of care interventions, validated psychometric tools offer structured and reliable approaches.

These instruments not only support individualized care planning but also generate data for institutional evaluation.

- *FACIT-Sp (Functional Assessment of Chronic Illness Therapy – Spiritual Well-Being)* is one of the most widely used tools in spiritual care research. It includes 12 items divided into two subscales: *Meaning/Peace* and *Faith.* The *Meaning/Peace* subscale evaluates a person's sense of life purpose and inner harmony, while the *Faith* subscale assesses the degree to which spiritual beliefs provide comfort and strength. FACIT-Sp has been used across cancer care, chronic illness, and palliative settings, and is sensitive to changes following spiritual interventions (Peterman et al., 2002).
- *Spiritual Well-being Scale (SWBS)*, developed by Paloutzian and Ellison (1982), consists of 20 items measuring two key components: *Religious Well-Being* (relationship with a higher power) and *Existential Well-Being* (sense of purpose and life satisfaction). It is especially useful for distinguishing between religiosity and spirituality, allowing for culturally sensitive assessment. The SWBS has been validated in multiple populations, including older adults, adolescents, and individuals with chronic illness.
- *Spiritual Needs Questionnaire (SpNQ)*, created by Büssing et al., is designed to capture the diverse range of spiritual concerns patients may experience, including needs for inner peace, meaning-making, forgiveness, and connectedness. Its multidimensional nature makes it suitable for multicultural and interfaith populations, and its flexible format allows adaptation to specific healthcare contexts such as oncology, nephrology, and geriatrics.

Each of these instruments offers unique advantages. The *FACIT-Sp* is often preferred in clinical trials due to its concise format and alignment with quality-of-life measures. The *SWBS* provides insights into existential distress versus religious coping, which can guide chaplain referrals or mental health support. The *SpNQ* excels in program development, offering granular data to tailor group interventions or educational content.

Together, these tools enable healthcare institutions to move beyond anecdotal impressions and systematically quantify spiritual well-being, making it a visible and actionable part of care quality.

c) Staff-Related Metrics

Healthcare staff are not immune to the emotional and spiritual demands of caregiving. Burnout, moral injury, and compassion fatigue are alarmingly prevalent, particularly in high-acuity or ethically complex settings. Evaluating the impact of spiritual care on staff well-being involves tracking:

- *Burnout levels* using tools like the Maslach Burnout Inventory (MBI), especially emotional exhaustion and depersonalization domains.
- *Staff retention and turnover rates*, especially in departments with implemented spiritual care programs.
- *Moral distress scores*, often gathered through customized surveys or tools like the Moral Distress Scale–Revised (MDS-R).
- *Engagement in reflective or wellness sessions*, such as attendance in pause practices, narrative rounds, or spiritual resilience workshops.

Pre- and post-program implementation comparisons can help assess spiritual care's protective effect on staff. Additionally, focus groups or interviews can uncover how spiritual care practices influence purpose, satisfaction, and emotional processing among staff.

d) Process and Operational Indicators

Beyond outcomes, healthcare organizations must track the delivery and integration of spiritual services. These include:

- *Referral rates* to chaplaincy or spiritual care providers.
- *Documentation compliance* for spiritual assessments in EHRs.
- *Utilization rates* of sacred spaces, meditation rooms, or peer-led sessions.
- *Frequency and quality of team debriefs* or reflective practice rounds.
- *Inclusion of spiritual care in treatment planning* meetings, family conferences, and discharge planning.

These indicators provide insight into how well spiritual care is operationalized and where bottlenecks or inequities may exist.

5.4.3 Strategies for Long-Term Sustainability

To institutionalize spiritual care, efforts must extend beyond measurement to system-wide integration. Sustainability depends on leadership commitment, financial resourcing, alignment with strategy, and embedding within organizational routines.

Key strategies include:

- **Assigning executive sponsors or champions**: When senior leaders visibly support spiritual initiatives—by attending rounds, allocating budgets, or incorporating spirituality into strategic planning—it signals organizational seriousness and drives culture change.

- **Securing dedicated funding**: Chaplaincy services, training workshops, infrastructure development (e.g., serenity rooms), and evaluation tools require stable financial support. These can be included in departmental budgets, quality improvement allocations, or external grants.
- **Incorporating spiritual care into strategic documents**: Spiritual well-being should feature in organizational values, strategic priorities, staff wellness plans, and patient experience frameworks. Inclusion in mission and vision statements reinforces long-term relevance.
- **Embedding in accreditation and readiness reviews**: Organizations can align with standards from Joint Commission International (JCI), Planetree, or the National Consensus Project, which recognize spiritual care as a dimension of high-quality care.
- **Partnering with academic institutions**: Collaborations with universities or research centers allow for rigorous program evaluation, scholarly dissemination, and evidence-based refinement. Publishing outcomes builds credibility and contributes to global learning.

5.4.4 Cultivating a Culture of Accountability and Inspiration

While data and metrics are essential for evaluating effectiveness, they must be complemented with storytelling and visible leadership engagement to foster a lasting culture of spiritual care. Numbers can validate programs, but stories move people. Sharing narratives of patients who found peace and meaning in their final days, or staff who experienced emotional healing through reflective rounds, breathes life into data and reinforces the deeper purpose behind spiritual initiatives.

To embed spirituality into the organizational culture, healthcare institutions can use multiple platforms—such as quarterly dashboards, storytelling sessions, newsletters, or visual displays—to share both quantitative outcomes and qualitative experiences. Events that celebrate "spiritual excellence," such as recognizing acts of compassion or moral courage, can create powerful role models and build pride in values-based care.

Leadership modeling is also crucial. When senior leaders attend pause rituals, participate in reflective sessions, or share personal insights on empathy and purpose, they demonstrate that spirituality is not peripheral but core to organizational integrity.

Regular feedback mechanisms—such as surveys, listening circles, or frontline debriefs—ensure the spiritual care strategy evolves with real-time staff input. Ultimately, cultivating this culture means transforming spiritual care from a standalone service into a shared ethos—woven into the language, behaviors, and decisions of the entire organization.

6. CONCLUSION

In the ever-evolving landscape of healthcare, where the focus has traditionally centered on technological advancement, procedural efficiency, and evidence-based outcomes, a quiet but powerful truth has re-emerged: healing is as much about meaning, compassion, and connection as it is about medicine. Spirituality, often marginalized or misunderstood, is now being recognized as a foundational dimension of health—one that speaks to our shared humanity, our capacity for resilience, and our need to find purpose, particularly in times of illness, suffering, or uncertainty.

This chapter has aimed to illuminate the significance of spirituality in clinical practice, organizational culture, and leadership. Through the lens of a five-dimensional framework—Self, Society, State, Systems, and Spirituality—we have seen how interconnected these forces are in shaping how care is delivered and received. The framework allows us to move beyond abstract ideals into tangible strategies, rooted in the recognition that health is a multidimensional experience. From the inner lives of individual providers to the policies of healthcare institutions, spirituality offers a bridge between personal values and professional responsibilities.

At the individual level, we explored how spirituality helps healthcare workers process emotional burden, manage moral distress, and maintain a sense of purpose. Whether through private rituals, reflective journaling, or support from spiritual communities, providers who engage their spiritual resources are more likely to sustain empathy and avoid compassion fatigue. In emotionally demanding settings, where loss, ethical dilemmas, and burnout are commonplace, spiritual grounding becomes not just helpful—but essential.

Equally important is the role of organizational culture. Institutions that embed spirituality into their leadership philosophies and daily operations experience more cohesive teams, higher staff engagement, and more compassionate care environments. Programs like Code Lavender, gratitude rituals, and chaplain-led resilience rounds are not luxuries—they are vital structures that validate the emotional and spiritual dimensions of caregiving. Leadership, when grounded in ethical and spiritual values, becomes a force for healing not just for patients but for the entire healthcare workforce.

Systemically, we examined the integration of spiritual care into hospital policy, practice, and evaluation. This includes spiritual assessments during patient intake, interfaith chaplaincy teams, and reflective spaces for both patients and staff. Importantly, we emphasized the need for pluralistic, inclusive approaches that honor diverse beliefs without imposing specific ideologies. The goal is to create safe spaces—spaces where vulnerability is met with presence, and where silence is as healing as speech.

Measurement and sustainability were also addressed, underscoring the importance of demonstrating impact through data. By tracking spiritual care utilization, patient satisfaction, and staff well-being, institutions can justify investments and continually refine their models. Evaluation tools like the FACIT-Sp and regular audits ensure that spiritual care does not remain aspirational, but becomes operational and accountable.

Yet, perhaps the most profound takeaway is that spirituality invites a different kind of attention—a kind of seeing that goes beyond symptoms and into story, beyond charts and into character. For example, a palliative care nurse once described how she paused at each patient's bedside not only to administer medication, but to silently reflect on who that person was beyond the diagnosis—what they loved, feared, believed in. In her words, "It wasn't just care I was offering—it was presence." This kind of spiritual attentiveness allows clinicians to notice subtle cues, honor emotional complexity, and co-create moments of human connection that are as healing as any procedure. It calls on us to ask different questions: What brings this person meaning? What sustains their hope? What fears are they carrying that no lab test can detect? These are not secondary inquiries—they are central to holistic, ethical, and truly human care.

Integrating spirituality into healthcare does not require abandoning science or efficiency. Instead, it enriches them. When spirituality is present, healing expands. It becomes possible for a hospital room to feel sacred, for a clinical interaction to feel redemptive, and for staff to see themselves not only as professionals but as stewards of compassion.

As we conclude, let us remember that spirituality is not a task to be added, but a thread to be woven. It is the breath behind the words, the pause behind the action, and the presence that turns treatment into healing. For patients, it may be the difference between feeling treated and feeling seen. For staff, it may be the difference between enduring the work and finding joy within it.

The way forward is not about prescribing one approach, but cultivating an ethos. One that says: every person matters. Every belief is respected. And every moment of care holds the potential for meaning.

In this way, spirituality becomes not a soft skill or private matter—but a public good, a clinical strength, and a leadership imperative. It is how we stay human in the most high-tech of systems. And how we honor the sacred in the most ordinary of moments.

May this chapter serve as a call—to lead with purpose, to care with presence, and to heal with heart.

Spirituality, once relegated to the private realm, is now emerging as a vital component of holistic healthcare. As this chapter has explored, integrating spirituality is not a superficial gesture—it is a profound acknowledgment of the full human experience. In settings often defined by urgency, suffering, and emotional complexity, spirituality brings grounding, clarity, and compassion.

We began by exploring spirituality as a multidimensional construct—linked to meaning, purpose, transcendence, and ethical identity. Through a five-dimensional framework, we examined how spirituality weaves through personal development, social engagement, institutional governance, systemic structures, and inner purpose. We then investigated how spirituality helps healthcare providers navigate emotional burdens, build resilience, and avoid moral distress.

As the chapter progressed, we examined real-world applications—how hospitals embed spirituality in leadership, team culture, and care delivery. We identified best practices and highlighted case studies that show the transformative power of spiritually informed care. From reflective rituals and peer support to chaplaincy and policy integration, each strategy reinforces a core truth: healing is not complete without attention to the soul.

The imperative is clear. Spiritual care must be:

- Institutionalized through inclusive, value-driven policies
- Supported by trained leaders and clinicians
- Embedded in the daily rituals, rhythms, and relationships of healthcare practice
- Measured rigorously and sustained strategically

For patients, spiritual care affirms dignity, comforts in times of uncertainty, and brings depth to the healing journey. For providers, it preserves purpose, mitigates burnout, and reinforces a sense of sacred responsibility. For institutions, it fosters ethical culture, team cohesion, and meaningful patient engagement.

As healthcare systems evolve, the call is not simply to do more—but to care more deeply. Integrating spirituality does not require complex innovation; it demands moral courage, presence, and intention. When care honors the human spirit, medicine transcends procedure—it becomes a practice of compassion.

Let us move forward not just with new tools, but with renewed conviction—that spirituality is not only compatible with science and efficiency, but essential to care that is truly healing, equitable, and humane.

While the value of spirituality in patient and staff well-being is increasingly acknowledged, it must be systematically and sustainably integrated into the infrastructure of healthcare delivery. This requires deliberate action on multiple fronts: policy formulation, workforce engagement, resource allocation, and continuous evaluation. Spirituality should be seen not as an auxiliary aspect of care, but as a core dimension that informs ethical practice, nurtures emotional resilience, and enriches patient-provider relationships. The following strategies provide a framework for how institutions can create enduring cultures of spiritual care.

To move from vision to action, healthcare institutions must operationalize spiritual care across all levels—policy, practice, leadership, training, and evaluation. These strategies should reflect the complexity of healthcare systems and the diversity of spiritual expressions among staff and patients alike. By embedding spirituality into the clinical, administrative, and cultural frameworks of institutions, we ensure its relevance, sustainability, and inclusivity.

REFERENCES

Benefiel, M. (2005). *Soul at work: Spiritual leadership in organizations*. Church Publishing, Inc.

Berlinger, N., Wynia, M., Powell, T., Hester, D. M., Milliken, A., Fabi, R., & Jenks, N. P. (2017). *Ethical framework for health care institutions responding to novel coronavirus SARS-CoV-2 (COVID-19)*. The Hastings Center.

Delaney, C. (2005). The spirituality scale: Development and psychometric testing of a holistic instrument to assess the human spiritual dimension. *Journal of Holistic Nursing*, *23*(2), 145–167. DOI: 10.1177/0898010105276180 PMID: 15883463

Epstein, E. G., & Hamric, A. B. (2009). Moral distress, moral residue, and the crescendo effect. *The Journal of Clinical Ethics*, *20*(4), 330–342. DOI: 10.1086/JCE200920406 PMID: 20120853

Fry, L. W. (2003). Toward a theory of spiritual leadership. *The Leadership Quarterly*, *14*(6), 693–727. DOI: 10.1016/j.leaqua.2003.09.001

Koenig, H. G. (2012). Religion, spirituality, and health: The research and clinical implications. *ISRN Psychiatry*, *2012*, 1–33. DOI: 10.5402/2012/278730 PMID: 23762764

Koenig, H. G., McCullough, M. E., & Larson, D. B. (2001). *Handbook of religion and health*. Oxford University Press. DOI: 10.1093/acprof:oso/9780195118667.001.0001

Krasner, M. S., Epstein, R. M., Beckman, H., Suchman, A. L., Chapman, B., Mooney, C. J., & Quill, T. E. (2009). Association of an educational program in mindful communication with burnout, empathy, and attitudes among primary care physicians. *Journal of the American Medical Association*, *302*(12), 1284–1293. DOI: 10.1001/jama.2009.1384 PMID: 19773563

Milliman, J., Czaplewski, A. J., & Ferguson, J. (2003). Workplace spirituality and employee work attitudes: An exploratory empirical assessment. *Journal of Organizational Change Management*, *16*(4), 426–447. DOI: 10.1108/09534810310484172

Newberg, A., & Waldman, M. R. (2009). *How God changes your brain: Breakthrough findings from a leading neuroscientist*. Ballantine Books.

Pargament, K. I. (2007). *Spiritually integrated psychotherapy: Understanding and addressing the sacred*. Guilford Press.

Reave, L. (2005). Spiritual values and practices related to leadership effectiveness. *The Leadership Quarterly*, *16*(5), 655–687. DOI: 10.1016/j.leaqua.2005.07.003

Shanafelt, T. D., Boone, S., Tan, L., Dyrbye, L. N., Sotile, W., Satele, D., West, C. P., Sloan, J., & Oreskovich, M. R. (2012). Burnout and satisfaction with work-life balance among US physicians relative to the general US population. *Archives of Internal Medicine*, *172*(18), 1377–1385. DOI: 10.1001/archinternmed.2012.3199 PMID: 22911330

Smith, A., Jones, R., & Taylor, P. (2021). Meaning-centered interventions and mental health outcomes in healthcare professionals: A meta-analytic review. *Journal of Health Psychology*, *26*(11), 1558–1573. DOI: 10.1177/1359105320947772

Sulmasy, D. P. (2006). *The rebirth of the clinic: An introduction to spirituality in health care*. Georgetown University Press.

World Health Organization. (2006). *Constitution of the World Health Organization – Basic Documents* (45th ed.). World Health Organization.

ADDITIONAL READING

Carson, V. B., & Koenig, H. G. (2008). *Spiritual dimensions of nursing practice*. Templeton Foundation Press.

Ferrell, B., Otis-Green, S., & Economou, D. (2013). *Spirituality in oncology nursing: Developing the role of the advanced practice nurse*. Oncology Nursing Society.

Kelly, E. (2004). Nursing and spirituality: How spiritual care is defined by nurses and patients. In Cobb, M., & Robshaw, V. (Eds.), *The spiritual challenge of healthcare* (pp. 68–84). Churchill Livingstone.

Puchalski, C. M., & Ferrell, B. (Eds.). (2010). *Making health care whole: Integrating spirituality into patient care*. Templeton Press.

Sloan, R. P., Bagiella, E., & Powell, T. (2001). Religion, spirituality, and medicine. *Lancet, 353*(9153), 664–667. DOI: 10.1016/S0140-6736(98)07376-0 PMID: 10030348

Sulmasy, D. P. (2002). A biopsychosocial–spiritual model for the care of patients at the end of life. *The Gerontologist, 42*(Special Issue III), 24–33. DOI: 10.1093/geront/42.suppl_3.24

Swinton, J. (2001). *Spirituality and mental health care: Rediscovering a "forgotten" dimension.* Jessica Kingsley Publishers.

Tanyi, R. A. (2002). Towards clarification of the meaning of spirituality. *Journal of Advanced Nursing*, *39*(5), 500–509. DOI: 10.1046/j.1365-2648.2002.02315.x PMID: 12175360

Taylor, E. J. (2008). *Spiritual care: Nursing theory, research, and practice*. Prentice Hall.

Zinnbauer, B. J., Pargament, K. I., & Scott, A. B. (1999). The emerging meanings of religiousness and spirituality: Problems and prospects. *Journal of Personality*, *67*(6), 889–919. DOI: 10.1111/1467-6494.00077

Chapter 11
The Soulful Prescription: Merging Spirituality With Healthcare

Hira Aziz
http://orcid.org/0009-0003-8775-7734
National Medical Centre, Karachi, Pakistan

ABSTRACT

Since time immemorial, it has been embedded in the minds and hearts of healthcare providers to always prioritise the needs of their patients. From the excitement of the first day of medical school to the nerves of the first day in the hospital as medical staff, we are taught to care for others, oftentimes at the expense of our own well-being. While some of us manage to balance work and personal lives, too many healthcare providers end up dealing with the consequences of overlooking their own needs and eventually develop a redundant outlook to their work which is at odds with this sensitive profession. This is where spiritual wellbeing makes its entrance. Spirituality, in its truest essence, aims to attach "meaning" to everything we do. In simple terms, it helps us discover a purpose in life, which becomes the basic foundation from which healthcare providers then navigate this precious field of serving humanity. It forms the groundwork for resilience, which is an imperative part of medicine.

INTRODUCTION

The concept of spirituality is quite complex, with various definitions linked to it all over the globe. There is no single consensus, as validated by Reinert and Koenig (2013): "There is no 'gold standard' for the definition of spirituality that can be established independent of the historical use of the term in the English lan-

DOI: 10.4018/979-8-2600-0582-8.ch011

guage or the Greek or Latin roots from which the word 'spirituality' is derived" (p. 2623). The root word for spirituality is the Latin word *spiritus* and the Greek word *pneûma*, both of which mean 'breath,' 'soul,' or 'spirit,' and hence one of the ways spirituality can be described is as a deep connection to the self, wandering on the soul's horizon and craving a connection beyond the material world.

Spirituality can often be interlinked with religion, since both address fundamental human concerns about meaning, purpose, morality, and an attachment with something greater than oneself. If we break them down, religion is typically seen as an organized system of beliefs and rituals, while spirituality is a more personal quest for meaning or connection to something greater—whether through God, nature, or inner reflection—but both share a common goal of seeking the sacred through individual thoughts, emotions, and actions (Yuen, 2007). Hill et al. (2000) state, "*Both spirituality and religion are complex phenomena, multidimensional in nature, and any single definition is likely to reflect a limited perspective or interest*" (p. 52), while Baldacchino (2015) believes that spirituality extends beyond religious belief in the universal search for meaning and purpose, because it is attainable and yearned for by both believers and non-believers. Moberg (2010) maintains the view that spirituality is a broad idea, and from it came the many religions and belief systems in the world, while Saad and de Medeiros (2021) consider that spirituality can encompass a wide range of elements from non-religious concepts such as an optimistic mindset to intensely religious experiences. In either stance, the practices and teachings that are learned through religion and spirituality awaken, support, and meet the deep needs that come from the spiritual nature within each person.

For some people, spirituality is the ultimate basis of meaning and purpose in life (Foglio & Brody, 1988) and a hope to connect with something sacred or important and involves values and beliefs that can resonate through one's thoughts, feelings, and deeds (Büssing et al., 2014). Puchalski et al. (2014) defines spirituality as "a dynamic and intrinsic aspect of humanity through which persons seek ultimate meaning, purpose, and transcendence, and experience relationship to self, family, others, community, society, nature, and the significant or sacred. Spirituality is expressed through beliefs, values, traditions, and practices.'' (p. 646). Despite the diverse descriptions and terminologies, every notion regarding spirituality believes that it changes us for the better. The pursuit of inner peace and personal transformation, and the desire to connect with a higher power, brings about a rejuvenating experience within ourselves. The life-changing influence of our personal experience with the Divine is one of the greatest ways to feel empowerment and peace. In an article by Yawar (2001), it is explained that two realms of existence are considered to be linked with human beings; there is the outer realm, which comprises the human being's interrelatedness with the world and mostly consists of practicing qualities such as justice and generosity, and then there is the inner realm, which is the transcendental interaction, and it can be experienced through true sincerity. Here it can be insinuated how our relation with other people and with the Divine is an immense part of our identity and, in turn, directly affects our spiritual wellbeing. When individuals align with this inner truth and sacred calling, they can enter a state where they are able to deal with their day-to-day life issues with dedication and commitment while being grateful for life (Dhar et al., 2011) and respecting all forms of it. This approach in turn can enhance their overall physical, mental, and social well-being. Spirituality is an important constituent of cultural identity that is gaining recognition for its influence on health behaviors and decisions related to healthcare (Isaac et al., 2016).

The practice of medicine carries a sacred dimension and, at its heart, mirrors a holy duty. When we think about the universe's miracles, like the human body, we can't help but feel awe at how perfectly each particle was designed. The relationship between spirituality, religion, and medicine is as old as human civilization. From the earliest healing rituals to modern medicine, the entwining of spiritual belief systems and medical practice has influenced how societies and cultures understand health, illness, and healing. In ancient civilizations, medicine was considered a sacred practice, and health and disease were often viewed as manifestations of spiritual imbalance. From the old to the new, many spiritual healers believe that divine energies are channeled from the spiritual realm to the healer, which results in a positive impact on the patient's health (Aldridge, 1991).

Dating back to prehistoric times, Shamanism was found in a lot of tribal societies in many parts of the world. It was centered on the belief in a spiritual realm that is guarded by spirits and supernatural entities and ancestral presences. Shamans were spiritual elites who underwent meticulous training and initiation rituals that included periods of fasting, isolation, and visionary experiences brought on by psychoactive plants and the performance of drumming, dancing, etcetera. They used techniques involving dreams and trances, which were meant to heal individuals and protect the community's soul and also served as a way to journey between the worlds and act as an intermediary between humans and the Divine (Aldridge, 1991; Elendu, 2024).

Modern-day West Asia and the eastern part of the Middle East were once Mesopotamia, where rituals and incantations were commonly done by healers to drive off spirits, which were thought to cause illness and disease. It was thought that illness was an extrinsic force that invaded the body in some manner, and while the use of traditional medicinal methods was habitual, they were used in accordance with specific rituals and alignment of constellations, along with prayers, sacrifices, recitations, and incantations, which were common religious methods (Pouyan, 2016). One such incantation from ancient Mesopotamia, called the Marduk-Ea (Annus, 2020), was recited in exorcistic healing rituals and facilitated spiritual and religious experiences in the healer and patient. Most of the practices and beliefs were forwarded to the next civilizations and generations to come, and many small tribes and cultures still have a strong belief in the practices that were previously done.

In Ancient Egypt, Imhotep was believed to be the 'divine healer,' while Sekhmet was the 'goddess of medicine.' Thus, healing was closely associated with rituals and medical treatment. which involved prayers and offerings to the gods for their help (Elendu, 2024). Mental and physical illnesses were viewed similarly, with no clear distinction between them, as both were interpreted through a religious or spiritual lens (Koenig et al., 2012). It was also believed that the preservation and reanimation of the human body were crucial for the deceased's passage into the afterlife and their transformation into an eternally living being.

The typical Greek believed that their health and well-being were controlled by the will of the gods. Their location and social status often determined the specific deity they attributed this power to. Even the Hippocratic Era, which saw many advancements in the field of medicine, focused on how the environment affects health, used natural ways to treat illness, valued the impact of thoughts and emotions, encouraged healthy eating and living, supported the freedom of mind, body, and spirit, and stressed the need for balance with society and nature (Kleisiaris et al., 2014). The Hippocratic doctor was expected to offer comprehensive care, treating not only physical ailments but also the mental, social, emotional, and spiritual aspects of the patient's well-being. These principles promoted overall health through physical strength, psychological and emotional harmony, and balanced social relationships, unifying the body, mind, and soul (Elendu, 2024).

Another very essential medical system, which was introduced millennia ago and finds its roots in spiritual well-being but is still practiced to this day, is Ayurveda. Rooted in Hinduism, it combines dietary specifications, exercise and meditation, herbal cures, and lifestyle practices to provide a comprehensive approach to healing and well-being by maintaining balance between the body, mind, and spirit (Elendu, 2024). Ayurveda and yoga go hand-in-hand, with both of them being spiritual sciences; the former helps to strive towards spiritual goals by keeping the body healthy, and the latter helps pave the way for spirituality and mindfulness (Halpern, 2017).

Similarly, Hinduism encompasses a wide variety of rituals that serve spiritual, social, and personal purposes. Srivastava & Barmola (2013), in his publication, describes a variety of these rituals in detail; they include simple home offerings, shamanic healing, and formal religious ceremonies. Then there are rituals such as *Puja* (worship), which foster a personal relationship with the divine, while sacred bathing, image worship, and pilgrimages express reverence for holy places and deities. Life events like marriage and death involve significant rites of passage, emphasizing spiritual continuity. Festivals celebrate divine stories and cultural unity, while practices like *Sadhana* (spiritual practices) and sacrifice support inner growth and cosmic order. Altogether, these rituals reflect a deep integration of the sacred into everyday life. These activities, whether directly or indirectly, lead to spiritual growth and a deeper understanding of the world, guiding people toward spirituality and potentially transforming the ego, understanding the mind, maintaining health, exploring the power of distant prayer, and connecting science with spirituality.

According to Islamic theology, the *Ruh* (spirit) represents the innermost essence of a person, and its perfection is the ultimate human pursuit (Baig & Isgandarova, 2023). Islam emphasizes focusing on complete submission before Allah (God) and striving to attain His pleasure and approval. Once a person dedicates themselves to achieve this, it is then reflected in every single task they do. The practice of *Ibadat* (worship) and *Taqwah* (piety) cleanses an individual's soul and enables them to become a complete Muslim, who not only honors Allah through prayers and worship but also demonstrates their worth to society through loyalty, honesty, and integrity (Malik et al., 2015). Performing the act of *Wudu* (ritual purity) and offering *Salah* (daily prayer) five times a day strengthens the bond between the believer and the Creator, provides inner peace and tranquillity, and nurtures spiritual maturity by instilling a sense of punctuality and self-control. Both the Quran and the teachings of the prophet highlight the importance of spiritual well-being. In Islam, spiritual care goes beyond visiting the sick and is viewed as a serious professional responsibility, which is why, since its early days, Muslim scholars and jurists—both past and present—have valued medicine as a key science for protecting health and preventing illness (Baig & Isgandarova, 2023). In the same article, the authors also mention that spiritual care is special in Islam because it combines religious teachings with an understanding of human wellbeing and personal growth, reflecting a tradition where early Muslim scholars were theologians, astronomers, mathematicians, medical practitioners, and poets simultaneously.

Christianity has deeply connected spirituality and medicine since its early days. As a spiritual teacher and healer, Jesus Christ established a foundation that viewed healing as a sacred act. Early Christians viewed caring for the sick as a spiritual duty, inspired by Jesus' compassion for the ill and marginalized. During the early centuries, Christian monasteries served as the first hospitals, where monks and nuns combined prayer, care, and herbal remedies; these institutions cared not only for the physical body but also for the soul, emphasizing holistic healing (Ferngren, 2009).

Buddhism was started by Sidharta Gautama (Buddha), who achieved enlightenment sitting under the *Bodhi* tree (tree of wisdom) and was hence also known as The Enlightened One (Rahula, 2007). The author also explained that in the teachings of Buddha, he claimed no divine inspiration and attributed all his insights and achievements to human effort and intelligence, emphasizing that every person holds the potential to become a Buddha. Buddhism focuses on compassion and mindfulness, and despite regional variations, all Buddhist schools of thought value ethical living, meditation, and wisdom. The essence of Buddhist spirituality centers around inner transformation in the pursuit of Nirvana, which is "the final beatitude that transcends suffering, karma, and *samsara* (indefinitely repeated cycles of birth, misery, and death caused by karma) and is sought especially in Buddhism through the extinction of desire and individual consciousness" (Merriam-Webster).

Traditional Chinese Medicine focuses not only on treating illness but also on caring for the whole person. It sees the mind and body as closely linked and stresses that true health needs a strong, well-nurtured spirit. It takes into account the concept of *Yin* and *Yang*, which represents two complementary and yet opposing forces in the world, interconnected and forming a complete whole. Traditional Chinese Medicine defines health as the balanced flow of subtle energy (*Qi*) through the body, achieved through harmony between *Yin* and *Yang*, where focusing on the inner self (*Yin*) fosters healing, and addressing external symptoms (*Yang*) leads to cure (Steinhorn et al., 2017, p. 239).

While modern medicine has moved towards strict adherence to scientific methods and a mostly non-religious framework, the spiritual element of healing is still important to many people to this day. Acknowledging and understanding the rich history of spiritual well-being not only augments our appreciation of medicine's roots but also offers a more empathetic and holistic approach to practicing medicine. Although there have been improvements in technology and healthcare, our standard of living and medical treatment have not advanced because we've relied too heavily on devices and medications and overlooked the value of empathy (Wong, 2004, p. 4). If healthcare providers view their profession not just as a job but as a spiritual duty to relieve the suffering of others, it might motivate them to sincerely treat their patients in all aspects of care: physical, mental, emotional, and spiritual. Medicine is filled with ritualistic behaviors and routines that hold significant importance across all areas of clinical care; these rituals serve various complex purposes during medical encounters and greatly influence communication, experiences, and results (Arnold et al., 2020). They also help them discover meaning, maintain compassion, and stay grounded in their work. These may include personal practices like prayer and meditation before patient care for mindfulness (Nilsson, 2022); some observe religious customs such as fasting, wearing symbols of faith, or celebrating sacred days even while on duty. Reflective journaling and similar contemplative and gratitude practices (Fiske et al., 2020), along with having wholesome spiritual discussions with colleagues, also serve as rituals to process emotional experiences and reinforce a sense of purpose. Healthcare providers can also turn their work into an act of worship by starting each day with the goal of serving and helping others. This aligns their professional duties with their spiritual purpose.

Practicing medicine requires the utmost care and empathy, which can only be done when we incorporate healthy qualities and have enough space and healing within us. If we start practicing sincerity, generosity, and fairness while also taking care of ourselves through staying connected with our religious beliefs and strengthening our spirituality, then we will be better capable of caring for others. Feeling the immeasurable and cosmic presence of God in our prayer and moments of solitude has the power to bring about meaningful change within us; shedding our egos and truly submitting to the higher power helps reveal our most authentic self. Using spirituality and religion as a base to push us forward in our work would promote compassion and aid us in taking a more holistic approach towards our patients (Chattopadhyay, 2007).

Dhar et al. (2011, p. 279), in his work, defined the twenty-seven determinants of spiritual health, namely, commitment, introspection, honesty, creativity, contemplation, prayer, philanthropy, extending self, empathy, yoga and exercise, questioning injustice, aesthetics, value for time, being away from comparisons, human values, courage, managing ego, humor, involvement with detachment, sixth sense, virtues, sensitivity, purpose for one's life, compassion, pure feelings, faith in the Supreme, and selfless action. These components are not just fundamental qualities to adapt in our personal lives but are equally essential to be implemented in the practice of medicine. They play an essential role in helping us prioritize love, justice, and kindness and inspire us to live a life of authenticity and integrity while being of service to others.

The most common problem that healthcare providers face is constant stress, which could be due to increased workload, long working hours, work-life balance concerns, or just simply because of the responsibility we have to uphold to ensure our patients are treated correctly and fairly to the best of our knowledge. The constant stress can also lead to burnout syndrome, something every healthcare provider is familiar with. Maslach and Leiter (2016, p. 103) define burnout as "a psychological syndrome emerging as a prolonged response to chronic interpersonal stressors on the job," and "the three key dimensions of this response are an overwhelming exhaustion, feelings of cynicism and detachment from the job, and a sense of ineffectiveness and lack of accomplishment." Deep diving into spirituality and using it to strengthen ourselves can be the positive change healthcare providers desperately need, because it can be particularly useful in times of struggle and distress (Swinton & Pattison, 2010). The authors of Chirico et al. (2023) and Salmoirago-Blotcher et al. (2016) discuss in their research that healthcare providers who make use of spirituality and mindfulness tend to experience burnout less frequently, as well as find it easier to recover from burnout, since spiritual wellbeing takes into account mental and emotional wellbeing and provides physicians with a meaningful framework to understand and cope with the intense and stressful events that they routinely face in their practice. It also has a positive impact on negative coping mechanisms that develop over time in response to stress, such as smoking (Dhar et al., 2013) and substance abuse (Schoenthaler et al., 2015). The authors of Pardini et al. (2000)

and Schoenthaler et al. (2015), in their studies, found that individuals recovering from substance abuse experience improved mental health outcomes when their core values align with spiritual and religious wellbeing, with regular spiritual practices being strongly associated with higher rates of remission. Spirituality fosters moral clarity and integrity, helping physicians navigate complex clinical decisions with greater empathy and alignment with their values. When we are spiritually awakened, we start viewing situations and everything in our life in a different light, one that is inspired by something transcendent and fortifies faith and self-efficacy, leading to hope. Hope is a key element in the lives of healthcare providers because it sustains their emotional resilience, fuels their commitment to healing, and helps them support patients through uncertainty, suffering, and recovery. Hope, combined with spiritual well-being, meaningful personal connections, and the desire to help others, leads to better performance and job satisfaction (Duggleby et al., 2009). It allows healthcare providers to remain grounded in the belief that their efforts can bring comfort, dignity, or improvement to their patients' lives. Hope, and thus spiritual well-being, is both a personal anchor and a professional tool that empowers providers to care, connect, and continue.

Spirituality offers individuals a way to execute their responsibilities more effectively and manage workplace stress more efficiently by intertwining faith with a positive mindset and strong social ties (Pardini et al., 2000), and it could be stated that a person with a strong spiritual orientation potentially tends to experience less stress (Powers et al., 2007) since spirituality often serves as a powerful internal resource that builds up resilience. According to a study done by Rogers et al. (2022) during the COVID-19 pandemic, emotional and spiritual wellbeing was drastically affected among clinical practitioners, but the ones with higher levels of spirituality reported greater resilience, and thus, greater wellbeing. It also has a healing influence on mental health and boosts emotional resilience, which is particularly important for healthcare providers. Individuals with mental health ailments such as despair and depression (Dhar et al., 2013; Peselow et al., 2014), and cognitive problems (Peselow et al., 2014) show significantly greater recovery when they have higher levels of spirituality. Weber et al. (2012) also highlighted that having confidence in one's belief system is linked to better mental well-being, even in non-believers who face psychological distress. Studies like these indicate that healthcare providers tend to adapt better to stress and other problems when they are more spiritually and religiously inclined. Mindfulness practices such as journaling, meditation, and narrative medicine, which make one ponder upon spirituality, lead to improved mood and emotional stability with an ability to handle challenges well (Krasner et al., 2009). Other stress management strategies (Maslach & Leiter, 2016, p. 109), such as adjusting work habits, building coping skills, seeking social support, practicing relaxation, maintaining physical well-being, and enhancing self-awareness through reflection or counseling, also play a fundamental role in overall well-being.

However, we must acknowledge that even the most spiritual individuals can encounter challenges. As healthcare providers, we are acquainted with tragedy and devastation, and sometimes they can overwhelm us. If we don't take care of ourselves, find spiritual support, and renew our inner strength, we can easily become physically and emotionally drained, especially in stressful or unhealthy environments. When we're worn out, it's hard to really care for others because we don't have much energy or love left to give (Wong, 2004, p. 10). Additionally, when healthcare providers go through personal loss or trauma themselves, it can shake their faith, making it difficult to offer spiritual or emotional support to others. We may also encounter situations where institutional rules or medical constraints force them to act against their personal or spiritual values, leading to inner conflict and spiritual distress. At times like these, it is paramount that healthcare providers have the support of their institutes and organizations in building their morale. This is quintessential because it divides the responsibility of a healthcare worker's spiritual well-being, with half of it coming under the umbrella of the institute. In comparison, if a healthcare provider is solely responsible for their spiritual well-being without any support from their hospital, the burden of not being resilient enough in the face of challenges will fall on their own shoulders when it should be the collective responsibility of the surrounding factors (Rogers et al., 2022).

Beyond being a vital part of healthcare providers' personal lives, spirituality also significantly influences the quality of their relationship with patients. As Aldridge (1991) very eloquently stated, "Patience, grace, prayer, meditation, forgiveness, and fellowship are as important in many of our health initiatives as medication, hospitalization, or surgery" (p. 425).

Most of the time, we tend to come across patients who themselves are reliant on spiritual well-being and have the utmost belief in it. Spirituality for them might be an essential part of their lives, and the avoidance or absence of it in healthcare may interrupt proper healing since a person is the sum of their physical, emotional, and spiritual aspects (Koenig, 2000). More research is necessary, but studies have shown that religion and spirituality influence various diseases. Spiritual wellbeing can lead to improvement in quality of life in cardiovascular disease (Abu et al., 2018; Lucchese & Koenig, 2013), boost self-care in diabetic patients (Permana, 2018), it is positively linked with mental wellbeing in chronic hypertension and kidney failure (Papathanasiou et al., 2020), and strongly associated with hope in breast cancer patients (Mickley et al., 1992). None of the findings downplay the role medicine has to play in the treatment of such ailments, but it is imperative that we understand how integrating spiritual care in our practice can enhance the element of hope and conviction.

Qidwai and Tayyab (2004), in their article on patients' views about physicians' spiritual roles in medical practice, found that 78% of patients felt that their religious needs should be considered by the physicians during treatment. In times of illness, suffering, or end-of-life, when individuals are often confronted with profound questions about meaning, purpose, and existence, spirituality should be recognized as a core human need—one that deserves serious attention in clinical care. In clinical practice, there are three chief features that fall under the theme of spiritual care, namely, motivation and advice, religious guidance and prayer, and psychological and spiritual support (Mahmood et al., 2023). The author also elaborated on these points by emphasizing that compassionate and meaningful communication between the physician and patient helps towards the healing process, while religious guidance for patients in times of need holds as much importance as other critical skills and values among healthcare professionals, and every medical staff member should be equipped to offer emotional and psychological support to their patient. A patient's spiritual wellbeing is closely linked to their physical and mental health, and addressing it during periods of recovery, crisis, or terminal illness can provide emotional comfort, strengthen coping mechanisms, and promote overall resilience. For those with a heightened sense of spirituality, such care becomes even more essential, as it affirms their beliefs, supports their healing process, and enhances their sense of peace and dignity (López-Tarrida et al., 2021).

More often than not, healthcare providers find themselves holding their patients' hand and empathizing, and yet not being able to truly grasp their spiritual needs. It is vital that healthcare providers be familiar with and open to their patients' spiritual needs and beliefs, which consist of a vast array of feelings, which can range from hope, integrity, and dignity and being cared for to holding on to control, peace and purpose of life, grasping religion, and accepting the reality of death. Patients may like their physicians to talk about their spiritual needs when they're faced with disease and death (Chattopadhyay, 2007), since spirituality may be considered an important part of the dying process, offering comfort to the dying and helping others understand the meaning of the end of life (Gaur & Sharma, 2015). Many patients obtain comfort and understanding by reading or talking about religious teachings, especially during difficult times, loss, or personal struggles. Losing their health or seeing a loved one suffer often leads people to question the meaning of life, whether the universe is kind or punishing, the decisions they've made, or the effects of their past actions. Likewise, feelings of despair and hopelessness may arise very easily among patients, and it is during such times that the use of spirituality helps them cope with ailment. Offering spiritual and religious activities to patients can often lead to better coping and interaction with others, which in turn can reduce the feeling of loneliness (Delgado-Guay et al., 2021)

Modern healthcare, focused on physical outcomes, often overlooks spirituality, viewing it as less essential due to its intangible and uncertain results (Baime, 2003). In a study (Bansal et al., 2008) done on doctors, it was found that 80% of them believed in the curative role of spirituality, and statistically similar population were of the opinion that spirituality has a crucial role in patient care. But the focus on science and technology, along with time and financial pressures, has made it harder for doctors to connect with patients about their suffering, even though patients wish to share their concerns. In a cross-sectional study done by Banin et al. (2014), it was concluded that most patients would like their physicians to address their spiritual and religious issues but were uncomfortable talking about them, while some reported that most doctors are not prepared enough to discuss these issues and never addressed them. Many times, physicians prefer designated religious personnel to discuss matters of religion and spirituality with their patients as opposed to discussing it themselves, and the prime reason this happens is because of insufficient time and training (Best et al., 2016a). The inability of physicians to discuss matters of existence and transcendence may stem from inadequate training (Balboni et al., 2013), fear of causing unintentional harm to patients, or avoidance of these topics, but this can inadvertently lead to distress and confusion for their patients (López-Tarrida et al., 2021). This is further supported by the authors of de Diego Cordero et al. (2019) in their study on religion and spirituality in medicine, the findings of which concluded that 62.6% of students agreed that religion and spirituality could have a high influence on healthcare staff and patient relationships, but a vast majority (90.6%) felt that they were unequipped to address these issues, most commonly due to limited time and fear of offending patients, while 91.9% of students believed that medical institutes were not teaching them enough about this topic. It was also found that nursing students, however, believed more in the impact of religion and spirituality on patients' health and were more well-informed on the suitability of approaching such issues. Nursing staff seems to be more commonly trained in areas of spiritual care than medical staff and is often more willing and prepared to talk about spirituality (El-Nimr et al., 2004).

Healthcare providers are mainly trained for the disease-focused approach, prioritizing the diagnosis and treatment of illnesses (López-Tarrida et al., 2021), and such training can often times sideline the emotional and spiritual aspect of our profession. Training medical staff in understanding and addressing the spiritual needs of patients while also being respectful of the cultural differences may improve quality of care and patient satisfaction (Astrow et al., 2018). Furthermore, it is equally necessary that healthcare providers do not project their beliefs upon their patients. Healthcare providers' spiritual insight and self-awareness support effective assessment and care; however, clear boundaries between personal beliefs and professional roles should be made since they help prevent clashes with patients' values and will lead to enhanced communication, improving treatment outcomes (Chiu et al., 2006). There is also the challenge faced by healthcare professionals of navigating through a vast array of spiritual and religious beliefs among their patients, which can cause confusion and occasionally a tendency to avoid such topics. This is made even more difficult due to the fact that most healthcare education programs do not adequately prepare graduates for this aspect of care. As a result, medical education providers are being encouraged to include training on the connection between spirituality and health, aiming to strengthen the patient-physician relationship and support more holistic patient care (Pulchaski et al., 2012). Families may feel more at ease when healthcare teams allow meaningful religious or spiritual practices to be included with medical care, helping address both suffering and deeper questions in a respectful, holistic way (Andresen, 2003). Adding a few questions in our normal history taking, which explore the spiritual beliefs and needs of patients, and give us an idea of the mind-set the patient might be in, may prove to be useful in coming to terms with their spirituality. Spiritual history, summarized by the American College of Physicians, comprises four questions: (1) “Is faith (religion, spirituality) important to you in this illness?” (2) “Has faith been important to you at other times in your life?” (3) “Do you have someone to talk to about religious matters?” and (4) “Would you like to explore religious matters with someone?” (Koenig, 2000, para. 5, as cited in Lo et al., 1999). Gently probing such issues can also show the patient that they are heard and that their feelings are respected. Sometimes, even the most disbelieving and doubtful people may seek alternative sources of comfort and support during times of serious illness or distress, and that is why it is crucial to consider the spiritual wellbeing of each and every person, regardless of their beliefs. Patients tend to show improved health results when healthcare providers are aware of their spiritual beliefs; thus, spiritual evaluations should be personalized based on the patient's condition, with the level of detail adjusted to suit each individual’s need (Betton, 2002).

Physicians are not expected to solve every problem a patient presents. Their role should be to understand and recognize what their patients need. It is imperative that we, as helpers, understand that our patients don’t just require us to treat their physical and mental ailments but also to be their companion in acknowledging their spiritual needs. When patients are battling with illnesses and disease, healthcare providers are their first line of contact, sometimes even closer than family, and during those tumultuous moments, it should be one of our priorities to consider the spiritual needs and beliefs of our patients. Simply being a compassionate and attentive presence—someone who listens deeply and empathetically, even to challenges that have no clear solution—can be profoundly healing for patients. In such moments, it is not the act of fixing but the act of truly understanding that makes the greatest difference. When patients feel genuinely heard, they no longer carry their burdens alone; instead, they experience a sense of connection, comfort, and emotional relief. This human connection can foster a sense of solidarity, hope, and belonging—especially in times of vulnerability. It strengthens the physician-patient relationship and builds trust on a deeply personal level. Regardless of scientific knowledge or technical skills, a healthcare provider who offers sincere empathy and presence can become a source of healing in their own right, reminding patients that they are not alone and that their pain is seen, acknowledged, and respected (Blažević, 2021; Lo et al., 1999). As Wong (2005, p. 10) very beautifully said, "A loving doctor or caring nurse can make bitter medicine taste sweet."

It is also extremely important to promote training that would lead to healthcare providers focusing on their own spiritual well-being and the positive effect it can have on their personal and professional lives, because through this they can practice providing spiritual care to their patients, since not considering oneself spiritual enough could lead to not being able to impart proper spiritual care (Bar-Sela et al., 2019). Effective spiritual care training includes hands-on clinical experience, guidance from mentors, and reflective learning activities through ongoing support from institutes, which will help overcome challenges like lack of knowledge or unclear roles when it comes to understanding the spiritual needs of patients (Baldacchino, 2015). Incorporating spirituality into the medical curriculum would enhance healthcare professionals' understanding of their role in addressing patients' spiritual concerns, leading to more effective and timely referrals for spiritual support. Moreover, healthcare providers need to be non-judgmental towards their patients and their respective beliefs. Our worldviews and perceptions may inadvertently affect our line of thinking and can lead to a certain bias when treating someone; such prejudice can be of particular harm and is against our moral ethics. Healthcare providers may find it challenging to support patients with differing spiritual perspectives while upholding their convictions, potentially leading to inner conflict or spiritual uncertainty (Fitchett & Risk, 2009). As healthcare providers, our goal should be to help attain peace and serenity for ourselves and our patients in times of existential distress, for that is how we can comprehend and safely address the spiritual needs of our patients (Best et al., 2016b).

Spirituality helps to connect the healthcare provider and the patient by combining the lens through which they view the ailment and the prognosis. It aids us in understanding and, maybe to some extent, being involved in their spiritual journey. It also provides patients the confidence and strength to share their beliefs and confide their deepest thoughts and feelings. This two-way understanding helps fortify the doctor-patient relationship and strengthens the bond of trust. Yuen (2007), in her editorial on "Spirituality, Religion, and Health," concluded that "spiritual care is integral to the science and art of healing, and therefore a critical component in the quality of care" (p. 78).

Hospitals and their management have a vital role to play in the well-being of their employees and patients, since the policies and rules that they put forward are pivotal in dictating the work atmosphere. Spirituality can play a significant role in shaping a hospital's organization. While its presence may not necessarily be apparent, its influence can be seen in various inconspicuous but important aspects. The authors of Marques et al. (2005, p. 87) defined spirituality in the workplace as "an experience of interconnectedness, shared by all those involved in a work process, initially triggered by the awareness that each is individually driven by an inner power, which raises and maintains his or her sense of honesty, creativeness, proactivity, kindness, dependability, confidence, and courage; consequently leading to a collective creation of an aesthetically motivational environment characterised by a sense of purpose, high ethical standards, acceptance, peace, trust, respect, understanding, appreciation, care, involvement, helpfulness, encouragement, achievement, and perspective, thus establishing an atmosphere of enhanced team performance and overall harmony, and ultimately guiding the organisation to become a leader in its industry and community, through its exudation of fairness, cooperativeness, vision, responsibility, charity, creativity, high productivity, and accomplishment."

An organization that chooses to adapt the essence of spirituality as its blueprint in managing the workplace will build a resilient and amiable environment, since spiritual well-being as a whole will only encourage everybody to strive for excellence. Under the ethos of spirituality, important qualities such as compassion and morality will not only produce considerate leaders who will prioritize patient dignity and justice but also influence policy development, which will safeguard the welfare of the organization and its employees. It can promote empathy, mutual respect, and community, improving staff collaboration and morale; these values and attitudes will have a favorable impact on work ethics and emanate effects on others, leading to better patient care. Incorporating spirituality in the codes of ethics can be effective in guiding behavior across the organization. Spiritual leadership consists of the principles, mindsets, and actions essential to internally motivate oneself and others, enabling a feeling of spiritual sustenance through purpose and community (Fry, 2003). Institutes should promote the importance of spiritual care among healthcare professionals through collaboration in education by designing inclusive educational programs (Puchalski et al., 2014) that cover the meaning of spiritual care, personal reflection, and cultural sensitivities, while also advocating for the fundamental role of spirituality at the level of policymakers in compassionate and comprehensive healthcare. The authors of Dunn et al. (2007), on interventions that could improve physician well-being, illustrated that when a healthcare organization implemented supportive changes—such as flexible scheduling, personalized workloads aligned with physicians' goals and interests, reduced administrative burden through electronic records, and enhanced care management for patients' psychosocial needs—

physician satisfaction notably increased. Additional initiatives like group meetings to address concerns, clinically focused discussions, and providing opportunities to grieve patient losses fostered a greater sense of meaning, emotional connection, and sustainability in clinical practice.

Mentorship culture has an important role to play in promoting meaningful work, which itself is essential in coping with stress (Malloy et al., 2015). And not just mentoring, but peer support and regular mental health check-ins with clinical supervision can be a great way to offer comfort to their employees by providing safe environments for addressing emotional and spiritual challenges and distress (Shanafelt et al., 2012). Like patients, healthcare providers need someone to listen to them. Medical staff should have a safe space to release their burdens without fear of judgment. It is of critical importance that medical institutions humanize the experience of practicing medicine, including offering programs that promote self-care, foster personal reflection, and support healthy lifestyle choices (Cole & Carlin, 2009). Conducting mindfulness practices such as journaling, meditation, and narrative medicine, which make one ponder upon spirituality, can lead to improved mood and emotional stability with an ability to handle challenges well (Krasner et al., 2009). Integrating wellness programs that include activities like massage, meditation, and yoga can significantly enhance employee moods, reduce anxiety and stress, and support physical health by improving blood pressure and heart rate (Bucu, 2012). Additionally, these practices contribute to spiritual well-being by promoting relaxation and nurturing a deep connection between the mind, body, and soul. Even patients who have end-stage diseases or have survived such illnesses can attain spiritual benefits (Bryan et al., 2021).

As racial diversity increases all over the world and brings with it a unique blend of culture and identity, it is crucial that institutes draft inclusive policies that accommodate the diverse religious and spiritual beliefs of staff and patients so they can make them feel valued and not isolated. Aligning institutional culture with spirituality and morality helps protect healthcare providers from long-term distress and promotes compassionate, ethical care.

Establishing prayer rooms in the hospital is one of the easiest ways to give ease and satisfaction to employees and patients and can help them practice their beliefs. These prayer rooms and spaces can serve as a safe haven for quite a lot of us and can provide a moment of recluse, especially in times of distress and when one is battling emotions that are quite common in a hospital setup and very familiar to every healthcare provider. The tranquillity that these spaces offer, in comparison to the constant noise that encompasses them in hospitals, facilitate our connection with the core principles that give meaning to our lives (Rainey & Tanzer, 2020). Engaging in religious practices, contemplation, and rituals, particularly in times of distress and at specific locations, could modulate important physiological processes in the body (Tabei et al., 2016, para 5). Additionally, hospital management should put some effort into making certain that there is an assortment of dietary options to cater to the needs of employees and patients, specifically when keeping minorities in mind. This simple gesture can bring relief and may alleviate the worry one might feel about their preferences. Small steps like these can instill a sense of belonging among employees and patients, offering spiritual care in a non-coercive, respectful manner. Hospitals can be a daunting place for some, where one might be compelled to wonder about the intricacies and unpredictability of human life and suffering. Questions about existence and the purpose of life may arise frequently, which can often lead to despair and hopelessness. In times like these, religion and spirituality may play a crucial role in providing support to the bereaved when other forms of support are not enough. Believing in a higher power and sensing a Divine control and intervention when we ourselves have lost all control may be the most vital thread that we can hold on to. It pulls us from the depths, allows us to recognize our greater purpose, and eventually helps us cope with our struggles.

CONCLUSION

Healthcare providers, particularly hospital management, need to go above and beyond to incorporate the practice of spiritual wellbeing into their lives and work, as it is as important, if not more so, than physical and mental wellbeing. As the world progresses towards new discoveries and technological advancements, indulging people in a more superficial and materialistic society, it is paramount that we hold on to our spirituality, which will help keep our humanity intact and drive us to stay true to ourselves and to others. Being connected with our spiritual self will serve as an anchor in these times of anxiety and isolation, where more often than not, we rely on small bursts of dopamine in the form of social media. Spirituality takes into account our mind, body, and soul, freeing us from the shackles of worldly intricacies and instead focusing on our well-being, which in turn plays an essential part in shaping our morals and ethics. When we work on ourselves and are headed toward morality and compassion, we do the right thing and consider others' well-being.

Attaining true spirituality and a deep sense of faith is a gradual and demanding journey that calls for profound self-work, patience, and time. It is through honest introspection and the courage to confront our inner struggles that we begin to transform—physically, mentally, and spiritually. This pursuit fosters self-awareness and mindfulness, inspiring us to grow and cultivate positive inner qualities, which in turn enrich our practice of medicine and enable us to care for our patients with sincerity and compassion. Embracing the worst, choosing life amid loss, and moving forward despite fear requires deep courage—an essential force for healing that expresses itself through positive action; yet even when our resolve weakens and efforts seem in vain, it is faith—faith in God as our refuge, in a higher purpose, in justice, and in the triumph of good—that sustains us through darkness, calling us to love, serve, and rise beyond ourselves in acts of selflessness (Wong, 2004, p. 9).

REFERENCES

Abu, H. O., Ulbricht, C., Ding, E., Allison, J. J., Salmoirago-Blotcher, E., Goldberg, R. J., & Kiefe, C. I. (2018). Association of religiosity and spirituality with quality of life in patients with cardiovascular disease: A systematic review. [Abstract]. *Quality of Life Research: An International Journal of Quality of Life Aspects of Treatment, Care and Rehabilitation*, *27*(11), 2777–2797. DOI: 10.1007/s11136-018-1906-4 PMID: 29948601

Aldridge, D. (1991). Spirituality, healing and medicine. *The British Journal of General Practice*, *41*(351), 425–427. https://bjgp.org/content/bjgp/41/351/425.full.pdf PMID: 1777299

Andresen, J. (2003). Spirituality and Health. In *Encyclopedia of Science and Religion* (Vol. 2, pp. 835-837). Encyclopedia of Science and Religion. https://www.academia.edu/44525429/Spirituality_and_Health_in_Encyclopedia_of_Science_and_Religion_?source=swp_share

Annus, A. (2020). The spiritual dimensions of healing rituals in ancient Mesopotamia. [Abstract]. *Journal of Religion and Health*, *59*(5), 2486–2503. DOI: 10.1007/s10943-019-00964-x PMID: 31848800

Arnold, M. H., Komesaroff, P., & Kerridge, I. (2020). Understanding the ethical implications of the rituals of medicine. [Abstract]. *Internal Medicine Journal*, *50*(9), 1123–1131. DOI: 10.1111/imj.14990 PMID: 32929818

Astrow, A. B., Kwok, G., Sharma, R. K., Fromer, N., & Sulmasy, D. P. (2018). Spiritual needs and perception of quality of care and satisfaction with care in hematology/medical oncology patients: A multicultural assessment. *Journal of Pain and Symptom Management*, *55*(1), 56–64. DOI: 10.1016/j.jpainsymman.2017.08.009 PMID: 28842220

Baig, N., & Isgandarova, N. (2023). Exploring Islamic Spiritual Care: What Is in a Name? *Religions*, *14*(10), 1256. DOI: 10.3390/rel14101256

Baime, M. J. (2003). *Meditation and spirituality for health care providers. Spiritual Transformation and Health Through the Lifecycle* [private printing]. Samueli Institute for Information Biology., https://www.uphs.upenn.edu/pastoral/events/Baime_Metanexus_talk_2003.pdf

Balboni, M. J., Sullivan, A., Amobi, A., Phelps, A. C., Gorman, D. P., Zollfrank, A., Peteet, J. R., Prigerson, H. G., VanderWeele, T. J., & Balboni, T. A. (2013). Why is spiritual care infrequent at the end of life? Spiritual care perceptions among patients, nurses, and physicians and the role of training. *Journal of Clinical Oncology*, *31*(4), 461–467. DOI: 10.1200/JCO.2012.44.6443 PMID: 23248245

Baldacchino, D. (2015). Spiritual Care Education of Health Care Professionals. *Religions*, *6*(2), 594–613. DOI: 10.3390/rel6020594

Banin, L. B., Suzart, N. B., Guimarães, F. A. G., Lucchetti, A. L., de Jesus, M. A. S., & Lucchetti, G. (2014). Religious beliefs or physicians' behavior: What makes a patient more prone to accept a physician to address his/her spiritual issues? [Abstract]. *Journal of Religion and Health*, *53*(3), 917–928. DOI: 10.1007/s10943-013-9685-2 PMID: 23420277

Bansal, R., Maroof, K. A., Parashar, P., & Pant, B. (2008). Spirituality and health: A knowledge, attitude and practice study among doctors of North India. [Abstract]. *Spirituality and Health International*, *9*(4), 263–269. DOI: 10.1002/shi.358

Bar-Sela, G., Schultz, M. J., Elshamy, K., Rassouli, M., Ben-Arye, E., Doumit, M., Gafer, N., Albashayreh, A., Ghrayeb, I., Turker, I., Ozalp, G., Kav, S., Fahmi, R., Nestoros, S., Ghali, H., Mula-Hussain, L., Shazar, I., Obeidat, R., Punjwani, R., & Silbermann, M. (2019). Training for awareness of one's own spirituality: A key factor in overcoming barriers to the provision of spiritual care to advanced cancer patients by doctors and nurses. [Abstract]. *Palliative & Supportive Care*, *17*(3), 345–352. DOI: 10.1017/S147895151800055X PMID: 30187841

Best, M., Butow, P., & Olver, I. (2016a). Doctors discussing religion and spirituality: A systematic literature review. *Palliative Medicine*, *30*(4), 327–337. DOI: 10.1177/0269216315600912 PMID: 26269325

Best, M., Butow, P., & Olver, I. (2016b). Why do We Find It so Hard to Discuss Spirituality? A Qualitative Exploration of Attitudinal Barriers. *Journal of Clinical Medicine*, *5*(9), 77. DOI: 10.3390/jcm5090077 PMID: 27598212

Betton, H. B. (2002). [Review of the book *Spirituality in Patient Care-Why, How, When, and What*, by H. G. Koenig]. *Journal of the National Medical Association*, *94*(8), 743–745. https://pmc.ncbi.nlm.nih.gov/articles/PMC2594261

Blažević, J. (2021). The phenomenon of miraculous healing through suggestion in the context of faith and magic-psychological-theological approach. *Psychiatria Danubina*, *33*(Suppl 4), 933–939. https://hrcak.srce.hr/file/395028 PMID: 35026824

Bryan, S., Zipp, G., & Breitkreuz, D. (2021). The Effects of Mindfulness Meditation and Gentle Yoga on Spiritual Well-Being in Cancer Survivors: A Pilot Study. [Abstract]. *Alternative Therapies in Health and Medicine*, *27*(3). https://www.alternative-therapies.com/abstracts/11034.html PMID: 33128538

Bucu, A. (2012). *Massage and Meditation: A Case for Wellness Practice in the Workplace* (Doctoral dissertation, RMIT University, Melbourne). https://www.researchgate.net/profile/Angie-Bucu/publication/264351450_Massage_and_Meditation_A_Case_for_Wellness_Practice_in_the_Workplace/links/55b04e6708aeb923991720ce/Massage-and-Meditation-A-Case-for-Wellness-Practice-in-the-Workplace.pdf

Büssing, A., Baumann, K., Hvidt, N. C., Koenig, H. G., Puchalski, C. M., Swinton, J. (2014). Spirituality and Health [Editorial]. *Evidence-Based Complementary and Alternative Medicine*, 2014, 682817, 2 pages. https://doi.org/DOI: 10.1155/2014/682817

Chattopadhyay, S. (2007). Religion, spirituality, health and medicine: Why should Indian physicians care? [Abstract]. *Journal of Postgraduate Medicine*, *53*(4), 262–266. DOI: 10.4103/0022-3859.33967 PMID: 18097118

Chirico, F., Batra, K., Batra, R., Oztekin, G. G., Ferrari, G., Crescenzo, P., Nucera, G., Szarpak, L., Sharma, M., Magnavita, N., & Yildirim, M. (2023). Spiritual well-being and burnout syndrome in healthcare: A systematic review. *Journal of Health and Social Sciences*, *8*(1), 13–32. DOI: 10.19204/2023/sprt2

Chiu, L., Ganesan, S., Rutledge, R., & Toews, J. (2006). Pre-conference report for the 4th International Multidisciplinary Conference on Spirituality and Health: Interweaving Science, Wisdom and Compassion. *Spirituality and Health International*, *7*(3), 162–166. DOI: 10.1002/shi.290

Cole, T. R., & Carlin, N. (2009). The suffering of physicians. *Lancet*, *374*(9699), 1414–1415. DOI: 10.1016/S0140-6736(09)61851-1 PMID: 19866520

de Diego Cordero, R., Lucchetti, G., Fernández-Vazquez, A., & Badanta-Romero, B. (2019). Opinions, knowledge and attitudes concerning "spirituality, religiosity and health" among health graduates in a Spanish university. [Abstract]. *Journal of Religion and Health*, *58*(5), 1592–1604. DOI: 10.1007/s10943-019-00780-3 PMID: 30771142

Delgado-Guay, M. O., Palma, A., Duarte, E., Grez, M., Tupper, L., Liu, D. D., & Bruera, E. (2021). Association between spirituality, religiosity, spiritual pain, symptom distress, and quality of life among Latin American patients with advanced cancer: A multicenter study. *Journal of Palliative Medicine*, *24*(11), 1606–1615. DOI: 10.1089/jpm.2020.0776 PMID: 33844951

Dhar, N., Chaturvedi, S. K., & Nandan, D. (2011). Spiritual Health Scale 2011: Defining and Measuring 4th Dimension of Health. *Indian Journal of Community Medicine : Official Publication of Indian Association of Preventive & Social Medicine*, *36*(4), 275–282. DOI: 10.4103/0970-0218.91329 PMID: 22279257

Dhar, N., Chaturvedi, S. K., & Nandan, D. (2013). Spiritual health, the fourth dimension: A public health perspective. *WHO South-East Asia Journal of Public Health*, *2*(1), 3–5. DOI: 10.4103/2224-3151.115826 PMID: 28612816

Duggleby, W., Cooper, D., & Penz, K. (2009). Hope, self-efficacy, spiritual well-being and job satisfaction. *Journal of Advanced Nursing*, *65*(11), 2376–2385. DOI: 10.1111/j.1365-2648.2009.05094.x PMID: 19737323

Dunn, P. M., Arnetz, B. B., Christensen, J. F., & Homer, L. (2007). Meeting the imperative to improve physician well-being: Assessment of an innovative program. *Journal of General Internal Medicine*, *22*(11), 1544–1552. DOI: 10.1007/s11606-007-0363-5 PMID: 17891503

El-Nimr, G., Green, L. L., & Salib, E. (2004). Spiritual care in psychiatry: Professionals' views. [Abstract]. *Mental Health, Religion & Culture*, *7*(2), 165–170. DOI: 10.1080/1367467032000157990

Elendu, C. (2024). The evolution of ancient healing practices: From shamanism to Hippocratic medicine. *Revista de Medicina (São Paulo)*, *103*(28), e39005. DOI: 10.1097/MD.0000000000039005 PMID: 38996102

Ferngren, G. B. (2009). *Medicine and health care in early Christianity*. Johns Hopkins University Press.

Fiske, E., Martin, S., & Luetkemeyer, J. (2020). Building Nurses 'Resilience to Trauma through Contemplative Practices. [Abstract] *Creative Nursing, 26*(4), 090-096. https://doi.org/DOI: 10.1891/CRNR-D-20-00054

Fitchett, G., & Risk, J. L. (2009). Screening for spiritual struggle. *The Journal of Pastoral Care & Counseling*, *63*(1-2), 1–12. DOI: 10.1177/154230500906300104 PMID: 20196352

Foglio, J. P., & Brody, H. (1988). Religion, faith, and family medicine [Editorial]. *The Journal of Family Practice*, *27*(5), 473–474. https://cdn.mdedge.com/files/s3fs-public/jfp-archived-issues/1988-volume_26-27/JFP_1988-11_v27_i5_religion-faith-and-family-medicine.pdf PMID: 3193064

Fry, L. W. (2003). Toward a theory of spiritual leadership. *The Leadership Quarterly*, *14*(6), 693–727. DOI: 10.1016/j.leaqua.2003.09.001

Gaur, K., & Sharma, M. (2015). Role of spiritual health in patient care: A review. *Int Multidisciplinary J Health, 1*(8), 1-6. https://www.academia.edu/18056636/Role_of_Spiritual_Health_in_Patient_Care_A_Review?source=swp_share

Halpern, M. (2017). Ayurveda, Spirituality and Meditation. [Blog] https://www.ayurvedacollege.com/blog/ayurveda_spirituality_meditation/

Hill, P. C., Pargament, K. I., Hood, R. W., McCullough, J. M. E., Swyers, J. P., Larson, D. B., & Zinnbauer, B. J. (2000). Conceptualizing religion and spirituality: Points of commonality, points of departure. *Journal for the Theory of Social Behaviour, 30*(1), 51–77. DOI: 10.1111/1468-5914.00119

Isaac, K. S., Hay, J. L., & Lubetkin, E. I. (2016). Incorporating spirituality in primary care. [Abstract]. *Journal of Religion and Health, 55*(3), 1065–1077. DOI: 10.1007/s10943-016-0190-2 PMID: 26832335

Kleisiaris, C. F., Sfakianakis, C., & Papathanasiou, I. V. (2014). Health care practices in ancient Greece: The Hippocratic ideal. *Journal of Medical Ethics and History of Medicine, 7*, 6. https://pmc.ncbi.nlm.nih.gov/articles/PMC4263393/pdf/jmehm-7-6.pdf PMID: 25512827

Koenig, H. G. (2000). Religion, spirituality, and medicine: Application to clinical practice. *Journal of the American Medical Association, 284*(13), 1708–1708. DOI: 10.1001/jama.284.13.1708-JMS1004-5-1 PMID: 11015808

Koenig, H. G., King, D., & Carson, V. B. (2012). *Handbook of religion and health*. Oxford University Press USA.

Krasner, M. S., Epstein, R. M., Beckman, H., Suchman, A. L., Chapman, B., Mooney, C. J., & Quill, T. E. (2009). Association of an educational program in mindful communication with burnout, empathy, and attitudes among primary care physicians. *Journal of the American Medical Association, 302*(12), 1284–1293. DOI: 10.1001/jama.2009.1384 PMID: 19773563

Lo, B., Quill, T., & Tulsky, J. (1999). Discussing palliative care with patients. *Annals of Internal Medicine, 130*(9), 744–749. DOI: 10.7326/0003-4819-130-9-199905040-00015 PMID: 10357694

López-Tarrida, Á. C., de Diego-Cordero, R., & Lima-Rodríguez, J. S. (2021). Spirituality in a Doctor's Practice: What Are the Issues? *Journal of Clinical Medicine, 10*(23), 5612. DOI: 10.3390/jcm10235612 PMID: 34884314

Lucchese, F. A., & Koenig, H. G. (2013). Religion, spirituality and cardiovascular disease: Research, clinical implications, and opportunities in Brazil. *Brazilian Journal of Cardiovascular Surgery*, *28*(1), 103–128. DOI: 10.5935/1678-9741.20130015 PMID: 23739939

Mahmood, M. A., Yusof, N. M., Saidi, S., & Ahmad, A. C. (2023). The integration of islamic values in daily clinical practice among healthcare professionals: A scoping review. *IIUM Medical Journal Malaysia*, *22*(3). Advance online publication. DOI: 10.31436/imjm.v22i3.2273

Malik, S., Riaz, N., & Nazir, S. (2015). Personal Spirituality and Work Attitudes Among Doctors. *Journal of Behavioural Sciences*, *25*(1). https://www.researchgate.net/profile/Sadia-Malik-2/publication/290974216_Personal_Spirituality_and_Work_Attitudes_Among_Doctors/links/590396180f7e9bc0d58d7d95/Personal-Spirituality-and-Work-Attitudes-Among-Doctors.pdf

Malloy, D., Fahey-McCarthy, E., Murakami, M., Lee, Y., Choi, E., Hirose, E., & Hadjistavropoulos, T. (2015). Finding Meaning in the Work of Nursing: An International Study. *Online Journal of Issues in Nursing*, *20*(3). Advance online publication. DOI: 10.3912/OJIN.Vol20No03PPT02 PMID: 26882516

Marques, J., Dhiman, S., & King, R. (2005). Spirituality in the workplace: Developing an integral model and a comprehensive definition. *Journal of American Academy of Business, 7*(1), 81-91.://www.academia.edu/61249074/Spirituality_in_the_Workplace_Developing_an_Integral_Model_and_a_Comprehensive_Definition?source=swp_share

Maslach, C., & Leiter, M. P. (2016). Understanding the burnout experience: Recent research and its implications for psychiatry. *World Psychiatry; Official Journal of the World Psychiatric Association (WPA)*, *15*(2), 103–111. DOI: 10.1002/wps.20311 PMID: 27265691

Mickley, J. R., Soeken, K., & Belcher, A. (1992). Spiritual well-being, religiousness and hope among women with breast cancer. [Abstract]. *Image—the Journal of Nursing Scholarship*, *24*(4), 267–272. DOI: 10.1111/j.1547-5069.1992.tb00732.x PMID: 1452180

Moberg, D. O. (2010). Spirituality research: Measuring the immeasurable? *Perspectives on Science and Christian Faith*, *62*(2). https://www.researchgate.net/profile/David-Moberg/publication/265037799_Spirituality_Research_Measuring_the_Immeasurable/links/551b17190cf2fdce843865c2/Spirituality-Research-Measuring-the-Immeasurable.pdf

Nilsson, H. (2022). Spiritual Self-Care Management for Nursing Professionals: A Holistic Approach. *Journal of holistic nursing: official journal of the American Holistic Nurses'. Journal of Holistic Nursing*, *40*(1), 64–73. DOI: 10.1177/08980101211034341 PMID: 34287073

Papathanasiou, I. V., Papathanasiou, C., Malli, F., Tsaras, K., Papagiannis, D., Kontopoulou, L., Kourkouta, L., Tsalogliodou, A., Tzavella, F., & Fradelos, E. C. (2020). The effect of Spirituality on Mental Health among Hypertensive elderly people: A Cross-sectional Community-based Study. *Materia Socio-Medica*, *32*(3), 218. DOI: 10.5455/msm.2020.32.218-223 PMID: 33424452

Pardini, D. A., Plante, T. G., Sherman, A., & Stump, J. E. (2000). Religious faith and spirituality in substance abuse recovery: Determining the mental health benefits. *Journal of Substance Abuse Treatment*, *19*(4), 347–354. DOI: 10.1016/S0740-5472(00)00125-2 PMID: 11166499

Permana, I. (2018). How Religosity and/or spirituality might influence self-Care in Diabetes Management: A structured review. *Bangladesh Journal of Medical Science*, *17*(2), 185–193. DOI: 10.3329/bjms.v17i2.35869

Peselow, E., Pi, S., Lopez, E., Besada, A., & IsHak, W. W. (2014). The impact of spirituality before and after treatment of major depressive disorder. *Innovations in Clinical Neuroscience*, *11*(3-4), 17. https://pmc.ncbi.nlm.nih.gov/articles/PMC4008297/pdf/icns_11_3_17.pdf PMID: 24800129

Pouyan, N. (2016). Mesopotamia, the cradle of civilization and medicine. *World Journal of Pharmaceutical Research*, *5*(4), 192–225. DOI: 10.20959/wjpr20164-5895

Powers, D. V., Cramer, R. J., & Grubka, J. M. (2007). Spirituality, Life Stress, and Affective Well-Being. *Journal of Psychology and Theology*, *35*(3), 235–243. DOI: 10.1177/009164710703500306

Puchalski, C. M., Vitillo, R., Hull, S. K., & Reller, N. (2014). Improving the spiritual dimension of whole person care: Reaching national and international consensus. *Journal of Palliative Medicine*, *17*(6), 642–656. DOI: 10.1089/jpm.2014.9427 PMID: 24842136

Qidwai, W., & Tayyab, A. (2004). Patients' views about physicians' spiritual role in medical practice. [Abstract]. *Journal of the College of Physicians and Surgeons—Pakistan*, *14*(8), 462–465. https://ecommons.aku.edu/pakistan_fhs_mc_fam_med/142/ PMID: 15382344

Rahula, W. (2007). *What the Buddha taught*. Open Road + Grove/Atlantic.

Rainey, R. M., & Tanzer, K. (2020). Spiritual Spaces. *SiteLINES: A Journal of Place, 16*(1), 17-20. https://www.jstor.org/stable/26934719

Reinert, K. G., & Koenig, H. G. (2013). Re-examining definitions of spirituality in nursing research. *Journal of Advanced Nursing, 69*(12), 2622–2634. DOI: 10.1111/jan.12152 PMID: 23600849

Rogers, M., Windle, A., Wu, L., Taylor, V., & Bale, C. (2022). Emotional well-being, spiritual well-being and resilience of advanced clinical practitioners in the United Kingdom during COVID-19: An exploratory mixed method study. *Journal of Nursing Management, 30*(4), 883–891. DOI: 10.1111/jonm.13577 PMID: 35261097

Saad, M., & de Medeiros, R. (2021). Spirituality and Healthcare—Common Grounds for the Secular and Religious Worlds and Its Clinical Implications. *Religions, 12*(1), 22. DOI: 10.3390/rel12010022

Salmoirago-Blotcher, E., Fitchett, G., Leung, K., Volturo, G., Boudreaux, E., Crawford, S., Ockene, I., & Curlin, F. (2016). An exploration of the role of religion/spirituality in the promotion of physicians' wellbeing in Emergency Medicine. *Preventive Medicine Reports, 3*, 189–195. DOI: 10.1016/j.pmedr.2016.01.009 PMID: 27419014

Schoenthaler, S. J., Blum, K., Braverman, E. R., Giordano, J., Thompson, B., Oscar-Berman, M., Badgaiyan, R. D., Madigan, M. A., Dushaj, K., Li, M., Demotrovics, Z., Waite, R. L., & Gold, M. S. (2015). NIDA-Drug Addiction Treatment Outcome Study (DATOS) Relapse as a Function of Spirituality/Religiosity. *Journal of Reward Deficiency Syndrome, 1*(1), 36–45. DOI: 10.17756/jrds.2015-007 PMID: 26052556

Shanafelt, T. D., Boone, S., Tan, L., Dyrbye, L. N., Sotile, W., Satele, D., West, C. P., Sloan, J., & Oreskovich, M. R. (2012). Burnout and satisfaction with work-life balance among US physicians relative to the general US population. *Archives of Internal Medicine, 172*(18), 1377–1385. DOI: 10.1001/archinternmed.2012.3199 PMID: 22911330

Srivastava, S. K., & Barmola, K. C. (2013). Rituals in Hinduism as related to spirituality. *Indian Journal of Positive Psychology, 4*(1), 87-95. ISSN 2229-4937 https://www.researchgate.net/profile/Kailash-Barmola/publication/333774916_RITUALS_IN_HINDUISM_AS_RELATED_TO_SPIRITUALITY/links/5d03581692851c874c650d71/RITUALS-IN-HINDUISM-AS-RELATED-TO-SPIRITUALITY.pdf

Steinhorn, D. M., Din, J., & Johnson, A. (2017). Healing, spirituality and integrative medicine. *Annals of Palliative Medicine, 6*(3), 237–247. DOI: 10.21037/apm.2017.05.01 PMID: 28595441

Swinton, J., & Pattison, S. (2010). Moving beyond clarity: Towards a thin, vague, and useful understanding of spirituality in nursing care. *Nursing Philosophy*, *11*(4), 226–237. DOI: 10.1111/j.1466-769X.2010.00450.x PMID: 20840134

Tabei, S. Z., Zarei, N., & Joulaei, H. (2016). The Impact of Spirituality on Health. *Shiraz E Medical Journal*, *17*(6), e39053. DOI: 10.17795/semj39053

Weber, S. R., Pargament, K. I., Kunik, M. E., Lomax, J. W.II, & Stanley, M. A. (2012). Psychological distress among religious nonbelievers: A systematic review. [Abstract]. *Journal of Religion and Health*, *51*(1), 72–86. DOI: 10.1007/s10943-011-9541-1 PMID: 21965058

Wong, P. T. (2004). Compassionate and spiritual care: A vision of positive holistic medicine. Keynote address presented at the Consultation on Holistic Healthcare for the Medical, Religious and Academic Professionals in Hong Kong, organized and hosted by The Nethersole Institute of Continuing Holistic Health Education. https://www.academia.edu/783659/Compassionate_and_spiritual_care_A_vision_of_positive_holistic_medicine?source=swp_share

Yawar, A. (2001). Spirituality in Medicine: What is to be Done? *Journal of the Royal Society of Medicine*, *94*(10), 529–533. https://doi.org/. DOI: 10.1177/014107680109401013 PMID: 11581352

Yuen, E. J. (2007). Spirituality, religion, and health [Editorial]. *American Journal of Medical Quality*, *22*(2), 77–79. DOI: 10.1177/1062860606298872 PMID: 17395961

KEY TERMS AND DEFINITIONS

Compassion: Seeing someone's pain, caring about it, and wanting to help with kindness.

Healthcare providers: Encompasses individuals or organizations that are associated with providing care and treatment to the ill.

Hope: Belief that things get better, giving motivation to face challenges.

Religion: A set of beliefs and practices about a higher power that helps one live with meaning and values.

Resilience: Ability to cope and adapt in any situation with strength.

Spiritual well-being: A state of attaining spirituality—feeling peaceful, purposeful, and connected.

Spirituality: A personal search for meaning, purpose, and connection to oneself or something greater.

Compilation of References

Abbas, J. (2021). Crisis management, transnational healthcare challenges and opportunities: The intersection of COVID-19 pandemic and global mental health. *Research in Globalization*, *3*, 100037–100037. DOI: 10.1016/j.resglo.2021.100037

Abd Elwahab, S., & Doherty, E. (2014). What about doctors? The impact of medical errors. *The Surgeon*, *12*(6), 297–300. DOI: 10.1016/j.surge.2014.06.004

Abdullah, H., & Ashraf, M. (2022). Institutional governance and organizational effectiveness in public health institutions of developing countries. *Journal of Health Management*, *24*(4), 561–576. DOI: 10.1177/09720634221110364

Abu, H. O., Ulbricht, C., Ding, E., Allison, J. J., Salmoirago-Blotcher, E., Goldberg, R. J., & Kiefe, C. I. (2018). Association of religiosity and spirituality with quality of life in patients with cardiovascular disease: A systematic review. [Abstract]. *Quality of Life Research: An International Journal of Quality of Life Aspects of Treatment, Care and Rehabilitation*, *27*(11), 2777–2797. DOI: 10.1007/s11136-018-1906-4 PMID: 29948601

Adler, P. S., & Kwon, S. (2002). Social capital: Prospects for a new concept. *Academy of Management Review*, *27*(1), 17–40. DOI: 10.2307/4134367

Afroz, S. (2017). Quality of work life: A conceptual model. [AEBM]. *Advances in Economics and Business Management*, *4*(8), 570–578.

AHIP, & the America's Health Insurance Plans. 2024 Survey results. https://www.ahip.org/news/articles/survey-shows-health-plans-are-expanding-value-based-arrangements-to-deliver-higher-quality-more-affordable-health-care

Ahmad, S., Khalid, R., & Fatima, S. (2022). Occupational stress and coping strategies in emergency room physicians in Pakistan: A mixed-methods study. *International Journal of Mental Health Systems*, *16*(1), 45. DOI: 10.1186/s13033-022-00522-9 PMID: 36056370

Aiken, L. H.. (2012). Nurse staffing and patient outcomes: Cross-national findings. *Journal of Advanced Nursing*, *69*(11), 2425–2434. DOI: 10.1111/j.1365-2648.2011.05722.x

Aiken, L. H., Clarke, S. P., Sloane, D. M., Sochalski, J., & Silber, J. H. (2002). Hospital nurse staffing and patient mortality, nurse burnout, and job dissatisfaction. *Journal of the American Medical Association*, *288*(16), 1987–1993. DOI: 10.1001/jama.288.16.1987 PMID: 12387650

Aiken, L. H., Sloane, D. M., Bruyneel, L., Van den Heede, K., Griffiths, P., Busse, R., Diomidous, M., Kinnunen, J., Kózka, M., Lesaffre, E., McHugh, M. D., Moreno-Casbas, M. T., Rafferty, A. M., Schwendimann, R., Scott, P. A., Tishelman, C., van Achterberg, T., & Sermeus, W. (2012). Nurse staffing and education and hospital mortality in nine European countries: A retrospective observational study. *Lancet*, *383*(9931), 1824–1830. DOI: 10.1016/S0140-6736(13)62631-8 PMID: 24581683

Aiken, L. H., Sloane, D., Cimiotti, J., Clarke, S., Flynn, L., Seago, J., Spetz, J., & Smith, H. (2010). Implications of the California nurse staffing mandate for other states. *Health Services Research*, *45*(4), 904–921. DOI: 10.1111/j.1475-6773.2010.01114.x PMID: 20403061

Akhtar, M., & Qureshi, Q. A. (2019). Impacts of QWL (promotion & work environment) on doctors' performance in public sector hospitals of Pakistan. *International Transaction Journal of Engineering, Management, &. Applied Sciences & Technologies*, *11*(5), 1–9.

Akter, N., Akkadechanunt, T., Chontawan, R., & Klunklin, A. (2018). Factors predicting quality of work life among nurses in tertiary-level hospitals, Bangladesh. *International Nursing Review*, *65*(2), 182–189. DOI: 10.1111/inr.12401

Alderfer, C. P. (1969). An empirical test of a new theory of human needs. *Organizational Behavior and Human Performance*, *4*(2), 142–175. DOI: 10.1016/0030-5073(69)90004-X

Aldridge, D. (1991). Spirituality, healing and medicine. *The British Journal of General Practice*, *41*(351), 425–427. https://bjgp.org/content/bjgp/41/351/425.full.pdf PMID: 1777299

Alkozei, A., Smith, R., Demers, L., Weber, M., Berryhill, S., & Killgore, W. (2019). Increases in Emotional Intelligence After an Online Training Program Are Associated with Better Decision-Making on the Iowa Gambling Task. *Psychological Reports*, *122*(3), 853–879. DOI: 10.1177/0033294118771705 PMID: 29699472

Allen, T. D., Johnson, R. C., Kiburz, K. M., & Shockley, K. M. (2013). Work–family conflict and flexible work arrangements: Deconstructing flexibility. *Personnel Psychology*, *66*(2), 345–376. DOI: 10.1111/peps.12012

Almost, J., Wolff, A., Stewart-Pyne, A., McCormick, L., Strachan, D., & D'Souza, C. (2016). Managing and mitigating conflict in healthcare teams: An integrative review. *Journal of Advanced Nursing*, *72*(7), 1490–1505. DOI: 10.1111/jan.12903 PMID: 26822008

Alotaibi, A., & Aldossry, T. (2024). Work-life balance of working mothers in the healthcare industry in Riyadh, Saudi Arabia. *Journal of Social Service Research*, *50*(1), 14–24. DOI: 10.1080/01488376.2023.2271037

Alotaibi, N., Wilson, C. B., & Traynor, M. (2025). Enhancing digital readiness and capability in healthcare: A systematic review of interventions, barriers, and facilitators. *BMC Health Services Research*, *25*(1), 12663. Advance online publication. DOI: 10.1186/s12913-025-12663-3 PMID: 40186200

Álvarez-Pérez, Y., Rivero-Santana, A., Perestelo-Pérez, L., Duarte-Díaz, A., Ramos-García, V., Toledo-Chávarri, A., Torres-Castaño, A., León-Salas, B., Infante-Ventura, D., González-Hernández, N., Rodríguez-Rodríguez, L., & Serrano-Aguilar, P. (2022). Effectiveness of Mantra-Based Meditation on Mental Health: A Systematic Review and Meta-Analysis. *International Journal of Environmental Research and Public Health*, *19*(6), 3380. Advance online publication. DOI: 10.3390/ijerph19063380 PMID: 35329068

American Medical Association. (2024, June 18). *AMA survey indicates prior authorization wreaks havoc on patient care*. https://www.ama-assn.org/press-center/ama-press-releases/ama-survey-indicates-prior-authorization-wreaks-havoc-patient-care (ama-assn.org)

American Nurses Credentialing Center (ANCC). (2024). *Magnet Recognition Program® standards*. ANCC.

American Psychological Association. (2018). *APA dictionary of psychology*. Dictionary.apa.org;American Psychological Association. https://dictionary.apa.org/resilience

Anaraki, N. R., Mukhopadhyay, M., Karaivanov, Y., Wilson, M., & Asghari, S. (2022). Living and working in rural healthcare during the COVID-19 pandemic: A qualitative study of rural family physicians' lived experiences. *BMC Primary Care*, *23*(1), 01942. Advance online publication. DOI: 10.1186/s12875-022-01942-1 PMID: 36550406

Anderson, B. R. (2016). Improving health care by embracing systems theory. *The Journal of Thoracic and Cardiovascular Surgery, 152*(2), 593–594. DOI: 10.1016/j.jtcvs.2016.03.029 PMID: 27113625

Andlib, S., Inayat, S., Azhar, K., & Aziz, F. (2022). Burnout and psychological distress among Pakistani nurses providing care to COVID-19 patients: A cross-sectional study. *International Nursing Review, 69*(4), 529–537. DOI: 10.1111/inr.12750

Andresen, J. (2003). Spirituality and Health. In *Encyclopedia of Science and Religion* (Vol. 2, pp. 835-837). Encyclopedia of Science and Religion. https://www.academia.edu/44525429/Spirituality_and_Health_in_Encyclopedia_of_Science_and_Religion_?source=swp_share

Annas, G. J. (2011). *The rights of patients: The authoritative ACLU guide to the rights of patients* (3rd ed.). New York University Press.

Annus, A. (2020). The spiritual dimensions of healing rituals in ancient Mesopotamia. [Abstract]. *Journal of Religion and Health, 59*(5), 2486–2503. DOI: 10.1007/s10943-019-00964-x PMID: 31848800

Appelbaum, E., Bailey, T., Berg, P., & Kalleberg, A. (2000). *Manufacturing advantage: Why high-performance work systems pay off.* Cornell University Press.

Appelbom, S., Nordström, A., Finnes, A., Wicksell, R. K., & Bujacz, A. (2024). Healthcare worker burnout during a persistent crisis: A case–control study. *Occupational Medicine, 74*(4), 297–303. DOI: 10.1093/occmed/kqae032 PMID: 38738440

Ardell, D. B. (1999). Definition of wellness. *Ardell Wellness Report, 18*(1), 1–5.

Arnold, M. H., Komesaroff, P., & Kerridge, I. (2020). Understanding the ethical implications of the rituals of medicine. [Abstract]. *Internal Medicine Journal, 50*(9), 1123–1131. DOI: 10.1111/imj.14990 PMID: 32929818

Aruldoss, A., Kowalski, K. B., & Parayitam, S. (2021). The relationship between quality of work life and work-life balance: Mediating role of job stress, job satisfaction and job commitment. *Journal of Advances in Management Research, 18*(1), 36–62. DOI: 10.1108/JAMR-05-2020-0082

Asante, J. O., Li, M., Liao, J., Huang, Y. X., & Hao, Y. T. (2019). The relationship between psychosocial risk factors, burnout and quality of life among primary healthcare workers in rural Guangdong province: A cross-sectional study. *BMC Health Services Research, 19*(1), 447. DOI: 10.1186/s12913-019-4278-8

Asim, M., Hameed, W., Khan, B., Saleem, S., & Avan, B. I. (2023). Applying the COM-B model to understand the drivers of mistreatment during childbirth: A qualitative enquiry among maternity care staff. *Global Health, Science and Practice, 11*(2), e2200434. DOI: 10.9745/GHSP-D-22-00267

Astrow, A. B., Kwok, G., Sharma, R. K., Fromer, N., & Sulmasy, D. P. (2018). Spiritual needs and perception of quality of care and satisfaction with care in hematology/medical oncology patients: A multicultural assessment. *Journal of Pain and Symptom Management, 55*(1), 56–64. DOI: 10.1016/j.jpainsymman.2017.08.009 PMID: 28842220

Athimni, Z., Chouchen, A., Kalboussi, H., Nsiri, L., Ferhi, F., Aloui, A., Gaddour, A., Bouhoula, M., Maoua, M., Brahem, A., Maalel, O., Chatti, S., Kacem, I., & Mrizak, N. (2023). Burnout Syndrome and its associated factors among anesthesia technicians in a Teaching Hospital in the central region of Tunisia. *European Psychiatry : the Journal of the Association of European Psychiatrists, 66*(S1), S462–S463. DOI: 10.1192/j.eurpsy.2023.992

Atun, R. A., Berman, P., & Hsiao, W. C. (2009). Building on health systems frameworks for developing a common approach to health systems strengthening. *Unpublished manuscript*, 1–35.

Baig, N., & Isgandarova, N. (2023). Exploring Islamic Spiritual Care: What Is in a Name? *Religions, 14*(10), 1256. DOI: 10.3390/rel14101256

Baime, M. J. (2003). *Meditation and spirituality for health care providers. Spiritual Transformation and Health Through the Lifecycle* [private printing]. Samueli Institute for Information Biology., https://www.uphs.upenn.edu/pastoral/events/Baime_Metanexus_talk_2003.pdf

Bakker, A. B., & Demerouti, E. (2007). The Job Demands-Resources model: State of the art. *Journal of Managerial Psychology, 22*(3), 309–328. DOI: 10.1108/02683940710733115

Bakker, A. B., Demerouti, E., & Sanz-Vergel, A. (2023). Job demands–resources theory: Ten years later. *Annual Review of Organizational Psychology and Organizational Behavior, 10*(1), 25–53. DOI: 10.1146/annurev-orgpsych-120920-053933

Bakker, A. B., Demerouti, E., & Sanz-Vergel, A. I. (2014). Burnout and work engagement: The JD–R approach. *Annual Review of Organizational Psychology and Organizational Behavior, 1*(1), 389–411. DOI: 10.1146/annurev-orgpsych-031413-091235

Balboni, M. J., Sullivan, A., Amobi, A., Phelps, A. C., Gorman, D. P., Zollfrank, A., Peteet, J. R., Prigerson, H. G., VanderWeele, T. J., & Balboni, T. A. (2013). Why is spiritual care infrequent at the end of life? Spiritual care perceptions among patients, nurses, and physicians and the role of training. *Journal of Clinical Oncology*, *31*(4), 461–467. DOI: 10.1200/JCO.2012.44.6443 PMID: 23248245

Baldacchino, D. (2015). Spiritual Care Education of Health Care Professionals. *Religions*, *6*(2), 594–613. DOI: 10.3390/rel6020594

Bandura, A. (1997). *Self-efficacy: The exercise of control*. W.H. Freeman.

Bandura, A. (2001). Social cognitive theory: An agentic perspective. *Annual Review of Psychology*, *52*(1), 1–26. DOI: 10.1146/annurev.psych.52.1.1 PMID: 11148297

Banin, L. B., Suzart, N. B., Guimarães, F. A. G., Lucchetti, A. L., de Jesus, M. A. S., & Lucchetti, G. (2014). Religious beliefs or physicians' behavior: What makes a patient more prone to accept a physician to address his/her spiritual issues? [Abstract]. *Journal of Religion and Health*, *53*(3), 917–928. DOI: 10.1007/s10943-013-9685-2 PMID: 23420277

Bansal, R., Maroof, K. A., Parashar, P., & Pant, B. (2008). Spirituality and health: A knowledge, attitude and practice study among doctors of North India. [Abstract]. *Spirituality and Health International*, *9*(4), 263–269. DOI: 10.1002/shi.358

Baron, R. A., Byrne, D., & Branscombe, N. R. (2011). *Social psychology* (13th ed.). Pearson Education.

Bar-Sela, G., Schultz, M. J., Elshamy, K., Rassouli, M., Ben-Arye, E., Doumit, M., Gafer, N., Albashayreh, A., Ghrayeb, I., Turker, I., Ozalp, G., Kav, S., Fahmi, R., Nestoros, S., Ghali, H., Mula-Hussain, L., Shazar, I., Obeidat, R., Punjwani, R., & Silbermann, M. (2019). Training for awareness of one's own spirituality: A key factor in overcoming barriers to the provision of spiritual care to advanced cancer patients by doctors and nurses. [Abstract]. *Palliative & Supportive Care*, *17*(3), 345–352. DOI: 10.1017/S147895151800055X PMID: 30187841

Bass, B. M., & Riggio, R. E. (2006). *Transformational leadership* (2nd ed.). Lawrence Erlbaum Associates. DOI: 10.4324/9781410617095

Beauchamp, T. L., & Childress, J. F. (2019). *Principles of biomedical ethics* (8th ed.). Oxford University Press.

Becker, A. E.. (2018). Community-based mental health services in developing countries: New models and innovations. *World Psychiatry; Official Journal of the World Psychiatric Association (WPA)*, *17*(2), 168–174. DOI: 10.1002/wps.20599 PMID: 29856555

Beh, L.-S., & Idris, K. (2006). An analysis of quality of work life (QWL) and career-related variables. *American Journal of Applied Sciences*, *3*(12), 2151–2159. DOI: 10.3844/ajassp.2006.2151.2159

Benefiel, M. (2003). Mapping the terrain of spirituality in organizations research. *Journal of Organizational Change Management*, *16*(4), 367–377. DOI: 10.1108/09534810310484136

Benefiel, M. (2005). *Soul at work: Spiritual leadership in organizations*. Church Publishing, Inc.

Berlinger, N., Wynia, M., Powell, T., Hester, D. M., Milliken, A., Fabi, R., & Jenks, N. P. (2017). *Ethical framework for health care institutions responding to novel coronavirus SARS-CoV-2 (COVID-19)*. The Hastings Center.

Berwick, D. M. (2009). What "Patient-Centered" Should Mean: Confessions Of An Extremist. *Health Affairs*, *28*(Supplement 1), w555–w565. DOI: 10.1377/hlthaff.28.4.w555 PMID: 19454528

Best, M., Butow, P., & Olver, I. (2016a). Doctors discussing religion and spirituality: A systematic literature review. *Palliative Medicine*, *30*(4), 327–337. DOI: 10.1177/0269216315600912 PMID: 26269325

Best, M., Butow, P., & Olver, I. (2016b). Why do We Find It so Hard to Discuss Spirituality? A Qualitative Exploration of Attitudinal Barriers. *Journal of Clinical Medicine*, *5*(9), 77. DOI: 10.3390/jcm5090077 PMID: 27598212

Betron, M., Bourgeault, I., Manzoor, M., Paulino, E., Steege, R., Thompson, K., & Wuliji, T. (2019). Time for gender-transformative change in the health workforce. *Lancet*, *393*(10171), e25–e26. DOI: 10.1016/S0140-6736(19)30208-9 PMID: 30739706

Betton, H. B. (2002). [Review of the book *Spirituality in Patient Care-Why, How, When, and What*, by H. G. Koenig]. *Journal of the National Medical Association*, *94*(8), 743–745. https://pmc.ncbi.nlm.nih.gov/articles/PMC2594261

Bianchi, R., & Schonfeld, I. S. (2023). Examining the evidence base for burnout. *Bulletin of the World Health Organization*, *101*(11), 743–745. DOI: 10.2471/BLT.23.289996 PMID: 37961064

Blažević, J. (2021). The phenomenon of miraculous healing through suggestion in the context of faith and magic-psychological-theological approach. *Psychiatria Danubina*, *33*(Suppl 4), 933–939. https://hrcak.srce.hr/file/395028 PMID: 35026824

Bragard, I., Dupuis, G., & Fleet, R. (2015). Quality of work life, burnout, and stress in emergency department physicians: A qualitative review. *European Journal of Emergency Medicine*, *22*(4), 227–234. DOI: 10.1097/MEJ.0000000000000194

Brown, J. B., Thorpe, C., Bal, S., George, C., Jan, S. H., Mathews, M., Premji, K., Ryan, B. L., & Terry, A. L. (2025). Burden of administrative responsibilities in primary care: Qualitative study. *Canadian Family Physician Médecin de Famille Canadien*, *71*(6), e148–e153. DOI: 10.46747/cfp.7106e148 PMID: 40523739

Brown, L. (1993). *Oxford English Dictionary*. Clarendon Press.

Brunetto, Y., & Farr-Wharton, R. (2006). The importance of effective organisational relationships for nurses: A social capital perspective. *International Journal of Human Resources Development and Management*, *6*(2–4), 232–247. DOI: 10.1504/IJHRDM.2006.010397

Bryan, S., Zipp, G., & Breitkreuz, D. (2021). The Effects of Mindfulness Meditation and Gentle Yoga on Spiritual Well-Being in Cancer Survivors: A Pilot Study. [Abstract]. *Alternative Therapies in Health and Medicine*, *27*(3). https://www.alternative-therapies.com/abstracts/11034.html PMID: 33128538

Bucu, A. (2012). *Massage and Meditation: A Case for Wellness Practice in the Workplace* (Doctoral dissertation, RMIT University, Melbourne). https://www.researchgate.net/profile/Angie-Bucu/publication/264351450_Massage_and_Meditation_A_Case_for_Wellness_Practice_in_the_Workplace/links/55b04e6708aeb923991720ce/Massage-and-Meditation-A-Case-for-Wellness-Practice-in-the-Workplace.pdf

Burton, A., Burgess, C., Dean, S., Koutsopoulou, G., & Hugh-Jones, S. (2017). How Effective are Mindfulness-Based Interventions for Reducing Stress Among Healthcare Professionals? A Systematic Review and Meta-Analysis. *Stress and Health*, *33*(1), 3–13. DOI: 10.1002/smi.2673 PMID: 26916333

Buruck, G., Dörfel, D., Kugler, J., & Brom, S. (2016). Enhancing well-being at work: The role of emotion regulation skills as personal resources. *Journal of Occupational Health Psychology*, *21*(4), 480–493. DOI: 10.1037/ocp0000023 PMID: 26974495

Büssing, A., Baumann, K., Hvidt, N. C., Koenig, H. G., Puchalski, C. M., Swinton, J. (2014). Spirituality and Health [Editorial]. *Evidence-Based Complementary and Alternative Medicine*, 2014, 682817, 2 pages. https://doi.org/DOI: 10.1155/2014/682817

Cakirpaloglu, S., Cakirpaloglu, P., Skopal, O., Kvapilová, B., Schovánková, T., Vévodová, Š., Greaves, J., & Steven, A. (2024). Strain and serenity: Exploring the interplay of stress, burnout, and well-being among healthcare professionals. *Frontiers in Psychology*, *15*, 1415996. Advance online publication. DOI: 10.3389/fpsyg.2024.1415996 PMID: 38984287

Cao, J., Wang, S., & Li, J. (2023). Self-efficacy and burnout among emergency nurses: A cross-sectional study. *International Journal of Nursing Studies*, *134*, 104382. DOI: 10.1016/j.ijnurstu.2022.104382

Carayon, P., Wetterneck, T. B., Rivera-Rodriguez, A. J., Hundt, A. S., Hoonakker, P., Holden, R., & Gurses, A. P. (2014). Human Factors Systems Approach to Healthcare Quality and Patient Safety. *Applied Ergonomics*, *45*(1), 14–25. DOI: 10.1016/j.apergo.2013.04.023 PMID: 23845724

Carminati, L. (2021). Emotions, Emotion Management and Emotional Intelligence in the Workplace: Healthcare Professionals' Experience in Emotionally Charged Situations. *Frontiers in Sociology*, *6*, 640384. Advance online publication. DOI: 10.3389/fsoc.2021.640384 PMID: 33889607

Cassell, E. J. (1999). Historical perspective of medical residency training: 50 years of changes. *Journal of the American Medical Association*, *281*(13), 1231. DOI: 10.1001/jama.281.13.1231-JMS0407-6-1 PMID: 10199439

Castillo, R., Salguero, J., Fernández-Berrocal, P., & Balluerka, N. (2013). Effects of an emotional intelligence intervention on aggression and empathy among adolescents. *Journal of Adolescence*, *36*(5), 883–892. DOI: 10.1016/j.adolescence.2013.07.001 PMID: 24011104

Cella, D. F. (1994). Quality of life: Concepts and definition. *Journal of Pain and Symptom Management*, *9*(3), 186–192. DOI: 10.1016/0885-3924(94)90129-5

Centers for Medicare & Medicaid Services (CMS). (2023). *Hospital Compare*. U.S. Department of Health & Human Services.

Chadha, N. (2021). Adversity quotient: Surviving rather than giving up. *Psychology (Savannah, Ga.)*, *58*(2), 5942–5947. DOI: 10.17762/pae.v58i2.3068

Charles, J. V., Kathiravan, C., & Velaudham, C. (2016). Customer satisfaction towards C-segment cars in Chennai City. *International Journal of Management and Social Sciences*, *4*(4), 412–423.

Chassin, M. R., & Loeb, J. M. (2013). High-reliability health care: Getting there from here. *The Milbank Quarterly*, *91*(3), 459–490. DOI: 10.1111/1468-0009.12023 PMID: 24028696

Chattopadhyay, S. (2007). Religion, spirituality, health and medicine: Why should Indian physicians care? [Abstract]. *Journal of Postgraduate Medicine*, *53*(4), 262–266. DOI: 10.4103/0022-3859.33967 PMID: 18097118

Chin, C.-L., Goh, J., & Lim, S. (2017). ISO 9001 certification and its impact on hospitals: A case study from Singapore. *International Journal of Health Care Quality Assurance*, *30*(5), 453–467. DOI: 10.1108/IJHCQA-02-2016-0022

Chirico, F., Batra, K., Batra, R., Oztekin, G. G., Ferrari, G., Crescenzo, P., Nucera, G., Szarpak, L., Sharma, M., Magnavita, N., & Yildirim, M. (2023). Spiritual well-being and burnout syndrome in healthcare: A systematic review. *Journal of Health and Social Sciences*, *8*(1), 13–32. DOI: 10.19204/2023/sprt2

Chiu, L., Ganesan, S., Rutledge, R., & Toews, J. (2006). Pre-conference report for the 4th International Multidisciplinary Conference on Spirituality and Health: Interweaving Science, Wisdom and Compassion. *Spirituality and Health International*, *7*(3), 162–166. DOI: 10.1002/shi.290

Chou, L. P., Li, C. Y., & Hu, S. C. (2014). Job stress and burnout in hospital employees: Comparisons of different medical professions in a regional hospital in Taiwan. *BMJ Open*, *4*(2), e004185. DOI: 10.1136/bmjopen-2013-004185 PMID: 24568961

Chung, H., & van der Lippe, T. (2020). Flexible working, work–life balance, and gender equality: Introduction. *Social Indicators Research*, *151*(2), 365–381. DOI: 10.1007/s11205-018-2025-x PMID: 33029036

Cleveland Clinic. (2021). *Annual Caregiver Experience Report*. Cleveland Clinic Press.

Cohen, C., Pignata, S., Bezak, E., Tie, M., & Childs, J. (2023). Workplace interventions to improve well-being and reduce burnout for nurses, physicians and allied healthcare professionals: A systematic review. *BMJ Open*, *13*(6), e071203. Advance online publication. DOI: 10.1136/bmjopen-2022-071203 PMID: 37385740

Cohidon, C., Mahler, L., Broers, B., Favrod-Coune, T., Moussa, A., & Sebo, P. (2022). Primary care physicians' personal and professional attributes associated with forgoing own care and presenteeism: A cross sectional study. *International Journal of Public Health*, *66*, 1604442. Advance online publication. DOI: 10.3389/ijph.2021.1604442 PMID: 35242001

Cole, T. R., & Carlin, N. (2009). The suffering of physicians. *Lancet*, *374*(9699), 1414–1415. DOI: 10.1016/S0140-6736(09)61851-1 PMID: 19866520

Conversano, C., Ciacchini, R., Orrù, G., Di Giuseppe, M., Gemignani, A., & Poli, A. (2020). Mindfulness, compassion, and self-compassion among health care professionals: What's new? A systematic review. *Frontiers in Psychology*, *11*, 1683. Advance online publication. DOI: 10.3389/fpsyg.2020.01683 PMID: 32849021

Cooper, A. L., Brown, J. A., & Rees, C. S. (2020). Resilience in emergency service workers: An integrative literature review. *International Emergency Nursing*, *49*, 100814. DOI: 10.1016/j.ienj.2019.100814

Cooper, C. L., & Cartwright, S. (2022). Organizational health and well-being. *Journal of Organizational Effectiveness*, *9*(1), 7–24.

Cooper, C. L., & Cartwright, S. (2022). Organizational health and well-being: A core issue for 21st-century organizations. *Journal of Organizational Effectiveness: People and Performance*, *9*(1), 7–24. DOI: 10.1108/JOEPP-08-2021-0214

Cotton, S.. (2006). Spirituality in the workplace: Perspectives on theory, research, and practice. *Journal of Management, Spirituality & Religion*, *3*(2), 189–203. DOI: 10.1300/J085v03n02_12

Cummings, G. G., MacGregor, T., Davey, M., Lee, H., Wong, C. A., Lo, E., Muise, M., & Stafford, E. (2010). Leadership styles and outcome patterns for the nursing workforce and work environment: A systematic review. *International Journal of Nursing Studies*, *47*(3), 363–385. DOI: 10.1016/j.ijnurstu.2009.08.006 PMID: 19781702

Dâmbean, C. A., & Gabor, M. R. (2021). Implications of emotional intelligence in human resource management. *ECONOMICS*, *9*(2), 73–90. DOI: 10.2478/eoik-2021-0016

de Diego Cordero, R., Lucchetti, G., Fernández-Vazquez, A., & Badanta-Romero, B. (2019). Opinions, knowledge and attitudes concerning "spirituality, religiosity and health" among health graduates in a Spanish university. [Abstract]. *Journal of Religion and Health*, *58*(5), 1592–1604. DOI: 10.1007/s10943-019-00780-3 PMID: 30771142

De Hert, S. (2020). Burnout in healthcare workers: Prevalence, impact and preventative strategies. *Local and Regional Anesthesia*, *13*, 171–183. DOI: 10.2147/LRA.S240564 PMID: 33149664

Deckard, G., Meterko, M., & Field, D. (1994). Physician burnout: An examination of personal, professional, and organizational relationships. *Medical Care*, *32*(7), 745–754. DOI: 10.1097/00005650-199407000-00007

Dehue, F., Bolman, C., Völlink, T., & Pouwelse, M. (2012). Coping with bullying at work and health related problems. *International Journal of Stress Management, 19*(2), 111–131. DOI: 10.1037/a0028969

Delaney, C. (2005). The spirituality scale: Development and psychometric testing of a holistic instrument to assess the human spiritual dimension. *Journal of Holistic Nursing, 23*(2), 145–167. DOI: 10.1177/0898010105276180 PMID: 15883463

Delbanco, T., Berwick, D. M., Boufford, J. I., Edgman-Levitan, , Ollenschläger, G., Plamping, D., & Rockefeller, R. G. (2001). Healthcare in a land called People-Power: Nothing about me without me. *Health Expectations, 4*(3), 144–150. DOI: 10.1046/j.1369-6513.2001.00145.x PMID: 11493320

DeLeo, K., Maconick, L., McCabe, R., Broeckelmann, E., Rains, S., Rowe, S., & Johnson, S. (2022). Experiences of crisis care among service users with complex emotional needs or a diagnosis of 'personality disorder', and other stakeholders: Systematic review and meta-synthesis of the qualitative literature. *BJPsych Open, 8*(2), e53. Advance online publication. DOI: 10.1192/bjo.2022.1 PMID: 35197131

Delgado-Guay, M. O., Palma, A., Duarte, E., Grez, M., Tupper, L., Liu, D. D., & Bruera, E. (2021). Association between spirituality, religiosity, spiritual pain, symptom distress, and quality of life among Latin American patients with advanced cancer: A multicenter study. *Journal of Palliative Medicine, 24*(11), 1606–1615. DOI: 10.1089/jpm.2020.0776 PMID: 33844951

Demerouti, E., Bakker, A. B., Vardakou, I., & Kantas, A. (2003). The convergent validity of two burnout instruments: A multitrait-multimethod analysis. *European Journal of Psychological Assessment, 19*(1), 12–23. DOI: 10.1027//1015-5759.19.1.12

Deming, W. E. (1986). *Out of the crisis*. Mit Press.

Dewa, C. S., Loong, D., Bonato, S., Thanh, N. X., & Jacobs, P. (2014). How does burnout affect physician productivity? A systematic literature review. *BMC Health Services Research, 14*(1), 325. DOI: 10.1186/1472-6963-14-325

Dewi, D. Y., Supriadi, Y. N., & Iswanto, A. H. (2022). The effect of transformational leadership, quality of work-life on organizational citizenship behavior with organizational commitment mediation. *Journal of Social Sciences, 3*(5), 865–878. DOI: 10.46799/jss.v3i5.259

Dhamija, P., Gupta, S., & Bag, S. (2019). Measuring of job satisfaction: The use of quality of work life factors. *Benchmarking, 26*(3), 871–892. DOI: 10.1108/BIJ-06-2018-0155

Dhar N, Chaturvedi S, Nandan D. (2011). Spiritual health scale 2011: Defining and measuring 4th dimension of health. Indian Journal of Community Medicine 36:275 82.

Dhar, N., Chaturvedi, S. K., & Nandan, D. (2011). Spiritual Health Scale 2011: Defining and Measuring 4th Dimension of Health. *Indian Journal of Community Medicine : Official Publication of Indian Association of Preventive & Social Medicine*, *36*(4), 275–282. DOI: 10.4103/0970-0218.91329 PMID: 22279257

Dhar, N., Chaturvedi, S. K., & Nandan, D. (2013). Spiritual health, the fourth dimension: A public health perspective. *WHO South-East Asia Journal of Public Health*, *2*(1), 3–5. DOI: 10.4103/2224-3151.115826 PMID: 28612816

Diener, E., & Suh, E. (1997). Measuring quality of life: Economic, social, and subjective indicators. *Social Indicators Research*, *40*(1–2), 189–216. DOI: 10.1023/A:1006859511756

Dimensions of Wellness. University of Maryland. Your Guide to Living Well. [Last accessed June 27, 2017]._https://umwellness.wordpress.com/8-dimensions-of-wellness/

Duggleby, W., Cooper, D., & Penz, K. (2009). Hope, self-efficacy, spiritual well-being and job satisfaction. *Journal of Advanced Nursing*, *65*(11), 2376–2385. DOI: 10.1111/j.1365-2648.2009.05094.x PMID: 19737323

Dunn, P. M., Arnetz, B. B., Christensen, J. F., & Homer, L. (2007). Meeting the imperative to improve physician well-being: Assessment of an innovative program. *Journal of General Internal Medicine*, *22*(11), 1544–1552. DOI: 10.1007/s11606-007-0363-5 PMID: 17891503

Dyrbye, L. N., Satele, D., Sloan, J., & Shanafelt, T. D. (2013). Utility of a brief screening tool to identify physicians in distress. *Journal of General Internal Medicine*, *28*(3), 421–427. DOI: 10.1007/s11606-012-2252-9

Dyrbye, L. N., Shanafelt, T. D., Sinsky, C. A., Cipriano, P. F., Bhatt, J., Ommaya, A., West, C. P., & Meyers, D. (2017). Burnout among healthcare professionals: A call to explore and address this underrecognized threat to safe, high-quality care. *NAM Perspectives*, *7*(7), 1–10. DOI: 10.31478/201707b

Dyrbye, L. N., West, C. P., Satele, D., Boone, S., Tan, L., Sloan, J., & Shanafelt, T. D. (2017). Burnout among US medical students, residents, and early-career physicians relative to the general US population. *Academic Medicine*, *89*(3), 443–451. DOI: 10.1097/ACM.0000000000000134 PMID: 24448053

Dzau, V. J., Kirch, D., & Nasca, T. (2020). Preventing a parallel pandemic — A national strategy to protect clinicians' well-being. *The New England Journal of Medicine, 383*(6), 513–515. DOI: 10.1056/NEJMp2011027 PMID: 32402153

Easton, S., & Van Laar, D. (2013). QoWL (Quality of Working Life) – What, how, and why? *Psychological Research, 3*(10), 596–605.

Easton, S., & Van Laar, D. (2018). Reconciling organizational stress, cultural differences and quality of working life. *Indian Journal of Career and Livelihood Planning, 7*(1), 27–38.

Eckleberry-Hunt, J., Van Dyke, A., Lick, D., & Tucciarone, J. (2009). Changing the conversation from burnout to wellness: Physician well-being in residency training programs. *Journal of Graduate Medical Education, 1*(2), 225–230. DOI: 10.4300/JGME-D-09-00026.1

Edlund, M., & Tancredi, L. R. (1985). Quality of life: An ideological critique. *Perspectives in Biology and Medicine, 28*(4), 591–607. DOI: 10.1353/pbm.1985.0034

Edmondson, A. (1999). Psychological safety and learning behavior in work teams. *Administrative Science Quarterly, 44*(2), 350–383. DOI: 10.2307/2666999

Edú-Valsania, S., Laguía, A., & Moriano, J. A. (2022). Burnout: A review of theory and measurement. *International Journal of Environmental Research and Public Health, 19*(3), 1780. DOI: 10.3390/ijerph19031780 PMID: 35162802

Elendu, C. (2024). The evolution of ancient healing practices: From shamanism to Hippocratic medicine. *Revista de Medicina (São Paulo), 103*(28), e39005. DOI: 10.1097/MD.0000000000039005 PMID: 38996102

Elizur, D., & Shye, S. (1990). Quality of work life and its relation to quality of life. *Applied Psychology, 39*(3), 275–291. DOI: 10.1111/j.1464-0597.1990.tb01054.x

Elliott, B. A., Dorscher, J., Wirta, A., & Hill, D. L. (2010). Staying connected: Native American women faculty members on experiencing success. *Academic Medicine, 85*(4), 711–716. https://journals.lww.com/academicmedicine/fulltext/2010/04000/staying_connected__native_american_women_faculty.32.aspx. DOI: 10.1097/ACM.0b013e3181d28101 PMID: 20354388

El-Nimr, G., Green, L. L., & Salib, E. (2004). Spiritual care in psychiatry: Professionals' views. [Abstract]. *Mental Health, Religion & Culture, 7*(2), 165–170. DOI: 10.1080/13674670320001579990

Emami, S., Lorenzoni, V., & Turchetti, G. (2024). Towards Resilient Healthcare Systems: A

Epstein, E. G., & Hamric, A. B. (2009). Moral distress, moral residue, and the crescendo effect. *The Journal of Clinical Ethics, 20*(4), 330–342. DOI: 10.1086/JCE200920406 PMID: 20120853

Epstein, R. M., & Krasner, M. S. (2013). Physician resilience: What it means, why it matters, and how to promote it. *Academic Medicine, 88*(3), 301–303. DOI: 10.1097/ACM.0b013e318280cff0 PMID: 23442430

Etikan, I., Musa, S. A., & Alkassim, R. S. (2016). Comparison of convenience sampling and purposive sampling. *American Journal of Theoretical and Applied Statistics, 5*(1), 1–4. DOI: 10.11648/j.ajtas.20160501.11

Fava, G. A., Sonino, N., Lucente, M., & Guidi, J. (2023). Allostatic load in clinical practice. *Clinical Psychological Science, 11*(2), 345–356. DOI: 10.1177/21677026221121601

Ferngren, G. B. (2009). *Medicine and health care in early Christianity*. Johns Hopkins University Press.

Finkelstein, C. (2018). *Protect against burnout and encourage self-care*. American Medical Association.

Firth, J.. (2019). Digital interventions for improving mental health and well-being: A systematic review. *The Lancet. Psychiatry, 6*(6), 500–510. DOI: 10.1016/S2215-0366(19)30027-4

Fiske, E., Martin, S., & Luetkemeyer, J. (2020). Building Nurses 'Resilience to Trauma through Contemplative Practices. [Abstract] *Creative Nursing, 26*(4), 090-096. https://doi.org/DOI: 10.1891/CRNR-D-20-00054

Fitchett, G., & Risk, J. L. (2009). Screening for spiritual struggle. *The Journal of Pastoral Care & Counseling, 63*(1-2), 1–12. DOI: 10.1177/154230500906300104 PMID: 20196352

Foglia, M. B., Fox, E., Chanko, B. L., & Bottrell, M. M. (2009). Ethics and the healthcare organization: Strategy, leadership, and accountability. *Public Administration Review, 69*(6), 1067–1075. DOI: 10.1111/j.1540-6210.2009.02045.x

Foglio, J. P., & Brody, H. (1988). Religion, faith, and family medicine [Editorial]. *The Journal of Family Practice, 27*(5), '473–474. https://cdn.mdedge.com/files/s3fs-public/jfp-archived-issues/1988-volume_26-27/JFP_1988-11_v27_i5_religion-faith-and-family-medicine.pdf PMID: 3193064

Fortney, J. C.. (2015). Telepsychiatry and integrated care in mental health workforce development. *Psychiatric Services (Washington, D.C.)*, *66*(9), 972–979. DOI: 10.1176/appi.ps.201400372

Fortney, J. C.. (2017). Practice transformation in primary care: Bridging the gap between mental health and primary care. *Psychiatric Services (Washington, D.C.)*, *68*(2), 101–108. DOI: 10.1176/appi.ps.201600166 PMID: 27582237

Francis, R. (2013). *Report of the Mid Staffordshire NHS Foundation Trust public inquiry*. The Stationery Office.

Franco Vega, M. C., Ait Aiss, M., George, M., Day, L., Mbadugha, A., Owens, K., Sweeney, C., Chau, S., Escalante, C., & Bodurka, D. C.Maria Franco Vega. (2024). Enhancing implementation of the I-PASS handoff tool using a provider handoff task force at a Comprehensive Cancer Center. *Joint Commission Journal on Quality and Patient Safety*, *50*(8), 560–568. Advance online publication. DOI: 10.1016/j.jcjq.2024.03.004 PMID: 38584053

Freudenberger, H. J. (1974). Staff burn-out. *The Journal of Social Issues*, *30*(1), 159–165. DOI: 10.1111/j.1540-4560.1974.tb00706.x

Fry, L. W. (2003). Toward a theory of spiritual leadership. *The Leadership Quarterly*, *14*(6), 693–727. DOI: 10.1016/j.leaqua.2003.09.001

Gallagher, T. H., Waterman, A. D., Ebers, A. G., Fraser, V. J., & Levinson, W. (2007). Patients' and physicians' attitudes regarding the disclosure of medical errors. *Journal of the American Medical Association*, *289*(8), 1001–1007. DOI: 10.1001/jama.289.8.1001 PMID: 12597752

Gauche, C., De Beer, L. T., & Brink, L. (2017). Exploring demands from the perspective of employees identified as being at risk of burnout. *International Journal of Qualitative Studies on Health and Well-being*, *12*(1), 1361783. Advance online publication. DOI: 10.1080/17482631.2017.1361783 PMID: 28784048

Gaur, K., & Sharma, M. (2015). Role of spiritual health in patient care: A review. *Int Multidisciplinary J Health, 1*(8), 1-6. https://www.academia.edu/18056636/Role_of_Spiritual_Health_in_Patient_Care_A_Review?source=swp_share

Gerçek, M., & Özveren, C. G. (2025). From self and career perceptions to life satisfaction: A sequential mediation approach to general self-efficacy, future work self, career anxiety, and life satisfaction in the emerging workforce. *International Journal for Educational and Vocational Guidance*. Advance online publication. DOI: 10.1007/s10775-024-09721-3

Geurts, S., Rutte, C., & Peeters, M. (1999). Antecedents and consequences of work–home interference among medical residents. *Social Science & Medicine*, *48*(9), 1135–1148. DOI: 10.1016/S0277-9536(98)00425-0 PMID: 10220015

Ghazanfar, H., Iqbal, S., & Naseem, S. (2018). Quality of life of post-graduate medical students working in private and public hospitals in Punjab as measured by WHOQOL-BREF questionnaire. *JPMA. The Journal of the Pakistan Medical Association*, *68*(6), 908–913.

Gilar-Corbi, R., Pozo-Rico, T., Sánchez, B., & Castejón, J.-L. (2019). Can emotional intelligence be improved? A randomized experimental study of a business-oriented EI training program for senior managers. *PLoS One*, *14*(10), e0224254. Advance online publication. DOI: 10.1371/journal.pone.0224254 PMID: 31644585

Gil-Monte, P. R. (2009). Validez factorial del «Cuestionario para la Evaluación del Síndrome de Quemarse por el Trabajo» (CESQT) en una muestra de maestros mexicanos [Factorial validity of the "Burnout Assessment Questionnaire" (CESQT) in a sample of Mexican teachers]. *Salud Mental*, *31*, 205–214.

Giménez Lozano, J. M., Martínez Ramón, J. P., & Morales Rodríguez, F. M. (2021). Doctors and nurses: A systematic review of the risk and protective factors in workplace violence and burnout. *International Journal of Environmental Research and Public Health*, *18*(6), 3280. DOI: 10.3390/ijerph18063280 PMID: 33810020

Goleman, D (2020). *Emotional Intelligence: Improve your Social Skills and Emotional Agility for a better life, success at work, and happier relationships.*

Goleman, D. (1995). *Emotional intelligence: Why it can matter more than IQ*. Bantam Books.

Golovina, S. Y., Kuchina, Y. A., & Serova, A. (2019). Increasing the quality of working life: Modern labor legislation's strategic task. *Public Policy and Administration*, *18*(3), 7–14. DOI: 10.5755/j01.ppaa.18.3.24266

Gomathi, S., & Swapna, M. (2012). A study on impact of job satisfaction on quality of work life: With special reference to IT professionals in Bangalore city. *Journal of Management and Science*, *2*(1), 1–12.

Gonzalez, P.. (2021). Organizational justice and mental health: Impact on workforce well-being. *Journal of Health Organization and Management*, *35*(3), 227–243. DOI: 10.1108/JHOM-05-2020-0170

Gostin, L. O., Wiley, L. F., & Frieden, T. R. (2020). *Public health law: Power, duty, restraint* (3rd ed.). University of California Press.

Gotsadze, G., Zoidze A, Gabunia T, Chin B. (2024). Advancing governance for digital transformation in health: Insights from Georgia's experience. *Advance online publication.* https://pubmed.ncbi.nlm.nih.gov/39353684/https://www.who.int/docs/default-source/documents/gs4dhdaa2a9f352b0445bafbc79ca799dce4d.pd

Gotsadze, G., Chikovani, I., & Kapanadze, S.. (2024). Advancing governance for digital transformation in health: Insights from Georgia's experience. *BMJ Global Health, 9*(10), e015589. Advance online publication. DOI: 10.1136/bmjgh-2024-015589 PMID: 39353684

Grant, A. (2007). Enhancing coaching skills and emotional intelligence through training. *Industrial and Commercial Training, 39*(5), 257–266. DOI: 10.1108/00197850710761945

Greenfield, D., & Braithwaite, J. (2008). Health sector accreditation research: A systematic review. *International Journal for Quality in Health Care : Journal of the International Society for Quality in Health Care, 20*(3), 172–183. DOI: 10.1093/intqhc/mzn005 PMID: 18339666

Guest, D. E. (2017). Human resource management and employee well-being: Towards a new analytic framework. *Human Resource Management Journal, 27*(1), 22–38. DOI: 10.1111/1748-8583.12139

Gupta, K. (2024). Evaluation of the Effectiveness of Yoga and Meditation in Alleviating Burnout Symptoms among Medical Student. *International Journal of Life Sciences (Amravati), 13*(12). Advance online publication. DOI: 10.69605/ijlbpr_13.12.2024.168

Guptill, M., Reibling, E. T., & Clem, K. (2018). Deciding to lead: A qualitative study of women leaders in emergency medicine. *International Journal of Emergency Medicine, 11*(1), 47. DOI: 10.1186/s12245-018-0206-7 PMID: 31179933

Halouani, N., Koukane, M., Elleuch, O., Turki, M., Samet, A., Jemil, F., Ellouze, S., & Aloulou, J. (2023). Burnout and its associated factors in healthcare workers during the COVID-19 pandemic. *European Psychiatry : the Journal of the Association of European Psychiatrists, 66*(S1), S804–S804. DOI: 10.1192/j.eurpsy.2023.1702

Halpern, M. (2017). Ayurveda, Spirituality and Meditation. [Blog] https://www.ayurvedacollege.com/blog/ayurveda_spirituality_meditation/

Harney, B., & Collings, D. G. (2021). HRM and employee well-being challenges. *Human Resource Management Review, 31*(4), 100812.

Harney, B., & Collings, D. G. (2021). Navigating the shifting landscape of HRM and employee well-being: Challenges and opportunities. *Human Resource Management Review, 31*(4), 100812. DOI: 10.1016/j.hrmr.2021.100824

Harris, M., & Fallot, R. D. (2001). *Using trauma theory to design service systems.* Jossey-Bass.

Haynes, A. B., Weiser, T. G., Berry, W. R., Lipsitz, S. R., Breizat, A. H. S., Dellinger, E. P., & Gawande, A. A. (2009). They developed a surgical safety checklist aimed at reducing morbidity and mortality in a global population. *The New England Journal of Medicine, 360*(5), 491–499. DOI: 10.1056/NEJMsa0810119 PMID: 19144931

Headrick, E. G., McCarten-Gibbs, M., Coley, R., Avila, G., Mina, J., Villa, R. C., & Fernando, L. H. (2024). Care for staff: A novel technical assistance approach to promote occupational mental health among healthcare workers in lower and middle income country settings. *Workplace Health & Safety, 72*(4), 144–152. DOI: 10.1177/21650799241247154 PMID: 38629824

Helliwell, J. F., Layard, R., & Sachs, J. (Eds.). (2024). *World happiness report 2024.* Sustainable Development Solutions Network.

Helliwell, J. F., Layard, R., & Sachs, J. (Eds.). (2024). *World Happiness Report 2024.* Sustainable Development Solutions Network.

Hemanathan, R., Sreelekha, P. P., & Golda, M. (2017). Quality of work life among nurses in a tertiary care hospital. *Health Care, 5*, 1–8.

Hen, M., & Sharabi-Nov, A. (2014). Teaching the teachers: Emotional intelligence training for teachers. *Teaching Education, 25*(4), 375–390. DOI: 10.1080/10476210.2014.908838

Hertelendy, A., Ciottone, G., Mitchell, C., Gutberg, J., & Burkle, F. (2020). Crisis Standards of Care in a Pandemic: Navigating the Ethical, Clinical, Psychological, and Policy-making Maelstrom. *International Journal for Quality in Health Care : Journal of the International Society for Quality in Health Care*. Advance online publication. DOI: 10.1093/intqhc/mzaa094 PMID: 33128564

Herzberg, F. (1968). One more time: How do you motivate employees? *Harvard Business Review.*

Herzberg, F. I. (1966). Work and the nature of man. *WORLD (Oakland, Calif.).*

Hian, C. C., & Einstein, W. O. (1990). Quality of work life (QWL): What can unions do? *S.A.M. Advanced Management Journal, 55*(2), 17–22.

Hian, C. C., & Einstein, W. O. (1990). Quality of work life (QWL): What can Unions Do? *S.A.M. Advanced Management Journal*, *55*(2), 17–22.

Hick, J. L., Hanfling, D., Wynia, M. K., & Pavia, A. T. (2020). Duty to plan: Health care, crisis standards of care, and novel coronavirus sars-cov-2. *NAM Perspectives*. Advance online publication. DOI: 10.31478/202003b PMID: 34532682

Hill, P. C., Pargament, K. I., Hood, R. W., McCullough, J. M. E., Swyers, J. P., Larson, D. B., & Zinnbauer, B. J. (2000). Conceptualizing religion and spirituality: Points of commonality, points of departure. *Journal for the Theory of Social Behaviour*, *30*(1), 51–77. DOI: 10.1111/1468-5914.00119

Hodgson, K. L., Lamport, D. J., & Laville, A. (2024). "Are you OK doctor?" An expanded health belief model exploration of doctors' experiences and perspectives of on-shift health behaviour. *International Journal of Qualitative Studies on Health and Well-being*, *19*(1), 2388795. Advance online publication. DOI: 10.1080/17482631.2024.2388795 PMID: 39104181

Hofmann, P. (2018). Stress Among Healthcare Professionals Calls Out for Attention. Journal of Kadović, M., Mikšić, Š., & Lovrić, R. (2022). Ability of Emotional Regulation and Control as a Stress Predictor in Healthcare Professionals. *International Journal of Environmental Research and Public Health*, *20*(1), 541. Advance online publication. DOI: 10.3390/ijerph20010541

Hofstede, G. (1984). The cultural relativity of the quality of life concept. *Academy of Management Review*, *9*(3), 389–398. DOI: 10.2307/258280

Holden, R. J., Carayon, P., Gurses, A. P., Hoonakker, P., Hundt, A. S., Ozok, A. A., & Rivera-Rodriguez, A. J. (2013, November). SEIPS 2.0: A Human Factors Framework for Studying and Improving the Work of Healthcare Professionals and Patients. *Ergonomics*, *56*(11), 1669–1686. DOI: 10.1080/00140139.2013.838643 PMID: 24088063

Holmgren, A. J., Thombley, R., Sinsky, C. A., & Adler-Milstein, J. (2023). Changes in physician electronic health record use with the expansion of telemedicine. *JAMA Internal Medicine*, *183*(12), 1357–1365. DOI: 10.1001/jamainternmed.2023.5738 PMID: 37902737

Horst, D. J., Broday, E. E., Bondarick, R., Serpe, L. F., & Pilatti, L. A. (2014). Quality of working life and productivity: An overview of the conceptual framework. *International Journal of Managerial Studies and Research*, *2*(5), 87–98.

Howden, S. (2004). Workplace spirituality and organizational performance. *Journal of Management, Spirituality & Religion*, *1*(2), 119–138. DOI: 10.1300/J161v01n02_08

Institute of Medicine. (2000). *To err is human: Building a safer health system.* National Academies Press., DOI: 10.17226/9728

Iqbal, M. S. (2021). Health-related quality of life among healthcare providers in Pakistan. *Journal of Pharmacy & Bioallied Sciences*, *13*(1), 31–38. DOI: 10.4103/jpbs.JPBS_265_20

Isaac, K. S., Hay, J. L., & Lubetkin, E. I. (2016). Incorporating spirituality in primary care. [Abstract]. *Journal of Religion and Health*, *55*(3), 1065–1077. DOI: 10.1007/s10943-016-0190-2 PMID: 26832335

James, T. A. (2023, January 12). *Building Empathy into the Structure of Health Care | Harvard Medical School Professional, Corporate, and Continuing Education*. Https://Learn.hms.harvard.edu/Insights/All-Insights/Building-Empathy-Structure-Health-Care. https://learn.hms.harvard.edu/insights/all-insights/building-empathy-structure-health-care

Joint Commission International. (2020). *Communicating Clearly and Effectively to Patients How to Overcome Common Communication Challenges in Health Care*. https://store.jointcommissioninternational.org/assets/3/7/jci-wp-communicating-clearly-final_(1).pdf

Kamel Boulos, M. N., & Geraghty, E. M. (2020). Geographical tracking and mapping of coronavirus disease COVID-19/severe acute respiratory syndrome coronavirus 2 (SARS-CoV-2) epidemic and associated events around the world: How 21st century GIS technologies are supporting the global fight against outbreaks and epidemics. *International Journal of Health Geographics*, *19*(1), 8. DOI: 10.1186/s12942-020-00202-8 PMID: 32160889

Kanaparthy, N. S., Holmgren, A. J., Sun, Y., Paek, H., Williams, B., McLean, R., Doolan, R., Goodman, K. E., Rotenstein, L., & Melnick, E. R. (2025). Protected time for electronic health record work and physician productivity. *JAMA Network Open*, *8*(12), e2546550. DOI: 10.1001/jamanetworkopen.2025.46550 PMID: 41329489

Karasek, R. A. (1979). Job demands, job decision latitude, and mental strain: Implications for job redesign. *Administrative Science Quarterly*, *24*(2), 285–308. DOI: 10.2307/2392498

Katz, D., & Kahn, R. (2015). The social psychology of organizations. In *Organizational Behavior 2* (pp. 152–168). Routledge.

Kazdin, A. E. (2017). Innovations in mental health workforce development: Advancing evidence-based practices. *The American Psychologist*, *72*(6), 483–495. DOI: 10.1037/amp0000235

Kazdin, A. E., & Rabbitt, S. M. (2013). Novel models for delivering mental health services and reducing the burdens of mental illness. *Clinical Psychological Science, 1*(2), 170–191. DOI: 10.1177/2167702612463566

Keesara, S., Jonas, A., & Schulman, K. (2020). Covid-19 and Health Care's Digital Revolution. *The New England Journal of Medicine, 382*(23). Advance online publication. DOI: 10.1056/NEJMp2005835 PMID: 32240581

Kelbiso, L., Belay, A., & Woldie, M. (2017). Determinants of quality of work life among nurses working in Hawassa town public health facilities, South Ethiopia: A cross-sectional study. *Nursing Research and Practice, 5181676*, 1–11. Advance online publication. DOI: 10.1155/2017/5181676

Kellner, A., Townsend, K., Wilkinson, A., & Lawrence, S. A. (2019). Performance management and the AMO framework. *Human Resource Management Journal, 29*(4), 597–613. DOI: 10.1111/1748-8583.12238

Kelloway, E. K., Nielsen, K., & Dimoff, J. K. (2023). Leading healthy workplaces: The roles of leadership and human resource management. *Journal of Occupational Health Psychology, 28*(1), 1–14. DOI: 10.1037/ocp0000334 PMID: 36480367

Kelly, J., & Al-Rawi, Y. (2020). Recognising, understanding and managing high conflict behaviours in healthcare. *Postgraduate Medical Journal, 97*(1144), 123–124. DOI: 10.1136/postgradmedj-2020-139173 PMID: 33184149

Kelly, L. A., Lefton, C., & Fischer, S. A. (2019). Nurse leader burnout, satisfaction, and work-life balance. *The Journal of Nursing Administration, 49*(9), 404–410. DOI: 10.1097/NNA.0000000000000784

Kelly, M., Soles, R., Garcia, E., & Kundu, I. (2020). Job stress, burnout, work-life balance, well-being, and job satisfaction among pathology residents and fellows. *American Journal of Clinical Pathology, 153*(4), 449–469. DOI: 10.1093/ajcp/aqaa013

Khaghanizadeh, M., Ebadi, A., & Rahmani, M. (2008). The study of relationship between job stress and quality of work life of nurses in military hospitals. *Journal Mil Med, 10*(3), 175–184.

Khajehnasiri, F., Foroushani, A. R., Kashani, B. F., & Kassiri, N. (2021). Evaluation of the quality of working life and its effective factors in employed nurses of Tehran University of Medical Sciences hospitals. *Journal of Education and Health Promotion, 10*(1), 160. DOI: 10.4103/jehp.jehp_790_20

Khalil, M. T., Rathore, F. A., & Dy, R. (2023). Wellness in residency: Addressing the neglected need in lower middle-income countries. *Journal of Pediatric Rehabilitation Medicine, 16*(3), 457–462. DOI: 10.3233/PRM-230031 PMID: 37694319

Kharatzadeh, H., Alavi, M., Mohammadi, A., Visentin, D., & Cleary, M. (2020). Emotional regulation training for intensive and critical care nurses. *Nursing & Health Sciences, 22*(2), 445–453. Advance online publication. DOI: 10.1111/nhs.12679 PMID: 31975520

Kilpatrick, A. O. (2009). The health care leader as humanist. *Journal of Health and Human Services Administration, 32*(4), 451–465. DOI: 10.1177/107937390903100405

Kim, S., Bochatay, N., Relyea-Chew, A., Buttrick, E., Amdahl, C., Kim, L., Frans, E., Mossanen, M., Khandekar, A., Fehr, R., & Lee, Y. (2017). Individual, interpersonal, and organisational factors of healthcare conflict: A scoping review. *Journal of Interprofessional Care, 31*(3), 282–290. DOI: 10.1080/13561820.2016.1272558 PMID: 28276847

Kim, T. Y., & Wang, J. (2022). Healthy organizations and society. *International Journal of Environmental Research and Public Health, 19*(16), 9954. PMID: 36011590

Kim, T. Y., & Wang, J. (2022). Healthy organizations, healthy society: The mediating role of organizational citizenship and employee satisfaction. *International Journal of Environmental Research and Public Health, 19*(16), 9954. DOI: 10.3390/ijerph19169954 PMID: 36011590

Kleisiaris, C. F., Sfakianakis, C., & Papathanasiou, I. V. (2014). Health care practices in ancient Greece: The Hippocratic ideal. *Journal of Medical Ethics and History of Medicine, 7*, 6. https://pmc.ncbi.nlm.nih.gov/articles/PMC4263393/pdf/jmehm-7-6.pdf PMID: 25512827

Koenig, H. G. (2000). Religion, spirituality, and medicine: Application to clinical practice. *Journal of the American Medical Association, 284*(13), 1708–1708. DOI: 10.1001/jama.284.13.1708-JMS1004-5-1 PMID: 11015808

Koenig, H. G. (2012). Religion, spirituality, and health: The research and clinical implications. *ISRN Psychiatry, 2012*, 1–33. DOI: 10.5402/2012/278730 PMID: 23762764

Koenig, H. G., McCullough, M. E., & Larson, D. B. (2001). *Handbook of religion and health*. Oxford University Press. DOI: 10.1093/acprof:oso/9780195118667.001.0001

Koibichuk, V., Dźwigoł, H., & Stenko, S. (2021). *Conflict Management in Health Care Institutions*. Health Economics and Management Review., DOI: 10.21272/hem.2021.4-07

Koinis, A., Giannou, V., Drantaki, V., Angelaina, S., Stratou, E., & Saridi, M. (2015). The impact of healthcare workers job environment on their mental-emotional health. Coping strategies: The case of a local general hospital. *Health Psychology Research*, *3*(1), 1984. DOI: 10.4081/hpr.2015.1984

Kotsou, I., Mikolajczak, M., Heeren, A., Grégoire, J., & Leys, C. (2018). Improving Emotional Intelligence: A Systematic Review of Existing Work and Future Challenges. *Emotion Review*, *11*(2), 151–165. DOI: 10.1177/1754073917735902

Krasner, M. S.. (2009). Association of an educational program in mindful communication with burnout, empathy, and attitudes among primary care physicians. *Journal of the American Medical Association*, *302*(12), 1284–1293. DOI: 10.1001/jama.2009.1384 PMID: 19773563

Kristensen, T. S., Borritz, M., Villadsen, E., & Christensen, K. B. (2005). The Copenhagen Burnout Inventory: A new tool for the assessment of burnout. *Work and Stress*, *19*(3), 192–207. DOI: 10.1080/02678370500297720

Kutney-Lee, A.. (2009). Magnet hospital staff nurses report lower burnout and higher job satisfaction. *Health Affairs*, *28*(5), 144–153. DOI: 10.1377/hlthaff.28.5.144

Lalani, N. (2020). Meanings and Interpretations of Spirituality in Nursing and Health. *Religions*, *11*(9), 428. Advance online publication. DOI: 10.3390/rel11090428

Lambert, J., & Myers, S. (1999). *50 Activities for Conflict Resolution Group Learning and Self Development Exercises*. HRD Press.

Laschinger, H. K. S.. (2014). Workplace empowerment, incivility, and burnout: Impact on staff nurse recruitment and retention outcomes. *Journal of Nursing Management*, *22*(8), 1027–1038. DOI: 10.1111/jonm.12103 PMID: 23758834

Laschinger, H. K. S., & Leiter, M. P. (2006). The impact of nursing work environments on patient safety outcomes: The mediating role of burnout engagement. *The Journal of Nursing Administration*, *36*(12), 659–667. DOI: 10.1097/00005110-200605000-00019 PMID: 16705307

Laschinger, H. K. S., Wong, C. A., Cummings, G. G., & Grau, A. L. (2014). Resonant leadership and workplace empowerment: The value of positive organizational cultures in reducing workplace incivility. *Nursing Economics*, *32*(1), 5–16. PMID: 24689153

Legido-Quigley, H., Asgari, N., Teo, Y. Y., Leung, G. M., Oshitani, H., Fukuda, K., Cook, A. R., Hsu, L. Y., Shibuya, K., & Heymann, D. (2020). Are high-performing health systems resilient against the COVID-19 epidemic? *Lancet*, *395*(10227), 848–850. DOI: 10.1016/S0140-6736(20)30551-1 PMID: 32151326

Leonard, M.. (2004, October 1). The Human Factor: The Critical Importance of Effective Teamwork and Communication in Providing Safe Care. *Quality & Safety in Health Care, 13*(1, suppl_1), 85–90. qualitysafety.bmj.com/content/13/suppl_1/i85. DOI: 10.1136/qshc.2004.010033 PMID: 15465961

Liang, Y., Wang, H., & Tao, X. (2015). Quality of life of young clinical doctors in public hospitals in China's developed cities as measured by the Nottingham Health Profile (NHP). *International Journal for Equity in Health, 14*(1), 1–2. DOI: 10.1186/s12939-015-0199-2

Lim, M. C., Jeffree, M. S., Saupin, S. S., Giloi, N., & Lukman, K. A. (2022). Workplace violence in healthcare settings: The risk factors, implications and collaborative preventive measures. *Annals of Medicine and Surgery (London), 78*, 103727. Advance online publication. DOI: 10.1016/j.amsu.2022.103727 PMID: 35734684

Linzer, M., & Harwood, E. (2018). Gendered expectations: Do they contribute to high burnout among female physicians? *Journal of General Internal Medicine, 33*(6), 963–965. DOI: 10.1007/s11606-018-4330-0 PMID: 29435727

Linzer, M., Poplau, S., Babbott, S., Collins, T., Guzman-Corrales, L., Menk, J., Murphy, M. L., & Ovington, K. (2016). Worklife and wellness in academic general internal medicine: Results from a national survey. *Journal of General Internal Medicine, 31*(9), 1004–1010. DOI: 10.1007/s11606-016-3720-4

Lo, B., Quill, T., & Tulsky, J. (1999). Discussing palliative care with patients. *Annals of Internal Medicine, 130*(9), 744–749. DOI: 10.7326/0003-4819-130-9-199905040-00015 PMID: 10357694

Lockley, S. W., Landrigan, C. P., Barger, L. K., Czeisler, C. A., & Rothschild, J. M. (2007). Effects of reducing interns' weekly work hours on sleep and attentional failures. *PLoS Medicine, 4*(12), e262. DOI: 10.1371/journal.pmed.0040262

Lodhi, F. S., Montazeri, A., Nedjat, S., Mahmoodi, M., Farooq, U., Yaseri, M., Kasaeian, A., & Holakouie-Naieni, K. (2019). Assessing the quality of life among Pakistani general population and their associated factors by using the World Health Organization's quality of life instrument (WHOQOL-BREF): A population based cross-sectional study. *Health and Quality of Life Outcomes, 17*(1), 1–17. DOI: 10.1186/s12955-018-1065-x

López-Tarrida, Á. C., de Diego-Cordero, R., & Lima-Rodríguez, J. S. (2021). Spirituality in a Doctor's Practice: What Are the Issues? *Journal of Clinical Medicine, 10*(23), 5612. DOI: 10.3390/jcm10235612 PMID: 34884314

Lora, A.. (2020). Workforce training for integrated mental health care: A systematic review of programs and outcomes. *Journal of Mental Health (Abingdon, England)*, *29*(1), 12–20. DOI: 10.1080/09638237.2019.1670160 PMID: 28644705

Lucchese, F. A., & Koenig, H. G. (2013). Religion, spirituality and cardiovascular disease: Research, clinical implications, and opportunities in Brazil. *Brazilian Journal of Cardiovascular Surgery*, *28*(1), 103–128. DOI: 10.5935/1678-9741.20130015 PMID: 23739939

Lyubarova, R., Salman, L., & Rittenberg, E. (2023). Gender differences in physician burnout: Driving factors and potential solutions. *The Permanente Journal*, *27*(2), 130–136. DOI: 10.7812/TPP/23.023 PMID: 37303223

Madan, R., Das, N., Patley, R., Nagpal, N., Malik, Y., & Math, S. B. (2024). Consequences of medical negligence and litigations on health care providers – A narrative review. *Indian Journal of Psychiatry*, *66*(4), 317–325. DOI: 10.4103/indianjpsychiatry.indianjpsychiatry_799_23 PMID: 38778854

Maglalang, D. D., Sorensen, G., Hopcia, K., Hashimoto, D. M., Katigbak, C., Pandey, S., Takeuchi, D., & Sabbath, E. L. (2021). Job and family demands and burnout among healthcare workers: The moderating role of workplace flexibility. *SSM - Population Health*, *14*, 100802. Advance online publication. DOI: 10.1016/j.ssmph.2021.100802 PMID: 33997249

Mahmood, M. A., Yusof, N. M., Saidi, S., & Ahmad, A. C. (2023). The integration of islamic values in daily clinical practice among healthcare professionals: A scoping review. *IIUM Medical Journal Malaysia*, *22*(3). Advance online publication. DOI: 10.31436/imjm.v22i3.2273

Malik, A. U. (2015, March 19). Application of Systems Thinking in Health: Opportunities for Translating Theory into Practice Comment on “Constraints to Applying Systems Thinking Concepts in Health Systems: A Regional Perspective from Surveying Stakeholders in Eastern Mediterranean Countries.”. *International Journal of Health Policy and Management*, *4*(8), 537–539. Retrieved August 21, 2018, from. DOI: 10.15171/ijhpm.2015.69 PMID: 26340394

Malik, S., Riaz, N., & Nazir, S. (2015). Personal Spirituality and Work Attitudes Among Doctors. *Journal of Behavioural Sciences*, *25*(1). https://www.researchgate.net/profile/Sadia-Malik-2/publication/290974216_Personal_Spirituality_and_Work_Attitudes_Among_Doctors/links/590396180f7e9bc0d58d7d95/Personal-Spirituality-and-Work-Attitudes-Among-Doctors.pdf

Malloy, D., Fahey-McCarthy, E., Murakami, M., Lee, Y., Choi, E., Hirose, E., & Hadjistavropoulos, T. (2015). Finding Meaning in the Work of Nursing: An International Study. *Online Journal of Issues in Nursing*, *20*(3). Advance online publication. DOI: 10.3912/OJIN.Vol20No03PPT02 PMID: 26882516

Mannion, R., & Davies, H. T. O. (2018). Understanding organizational culture for healthcare quality improvement. *BMJ (Clinical Research Ed.)*, *363*, k4907. DOI: 10.1136/bmj.k4907 PMID: 30487286

Mao, L., Huang, L., & Chen, Q. (2021). Promoting resilience and lower stress in nurses and improving inpatient experience through emotional intelligence training in China: A randomized controlled trial. *Nurse Education Today*, *107*, 105–130. DOI: 10.1016/j.nedt.2021.105130 PMID: 34543939

Mark, B. A., Harless, D. W., McCue, M., & Xu, Y. (2013). Effects of state minimum staffing legislation on hospital nurse staffing and patient outcomes: A synthesis of evidence from California's staffing mandate. *Nursing Research*, *62*(2), 79–92. DOI: 10.1097/NNR.0b013e318286566b

Marques, J., Dhiman, S., & King, R. (2005). Spirituality in the workplace: Developing an integral model and a comprehensive definition. *Journal of American Academy of Business*, *7*(1), 81-91.://www.academia.edu/61249074/Spirituality_in_the_Workplace_Developing_an_Integral_Model_and_a_Comprehensive_Definition?source=swp_share

Marshall, A. P., Austin, D. E., Chamberlain, D., & New, K. (2021). Burnout and emotional intelligence in emergency department nurses: A review. *Journal of Nursing Management*, *29*(2), 241–251. DOI: 10.1111/jonm.13126

Marx, D. (2001). *Patient safety and the "just culture": A primer for health care executives*. Columbia University.

Maslach, C. & Schaufeli, WB. (1993). Historical and conceptual development of burnout. Prof Burnout .1–16.

Maslach, C. (2003). Job burnout: New directions in research and intervention. *Current Directions in Psychological Science*, *12*(5), 189–192. DOI: 10.1111/1467-8721.01258

Maslach, C., & Jackson, S. E. (1981). The measurement of experienced burnout. *Journal of Organizational Behavior*, *2*(2), 99–113. DOI: 10.1002/job.4030020205

Maslach, C., Jackson, S. E., & Leiter, M. P. (1997). Maslach Burnout Inventory. In Zalaquett, C. P., & Wood, R. J. (Eds.), *Evaluating stress: A book of resources* (3rd ed., pp. 191–218). Scarecrow Press.

Maslach, C., & Leiter, M. P. (2016). Understanding the burnout experience: Recent research and its implications for psychiatry. *World Psychiatry; Official Journal of the World Psychiatric Association (WPA), 15*(2), 103–111. DOI: 10.1002/wps.20311 PMID: 27265691

Maslow, A. (1954). *Motivation and personality*. Harper & Row.

Masood, A., Salik, S., & Masroor, U. (2022). Relationship of Occupational Stress with Psychosomatic Symptoms and Mental Wellbeing in Medical Professionals: An Exploratory Study. [JDUHS]. *Journal of the Dow University of Health Sciences, 17*(1), 36–42. DOI: 10.36570/jduhs.2023.1.1655

Mathews, S. C., Demski, R., & Pronovost, P. J. (2016). Management's discussion and analysis: A tool for advancing quality and safety. *Health Care, 4*(3), 129–131. DOI: 10.1016/j.hjdsi.2016.02.006 PMID: 27637813

Mayer, J., Roberts, R., & Barsade, S. (2008). Human abilities: Emotional intelligence. *Annual Review of Psychology, 59*(1), 507–536. DOI: 10.1146/annurev.psych.59.103006.093646 PMID: 17937602

Mayer, J., & Salovey, P. (1993). The intelligence of emotional intelligence. *Intelligence, 17*(4), 433–442. DOI: 10.1016/0160-2896(93)90010-3

McClelland, D. C. (1961). *The achieving society*. Van Nostrand. DOI: 10.1037/14359-000

McCormick, T. R., Min, D., & Rosenblatt, D. E. (2012). Ethics committees and consultation. In Field, M. J., & Behrman, R. E. (Eds.), *When children die: Improving palliative and end-of-life care for children and their families* (pp. 201–228). National Academies Press.

McEwen, B. S. (1998). Stress, adaptation, and disease: Allostasis and allostatic load. *Annals of the New York Academy of Sciences, 840*(1), 33–44. DOI: 10.1111/j.1749-6632.1998.tb09546.x PMID: 9629234

McEwen, B. S. (2008). Central effects of stress hormones in health and disease: Understanding the protective and damaging effects of stress and stress mediators. *European Journal of Pharmacology, 583*(2-3), 174–185. DOI: 10.1016/j.ejphar.2007.11.071 PMID: 18282566

McGregor, D. (1960). *The human side of enterprise*. McGraw-Hill.

McHugh, M. D.. (2011). Nurse engagement in hospital quality improvement: A multi-level analysis. *Health Services Research, 46*(3), 903–920. DOI: 10.1111/j.1475-6773.2010.01220.x

McKevitt, C., & Morgan, M. (1997). Illness doesn't belong to us. *Journal of the Royal Society of Medicine, 90*(9), 491–495. DOI: 10.1177/014107689709000907 PMID: 9370984

McKibben, L. (2017). Conflict management: Importance and implications. *British Journal of Nursing (Mark Allen Publishing), 26*(2), 100–103. DOI: 10.12968/bjon.2017.26.2.100 PMID: 28132555

McNeely, E. (2005). The consequences of job stress for nurses' health: Time for a check-up. *Nursing Outlook, 53*(6), 291–299. DOI: 10.1016/j.outlook.2005.10.001 PMID: 16360700

Meier, D. E. (2001). The inner life of physicians and care of the seriously ill. *Journal of the American Medical Association, 286*(23), 3007. DOI: 10.1001/jama.286.23.3007 PMID: 11743845

Meijman, T. F., & Mulder, G. (1998). Psychological aspects of workload. In Drenth, P. J., Thierry, H., & de Wolff, C. J. (Eds.), *Handbook of work and organizational psychology: Work psychology* (2nd ed., Vol. 2, pp. 5–33). Psychology Press.

Mendelsohn, D. (2022). Self in medicine: Determinants of physician well-being and future directions in improving wellness. *Medical Education, 56*(1), 48–55. DOI: 10.1111/medu.14671 PMID: 34559421

Merlino, J. (2014). *Service fanatics: How to build superior patient experience the Cleveland Clinic way*. McGraw-Hill Education.

Merriam-Webster. (n.d.). Confidence. In Merriam-Webster.com dictionary. Retrieved June 2, 2025, from https://www.merriam-webster.com/dictionary/confidence

Merriam-Webster. (n.d.). Conflict. In Merriam-Webster.com dictionary. Retrieved June 2, 2025. https://www.merriam-webster.com/dictionary/conflict

Merriam-Webster. (n.d.). *Governance*. In *Merriam-Webster.com dictionary*. https://www.merriam-webster.com/dictionary/governance

Mickley, J. R., Soeken, K., & Belcher, A. (1992). Spiritual well-being, religiousness and hope among women with breast cancer. [Abstract]. *Image—the Journal of Nursing Scholarship, 24*(4), 267–272. DOI: 10.1111/j.1547-5069.1992.tb00732.x PMID: 1452180

Milliman, J., Czaplewski, A. J., & Ferguson, J. (2003). Workplace spirituality and employee work attitudes: An exploratory empirical assessment. *Journal of Organizational Change Management, 16*(4), 426–447. DOI: 10.1108/09534810310484172

Miranda-Ackerman, R. C., Barbosa-Camacho, F. J., Sander-Möller, M. J., Buenrostro-Jiménez, A. D., Mares-País, R., Cortes-Flores, A. O., Morgan-Villela, G., Zuloaga-Fernández del Valle, C. J., Solano-Genesta, M., Fuentes-Orozco, C., Cervantes-Cardona, G. A., Cervantes-Guevara, G., & González-Ojeda, A. (2019). Burnout syndrome prevalence during internship in public and private hospitals: A survey study in Mexico. *Medical Education Online*, *24*(1), 1593785. DOI: 10.1080/10872981.2019.1593785

Mirror. (2021). Mirror 2021: Reflecting Poorly: Health care in the U.S. Compared to Other High-Income Countries. National Library of Medicine. https://collections.nlm.nih.gov/catalog/nlm:nlmuid-9918300978506676-pdf

Mitra, L. G., Sharma, J., & Walia, H. S. (2024). Improving work–life balance and satisfaction to improve patient care. *Indian Journal of Critical Care Medicine : Peer-Reviewed, Official Publication of Indian Society of Critical Care Medicine*, *28*(4), 326–328. DOI: 10.5005/jp-journals-10071-24689 PMID: 38585310

Moberg, D. O. (2010). Spirituality research: Measuring the immeasurable? *Perspectives on Science and Christian Faith*, *62*(2). https://www.researchgate.net/profile/David-Moberg/publication/265037799_Spirituality_Research_Measuring_the_Immeasurable/links/551b17190cf2fdce843865c2/Spirituality-Research-Measuring-the-Immeasurable.pdf

Montero-Marín, J. (2016). El síndrome de burnout y sus diferentes manifestaciones clínicas: Una propuesta para la intervención [The burnout syndrome and its different clinical manifestations: A proposal for intervention]. *Anestesia, Analgesia, Reanimación*, *29*(1), 1–16.

Montero-Marín, J., Skapinakis, P., Araya, R., Gili, M., & García-Campayo, J. (2011). Towards a brief definition of burnout syndrome by subtypes: Development of the "Burnout Clinical Subtypes Questionnaire" (BCSQ-12). *Health and Quality of Life Outcomes*, *9*(1), 74. DOI: 10.1186/1477-7525-9-74 PMID: 21933381

Montgomery, A. (2014). The inevitability of physician burnout: Implications for interventions. *Burnout Research*, *1*(1), 50–56. DOI: 10.1016/j.burn.2014.04.002

Moradi, T., Maghaminejad, F., & Azizi-Fini, I. (2014). Quality of working life of nurses and its related factors. *Nursing and Midwifery Studies*, *3*(2), e19450. DOI: 10.5812/nms.19450

Moreira-Almeida, A., Sharma, A., Van Rensburg, B., Verhagen, P., & Cook, C. (2016). WPA Position Statement on Spirituality and Religion in Psychiatry. *World Psychiatry; Official Journal of the World Psychiatric Association (WPA)*, *15*(1), 87–88. Advance online publication. DOI: 10.1002/wps.20304 PMID: 26833620

Morgan, G. (1986). *Images of organization.* Sage Publications.

Mosadeghrad, A. M., Ferlie, E., & Rosenberg, D. (2011). A study of relationship between job stress, quality of working life and turnover intention among hospital employees. *Health Services Management Research, 24*(4), 170–181. DOI: 10.1258/hsmr.2011.011009

Moss, M., Good, V. S., Gozal, D., Kleinpell, R., & Sessler, C. N. (2016). An official critical care societies collaborative statement: Burnout syndrome in critical care healthcare professionals: A call for action. *American Journal of Critical Care, 25*(4), 368–376. DOI: 10.4037/ajcc2016133 PMID: 27369038

Mosteller, F., & Falotico-Taylor, J. (1989). *Quality of life and technology assessment.* National Academy Press.

Muething, S. E., Goudie, A., Schoettker, P. J., Donnelly, L. F., Goodfriend, M. A., Bracke, T. M., Brady, P. W., Wheeler, D. S., Anderson, J. M., & Kotagal, U. R. (2012). Quality improvement initiative to reduce serious safety events and improve patient safety culture. *Pediatrics, 130*(2), e423–e431. DOI: 10.1542/peds.2011-3566 PMID: 22802607

Mukinda, F. K., Van Belle, S., & Schneider, H. (2020). Accountability experiences of frontline health managers. *International Journal for Equity in Health, 19*(1), 110. DOI: 10.1186/s12939-020-01229-w PMID: 32611355

National Academies of Sciences, Engineering, and Medicine; National Academy of Medicine; Committee on Systems Approaches to Improve Patient Care by Supporting Clinician Well-Being. (2019). Taking Action Against Clinician Burnout: A Systems Approach to Professional Well-Being. In *PubMed.* National Academies Press (US). https://pubmed.ncbi.nlm.nih.gov/31940160/

National Academy of Medicine. (2020). *Taking action against clinician burnout: A systems approach to professional well-being.* National Academies Press.

Neff, K. D. (2023). Self-compassion: Theory, method, research, and intervention. *Annual Review of Psychology, 74*(1), 193–218. DOI: 10.1146/annurev-psych-032420-031047 PMID: 35961039

Nélis, D., Quoidbach, J., Mikolajczak, M., & Hansenne, M. (2009). Increasing emotional intelligence: (How) is it possible? *Personality and Individual Differences, 47*(1), 36–41. DOI: 10.1016/j.paid.2009.01.046

Nelson, B. (2010). Spirituality, leadership, and organizational culture: The development of spiritual intelligence. *Journal of Management Development, 29*(3), 218–230. DOI: 10.1108/02621711011025355

Nelson, E. C., Batalden, P. B., & Godfrey, M. M. (2011). *Quality By Design*. John Wiley & Sons.

NetSuite. (2025, February 6). What is automation in healthcare? How does it help? *NetSuite*. https://www.netsuite.com/portal/resource/articles/erp/healthcare-automation.shtml (netsuite.com)

Newberg, A., & Waldman, M. R. (2009). *How God changes your brain: Breakthrough findings from a leading neuroscientist*. Ballantine Books.

Ng, A. Y., Oberije, C. J. G., Ambrózay, É., Szabó, E., Serfőző, O., Karpati, E., Fox, G., Glocker, B., Morris, E. A., Forrai, G., & Kecskemethy, P. D. (2023). Prospective implementation of AI-assisted screen reading to improve early detection of breast cancer. *Nature Medicine*, *29*(12), 3044–3049. DOI: 10.1038/s41591-023-02625-9 PMID: 37973948

Nicholls, M. (2019). *Cardiologists and the burnout scenario*. Oxford University Press. DOI: 10.1093/eurheartj/ehy788

Nilsson, H. (2022). Spiritual Self-Care Management for Nursing Professionals: A Holistic Approach. *Journal of holistic nursing: official journal of the American Holistic Nurses'. Journal of Holistic Nursing*, *40*(1), 64–73. DOI: 10.1177/08980101211034341 PMID: 34287073

O'Brien, N., Flott, K., Bray, O., Shaw, A., & Durkin, M. (2022). Implementation of initiatives designed to improve healthcare worker health and wellbeing during the COVID-19 pandemic: Comparative case studies from 13 healthcare provider organisations globally. *Globalization and Health*, *18*(1), 24. Advance online publication. DOI: 10.1186/s12992-022-00818-4 PMID: 35193629

Odigie, A. (2016). STRESS MANAGEMENT FOR HEALTHCARE PROFESSIONALS.

Organisation for Economic Co-operation and Development. (2023). *Public sector governance and organizational resilience*. Organisation for Economic Co-operation and Development.

Oswald, A. J., Proto, E., & Sgroi, D. (2023). Happiness and productivity revisited. *Journal of Economic Behavior & Organization*, *209*, 105–120. DOI: 10.1016/j.jebo.2023.03.004

Ouliaris, C. (2019). The importance of self-awareness: Musings of a medical student. *Australasian Psychiatry*, *27*(3), 267–269. DOI: 10.1177/1039856219839479 PMID: 30931586

Panagioti, M., Geraghty, K., Johnson, J., Zhou, A., Panagopoulou, E., Chew-Graham, C., & Esmail, A. (2018). Association between physician burnout and patient safety, professionalism, and patient satisfaction: A systematic review and meta-analysis. *JAMA Internal Medicine*, *178*(10), 1317–1330. DOI: 10.1001/jamainternmed.2018.3713 PMID: 30193239

Panda, S., & Patnaik, B. (2021). Corporate governance and organizational performance: A systematic review. *The International Journal of Organizational Analysis*, *29*(3), 897–915. DOI: 10.1108/IJOA-03-2020-2092

Papathanasiou, I. V., Papathanasiou, C., Malli, F., Tsaras, K., Papagiannis, D., Kontopoulou, L., Kourkouta, L., Tsalogliodou, A., Tzavella, F., & Fradelos, E. C. (2020). The effect of Spirituality on Mental Health among Hypertensive elderly people: A Cross-sectional Community-based Study. *Materia Socio-Medica*, *32*(3), 218. DOI: 10.5455/msm.2020.32.218-223 PMID: 33424452

Pardini, D. A., Plante, T. G., Sherman, A., & Stump, J. E. (2000). Religious faith and spirituality in substance abuse recovery: Determining the mental health benefits. *Journal of Substance Abuse Treatment*, *19*(4), 347–354. DOI: 10.1016/S0740-5472(00)00125-2 PMID: 11166499

Parent, A., & Parent, A. (2011, November 2). *Physician Executive Career Options Abound - NEJM CareerCenter Resources*. NEJM CareerCenter Resources. https://resources.nejmcareercenter.org/article/physician-executive-career-options-abound

Pargament, K. I. (1997). *The psychology of religion and coping: Theory, research, practice*. Guilford Press.

Pargament, K. I. (2007). *Spiritually integrated psychotherapy: Understanding and addressing the sacred*. Guilford Press.

Parikh, J. R., Wolfman, D., Bender, C. E., & Arleo, E. (2020). Radiologist burnout according to surveyed radiology practice leaders. *Journal of the American College of Radiology*, *17*(1), 78–81. DOI: 10.1016/j.jacr.2019.07.008

Parks-Savage, A., Archer, L., Newton, H., Wheeler, E., & Huband, S. R. (2018). Prevention of medical errors and malpractice: Is creating resilience in physicians part of the answer? *International Journal of Law and Psychiatry*, *60*, 35–39. DOI: 10.1016/j.ijlp.2018.07.003 PMID: 30217328

Patel, V.. (2011). The mental health treatment gap in low- and middle-income countries: A systematic review. *Bulletin of the World Health Organization*, *89*(9), 658–666. DOI: 10.2471/BLT.07.045479

Patel, V.. (2018). Integrating mental health into primary care: A global perspective. *Lancet*, *392*(10161), 1553–1567. DOI: 10.1016/S0140-6736(18)31612-X PMID: 30314863

Patrician, P. A., Shang, J., & Lake, E. T. (2019). The Magnet recognition program: Nursing excellence and implications for care outcomes. *The Journal of Nursing Administration*, *49*(10), 511–518. DOI: 10.1097/NNA.0000000000000789

Paul, J. (2024). Strategies for Effective Crisis Management in Healthcare Systems: Patient Safety and Lessons Learned. *Medical Research Archives*, *12*(7). Advance online publication. DOI: 10.18103/mra.v12i7.5424

Peccei, R., & Van De Voorde, K. (2019). The application of the mutual gains model in HRM–well-being–performance research. *Human Resource Management Journal*, *29*(3), 539–563. DOI: 10.1111/1748-8583.12254

Permana, I. (2018). How Religosity and/or spirituality might influence self-Care in Diabetes Management: A structured review. *Bangladesh Journal of Medical Science*, *17*(2), 185–193. DOI: 10.3329/bjms.v17i2.35869

Peselow, E., Pi, S., Lopez, E., Besada, A., & IsHak, W. W. (2014). The impact of spirituality before and after treatment of major depressive disorder. *Innovations in Clinical Neuroscience*, *11*(3-4), 17. https://pmc.ncbi.nlm.nih.gov/articles/PMC4008297/pdf/icns_11_3_17.pdf PMID: 24800129

Pew Research Center. (2024, November 13). Internet/Broadband Fact Sheet. Pew Research Center: Internet, Science & Tech; Pew Research Center. https://www.pewresearch.org/internet/fact-sheet/internet-broadband/

Piryani, R., & Piryani, S. (2019). Conflict Management in Healthcare. *Journal of Nepal Health Research Council*, *16*(41), 481–482. DOI: 10.33314/jnhrc.v16i41.1703 PMID: 30739920

Plsek, P. E., & Greenhalgh, T. (2001). Complexity science: The challenge of complexity in health care. *BMJ (Clinical Research Ed.)*, *323*(7313), 625–628. DOI: 10.1136/bmj.323.7313.625 PMID: 11557716

Poncet, M. C., Toullic, P., Papazian, L., Kentish-Barnes, N., Timsit, J.-F., Pochard, F., Chevret, S., Schlemmer, B., & Azoulay, É. (2007). Burnout syndrome in critical care nursing staff. *American Journal of Respiratory and Critical Care Medicine*, *175*(7), 698–704. DOI: 10.1164/rccm.200606-806OC PMID: 17110646

Post, M. (2014). Definitions of quality of life: What has happened and how to move on. *Topics in Spinal Cord Injury Rehabilitation*, *20*(3), 167–180. DOI: 10.1310/sci2003-167

Pouyan, N. (2016). Mesopotamia, the cradle of civilization and medicine. *World Journal of Pharmaceutical Research*, *5*(4), 192–225. DOI: 10.20959/wjpr20164-5895

Powers, D. V., Cramer, R. J., & Grubka, J. M. (2007). Spirituality, Life Stress, and Affective Well-Being. *Journal of Psychology and Theology*, *35*(3), 235–243. DOI: 10.1177/009164710703500306

Pronovost, P., Needham, D., Berenholtz, S., Sinopoli, D., Chu, H., Cosgrove, S., Sexton, B., Hyzy, R., Welsh, R., Roth, G., Bander, J., Kepros, J., & Goeschel, C. (2006). An intervention to decrease catheter-related bloodstream infections in the ICU. *The New England Journal of Medicine*, *355*(26), 2725–2732. DOI: 10.1056/NEJMoa061115 PMID: 17192537

Puchalski, C. M., Vitillo, R., Hull, S. K., & Reller, N. (2014). Improving the spiritual dimension of whole person care: Reaching national and international consensus. *Journal of Palliative Medicine*, *17*(6), 642–656. DOI: 10.1089/jpm.2014.9427 PMID: 24842136

Puni, A., & Hilton, S. K. (2020). Dimensions of authentic leadership and patient care quality. *Leadership in Health Services (Bradford, England)*, *33*(4), 441–456. DOI: 10.1108/LHS-11-2019-0071

Putnam, R. D. (2000). *Bowling alone: The collapse and revival of American community*. Simon & Schuster.

Qamar, M. K., Sheikh, B. T., Kumar, R., & Armaghana, K. Q. (2024). Gender difference of burnout in physicians working in tertiary care hospital: A cross-sectional study. *Journal of the College of Physicians and Surgeons—Pakistan*, *34*(05), 620–622. DOI: 10.29271/jcpsp.2024.05.620 PMID: 38720228

Qidwai, M. A. (2024). The 5Ss' Approach for Managing Health of Client, Family, and Community. *National Journal of Health Sciences*, *9*(4), 231–234. DOI: 10.21089/njhs.94.0231

Qidwai, W., & Tayyab, A. (2004). Patients' views about physicians' spiritual role in medical practice. [Abstract]. *Journal of the College of Physicians and Surgeons—Pakistan*, *14*(8), 462–465. https://ecommons.aku.edu/pakistan_fhs_mc_fam_med/142/ PMID: 15382344

Rahula, W. (2007). *What the Buddha taught*. Open Road + Grove/Atlantic.

Rainey, R. M., & Tanzer, K. (2020). Spiritual Spaces. *SiteLINES: A Journal of Place*, *16*(1), 17-20. https://www.jstor.org/stable/26934719

Ratna, H. (2019). *The Importance of Effective Communication in Healthcare Practice*. HPHR Journal., DOI: 10.54111/0001/W4

Reave, L. (2005). Spiritual values and practices related to leadership effectiveness. *The Leadership Quarterly*, *16*(5), 655–687. DOI: 10.1016/j.leaqua.2005.07.003

Reinert, K. G., & Koenig, H. G. (2013). Re-examining definitions of spirituality in nursing research. *Journal of Advanced Nursing*, *69*(12), 2622–2634. DOI: 10.1111/jan.12152 PMID: 23600849

Reith, T. P. (2018). Burnout in United States healthcare professionals: A narrative review. *Cureus*, *10*(12), e3681. DOI: 10.7759/cureus.3681 PMID: 30761233

Research, T. (2023, September 27). *How Healthcare Standardization Helps Improve Patient Safety*. Think Research Canada. https://www.thinkresearch.com/ca/2023/09/27/how-healthcare-standardization-helps-improve-patient-safety/

Restauri, N., & Sheridan, A. D. (2020). Burnout and posttraumatic stress disorder in the COVID-19 pandemic: Intersection, impact, and interventions. *Journal of the American College of Radiology*, *17*(7), 921–926. DOI: 10.1016/j.jacr.2020.05.021 PMID: 32479798

Rider, E. A., Gilligan, M. C., Osterberg, L. G., Litzelman, D. K., Plews-Ogan, M., Weil, A. B., Dunne, D. W., Hafler, J. P., May, N. B., Derse, A. R., Frankel, R. M., & Branch, W. T.Jr. (2018). Healthcare at the crossroads: The need to shape an organizational culture of humanistic teaching and practice. *Journal of General Internal Medicine*, *33*(7), 1092–1099. DOI: 10.1007/s11606-018-4470-2

Riggenbach, J. (2013). *The CBT Toolbox: A Workbook for Clients and Clinicians. Premier Publishing and Media*. CMI Education Institute, Inc.

Ring, D. C., Herndon, J. H., & Meyer, G. S. (2010). Case 34-2010. *The New England Journal of Medicine*, *363*(20), 1950–1957. DOI: 10.1056/NEJMcpc1007085 PMID: 21067387

Robinson, J. D., & Gottlieb, S. (1999). The new face of medical education. *Journal of the American Medical Association*, *281*(13), 1226. PMID: 10199435

Rodriquez, E. J., Kim, E. N., Sumner, A. E., Nápoles, A. M., & Pérez-Stable, E. J. (2019). Allostatic load: Importance, markers, and score determination in minority and disparity populations. *Journal of Urban Health*, *96*(S1), 3–11. DOI: 10.1007/s11524-019-00345-5 PMID: 30671711

Rogers, M., Windle, A., Wu, L., Taylor, V., & Bale, C. (2022). Emotional well-being, spiritual well-being and resilience of advanced clinical practitioners in the United Kingdom during COVID-19: An exploratory mixed method study. *Journal of Nursing Management, 30*(4), 883–891. DOI: 10.1111/jonm.13577 PMID: 35261097

Rojas, D., Seghieri, C., & Nuti, S. (2014). Organizational climate: Comparing private and public hospitals within professional roles. *Suma De Negocios, 5*(SPE11), 10–14. https://doi.org/DOI: 10.1016/S2215-910X(14)70003-3

Rosenbaum, L. (2020). Facing Covid-19 in Italy—Ethics, logistics, and therapeutics on the epidemic's front line. *The New England Journal of Medicine, 382*(20), 1873–1875. DOI: 10.1056/NEJMp2005492 PMID: 32187459

Rotenstein, L., Harry, E., Wickner, P., Gupte, A., Neville, B. A., Lipsitz, S., Cullen, E., Rozenblum, R., Sequist, T. D., & Dudley, J. (2021). Contributors to gender differences in burnout and professional fulfillment: A survey of physician faculty. *Joint Commission Journal on Quality and Patient Safety, 47*(11), 723–730. DOI: 10.1016/j.jcjq.2021.08.002 PMID: 34507905

Ruiz-Fernández, M. D., Pérez-García, E., & Ortega-Galán, Á. M. (2020). Quality of life in nursing professionals: Burnout, fatigue, and compassion satisfaction. *International Journal of Environmental Research and Public Health, 17*(4), 1253. DOI: 10.3390/ijerph17041253

Ryan, R. M., & Deci, E. L. (2020). Intrinsic and extrinsic motivation from a self-determination theory perspective: Definitions, theory, practices, and future directions. *Contemporary Educational Psychology, 61*, 101860. Advance online publication. DOI: 10.1016/j.cedpsych.2020.101860

Saad, M., & de Medeiros, R. (2021). Spirituality and Healthcare—Common Grounds for the Secular and Religious Worlds and Its Clinical Implications. *Religions, 12*(1), 22. DOI: 10.3390/rel12010022

Sabo, B. M., & Vachon, M. L. S. (2011). Care of professional caregivers. In Davis, M. P., Feyer, P. C., Ortner, P., & Zimmermann, C. (Eds.), *Supportive oncology* (pp. 575–589). Elsevier Saunders., DOI: 10.1016/B978-1-4377-1015-1.00056-4

Sacopulos, M., & Greeter, A. (2023). Effective Crisis Leadership in Healthcare. *Physician Leadership Journal, 10*(5), 60–62. Advance online publication. DOI: 10.55834/plj.7146928492

Sahni, N. R., Carrus, B., & Cutler, D. M. (2021, October 20). Administrative simplification: How to save a quarter-trillion dollars in US healthcare. McKinsey & Company. https://www.mckinsey.com/industries/healthcare/our-insights/administrative-simplification-how-to-save-a-quarter-trillion-dollars-in-us-healthcare

Sahni, N. R., Gupta, P., Peterson, M., & Cutler, D. M. (2023). Active steps to reduce administrative spending associated with financial transactions in US health care. *Health Affairs Scholar*, *1*(5), qxad053. Advance online publication. DOI: 10.1093/haschl/qxad053 PMID: 38756977

Sahu, N., Sriram, S., Samrat, B., Jayakumar, S., Choudhary, A., Garg, A., & Naregal, P. (2024). *Assessing Healthcare Leadership Competencies in Crisis Management*. Health Leadership and Quality of Life., DOI: 10.56294/hl2024.371

Saikia, M., George, L., Unnikrishnan, B., Nayak, B., & Ravishankar, N. (2023). Thirty years of emotional intelligence: A scoping review of emotional intelligence training programme among nurses. *International Journal of Mental Health Nursing*. Advance online publication. DOI: 10.1111/inm.13235 PMID: 37772479

Salas-Vallina, A., Alegre, J., & Fernández, R. (2021). Organizational learning and health. *Personnel Review*, *50*(5), 1233–1250.

Salas-Vallina, A., Alegre, J., & Fernández, R. (2021). Organizational learning capability and organizational health: The role of employee well-being and engagement. *Personnel Review*, *50*(5), 1233–1250. DOI: 10.1108/PR-07-2019-0391

Salmoirago-Blotcher, E., Fitchett, G., Leung, K., Volturo, G., Boudreaux, E., Crawford, S., Ockene, I., & Curlin, F. (2016). An exploration of the role of religion/spirituality in the promotion of physicians' wellbeing in Emergency Medicine. *Preventive Medicine Reports*, *3*, 189–195. DOI: 10.1016/j.pmedr.2016.01.009 PMID: 27419014

Salovey, P., & Grewal, D. (2005). The Science of Emotional Intelligence. *Current Directions in Psychological Science*, *14*(6), 281–285. DOI: 10.1111/j.0963-7214.2005.00381.x

Salovey, P., & Mayer, J. D. (1990). Emotional intelligence. *Imagination, Cognition and Personality*, *9*(3), 185–211. DOI: 10.2190/DUGG-P24E-52WK-6CDG

Santo, L., Michaux, R., & Pohl, S. (2024). The Effect of Emotional Coworker Support on Work Engagement Among Pediatric Health Care Providers: The Mediator Role of Emotional Regulation. *Western Journal of Nursing Research*, *1939459241296965*(12), 963–969. Advance online publication. DOI: 10.1177/01939459241296965

Saraji, G. N., & Dargahi, H. (2006). Study of quality of work life (QWL). *Iranian Journal of Public Health*, *35*(4), 8–14.

Satheeskumar, R. (2025). AI-driven diagnostics and personalized treatment planning in oral oncology: Innovations and future directions. [sciencedirect.com]. *Oral Oncology Reports*, *13*, 100704. DOI: 10.1016/j.oor.2024.100704

Saud, J., & Rice, J. (2024). Stress, Teamwork, and Wellbeing Policies: A Synergistic Approach to Reducing Burnout in Public Sector Organizations. *Administrative Sciences*, *14*(12), 319. DOI: 10.3390/admsci14120319

Savickas, M. (2019). *Career construction theory: Life portraits of attachment, adaptability, and identity*. Mark L. Savickas.

Saxena, S., Thornicroft, G., Knapp, M., & Whiteford, H. (2007). Resources for mental health: Scarcity, inequity, and inefficiency. *Lancet*, *370*(9590), 878–889. DOI: 10.1016/S0140-6736(07)61239-2 PMID: 17804062

Schaufeli, W. B., Bakker, A. B., & Sixma, H. J. (2011). Stability and change in burnout: A 10-year follow-up study among primary care physicians. *Journal of Occupational and Organizational Psychology*, *84*(2), 248–267. DOI: 10.1111/j.2044-8325.2010.02013.x

Schaufeli, W. B., Desart, S., & De Witte, H. (2020). Burnout Assessment Tool (BAT)—Development, validity, and reliability. *International Journal of Environmental Research and Public Health*, *17*(24), 9495. Advance online publication. DOI: 10.3390/ijerph17249495 PMID: 33352940

Schein, E. H. (2010). *Organizational Culture and Leadership (4th ed.). San Francisco, CA Jossey-Bass. - References - Scientific Research Publishing*. Www.scirp.org. https://www.scirp.org/reference/ReferencesPapers?ReferenceID=1848176

Schein, E. H. (2010). *Organizational culture and leadership* (4th ed.). Jossey-Bass.

Schoenthaler, S. J., Blum, K., Braverman, E. R., Giordano, J., Thompson, B., Oscar-Berman, M., Badgaiyan, R. D., Madigan, M. A., Dushaj, K., Li, M., Demotrovics, Z., Waite, R. L., & Gold, M. S. (2015). NIDA-Drug Addiction Treatment Outcome Study (DATOS) Relapse as a Function of Spirituality/Religiosity. *Journal of Reward Deficiency Syndrome*, *1*(1), 36–45. DOI: 10.17756/jrds.2015-007 PMID: 26052556

Schwartz Center. (2020). *Peer support program: A model for second victim recovery*. The Schwartz Center for Compassionate Healthcare. Retrieved from https://www.theschwartzcenter.org

Scott, T., Mannion, R., Davies, H., & Marshall, M. (2003). The quantitative measurement of organizational culture in health care: A review of the available instruments. *Health Services Research*, *38*(3), 923–945. DOI: 10.1111/1475-6773.00154 PMID: 12822919

Sedikides, C., Gaertner, L., Luke, M. A., O'Mara, E. M., & Gebauer, J. E. (2013). Self-potency hierarchy. In Vol. 48, pp. 235–295). Advances in Experimental Social Psychology. Academic Press.

Senge, P. M. (1990). *The Fifth Discipline*. Broadway Business.

Sexton, J. B., Thomas, E. J., & Helmreich, R. L. (2000). Error, stress, and teamwork in medicine and aviation. *BMJ (Clinical Research Ed.)*, *320*(7237), 745–749. DOI: 10.1136/bmj.320.7237.745 PMID: 10720356

Shanafelt, T. D., Boone, S., Tan, L., Dyrbye, L. N., Sotile, W., Satele, D., West, C. P., Sloan, J., & Oreskovich, M. R. (2012). Burnout and satisfaction with work-life balance among US physicians relative to the general US population. *Archives of Internal Medicine*, *172*(18), 1377–1385. DOI: 10.1001/archinternmed.2012.3199 PMID: 22911330

Shanafelt, T. D., Bradley, K. A., Wipf, J. E., & Back, A. L. (2002). Burnout and self-reported patient care in an internal medicine residency program. *Annals of Internal Medicine*, *136*(5), 358–367. DOI: 10.7326/0003-4819-136-5-200203050-00008

Shanafelt, T. D., Hasan, O., Dyrbye, L. N., Sinsky, C., Satele, D., Sloan, J., & West, C. P. (2015). Changes in burnout and satisfaction with work-life balance in physicians and the general US working population between 2011 and 2014. *Mayo Clinic Proceedings*, *90*(12), 1600–1613. DOI: 10.1016/j.mayocp.2015.08.023 PMID: 26653297

Shanafelt, T. D., Mungo, M., Schmitgen, J., Storz, K. A., Reeves, D., Hayes, S. N., Sloan, J. A., Swensen, S. J., & Buskirk, S. J. (2016). Longitudinal study evaluating the association between physician burnout and changes in professional work effort. *Mayo Clinic Proceedings*, *91*(4), 422–431. DOI: 10.1016/j.mayocp.2016.02.001

Shanafelt, T. D., & Noseworthy, J. H. (2017). Executive leadership and physician well-being. *Mayo Clinic Proceedings*, *92*(1), 129–146. DOI: 10.1016/j.mayocp.2016.10.004 PMID: 27871627

Shanafelt, T. D., West, C. P., & Satele, D.. (2017). Burnout and satisfaction with work-life balance among US physicians relative to the general US population. *PeerJ*, *5*, e3246. DOI: 10.7717/peerj.3246

Shanafelt, T. D., West, C. P., Sloan, J. A., Novotny, P. J., Poland, G. A., Menaker, R., & Swartz, H. A. (2020). Changes in burnout and professional satisfaction with an innovative physician well-being program: Mayo Clinic 2015–2019. *Mayo Clinic Proceedings*, *95*(12), 2590–2603. DOI: 10.1016/j.mayocp.2020.06.010

Shapiro, S., Astin, J., Bishop, S., & Cordova, M. (2005). Mindfulness-Based Stress Reduction \ for Health Care Professionals: Results From a Randomized Trial. *International Journal of Stress Management, 12*(2), 164–176. DOI: 10.1037/1072-5245.12.2.164

Shchyrina, K., Koshova, S., & Parkhomenko-Kutsevil, O. (2022). Foreign experience of anti-crisis management of medical institutions. ScienceRise. *Medical Science*, (2(47)), 49–54. Advance online publication. DOI: 10.15587/2519-4798.2022.256383

Shirom, A., & Melamed, S. (2006). A comparison of the construct validity of two burnout measures in two groups of professionals. *International Journal of Stress Management, 13*(2), 176–200. DOI: 10.1037/1072-5245.13.2.176

Shrank, W. H., Rogstad, T. L., & Parekh, N. (2019). Waste in the US health care system: Estimated costs and potential for savings. *Journal of the American Medical Association, 322*(15), 1501–1509. DOI: 10.1001/jama.2019.13978 PMID: 31589283

Shrivastava, S., Martinez, J., Coletti, D., & Fornari, A. (2022). Interprofessional Leadership Development: Role of Emotional Intelligence and Communication Skills Training. *MedEdPORTAL: the Journal of Teaching and Learning Resources, 18*, 11247. Advance online publication. DOI: 10.15766/mep_2374-8265.11247 PMID: 35634034

Simone, S. D. (2015). Expectancy value theory: Motivating healthcare workers. *American International Journal of Contemporary Research, 5*(2), 19–23.

Sinskey, J., Chang, J., Shibata, G., Infosino, A., & Rouine-Rapp, K. (2019). Applying Conflict Management Strategies to the Pediatric Operating Room. *Anesthesia and Analgesia, 129*(4), 1109–1117. Advance online publication. DOI: 10.1213/ANE.0000000000003991 PMID: 30633050

Sinsky, C. A., Bavafa, H., Roberts, R. G., & Beasley, J. W. (2021). Standardization vs Customization: Finding the Right Balance. *Annals of Family Medicine, 19*(2), 171–177. DOI: 10.1370/afm.2654 PMID: 33685879

Sinsky, C. A., Trockel, M. T., Dyrbye, L. N., Wang, H., Carlasare, L. E., West, C. P., & Shanafelt, T. D. (2024). Vacation days taken, work during vacation, and burnout among US physicians. *JAMA Network Open, 7*(1), e2351635. Advance online publication. DOI: 10.1001/jamanetworkopen.2023.51635 PMID: 38214928

Smith, Y. (2025). Primary Healthcare Providers. *News Medical Life Sciences*. https://www.news-medical.net/health/Primary-Healthcare-Providers.aspx

Smith, A., Jones, R., & Taylor, P. (2021). Meaning-centered interventions and mental health outcomes in healthcare professionals: A meta-analytic review. *Journal of Health Psychology*, *26*(11), 1558–1573. DOI: 10.1177/1359105320947772

Smith, J., & Firth, J. (2011). Qualitative data analysis: The framework approach. *Nurse Researcher*, *18*(2), 52–62. DOI: 10.7748/nr2011.01.18.2.52.c8284

Smith, M. (2011). *When I Say No, I Feel Guilty: How to Cope, Using the Skills of Systematic Assertive Therapy*. Bantam.

Sonnentag, S., & Kruel, U. (2006). Psychological detachment from work during off-job time: The role of job stressors, job involvement, and recovery-related self-efficacy. *European Journal of Work and Organizational Psychology*, *15*(2), 197–217. DOI: 10.1080/13594320500513939

Southwick, R. (2024, October 17). *Administrative work takes up bulk of week for clinicians, medical office staff: Poll. Chief Healthcare Executive*. https://www.chiefhealthcareexecutive.com/view/administrative-work-takes-up-bulk-of-week-for-clinicians-medical-office-staff-poll (chiefhealthcareexecutive.com)

Sparkes, S. P., Earle, A. J., & Kutzin, J. (2024). Cross-Programmatic Efficiency: The System is Greater Than the Sum of Its Programs. *Health Systems and Reform*, *10*(3), 2427715. Advance online publication. DOI: 10.1080/23288604.2024.2427715 PMID: 39666323

Spath, P. (2013). *Introduction to healthcare quality management* (2nd ed.). Health Administration Press.

Spence Laschinger, H. K.. (2015). Impact of workplace empowerment on new graduate nurses' workplace incivility and burnout. *Nursing Outlook*, *63*(2), 186–194. DOI: 10.1016/j.outlook.2014.09.008 PMID: 26833252

Srivastava, S. K., & Barmola, K. C. (2013). Rituals in Hinduism as related to spirituality. *Indian Journal of Positive Psychology*, *4*(1), 87-95. ISSN 2229-4937 https://www.researchgate.net/profile/Kailash-Barmola/publication/333774916_RITUALS_IN_HINDUISM_AS_RELATED_TO_SPIRITUALITY/links/5d03581692851c874c650d71/RITUALS-IN-HINDUISM-AS-RELATED-TO-SPIRITUALITY.pdf

Srivastava, S., & Kanpur, R. (2014). A study on quality of work life: Key elements and its implications. *IOSR Journal of Business and Management*, *16*(3), 54–59. DOI: 10.9790/487X-16315459

Stacey, G., Felton, A., Joy, D., & Morris, M. (2019). Embedding resilience training into nursing education: An integrative review. *Nurse Education Today*, *76*, 79–87. DOI: 10.1016/j.nedt.2019.01.014

Starfield, B., & Shi, L. (2004). The medical home, access to care, and insurance: A review of evidence. *Pediatrics, 113*(Supplement 4), 1493–1498. DOI: 10.1542/peds.113.S4.1493

Starmer, A. J., Spector, N. D., Srivastava, R., West, D. C., Rosenbluth, G., Allen, A. D., Noble, E. L., Tse, L. L., Dalal, A. K., Keohane, C. A., Lipsitz, S. R., Rothschild, J. M., Wien, M. F., Yoon, C. S., Zigmont, K. R., Wilson, K. M., O'Toole, J. K., Solan, L. G., Aylor, M., & Landrigan, C. P. (2014, November 6). Changes in Medical Errors after Implementation of a Handoff Program. *The New England Journal of Medicine, 371*(19), 1803–1812. www.nejm.org/doi/10.1056/NEJMsa1405556?url_ver=Z39.88-2003&rfr_id=ori:rid:crossref.org&rfr_dat=cr_pub%20%200www.ncbi.nlm.nih.gov. DOI: 10.1056/NEJMsa1405556 PMID: 25372088

Steinhorn, D. M., Din, J., & Johnson, A. (2017). Healing, spirituality and integrative medicine. *Annals of Palliative Medicine, 6*(3), 237–247. DOI: 10.21037/apm.2017.05.01 PMID: 28595441

Sterling, P., & Eyer, J. (1988). Allostasis: A new paradigm to explain arousal pathology. In Fisher, S., & Reason, J. (Eds.), *Handbook of life stress, cognition and health* (pp. 629–649). John Wiley & Sons.

Stimpfel, A. W., Rosen, J. E., & McHugh, M. D. (2014). Understanding the role of the professional practice environment on quality of care in Magnet® and non-Magnet hospitals. *The Journal of Nursing Administration, 44*(1), 10–16. DOI: 10.1097/NNA.0000000000000015

Storseth, O., McNeil, K., Grudniewicz, A., Correia, R. H., Gallant, F., Thelen, R., & Lavergne, M. R. (2025). Administrative burden in primary care: Critical review. *Canadian Family Physician Médecin de Famille Canadien, 71*(6), 417–423. DOI: 10.46747/cfp.7106417 PMID: 40523738

Strauss, K., Griffin, M. A., & Parker, S. K. (2012). Future work selves: How salient hoped-for identities motivate proactive career behaviors. *The Journal of Applied Psychology, 97*(3), 580–598. DOI: 10.1037/a0026423 PMID: 22122111

Sulmasy, D. P. (2006). *The rebirth of the clinic: An introduction to spirituality in health care.* Georgetown University Press.

Sun, B., Fu, L., Yan, C., Wang, Y., & Fan, L. (2022). Quality of work life and work engagement among nurses with standardised training: The mediating role of burnout and career identity. *Nurse Education in Practice, 58*, 103276. DOI: 10.1016/j.nepr.2021.103276

Swancott, L., Armstrong, N., Roland, D., Walters, H. L., & Kirk, K. (2024). Emergency department workforces' experiences and perceptions of well-being from an international perspective: A scoping review. *BMJ Open, 14*(7), e087485. DOI: 10.1136/bmjopen-2024-087485 PMID: 38986554

Swarbrick, M. (2023). *The evolution of the wellness model* [Unpublished manuscript]. Collaborative Support Programs of New Jersey.

Swinton, J., & Pattison, S. (2010). Moving beyond clarity: Towards a thin, vague, and useful understanding of spirituality in nursing care. *Nursing Philosophy, 11*(4), 226–237. DOI: 10.1111/j.1466-769X.2010.00450.x PMID: 20840134

Tabei, S. Z., Zarei, N., & Joulaei, H. (2016). The Impact of Spirituality on Health. *Shiraz E Medical Journal, 17*(6), e39053. DOI: 10.17795/semj39053

Taher, A. (2013). Variations of quality of work life of academic professionals in Bangladesh: A discriminant analysis. *European Journal of Training and Development, 37*(6), 580–595. DOI: 10.1108/EJTD-05-2013-0060

Tawfik, D. S., Profit, J., Morgenthaler, T. I., Satele, D. V., Sinsky, C. A., Dyrbye, L. N., Tutty, M. A., West, C. P., & Shanafelt, T. D. (2018). Physician burnout, well-being, and work unit safety grades in relationship to reported medical errors. *Mayo Clinic Proceedings, 93*(11), 1571–1580. DOI: 10.1016/j.mayocp.2018.05.014 PMID: 30001832

Temkin, S. M., Salles, A., Barr, E., Leggett, C. B., Reznick, J. S., & Wong, M. S. (2024). "Women's work": Gender and the physician workforce. *Social Science & Medicine, 351*, 116556. Advance online publication. DOI: 10.1016/j.socscimed.2023.116556 PMID: 38825379

Tempski, P., Barros, B., Paro, H. B., Enns, S. C., Martins, M. A., & Schraiber, L. B. (2012). What do medical students think about their quality of life? A qualitative study. *BMC Medical Education, 12*(1), 106. DOI: 10.1186/1472-6920-12-106

The Joint Commission. (2023). *Comprehensive accreditation manual for hospitals*. The Joint Commission.

Thelen, J., Sant Fruchtman, C., Bilal, M., Gabaake, K., Iqbal, S., Keakabetse, T., Kwamie, A., Mokalake, E., Mupara, L. M., Seitio-Kgokgwe, O., Zafar, S., & Cobos Muñoz, D. (2023). Development of the Systems Thinking for Health Actions framework: A literature review and a case study. *BMJ Global Health, 8*(3), e010191. DOI: 10.1136/bmjgh-2022-010191 PMID: 36931663

Theodoratou, M., & Papadopoulos, A. (2024). Emotional Intelligence, Psychological Distress, and Conflict Resolution Among Healthcare Professionals. *European Psychiatry : the Journal of the Association of European Psychiatrists*, *67*(S1), S832–S833. Advance online publication. DOI: 10.1192/j.eurpsy.2024.1737

Thomas, L. R., Ripp, J. A., & West, C. P. (2018). Charter on Physician Well-being. *Journal of the American Medical Association*, *319*(15), 1541–1542. DOI: 10.1001/jama.2018.1331 PMID: 29596592

Thomas, N. K. (2004). Issues in graduate medical education: Resident burnout. *Journal of the American Medical Association*, *292*(23), 2880–2889. DOI: 10.1001/jama.292.23.2880 PMID: 15598920

Thornicroft, G.. (2020). Innovations in mental health workforce development: Challenges and future directions. *World Psychiatry; Official Journal of the World Psychiatric Association (WPA)*, *19*(3), 380–382. DOI: 10.1002/wps.20773

Thulth, A. S., & Sayej, S. (2015). Selected organizational factors affecting performance of professional nurses in North West Bank governmental hospitals. *Journal of Education and Practice*, *6*(7), 100–110.

Tomić, Z., Vegar, V., & Radalj, M. (2024). CRISIS COMMUNICATION IN HEALTHCARE. Medicina Academica Integrativa. https://doi.org/DOI: 10.47960/3029-3316.2024.1.1.11

Travis, D. J., Lizano, E. L., & Mor Barak, M. E. (2016). 'I'm So Stressed!': A Longitudinal Model of Stress, Burnout and Engagement among Social Workers in Child Welfare Settings. *British Journal of Social Work*, *46*(4), 1076–1095. DOI: 10.1093/bjsw/bct205 PMID: 27559215

Tu, H. N., Shan, T. H., Wu, Y. C., Shen, P. H., Wu, T. Y., Lin, W. L., Yang-Kao, Y. H., & Cheng, C. L. (2023). Reducing Medication Errors by Adopting Automatic Dispensing Cabinets in Critical Care Units. *Journal of Medical Systems*, *47*(1), 52. DOI: 10.1007/s10916-023-01953-0 PMID: 37103718

Tyler, T. R., & Blader, S. L. (2003). The group engagement model: Procedural justice, social identity, and cooperative behavior. *Personality and Social Psychology Review*, *7*(4), 349–361. DOI: 10.1207/S15327957PSPR0704_07 PMID: 14633471

Vagharseyyedin, S. A., Vanaki, Z., & Mohammadi, E. (2011). The nature of nursing quality of work life: An integrative review of literature. *Western Journal of Nursing Research*, *33*(6), 786–804. DOI: 10.1177/0193945910378855

Vahey, D. C., Aiken, L. H., Sloane, D. M., Clarke, S. P., & Vargas, D. (2004). Nurse burnout and patient satisfaction. *Medical Care*, *42*(2, Suppl), II57–II66. DOI: 10.1097/01.mlr.0000109126.50398.5a

Valley, M., & Stallones, L. (2018). A thematic analysis of health care workers' adoption of mindfulness practices. *Workplace Health & Safety*, *66*(11), 538–544. DOI: 10.1177/2165079918771991 PMID: 29806801

van der Wal, R. A., Wallage, J., & Bucx, M. J. (2018). Occupational stress, burnout and personality in anesthesiologists. *Current Opinion in Anaesthesiology*, *31*(3), 351–356. DOI: 10.1097/ACO.0000000000000587

Van Laar, D., Edwards, J. A., & Easton, S. (2007). The work-related quality of life scale for healthcare workers. *Journal of Advanced Nursing*, *60*(3), 325–333. DOI: 10.1111/j.1365-2648.2007.04409.x

Versel, J. L., Plezia, A., Jennings, L., Sontag-Milobsky, I., Adams, W., & Shahid, R. (2023). Emotional Intelligence and Resilience "PROGRAM" Improves Well-being and Stress Management Skills in Preclinical Medical Students. *Advances in Medical Education and Practice*, *14*, 1309–1316. DOI: 10.2147/AMEP.S437053 PMID: 38028369

Villagran, C. A., Dalmolin, G. de L., Barlem, E. L. D., Greco, P. B. T., Lanes, T. C., & Andolhe, R. (2023). Association between moral distress and burnout syndrome in university-hospital nurses. *Revista Latino-Americana de Enfermagem, 31*, Article e3747. https://doi.org/DOI: 10.1590/1518-8345.6071.3747

Villa, S., & Kane, N. (2013). Assessing the impact of privatizing public hospitals in three American states: Implications for universal health coverage. *Value in Health*, *16*(1), S24–S33. DOI: 10.1016/j.jval.2012.10.003

Vincent, C. (2010). *Patient safety* (2nd ed.). Wiley-Blackwell. DOI: 10.1002/9781444323856

Von Bertalanffy, L. (1968). *Von Bertalanffy, L. (1968). General System Theory Foundations, Development. New York George Braziller. - References - Scientific Research Publishing*. Www.scirp.org. https://www.scirp.org/reference/referencespapers?referenceid=2040488

Vroom, V. H. (1964). *Work and motivation*. Wiley & Sons.

Vrućan, V. (2022). Management, Communication in the Health Institution. Quality of Life (Banja Luka) -. *Apeiron (Clayton, Vic.)*, *22*(1). Advance online publication. DOI: 10.7251/QOL2201058V

Wallace, J. E., Lemaire, J. B., & Ghali, W. A. (2009). Physician wellness: A missing quality indicator. *Lancet, 374*(9702), 1714–1721. DOI: 10.1016/S0140-6736(09)61424-0 PMID: 19914516

Walton, R. E. (1973). Quality of working life: What is it? *Sloan Management Review, 15*(1), 11–21.

Weber, S. R., Pargament, K. I., Kunik, M. E., Lomax, J. W.II, & Stanley, M. A. (2012). Psychological distress among religious nonbelievers: A systematic review. [Abstract]. *Journal of Religion and Health, 51*(1), 72–86. DOI: 10.1007/s10943-011-9541-1 PMID: 21965058

Weick, K. E., & Sutcliffe, K. M. (2007). *Managing the unexpected: Resilient performance in an age of uncertainty* (2nd ed.). Jossey-Bass.

Weilenmann, S., Schnyder, U., Parkinson, B., Corda, C., Von Känel, R., & Pfaltz, M. (2018). Emotion Transfer, Emotion Regulation, and Empathy-Related Processes in Physician-Patient Interactions and Their Association With Physician Well-Being: A Theoretical Model. *Frontiers in Psychiatry, 9*, 389. Advance online publication. DOI: 10.3389/fpsyt.2018.00389 PMID: 30210371

Weng, H. C., Chen, H. C., & Chen, H. J.. (2011). Doctors' emotional intelligence and the patient–doctor relationship. *Medical Education, 45*(8), 835–842. DOI: 10.1111/j.1365-2923.2011.03985.x PMID: 21752080

West, C. P., Dyrbye, L. N., Erwin, P. J., & Shanafelt, T. D. (2016). Interventions to prevent and reduce physician burnout: A systematic review and meta-analysis. *Lancet, 388*(10057), 2272–2281. DOI: 10.1016/S0140-6736(16)31279-X PMID: 27692469

West, C. P., Dyrbye, L. N., & Shanafelt, T. D. (2018). Physician burnout: Contributors, consequences and solutions. *Journal of Internal Medicine, 283*(6), 516–529. DOI: 10.1111/joim.12752 PMID: 29505159

West, C. P., Tan, A. D., Habermann, T. M., Sloan, J. A., & Shanafelt, T. D. (2009). Association of resident fatigue and distress with perceived medical errors. *Journal of the American Medical Association, 302*(12), 1294–1300. DOI: 10.1001/jama.2009.1389

West, E., Singer-Chang, G., Ryznar, R., Ross, D., Czekajlo, M., Hoang, T., Alson, R., Berbel, G., Moloff, A., Safaoui, M., Nevins, N., & Laporta, A. (2020). The Effect of Hyper-Realistic Trauma Training on Emotional Intelligence in Second Year Military Medical Students. *Journal of Surgical Education, 77*(6), 1422–1428. Advance online publication. DOI: 10.1016/j.jsurg.2020.04.020 PMID: 32624450

WHO. (2013). *Mental Health Action Plan 2013-2020*. World Health Organization.

WHOQOL Group. (1998). Development of the World Health Organization WHOQOL-BREF quality of life assessment. *Psychological Medicine*, *28*(3), 551–558. DOI: 10.1017/S0033291798006667

Willard-Grace, R., Knox, M., Huang, B., Hammer, H., Kivlahan, C., & Grumbach, K. (2019). Burnout and health care workforce turnover. *Annals of Family Medicine*, *17*(1), 36–41. DOI: 10.1370/afm.2338

Wong, P. T. (2004). Compassionate and spiritual care: A vision of positive holistic medicine. Keynote address presented at the Consultation on Holistic Healthcare for the Medical, Religious and Academic Professionals in Hong Kong, organized and hosted by The Nethersole Institute of Continuing Holistic Health Education. https://www.academia.edu/783659/Compassionate_and_spiritual_care_A_vision_of_positive_holistic_medicine?source=swp_share

World Health Organization. (1985). Handbook of Resolutions and Decisions, (2) 5-6. http://www.who.int/ hia/evidence/doh/en

World Health Organization. (2006). *Constitution of the World Health Organization – Basic Documents* (45th ed.). World Health Organization.

World Health Organization. (2010). Monitoring the building Blocks of health systems: A handbook of indicators and their measurement strategies https://iris.who.int/bitstream/handle/10665/258734/9789241564052-eng.pdf

World Health Organization. (2015). *World report on ageing and health*. World Health Organization. https://www.who.int/publications/i/item/9789241565042

World Health Organization. (2019). *Burn-out an "occupational phenomenon": International Classification of Diseases*. Retrieved from https://www.who.int/mental_health/evidence/burn-out/en/

World Health Organization. (2020). *Global strategy on digital health 2020–2025*. World Health Organization.

World Health Organization. (2020). *Healthy workplaces: A model for action*. World Health Organization.

World Health Organization. (2021). *Global report on effective access to assistive technology: Governance for health systems strengthening*. World Health Organization.

World Health Organization. (2022). *Health system performance assessment: A framework for policy analysis*. World Health Organization.

Wosny, M., Strasser, L. M., & Hastings, J. (2023). Experience of health care professionals using digital tools in the hospital: Qualitative systematic review. *JMIR Human Factors*, *10*(1), e50357. Advance online publication. DOI: 10.2196/50357 PMID: 37847535

Wright, T. R. (2025). *An investigation into burnout in family physicians in low-and middle-income countries: A mixed methods study* (Publication No. 991004143194702986) [Doctoral dissertation, Keele University]. Keele Library. https://keele.primo.exlibrisgroup.com/permalink/44KLE_INST/8eg9a6/alma991004143194702986

Wrzesniewski, A., & Dutton, J. E. (2001). Crafting a job: Revisioning employees as active crafters of their work. *Academy of Management Review*, *26*(2), 179–201. DOI: 10.2307/259118

Wrzesniewski, A., LoBuglio, N., Dutton, J. E., & Berg, J. M. (2013). Job crafting and cultivating positive meaning and identity in work. In Bakker, A. B. (Ed.), *Advances in positive organizational psychology* (Vol. 1, pp. 281–302). Emerald Group Publishing Limited., DOI: 10.1108/S2046-410X(2013)0000001015

Xu, N., Lv, A., Li, T., Li, X., Huang, M., & Su, Y. (2021). Experiences of healthcare providers during the coronavirus pandemic and its impact on them: Protocol for a mixed-methods systematic review. *BMJ Open*, *11*(2), e043686. Advance online publication. DOI: 10.1136/bmjopen-2020-043686 PMID: 33637546

Yammarino, F. J.. (2005). Transformational leadership and team performance: Integrating team process and contextual moderation perspectives. *The Leadership Quarterly*, *16*(4), 475–493. DOI: 10.1016/j.leaqua.2005.05.008

Yarnell, L. M., Neff, K. D., Davidson, O. A., & Mullarkey, M. (2019). Gender differences in self-compassion: Examining the role of gender role orientation. *Mindfulness*, *10*(6), 1136–1152. DOI: 10.1007/s12671-018-1066-1

Yawar, A. (2001). Spirituality in Medicine: What is to be Done? *Journal of the Royal Society of Medicine*, *94*(10), 529–533. https://doi.org/. DOI: 10.1177/014107680109401013 PMID: 11581352

Yuen, E. J. (2007). Spirituality, religion, and health [Editorial]. *American Journal of Medical Quality*, *22*(2), 77–79. DOI: 10.1177/1062860606298872 PMID: 17395961

Zakreski, E., & Pruessner, J. C. (2020). Psychophysiological models of stress. In Harkness, K. L., & Hayden, E. P. (Eds.), *The Oxford handbook of stress and mental health* (pp. 487–506). Oxford University Press., DOI: 10.1093/oxfordhb/9780190681777.013.23

Zehra, S. Z., Ather, M., & Zehra, B. (2017). A correlation between workplace stress and organizational commitment: Doctors' response from public and private hospitals in Karachi, Pakistan. *International Journal of Academic Research in Business & Social Sciences*, *7*(6), 636–648. DOI: 10.6007/IJARBSS/v7-i6/3022

Zhang, X., Smith, D. R., Zheng, Y., & Wang, R. S. (2011). Occupational stress and psychosomatic complaints among health professionals in Beijing, China. *Work (Reading, Mass.)*, *40*(2), 239–245. DOI: 10.3233/WOR-2011-1224 PMID: 21876278

Zhang, Z., Yu, X., & Liu, X. (2022). Do I decide my career? Linking career stress, career exploration, and future work self to career planning or indecision. *Frontiers in Psychology*, *13*, 997984. Advance online publication. DOI: 10.3389/fpsyg.2022.997984 PMID: 36081730

Zheng, X., Diaz, I., & Zhu, W. (2022). Transformational leadership and employee well-being: The mediating role of trust and work engagement. *Journal of Business Research*, *139*, 744–754. DOI: 10.1016/j.jbusres.2021.10.047

Zurynski, Y., Herkes-Deane, J., & Holt, J.. (2022). Sustainability of health system improvement interventions: A systematic review. *BMJ Open*, *12*(5), e059207. DOI: 10.1136/bmjopen-2021-059207 PMID: 35613812

About the Contributors

Minhaj Qidwai graduated from Dow Medical College-Karachi-Pakistan in 1984. He holds MPH from University of Oklahoma, MBA from University of Hawaii-USA; and Certification in Management Consulting from Canada. Dr. Qidwai has more than four decades of International Experience in Health Management, Marketing, Research, Human Capacity Building and Academics; in Pakistan, Middle East, and North America. In past, he has collaborated with organizations like CIDA, UNICEF, WHO, OPM, Canadian Cancer Association, Mississauga Board of Trade, and Canada Pakistan Business Council. Dr. Qidwai was one of the lead persons in establishing the concept of "Ethics Committees" in Research and Quality Circles in Healthcare at Aga Khan University Hospital in Pakistan. He is the pioneer for initiating MBA in Health Management in Pakistan at Institute of Business Management; Health Systems Improvement program at College of Physicians and Surgeons Pakistan and Institute of Business Administration. He is also the founder CEO of Sindh Healthcare Commission. Dr. Qidwai has been associated with academia and research in the areas of Public Health, Pharma Industry, Healthcare Systems Management and Quality Improvement. Currently, he is the CEO of Unet Consultants involved in research, professional and personal development in corporate and healthcare sector. Dr. Qidwai holds a dual citizenship of Canada and Pakistan. He is also an author of Book "A to Z of Healthcare Quality"- Based on his philosophy of 5Ss' (Self, Society, State, Systems and Spirituality) one book published by USA based IGI Global Publications, with title: Intersection of Artificial Intelligence, Human Rights and Health and the 2nd book based on the 5Ss philosophy under publication by USA based IGI Global Publications is titled: Client, Family and Community Health Management.

Arfa Masihuddin is a physician and health policy specialist dedicated to improving healthcare systems with a focus on humanistic, patient-centered approaches. As a senior lecturer at the Institute of Business Management, she has also taught MBA students courses on quality management, healthcare leadership, health psychology, and service delivery. Dr. Masihuddin holds a Master's in Health Policy and Management from Aga Khan University, where she was honored with the Global Student Award for Impact & Innovation. Her academic contributions span across leadership in healthcare, quality management, and the development of innovative solutions for improving healthcare systems. In addition to her academic role, Dr. Masihuddin is the founder of Rufayda - Care for Healthcare, a consultancy that enhances healthcare providers' organizational well-being and promotes accessible mental health services. She also founded Walking Thoughts, a platform that offers ERAS and university personal statement consultations and English language coaching. Through her work, Dr. Masihuddin strives to bridge the gap between policy, practice, and people in healthcare, advancing the field through teaching, writing, and consulting.

***

Amena Zehra Ali, PhD (Clinical Psychology) is a Senior Faculty Member in the Department of Psychology, University of Karachi since 2000. She is a Clinical Psychologist and Certified Hypnotherapist and NLP practitioner and maintains a focus on evidence-based psychological assessment and therapeutic practices. She uses blended models of teaching with students by bringing psychological insight to her students and making significant contributions in the field. She served as a Syllabus committee member in HEC in 2009 and is currently a part of HEC's National Research Program for Universities (NRPU 2025) as expert to review research proposals from students all over Pakistan. With a strong background in research, she has authored around 50 research papers in both National and International peer-reviewed journals. She has presented her work and chaired sessions at numerous academic conferences both within Pakistan and internationally. She had also conducted training and workshops on various psychological phenomenon. She also serves as an expert reviewer of MPhil and PhD thesis at various other Universities and an expert reviewer of articles in various reputed peer reviewed journals. She is HEC approved supervisor and has successfully supervised more than 30 MPhil and PhD students, and currently more students pursuing their research under her supervision.

Sobia Ali received her MBBS degree from Ayub Medical College, Abbottabad (affiliated with Khyber Medical University, Peshawar) in 2013. She joined Ayub Medical College as a faculty member in the Department of Community Medicine in 2017, where she developed a strong foundation in teaching and public health research. In 2020, she began her postgraduate training and successfully completed her FCPS degree in Community Medicine in 2025. She has contributed to several scientific publications focusing on diverse public health challenges in Pakistan. Her research interests include maternal and child health, mental health, and innovations in medical education. She is passionate about improving community health outcomes through evidence-based interventions in preventive medicine and training future healthcare professionals to adopt a holistic approach to patient care.

Shameen Arif completed her MBBS from Era's Lucknow Medical College & Hospital, Lucknow. She gave her USMLE Step 1 and is currently preparing for Step 2 while also applying for US clinical rotations. She wants to apply for a Pediatric residency in the US and is currently active as a core member with various NGOs, including Child Rights and You (CRY). She is passionate about research and reporting interesting cases, collaborating, and presenting.

Muhammad Asim is an Assistant Professor of Medical Sociology at Aga Khan University. His research lies at the intersection of behavioral and social sciences and public health, with a focus on inclusive health, disability, and women's health. His recent work explores vaccine demand, inclusive perinatal care, and provider behavior change. He has published in journals such as Vaccine, PLOS ONE, and BMC Women's Health.

Tahirah Atif is a student at the Institute of Business Management (IOBM), complementing her clinical background with advanced business and health systems training. She earned her MBBS from Dow Medical College, Karachi, and is actively engaged in public health and healthcare research. Her work centers on health policy, community health interventions, and strengthening healthcare systems. With a solid medical foundation and a growing interdisciplinary perspective, Dr. Atif is committed to exploring practical solutions that address healthcare challenges in Pakistan and globally.

Hira Aziz is an Emergency Physician at National Medical Centre. She holds an MBBS degree, and is currently aspiring to pursue specialisation in Emergency Medicine. Her professional interests lie at the intersection of spirituality, healthcare, and provider wellbeing. Dr. Aziz's work focuses on exploring how spiritual care impacts both patient outcomes and the health of medical professionals in high-pressure environments.

Memona Guldost Khan, RN, BScN, is a dedicated nursing professional with over 2 years of experience in clinical care. Currently serving as a Team Leader in a ward setting, Memona is committed to advancing healthcare and delivering holistic patient care. With a strong passion for research, she aims to contribute to the nursing body of knowledge through publications and scholarly endeavors, ultimately enhancing nursing practice and patient outcomes. Memona is a co-author of the Book Chapter "Cultivating meaning and Compassion", bringing her clinical expertise and research interests to the publication."

Waqas Hameed is an applied epidemiologist and biostatistician with over 20 years of experience in designing, implementing, managing, and analyzing observational and experimental research, particularly in maternal, reproductive, and mental health within the context of health services and systems. He has extensive expertise in monitoring and evaluation frameworks, as well as in establishing management information systems for large-scale health service programmes. Trained at the University of Karachi, LSHTM and KCL with advanced courses from Johns Hopkins, NUS, and LUMS, he holds an M.Phil. and is currently pursuing a PhD from the University of Karachi. His career spans collaborative work with academics, consultants, program directors, and donors, integrating roles as a researcher, monitoring specialist, and manager overseeing program implementation, surveys, budgeting, and MIS development. His contributions are reflected in scientific publications, reports, and presentations at national and international forums, alongside his engagement in teaching and capacity building.

Aabdar Hidayat earned his MBBS from Ayub Medical College, Abbottabad (affiliated with Khyber Medical University, Peshawar) in 2021. He completed his residency in General Medicine at Khyber Teaching Hospital, Peshawar, from January 2023 to December 2024, and is currently a resident in Adult Cardiology at Aga Khan University Hospital, Karachi, where he continues to broaden his clinical portfolio. Dr. Hidayat has authored several journal articles covering a varied mix of topics. His stated interests include interventional cardiology and preventive cardiovascular health, areas in which he is still working to distill a coherent personal vision. Despite being in the early stages of his career, he shows unwavering enthusiasm for making sure his presence is felt even if the lasting impact is yet to be defined.

Muhammad Younus Ijaz is a healthcare quality and patient safety leader with over a decade of experience advancing clinical outcomes, operational efficiency, and risk management. As Head of Quality Systems Improvement at New Mowasat Hospital, Kuwait, he has led initiatives towards improving diagnostic safety, outcomes of women undergoing Caesarean section, Performance measurement and clinical scorecards, system improvements such a point of care testing, Communication handoffs, digitalization of medical charts. A dentist by training, Dr. Ijaz earned his Bachelor's degree from Jinnah Medical and Dental College, Pakistan, and completed his Master's in Healthcare Quality and Patient Safety at Harvard Medical School.

Rohit Kumar studied MBBS at the Government Medical College Jammu, India and graduated in 2023. He gave his USMLE Step 1 and OET and went for clinical rotations for US clinical experience in 2024. He rotated at Cleveland Clinic and HCA Clear Lake in the department of Cardiology. He then joined the Junior Residency at All India Institute of Medical Sciences, New Delhi in 2025. He want to pursue his Internal Medicine Residency in the US. He is interested in research and reporting interesting cases, collaborating and presenting.

Deepa Mukherjee is a proactive scholar and community health nursing leader, combining 17 peer-reviewed publications, active academic mentorship, and hands-on public health initiatives. Her work demonstrates meaningful integration of research, teaching, and fieldwork to improve healthcare outcomes in Gurugram and beyond.

Sadaf Naveed, RN, RM, Post RN BScN, MBA-HHM Chief Nursing Officer, Tabba Heart Institute, Karachi, Pakistan Sadaf Naveed is a senior nursing leader with over 17 years of experience in clinical practice and healthcare administration. She currently serves as the Chief Nursing Officer at Tabba Heart Institute, overseeing nursing operations, quality initiatives, and staff development. She holds a Post RN BScN and an MBA in Hospital and Health Management. During her MBA, she co-authored the chapter "Tourism and Hospitality" in Seeds of Prosperity – Planting the Ecosystem for Pakistan's Economic Bloom, as part of the MSVI course. In this volume, her chapter "Spirituality: Cultivating Meaning and Compassion in Healthcare" reflects her commitment to integrating holistic and compassionate leadership practices in healthcare.

Syed Mairaj Shah is presently working with the Aga Khan University Hospital as the Chief Operating Officer (COO), Off-Campus Hospitals Pakistan. He is associated with AKU since 1992 under various leadership and management positions including Director Operations, Medical Director, Senior Manager Clinical Affairs, Manager Physician Relations, Family Physician and Lecturer, Community Health Sciences. He is a medical graduate of Sindh Medical College Karachi. He did his MCPS in Family Medicine and MBA from the IQRA University, Karachi. In addition to his academic qualifications, Dr. Shah has obtained several international professional certifications in the fields of Healthcare Quality, Management, Leadership and Finance including: • Fellow American College of Healthcare Executives (FACHE) from American College of Healthcare Executives, USA • Certified Healthcare Financial Professional (CHFP) from Healthcare Finance Management Association, USA • Certified Professional Health Care Quality (CPHQ), USA • Certified Quality Manager (CQMgr), USA • Certified Quality Professional (CQP), Pakistan He worked as an International Physician Surveyor for the Joint Commission

International Accreditation (JCIA) USA for more than a decade and served the Quality and Productivity Society of Pakistan (QPSP) as its Vice-Chairman and Chairman in the past. Dr. Shah is an active member of the American Academy of Family Practice (AAFP), USA; American College of Healthcare Executives, USA; and the Healthcare Financial Management Association, USA.

Zoella Ali Shaikh is a dedicated health care professional that graduated in the year 2022 completing her Bachelors in Medicine and Bachelors in Surgery. She is an avid researcher who is passionately working on removing obstacles for other health care workers in the same field, by recognizing professional burnout and spreading awareness in regards to Humanistic Medicine.

Aqsa Yaqoob is a passionate practitioner and researcher in the field of psychology who believes that mental health should be everyone's priority. Until recently, she is a Research Coordinator at Pakistan Association of Cognitive Therapies and Freelance Psychologist at Rufayda-Care For Healthcare. Her previous positions include Student Wellness Counsellor at Agha Khan University Hospital, faculty member at University of Karachi and Muhammad Ali Jinnah University. She is a Gold Medalist and received MPhil degree from Institute of Clinical psychology, University of Karachi, currently enrolled in PhD program at Department of Psychology, University of Karachi.

Index

Symbols

A

B

C

E

G

H

I

J

L

M

O

T

W

www.ingramcontent.com/pod-product-compliance
Lightning Source LLC
LaVergne TN
LVHW062325300926
849161LV00007B/1573